About These Stories

Fiction for Fiction Writers and Readers

About These Stories

Fiction for Fiction Writers and Readers

David Huddle
University of Vermont

Ghita Orth
University of Vermont

Allen Shepherd
University of Vermont

McGraw-Hill, Inc.

New York   St. Louis   San Francisco   Auckland   Bogotá   Caracas
Lisbon   London   Madrid   Mexico City   Milan   Montreal   New Delhi
San Juan   Singapore   Sydney   Tokyo   Toronto

This book was developed by STEVEN PENSINGER, Inc.

ABOUT THESE STORIES
Fiction for Fiction Writers and Readers

Acknowledgments appear on pages 291–292, and on this page by reference.

 This book is printed on recycled, acid-free paper containing 10% postconsumer
waste.

1 2 3 4 5 6 7 8 9 0 DOC DOC 9 0 9 8 7 6 5 4

ISBN 0-07-030851-9

This book was set in Palatino by Ruttle, Shaw & Wetherill, Inc.
The editors were Steve Pensinger and Jean Akers;
the designer was Carol A. Couch;
the production supervisor was Kathryn Porzio.
R. R. Donnelley & Sons Company was printer and binder.

Library of Congress Cataloging-in-Publication Data

About these stories: Fiction for fiction writers and readers / [edited by] David Huddle,
    Ghita Orth, Allen Shepherd.
        p.   cm.
    Includes index.
    ISBN 0-07-030851-9
    1. Short stories.   I. Huddle, David, (date).   II. Orth, Ghita, (date).   III.
Shepherd, Allen.
PN6120.2.A26   1995
808.83'1—dc20   94-11279

About the Authors

David Huddle has taught literature and creative writing at the University of Vermont since 1971. He has taught at the University of Idaho, Goddard College, Warren Wilson College, Middlebury College, the Bread Loaf Writers' Conference, and the Bread Loaf School of English, where he has been the Robert Frost Professor of American Literature. He has held two fellowships from the National Endowment for the Arts as well as fellowships from Yaddo, the Bread Loaf Writers' Conference, and the Virginia Center for the Creative Arts. He holds an Honorary Doctorate of Humanities from Shenandoah College and Conservatory. Huddle's books include *Paper Boy, Stopping by Home, The High Spirits, Only the Little Bone, The Nature of Yearning, The Writing Habit, Intimates,* and the recently published *A David Huddle Reader.* His poetry, fiction, and essays have appeared in *Esquire, Harper's, The New York Times Book Review, The New York Times Magazine, Los Angeles Times Book Review, Details, Epoch, Poetry, Plowshares, TriQuarterly, The Hudson Review, Kenyon Review, Virginia Quarterly Review, Prairie Schooner,* and *The Gettysburg Review.* He is currently Acting Editor of *New England Review.*

Ghita Orth is a Lecturer in English at the University of Vermont where she teaches creative writing and literature. She received her B.A. from Brandeis University, where she was elected to Phi Beta Kappa, and her M.A. from the University of Vermont. She is the author of a book of poems, *The Music Of What Happens,* and her work has appeared in a number of journals, including *New England Review, Poem, Appalachia,* and *Green Mountains Review.* With Allen Shepherd she co-authored the fiction section in *Angles of Vision* (McGraw-Hill) and with Allen Shepherd and David Huddle is currently writing a poetry text that will be the companion volume to *About These Stories.*

Allen Shepherd's degrees come from Harvard, Brown, and the University of Pennsylvania. Since 1965 he has taught nineteenth- and twentieth-century American literature at the University of Vermont. His fiction, poetry, and essays have appeared in *Colorado Quarterly, Mississippi Quarterly, Texas Studies in Literature and Language, Kansas Quarterly, Recherches Anglaises et Americaines, The New Yorker, Modern Fiction Studies, Cimarron Review, The Southern Review, The Georgia Review,* and *The New England Review.* With Arthur Biddle he wrote a chapter on short fiction in *Reading, Writing, and the Study of Literature* (Random House), with Ghita Orth the fiction section in *Angles of Vision* (McGraw-Hill), and with Ghita Orth and David Huddle is currently writing a poetry text that will be a companion volume to *About These Stories.*

This book is dedicated to Arraga Young, Marie Merrell, and Virginia Shepherd.

Contents

Preface

The essays in this book circle around three basic questions. First, they ask how the stories work. How are they put together—what decisions did the authors make regarding plot and characterization and point of view, for instance? Second, the essays reflect on what the stories mean. What, essentially, are the stories about, and how may their thematic concerns be defined? And third, the essays consider how good the stories are. What is there about them that seems particularly well done or memorable?

Not all the essays address all three questions, of course, but all three questions and the answers to them are intimately related. It is hard to talk about one without talking about the others. For instance, we come to our conclusions as to what a story is about (theme) by attending to what happens to the people in the story (plot and characterization). And if we think well of the author's development of these three short story components, we are well on our way to articulating a favorable judgment of the story.

In attempting our own answers to the three basic questions cited above, we do not presume to offer last words or definitive pronouncements. In fact, if you read carefully, you will see that the editors do not always agree with one another, which is as it should be. Each of us is—as you are—both reader and writer. Our essays derive from our experiences in reading fiction, in writing fiction, and in writing about fiction. We have consistently kept in mind the complementary interests of readers and writers. Accustoming yourself to reading fiction from a writer's perspective will lead you to ask questions of the story and to arrive at answers which might otherwise not present themselves to you.

We would like to thank Pat Carr, Western Kentucky University; Mili Clark, State University of New York at Buffalo; and Quentin Duval, Solano College, for their helpful comments and suggestions in reviewing the manuscript.

David Huddle
Ghita Orth
Allen Shepherd

About These Stories

Fiction for Fiction Writers and Readers

Introduction: Fiction for Fiction Writers and Readers

Fiction writers *make* fiction—what could possibly be said about these stories, already made by established writers, that could be useful to students learning to make stories of their own or continuing to read and write about them? How can the end results of a process of considering, choosing, and crafting help writers and readers better understand that process itself? "In terms of the craft of writing," poet Diane Wakoski says, "I think that you learn it by reading. I just don't see any other way for learning it. I think you learn more from reading than from hearing people talk."

So this book will not "talk" at you; it will not suggest exercises in plotting or character development, nor will it explain the elements of fiction or some "right" way to use images, symbols, or descriptive details. Instead, it will give you stories that work, by authors you may be familiar with and others entirely new to you, and it will ask you to read and reflect on these stories as a writer. "When writers look for certain suggestions or solutions, they find other writers," says Robert Creeley. "They find suggestions and possibilities for their own activity. I read for pleasure, obviously, too, but I read also to find out what's possible and who's got some useful answers."

Because we think the stories included here embody useful answers to the kinds of questions important to writers, we've followed each story with some thoughts about the fiction-writing possibilities it may reveal. To read fiction with a writer's eye or to write about fiction from a writer's perspective, therefore, is not to find models to imitate but rather to see the ways in which other writers handle, even juggle perhaps, those fictional concerns that you yourself are exploring. These stories don't offer the sole solutions to problems you might encounter, but, as the essays that follow them suggest, they do illustrate

1

ways of dealing with fictional material that can offer possibilities for your own creative or interpretive work.

They even demonstrate ways of generating that material. One of the first questions writers ask themselves every time they sit down to a fresh notebook or open a new computer file is "What do I write about?" Chekhov's story "A Dead Body" suggests one of the readiest answers—an autobiographical event. The essay examines the artful transmutation of what happened into finished fiction and offers informed speculation on why Chekhov proceeded as he did. Another story, Rosa's "The Third Bank of the River," demonstrates the ways material can grow from an imagined premise. In "A Hunger Artist," Kafka begins with an absurd concept—fasting as performance art—which he develops narratively into a powerful modern fable.

Once a writer has found material that challenges and engages, the next questions may well be, "What do I *do* with it? How can I find the shape that will allow it to be most effective?" The relationship of form and content is exemplified here both in the violent, dramatic events that unfold in Erdrich's "Fleur" and the seeming nonevents that make up the plot of Joyce's "Eveline." The way a structure based on narrative symmetry can hold a story together and unify its various elements is apparent in McPherson's "The Story of a Dead Man."

A writer's relation to the circumstances that a fictional plot recounts determines the story's focus of narration. The narrative perspective, the point of view, chosen by Hawthorne in "Wakefield" colors our response to the story, and Bambara's "My Man Bovanne" makes clear the ways in which language, narration, and character intertwine. But how much of characterization is dependent on information provided to the reader, and how much can be safely implied? The reader who compares the two versions of Carver's "So Much Water So Close to Home" will discover some possible answers to this question.

Plot, point of view, and characterization, however, are not the only concerns of fiction writers—events, from whatever vantage point we perceive them, happen to characters in specific places and at specific times. Mishima's "Swaddling Clothes" demonstrates some ways in which place and atmosphere can become components of meaning, while in "What I Did for Love" Schwartz uses the story's time frame and manipulation of chronology to emphasize its central concerns. The meanings any story emphasizes are, of course, embodied in the story itself—it shows rather than tells. In "The Garden Party" Mansfield uses a descriptive prose style that virtually acts out its meanings, and in "The Kiss" Alvarez builds a story around the single moment of a party game that conveys the powerful psychological, historical, and cultural forces at work on an immigrant family.

Conveying meaning is, after all, what fiction itself is "about"—each craft choice and narrative decision a writer makes affects the reader's response. In making their stories, therefore, writers share their ideas and feelings with us; they ask us to look at the world in ways that may not be our own. Hannah's "Love Too Long" and Price's "A Chain of Love" raise issues larger than the stories themselves and find ways to garner the reader's assent to their implications.

Through reading these stories then, fiction writers and fiction readers can come to recognize, as Creeley asserts, "suggestions and possibilities for their own activity." Moreover, by seeing what works in the fiction of established authors, writers and readers can find a healthy challenge to their own potential. Benjamin D. Carlisle wrote "In the Woods" as a student in an undergraduate creative writing workshop; as a junior, majoring in both English and environmental studies, Maria Hummel wrote the accompanying essay that discusses the balance of detail and conciseness in Carlisle's story. Out of our shared conviction that fiction writing and fiction reading are natural and mutually nourishing activities, we editors decided to include stories of our own and to provide accompanying essays that offer our readers some insight into how these stories came to us. To join our readers in the enterprise of coming to know a newly encountered work of fiction through writing about it, we've also included essays about one another's stories.

Reading fiction with a writer's concerns in mind does not lessen our pleasure in the work but rather can increase it by reminding us that we are not the first to have wrestled with recalcitrant material, or tested the possibilities of form and style, or tried to find a voice for our most deeply held concerns and convictions. These stories work because they have been made to work, and it is not only fiction *writers* who can benefit from considering the issues of craft involved. At any level of study, short story readers will find their sense of possibility enlarged by the ways these stories engage such questions as "What do I write about? And how?"

For the reader who is not trying to write fiction, each essay accompanying a story is offered as one approach to thinking carefully about that story. Implicitly, you are asked to compare your impressions with those of the essayist. To write about a story is to do homage to it, is to express one's regard—and in many cases, one's strong feeling—for a story. These essays are intended to be exemplary to the extent that each demonstrates one way in which a story inspired one reader to write about it. For the student carrying out a writing assignment in a literature class, it may be helpful to remember that the inspired essay is usually more warmly received than the one written out of an obligatory sense of "what the professor wants." Thus, in the early stages of thinking about writing about short stories, the first questions to be asked are "What really interests me?" "Which stories do I like best, and why do I like them?" and "What is it about this story that makes it affect me so strongly?"

A common misconception about the "critical" discussion of literature is that criticism somehow violates literary art—and indeed, insensitive criticism may be in opposition to the spirit of a literary work. However, the best critics are those who attempt most fully to understand a work of literature. Such essays come out of a reader's desire to gain a more intimate relationship with a particular story, and the measure of their success is the extent to which they enhance a reader's appreciation of the stories they accompany.

Writing about short stories is as natural as dancing to music; if you like the music, you want to get up and start moving your feet. If you like a short story, you usually want to tell somebody about it or find somebody else who has read it and wants to talk about it. Writing an essay about a story is a formalization of that impulse to "do something" in response to it. The essays here are natural responses to the stories they accompany, but they are certainly not exclusive responses. They are meant to serve readers merely as the opening remarks of a discussion that can go on indefinitely. Many more essays remain to be written about every one of these stories. The editors could hope for no more rewarding response to this book than that it inspire story writers to write more stories and story readers to have their say in writing about these stories.

ABOUT

Anton Chekhov

Anton Chekhov, grandson of a serf, was born in 1860 in the Russian provincial town of Taganrog and died at Badenweiler, Germany, in 1904. He wrote fiction (over eight hundred stories), nonfiction, and plays, of which *The Cherry Orchard* is perhaps best known. He was also a medical doctor.

A Dead Body

Anton Chekhov

A calm August night. The mist rose slowly from the fields, covering everything within view with a dull-colored winding sheet. When lit by the moon, the mist gave the impression of a quiet and limitless expanse of ocean, and at another time it resembled an immense white wall. The air was damp and chilly, and the morning still far away. There was a fire blazing a step or two beyond the pathway running along the edge of the forest. Near the small fire, under a young oak, lay a dead body covered from head to foot with a clean white linen sheet, and there was a small wooden icon lying on the dead man's chest. Beside the dead body, almost sitting in the pathway, were the "watchers," two peasants who were performing one of the most disagreeable and uninviting tasks ever given to peasants. One was a tall youngster with a faint mustache and thick black bushy eyebrows, wearing bast shoes and a tattered sheepskin jacket, his feet stretched out in front of him, as he sat in the damp grass. He was trying to make time go faster by getting down to work. His long neck was bent, and he wheezed loudly while he whittled a spoon from a big curved chunk of wood. The other was a small, thin pock-marked peasant with an ancient face, a scant mustache, and a little goatee beard. His hands had fallen on his knees, and he gazed listlessly and motionlessly into the flames.

The small pile of faggots that lay between them blazed up and threw a red glare on their faces. It was very quiet. The only sound came from the scraping of the knife on the wood and the crackling of the damp faggots in the flames.

"Don't fall asleep, Syoma," the young man said.

"Me? No, I'm not falling asleep," stammered the man with a goatee.

"That's good. It's hard sitting here alone, I'd get frightened. Talk to me, Syoma."

"I wouldn't know . . ."

"Oh, you're a strange fellow, Syomushka! Some people laugh, invent stories, and sing songs, but you—God knows what to make of you. You sit there like a scarecrow in a potato field and stare at the flames. You don't know how to put words together. . . . You're plain scared of talking. You must be getting on for fifty, but you've no more sense than a baby. Aren't you sorry you are such a fool?"

"Reckon so," said the man with a goatee gloomily.

"Well, we're sorry too. Wouldn't you say so? There you are, a good solid fellow, don't drink too much, and the only trouble is that you haven't a brain in your head. Still, if the good Lord afflicted you by making you witless, there's no reason why you shouldn't try to pick up some glimmering of intelligence, is there? Make an effort, Syoma. . . . If someone speaks a good word and you don't understand it, you ought to try to fathom it, get the sense of it somehow, keep on thinking and concentrating. If there's anything you don't understand, you should make an effort and think over exactly what it means. Do you understand me? Just make an effort! If you don't get some sense into your head, you'll die an idiot, you'll be the least important man in the world."

Suddenly a long-drawn-out moaning sound was heard from the direction of the forest. There was the sound of something being torn from the top of a tree, slithering down and rustling among the leaves, and falling to the ground, followed by a dull echo. The young man shuddered and looked searchingly at his companion.

"It's only an owl running after little birds," Syoma said gloomily.

"I'd have thought it was time for the birds to be flying to warm countries now."

"Yes, that's true."

"And the dawns are getting cold now—there's a chill in the air. Birds, too—cranes, for example—they feel the cold, they're delicate things. When it's cold like this, they die. Me, I'm not a crane, but I'm frozen. Put some more wood on!"

Syoma rose and vanished in the dark undergrowth. While he was wandering through the undergrowth, snapping off dry twigs, his companion shielded his eyes with his hands, shivering at every sound. Syoma brought back an armful of wood and threw it on the fire. Little tongues of flame licked the black twigs uncertainly, and then suddenly, as though at a word of command, the flames leapt up and enveloped their faces in a deep purple glow; and the pathway, and the white linen sheet which showed the dead man's hands and feet in relief, and the icon, all these shone with the same deep purple glow. The watchers remained silent. The young man bent his neck still lower and went back to work more nervously than ever. Meanwhile the old man with the goatee sat motionless, never taking his eyes from the fire.

"Oh, ye that love not Zion shall be ashamed in the face of the Lord!"—the silence of the night was suddenly broken by a high falsetto voice, and soft footsteps.

Into the purple firelight there emerged the dark figure of a man wearing a broad-brimmed hat and the short cassock of a monk, carrying a birch-bark sack on his shoulders.

"Thy will be done, O Lord! O Holy Mother!" he sang in a voice grown hoarse. "I saw the fire in the depths of night, and my soul leapt for joy! At first, I told myself they were keeping watch over horses, and then I told myself, it cannot be so, for there are no horses. Then, said I, they were thieves waiting to pounce upon some rich Lazarus, and then it crossed my mind they were gypsies preparing to sacrifice victims to their idols. My soul again leapt for joy! I said to myself: Go then, Theodosy, thou servant of God, receive a martyr's crown! So I flew to the fire on the gentle wings of a moth. Now I stand before you, and examine your physiognomies, and judge your souls, and I conclude you are neither thieves nor heathens! Peace be upon you!"

"Good evening to you."

"Dear brethren in God, pray tell me where I can find Makukhinsky's brick-yard?"

"It's not far. Straight down the road, and after a mile and a half you'll come to Ananova, which is our village. Turn right at the village, Father, follow the riverbank, and keep on going till you reach the brickyard. It's two miles from Ananova."

"God give you health! . . . Tell me, why are you sitting here?"

"We are keeping watch. Look over there—there's a dead body."

"Eh, what's that? A dead body! Holy Mother!"

When the stranger saw the white sheet and the icon, he shivered so violently that his legs involuntarily made little hopping motions. This unexpected sight produced an overwhelming effect. He shrank within himself and was rooted to the spot, his eyes glazed, his mouth wide open. For three minutes he remained completely silent, as though he could not believe his eyes, and then he muttered: "O Lord, O Holy Mother! I was wandering abroad and giving offense to none, and now am I consigned to punishment. . . ."

"What are you?" the young man asked. "Are you a member of the clergy?"

"No, no . . . I wander from one monastery to another. Do you know by chance Mikhail Polikarpich? He runs the brickyard, and I'm his nephew. . . . Thy will be done, O Lord! . . . What are you doing here?"

"We are the watchers. They told us to watch him."

"Yes, yes," muttered the man in the cassock, running his hands over his eyes. "Tell me—the dead man—where did he come from?"

"He was passing by."

"Well, such is life! So it is, dear brethren, and now I must go on my way. I'm all confused. I tell you, I'm more frightened of the dead than of anything else. And it comes to me that when he was living, no one paid any attention to him, and now that he is dead and delivered over to corruption, we tremble before him as though he were a great conqueror or a high official of the Church. . . . Such is life! . . . Tell me, was he murdered?"

"Christ knows! Maybe he was murdered, maybe he just died."

"Yes, yes. So it is! And who knows, dear brethren, even now his soul may be tasting the delights of Paradise."

"No, his soul is still clinging close to his body," the young man said. "It doesn't leave the body for three days."

"Hm, yes! How cold it is, eh? My teeth are chattering. . . . How do I go? Straight ahead, eh?"

"Till you reach the village, and then you turn to the right, by the river."

"By the river, eh? Why am I standing here? I must get going. Good-by, dear brethren!"

The man in the cassock took four or five steps along the path, and then stood still.

"I forgot to give a kopeck for the funeral," he said. "You are good religious people. May I—is it right for me to leave the money?"

"You should know best, since you go about from one monastery to another. Suppose he died a natural death—then it will go for the good of his soul. If he didn't, then it's a sin."

"That's true. Maybe he killed himself, and so I had better keep the money. Oh, so much evil in the world! Even if you gave me a thousand rubles, I wouldn't stay here. . . . Farewell, brothers!"

Slowly the man in the cassock moved away, and again he stood still.

"I don't know what to do," he muttered. "It's terrible to be staying here by the fire and waiting for daybreak, and it's terrible to be going along the road. I'll be haunted by him—he'll come out of the shadows! God is punishing me! I've walked for four hundred miles, and nothing ever happened to me, and now I am close to home, and there's all this misery. I can't go on. . . ."

"You're right. It's terrible."

"I'm not afraid of wolves. I'm not afraid of robbers, or the dark, but I'm afraid of the dead. I'm terrified, and that's the truth! Dear good religious brethren, I beg you on my knees to see me to the village."

"We have to stay with the body."

"Dear brethren, no one will ever know. Truly, no one will see you coming with me. God will reward you a hundredfold. You with a beard—come with me! Do me that kindness! Why doesn't he talk?"

"He hasn't got much sense," the young man said.

"Come with me, friend. I'll give you five kopecks!"

"I might, for five kopecks," the young man said, scratching the back of his head. "It's against orders, though. If Syoma, the poor fool, will stay here, then I'll come. Syoma, do you mind staying here alone?"

"I don't mind," the fool said.

"All right. Let's go."

So the young man rose and went with the man wearing a cassock, and soon the sound of their steps and the talk died away into the night.

Syoma closed his eyes and fell into a gentle sleep. The fire gradually went out, and soon the dead body was lost among great shadows.

Chekhov's Transmutation of Raw Material in "A Dead Body"

Allen Shepherd

Even if your renown as a fiction writer does not extend beyond your own family, you are likely to receive urgent, invariably well-intentioned, and always free suggestions as to the people, places, and events out of which you can, with a little work, certainly make a wonderful, publishable short story. Not to mention money, maybe lots of it. On such occasions richly decorated anecdotes are proffered; sometimes, indeed, whole life stories are put at your disposal. It is difficult to explain why someone else's facts aren't going to be the making of your fiction, but you could begin by confessing that even working up your own facts—memorable moments from your own life—is a tricky, dangerous, frustrating, and often unproductive business. Let me illustrate.

When I was a junior in college I visited a state mental institution in Massachusetts. We went in a gray bus in the rain, and it must have had something to do with a course I was taking. I don't remember the course, and it doesn't seem to me now like the sort of thing I would have done. It was thirty-seven years ago, that I know, which at least accounts for all the details I've forgotten. What I have remembered, however, could as well have happened yesterday, and I dream of it still.

The anecdote which I'm now launched into has to do with how one uses fact in fiction, how one takes possession of the material, or—in my case thus far—does not.

We were taken inside, given some sort of orientation, told to stay together and what time we were going to leave. I remember a succession of locked doors opened for us and seeing people strapped in chairs rocking as hard as they could and moaning. I ended up in a kind of game room (Alone? It doesn't seem likely). Four of us played Parcheesi. One woman sat in her chair and looked at me but did not play or speak or do anything at all. She was small and dirty. Another was larger and loud; she had red hair, and her tongue did not seem to fit inside her mouth. During the game she unbuttoned her dress to the waist and in answer to some innocent remark of mine she replied, "Full of fucks, you mean" and laughed.

The fourth person at the table could have been my grandmother. Not that she looked or sounded like her: she was probably younger and had a border state accent. I could tell that she had been, not too many years before, quite pretty. My grandmother was from Maine and was safely sane and comfortably housed outside Boston. But the woman who was not my grandmother wanted to know where I was in school, what classes I was taking, which I liked the most. She seemed pleased to discover that I was majoring in English. She apologized for the others and the circumstance. She was alone in life. Her husband had died. Her son had been killed in the South Pacific in the war. I learned her name (she introduced herself), but I can't now remember it, haven't been able to for years. We talked easily, it seemed, avoiding the present. But when I had to leave she began to get uneasy and visibly unhappy and almost cried.

It was an awful mistake, she said. She held my arm and told me that my coming was a breath of life to her and could I imagine what it was like for her to be here with these people all the time and asked would I please come back. I did not know what to do or say and was perfectly miserable. At the door (by this time someone—an attendant—had come for me, and I was late) she smiled up at me and said how much she had enjoyed our visit and that I wasn't to worry (this she whispered): everything would be all right because General MacArthur was coming up from Tennessee with an army to get her out.

As you can tell, that afternoon made a lasting impression. I have never made any notes, I have never needed to. If I were going to write a story about it, I could probably recover more details or, if not, invent some likely ones. But I have never been able to do a story wholly or partly based on that afternoon in the fall of 1957. I have God's plenty of details, my own facts, but don't (finally) know what they mean. I am trapped by the completeness of the story as given; I've never been able to take possession of it, convert it to my own use. This is to say that even using autobiographical facts entails an act of discovery.

It is the end of the story that is most troublesome. I had begun to worry that indeed she should *not* be there—she seemed so lucid, so understanding, so unhappy, so much the undefended victim. And then, of course, came the startling reversal, starring me as the innocent, though in company with a five-star general as the lady's deliverer. How to make the end of the story implicit in its beginning? Or is this simply another instance of yielding one's creative autonomy to raw factuality? Probably so.

By way of instructive contrast, consider what a master builder, Anton Chekhov, did with a scene from a Ukrainian afternoon in the 1880s—how he made "A Dead Body." First, however, a few contextual details. Chekhov passed his final round of medical examinations at the University of Moscow early in June 1884. The rest of that summer he spent as a not-very-busy attending physician at a provincial hospital at Voskresensk, near Moscow. On June 27, having heard that a murder had taken place nearby, he obtained permission to be present at the autopsy. Among Chekhov scholars, it is generally acknowledged that it was this event which inspired "A Dead Body," sometimes translated as "The Corpse." On that same day he wrote a long and colorfully detailed letter to a friend, Nikolay Leikin. Reading this letter, we are clearly looking over notes for a story, which in fact Chekhov wrote the next summer and published in September 1885. As you read the part of the letter which follows, consider what material Chekhov retained in the story, what he excluded, what he emphasized, and what he invented. Consider also how the tone changes from letter to story and why, in general, so far as you can judge, he does what he does.

> Today I attended a medico-legal autopsy which took place ten versts from V. I drove in a valiant troika with an ancient examining magistrate who could scarcely draw breath and who was almost entirely useless, a sweet little gray-haired man who had been dreaming for twenty-five years of a place on the bench. I conducted the post-mortem in a field with the help of the local district doctor, beneath the green leaves of a young oak tree, beside a country road. . . . The dead man was no one the villagers knew by name, and the peasants on whose land the body was found entreated us tearfully, by the Lord God, not to conduct the post-mortem in their village. "The women and children will be too terrified to sleep . . ." At first the examining magistrate made a wry face, because he was afraid it would rain, but later, realizing that he could make out a rough draft of his report in pencil, and seeing that we were perfectly prepared to cut up the body in the open air, he gave in to the desires of the peasants. A frightened little village, the witnesses, the village constable with his tin badge, the widow roaring away fifty yards from the post-mortem, and two peasants acting as custodians near the corpse. Near these silent custodians a small campfire was dying down. To guard over a corpse day and night until the arrival of the authorities is one of the unpaid duties of peasants. The body, in a red shirt and a pair of new boots, was covered with a sheet. On the sheet was a towel with an icon on top. We asked the policeman for water. There was water all right—a pond not far away, but no one offered us a bucket: we would pollute the water. The peasants tried to get round it; they would steal a bucket from a neighboring village. Where, how, and when they had the time to steal it remained a mystery, but they were terribly proud of their heroic feat and kept smiling to themselves. The post-mortem revealed twenty fractured ribs, emphysema, and a smell of alcohol from the stomach. The death was violent, brought about by suffocation. The chest of the drunken man had been crushed with something heavy, probably by a peasant's knee. The body was covered with abrasions produced by artificial respiration. The local peasants who found the body had applied artificial respiration so energetically for two hours that the future counsel for the defense would be justified in asking the medical expert whether the fracture of the ribs could have been caused by the attempts to revive the dead man. But I don't think the question will ever be asked. There won't be any counsel for the defense and there won't be any accused. The examining magistrate is so decrepit that he would hardly notice a sick bedbug, let alone a murderer. . . .

Quite a letter! Not surprisingly, given that the writer is a newly hatched MD, it is full of medical details, which he seems to relish. The anonymous peasant's death occasions no feeling whatsoever. Dr. Chekhov offers a whole cast of characters, a crowded scene, a sketch of the setting, a strong sense of the narrator's perspective, and a variety of humor ranging from wry to grim. At least a story and a half, one would think. Notice, in fact, how much promising material in the letter finds no place in the story. Chekhov, for example, excises the pond, the village, the policeman with his tin badge, the crowds of villagers, the local doctor, the decrepit examining magistrate, and all the business of the heroic bucket stealers. What Chekhov has done is to create a focus for his story, deliberately excluding superficially interesting, colorful, or comic details. This is to be a story of a body and two watchers—until, that is, they are joined by a fourth person, the wandering lay brother. His addition, it seems to me, is the making of the story.

Chekhov's fictional practice is astute and thoroughly professional. Between 1880 and 1884, indeed, he had published over three hundred pieces in various Moscow and Petersburg periodicals. At *Fragments,* edited by his friend Leikin and in whose pages his work had begun to appear in 1882, there were two ironclad rules which he had grudgingly assimilated. The first rule was to keep the censor always in mind; the second was that no story could run more than one hundred lines. Thus in the first instance the exclusion from the story of the letter's concluding reflections on the inadequacies of Russian justice, on murderers running free. Thus also the size of the story, carefully trimmed and shaped.

Chekhov makes a number of other strategic exclusions, consideration of which will carry us closer to thematic interpretation. Why not preserve the dead man's red shirt and new boots—wonderfully particular and authentic seeming and even poignant as these details are? I expect it is because, as the story's title, "A Dead Body" (emphasis added), suggests, Chekhov intends the dead man to remain substantially generic, anonymous, and mysterious. And if he could not allow the dead man to have new boots or a red shirt, he certainly couldn't admit his bawling widow to the story. The icon on top of the body, however, is preserved; its absence would have struck readers as unusual, odd, untypical. What begins to come clear is that thematically, the story is focused on three peasants' responses to the awful mystery of death. Who is this man? What happened to him? How did he get here? And probably, Is his soul still in the vicinity?

By comparing the first half of the letter to the story—before, that is, the peasant guardians are referred to—we remark another substantial change between letter and story. The letter, of course, is written in the first person, while the story is done in third-person point of view. The tone of the letter is that of a well-educated, intelligent, articulate man deliberately undertaking to engage and entertain his correspondent, who is also his occasional editor. Without contempt but with condescension, the peasants are represented as a lower order, other than and generically inferior to the writer. They are people by whom one is naturally amused. To read the letter is to be reminded of much unguarded nineteenth-century American writing about blacks by whites. The tone of the story is notably different, one reason for which being that in fiction Chekhov believed that by intervening to explain, judge, condemn, or absolve his characters, a writer overstepped his bounds. A writer, he thought, should be at the service of his characters, and not vice versa.

If we look at the story's first paragraph, we will see some other elements of Chekhovian strategy. In the letter Dr. Chekhov performs the postmortem in broad daylight in a field beside a road. Events in the story, however, transpire during "[a] calm August night." Though as "calm" would suggest, there is nought to fear, the fitfully illuminated darkness is preferable for atmospheric effects and for the awakening of superstitious alarm. The night derives, we may say, from the sentence in the letter which reads "To guard over a corpse day and night until the arrival of the authorities is one of the unpaid duties of peasants." Chekhov imagines how those two peasants in the letter might have passed their night and further invents for them a visitor, the lay brother.

In the scene setting of the first and second sentences of the first paragraph, mist is associated with death in the "dull-colored winding sheet," while in the third, death's awful mystery is intimated (the mist seems now a limitless ocean, now a blank wall). The fourth sentence registers further atmospheric detail (the "damp and chilly" air) but also more directly implies human response ("the morning still far away"). Next the fire (which was a "small campfire . . . dying down" in the letter), now "blazing," offers man-made illumination, warmth, cheer, and perhaps a delusive protection from the dangers of the woods. From the body, which has been undramatically educed but which will remain the focus of meaning in the story, attention shifts to the two peasant watchers.

These two peasants presumably derive from the pair Dr. Chekhov observed "acting as custodians near the corpse." About them he recorded very few details; they are said to be "silent" and "unpaid," and since they are still there after so long a wait, they may be honored as faithful. From the description of the other peasants which Chekhov provides, it appears that they are ignorant and superstitious (thus their horror at the prospect of an autopsy conducted within their village). From their determination to steal a bucket and their comic happiness at succeeding, we may conclude that they are innocently knavish, transparently hypocritical.

As we read "A Dead Body," we discover that these are substantially the qualities or circumstances which define the three living members of the cast. Syoma, for instance, is notably quiet; he is also, of the lot, the only faithful watcher. The other two are notably superstitious and hypocritical but are presented to us as comic rather than venal figures. Finally, it is the lay brother's willingness to pay the younger peasant which speeds their departure.

Chekhov indulges in no metaphysical or religious speculation; his satire is not bitter or penetrating but good humored and benign. In fact, Chekhov had been writing and performing in such scenes since childhood. "One evening," we read in Henri Troyat's biography, "he would transform himself into a dental surgeon and, armed with a pair of coal tongs and any number of grimaces, proceed to pull a recalcitrant patient's tooth. Or he was a benighted, decrepit priest being examined by his bishop. . . . Or else he would mimic the mayor . . . presiding at an endless church ceremony or reviewing a detachment of Cossacks" (Henri Troyat, *Chekhov*, trans. Michael Heim [New York: Dutton, 1986], p. 21).

From the very beginning, the two peasant watchers are played off against each other in visual and other respects. We recognize them as a Mutt-and-Jeff duo. One is tall, the other short. One is young, the other old. One is voluble, the other silent. Developing such contrasts is a basic and sometimes effective means of character differentiation but if maintained without variation is likely to seem mechanical and become tedious. Chekhov does offer variation: If we add the lay brother who is shortly to appear and if we count the dead body as a fourth character, it is apparent that the characters are presented in pairs. The two young men who so eagerly depart the scene are obviously alike in several respects; so, less obviously, are the two men who quietly remain behind.

Before the lay brother's appearance, the two peasants pursue a halting and one-sided conversation, prompted almost exclusively by the younger man's growing unease. Addressing Syoma, he assumes an air of didactic superiority. We understand why he runs on—he is comforted by the sound of his own voice—but what of his judgment of the older peasant? What is the reader to make of Syoma?

He stammers, he says little, and that "gloomily," he gazes "listlessly and motionlessly" into the fire and passively absorbs the younger man's instruction. He seems accustomed to it. It is Syoma, however, who explains the dreadful rustling in the woods, who goes unprotected into the dark to gather more twigs for the fire, and who, when at last left alone with the body, falls into a "gentle sleep." To the younger peasant, he is a "fool," and toward the end of the story the narrator assimilates the term. Thus "'I don't mind,' said the fool." But what we hear is an ironic echo, not authorial indictment of Syoma. Is Syoma a man of limited intelligence and little imagination? Is his "gentle sleep" simply a product of lethargy? Or are we to understand that Syoma's gloomy taciturnity is indicative of simplicity, self-possession, and wisdom? Maybe. All we can be sure of, however, is that like the body he keeps company with, Syoma is both as common as dirt and as impenetrable as death.

Theodosy, the lay brother, is the one character in the story who has no antecedent in the letter, unless he is a projection of the author. What sort of character is Theodosy, and why should Chekhov have invented him? He is a lineal descendant of the dentists, priests, and mayors of the author's childhood skits, a broadly comic figure, as is exemplified by his falsetto voice, his sonorous, formulaic biblical diction, his involuntary quaking, his incongruous ignorance of good religious practice, his horror at the presence of the corpse, even his destination—Makukhinsky's brickyard. Chekhov uses him principally as a catalyst, to move the story forward, to display the nature of the other two peasants, and to precipitate the conclusion. The story ends as it began, silence reestablished after brief disquiet as Syoma and the corpse are lost again "among great shadows."

Chekhov was, even at twenty-four, a writer who collected anecdotes, actively sought out material. I imagine he went to the autopsy with such thoughts somewhere in mind. Writing the letter (he kept copies of most of his letters) recorded the material, including more details than he could ever need, and suggested possibilities of characterization, plot, and theme. During the year between letter and story the narrative sorted itself out, achieved focus. As Chekhov later wrote, "I need to let a subject strain through my memory until only what is important or typical remains as in a filter."

As for the narrative of my afternoon visit to the institution those many years ago—what is to be done? General MacArthur is apparently not coming, but Chekhov's example might provide help. "A Dead Body" is a very slight story, anecdotal in its simplicity. It works as well as it does in part because of the detachment he achieved through use of the third-person point of view, removing Dr. Chekhov (of the letter) from the scene of the action. Maybe I should try the same thing, thereby escaping from the tyranny of fact. Specifically, how is the undergraduate visitor to be presented? How do the others, the patients, see him? Suppose I were also to set down the story in the present tense, a technique my colleague Professor Huddle has suggested—the aim being to get down on paper all the details that might work? I begin to see all kinds of possibilities.

ABOUT

João Guimarães Rosa

João Guimarães Rosa, born in Brazil in 1908, served in various European countries as a member of Brazil's diplomatic corps and, before his death in 1967, held a high position in the Ministry of Foreign Affairs. He was also considered his country's foremost fiction writer, publishing three collections of short stories, a two-volume edition of novellas, and a novel, *The Devil to Pay in the Backlands.* In 1963 he was made a member of the Brazilian Academy of Letters.

The Third Bank of the River

João Guimarães Rosa
(English translation by William Grossman)

My father was a dutiful, orderly, straightforward man. And according to several reliable people of whom I inquired, he had had these qualities since adolescence or even childhood. By my own recollection, he was neither jollier nor more melancholy than the other men we knew. Maybe a little quieter. It was mother, not father, who ruled the house. She scolded us daily—my sister, my brother, and me. But it happened one day that father ordered a boat.

He was very serious about it. It was to be made specially for him, of mimosa wood. It was to be sturdy enough to last twenty or thirty years and just large enough for one person. Mother carried on plenty about it. Was her husband going to become a fisherman all of a sudden? Or a hunter? Father said nothing. Our house was less than a mile from the river, which around there was deep, quiet, and so wide you couldn't see across it.

I can never forget the day the rowboat was delivered. Father showed no joy or other emotion. He just put on his hat as he always did and said goodbye to us. He took along no food or bundle of any sort. We expected mother to rant and rave, but she didn't. She looked very pale and bit her lip, but all she said was:

"If you go away, stay away. Don't ever come back!"

Father made no reply. He looked gently at me and motioned me to walk along with him. I feared my mother's wrath, yet I eagerly obeyed. We headed toward the river together. I felt bold and exhilarated, so much so that I said:

"Father, will you take me with you in your boat?"

He just looked at me, gave me his blessing, and, by a gesture, told me to go back. I made as if to do so but, when his back was turned, I ducked behind

16

some bushes to watch him. Father got into the boat and rowed away. Its shadow slid across the water like a crocodile, long and quiet.

Father did not come back. Nor did he go anywhere, really. He just rowed and floated across and around, out there in the river. Everyone was appalled. What had never happened, what could not possibly happen, was happening. Our relatives, neighbors, and friends came over to discuss the phenomenon.

Mother was ashamed. She said little and conducted herself with great composure. As a consequence, almost everyone thought (though no one said it) that father had gone insane. A few, however, suggested that father might be fulfilling a promise he had made to God or to a saint, or that he might have some horrible disease, maybe leprosy, and that he left for the sake of the family, at the same time wishing to remain fairly near them.

Travelers along the river and people living near the bank on one side or the other reported that father never put foot on land, by day or night. He just moved about on the river, solitary, aimless, like a derelict. Mother and our relatives agreed that the food which he had doubtless hidden in the boat would soon give out and that then he would either leave the river and travel off somewhere (which would be at least a little more respectable) or he would repent and come home.

How far from the truth they were! Father had a secret source of provisions: me. Every day I stole food and brought it to him. The first night after he left, we all lit fires on the shore and prayed and called to him. I was deeply distressed and felt a need to do something more. The following day I went down to the river with a loaf of corn bread, a bunch of bananas, and some bricks of raw brown sugar. I waited impatiently a long, long hour. Then I saw the boat, far off, alone, gliding almost imperceptibly on the smoothness of the river. Father was sitting in the bottom of the boat. He saw me but he did not row toward me or make any gesture. I showed him the food and then I placed it in a hollow rock on the river bank; it was safe there from animals, rain, and dew. I did this day after day, on and on and on. Later I learned, to my surprise, that mother knew what I was doing and left food around where I could easily steal it. She had a lot of feelings she didn't show.

Mother sent for her brother to come and help on the farm and in business matters. She had the schoolteacher come and tutor us children at home because of the time we had lost. One day, at her request, the priest put on his vestments, went down to the shore, and tried to exorcise the devils that had got into my father. He shouted that father had a duty to cease his unholy obstinacy. Another day she arranged to have two soldiers come and try to frighten him. All to no avail. My father went by in the distance, sometimes so far away he could barely be seen. He never replied to anyone and no one ever got close to him. When some newspapermen came in a launch to take his picture, father headed his boat to the other side of the river and into the marshes, which he knew like the palm of his hand but in which other people quickly got lost. There in his private maze, which extended for miles, with heavy foliage overhead and rushes on all sides, he was safe.

We had to get accustomed to the idea of father's being out on the river. We had to but we couldn't, we never could. I think I was the only one who understood to some degree what our father wanted and what he did not want. The thing I could not understand at all was how he stood the hardship. Day and night, in sun and rain, in heat and in the terrible midyear cold spells, with his old hat on his head and very little other clothing, week after week, month after month, year after year, unheedful of the waste and emptiness in which his life was slipping by. He never set foot on earth or grass, on isle or mainland shore. No doubt he sometimes tied up the boat at a secret place, perhaps at the tip of some island, to get a little sleep. He never lit a fire or even struck a match and he had no flashlight. He took only a small part of the food that I left in the hollow rock—not enough, it seemed to me, for survival. What could his state of health have been? How about the continual drain on his energy, pulling and pushing the oars to control the boat? And how did he survive the annual floods, when the river rose and swept along with it all sorts of dangerous objects—branches of trees, dead bodies of animals—that might suddenly crash against his little boat?

He never talked to a living soul. And we never talked about him. We just thought. No, we could never put our father out of mind. If for a short time we seemed to, it was just a lull from which we would be sharply wakened by the realization of his frightening situation.

My sister got married, but mother didn't want a wedding party. It would have been a sad affair, for we thought of him every time we ate some especially tasty food. Just as we thought of him in our cozy beds on a cold, stormy night, out there, alone and unprotected, trying to bail out the boat with only his hands and a gourd. But I knew that by then his hair and beard must have been shaggy and his nails long. I pictured him thin and sickly, black with hair and sunburn, and almost naked despite the articles of clothing I occasionally left for him.

He didn't seem to care about us at all. But I felt affection and respect for him, and, whenever they praised me because I had done something good, I said:

"My father taught me to act that way."

It wasn't exactly accurate but it was a truthful sort of lie. As I said, father didn't seem to care about us. But then why did he stay around there? Why didn't he go up the river or down to the river, beyond the possibility of seeing us or being seen by us? He alone knew the answer.

My sister had a baby boy. She insisted on showing father his grandson. One beautiful day we all went down to the river bank, my sister in her white wedding dress, and she lifted the baby high. Her husband held a parasol above them. We shouted to father and waited. He did not appear. My sister cried; we all cried in each other's arms.

My sister and her husband moved far away. My brother went to live in a city. Times changed, with their usual imperceptible rapidity. Mother finally moved too; she was old and went to live with her daughter. I remained behind, a leftover. I could never think of marrying. I just stayed there with the impedimenta of my life. Father, wandering alone and forlorn on the river, needed me.

I knew he needed me, although he never even told me why he was doing it. When I put the question to people bluntly and insistently, all they told me was that they heard that father had explained it to the man who made the boat. But now this man was dead and nobody knew or remembered anything. There was just some foolish talk, when the rains were especially severe and persistent, that my father was wise like Noah and had the boat built in anticipation of a new flood; I dimly remember people saying this. In any case, I would not condemn my father for what he was doing. My hair was beginning to turn gray.

I have only sad things to say. What bad had I done, what was my great guilt? My father always away and his absence always with me. And the river, always the river, perpetually renewing itself. The river, always. I was beginning to suffer from old age, in which life is just a sort of lingering. I had attacks of illness and of anxiety. I had a nagging rheumatism. And he? Why, why was he doing it? He must have been suffering terribly. He was so old. One day, in his failing strength, he might let the boat capsize; or he might let the current carry it downstream, on and on, until it plunged over the waterfall to the boiling turmoil below. It pressed upon my heart. He was out there and I was forever robbed of my peace. I am guilty of I know not what, and my pain is an open wound inside me. Perhaps I would know—if things were different. I began to guess what was wrong.

Out with it! Had I gone crazy? No, in our house that word was never spoken, never through all the years. No one called anybody crazy, for nobody is crazy. Or maybe everybody. All I did was go there and wave a handkerchief. So he would be more likely to see me. I was in complete command of myself. I waited. Finally he appeared in the distance, there, then over there, a vague shape sitting in the back of the boat. I called to him several times. And I said what I was so eager to say, to state formally and under oath. I said it as loud as I could:

"Father, you have been out there long enough. You are old. . . . Come back, you don't have to do it anymore. . . . Come back, and I'll go instead. Right now, if you want. Any time. I'll get into the boat. I'll take your place."

And when I had said this my heart beat more firmly.

He heard me. He stood up. He maneuvered with his oars and headed the boat toward me. He had accepted my offer. And suddenly I trembled, down deep. For he had raised his arm and waved—the first time in so many, so many years. And I couldn't . . . In terror, my hair on end, I ran, I fled madly. For he seemed to come from another world. And I'm begging forgiveness, begging, begging.

I experienced the dreadful sense of cold that comes from deadly fear, and I became ill. Nobody ever saw or heard about him again. Am I a man, after such a failure? I am what never should have been. I am what must be silent. I know it is too late. I must stay in the deserts and unmarked plains of my life, and I fear I shall shorten it. But when death comes I want them to take me and put me in a little boat in this perpetual water between the long shores; and I, down the river, lost in the river, inside the river . . . the river . . .

The What If? Story: João Guimarães Rosa's "The Third Bank of the River"

Ghita Orth

"What if . . . ?" is a question that has long held fascination for fiction writers. What if a man fell asleep for twenty years and woke into a world that had passed him by? What if a man got up one morning to find that overnight he had turned into a giant cockroach? What if these were not seen as dreams but as fictional realities? Imagining such possibilities, building a story on a "what if?" premise rather than your own or someone else's facts, can generate material as powerful as Washington Irving's "Rip Van Winkle," Franz Kafka's *Metamorphosis,* or João Guimarães Rosa's "The Third Bank of the River."

In this story, as in the life of its narrator, "what had never happened, what could not possibly happen, [is] happening." What if a previously responsible man decided to leave his family and spend the rest of his life rowing on a nearby river, "solitary, aimless, like a derelict"? Rosa asks us to confront the "phenomenon" of the story just as the narrator must confront his father's inexplicable behavior; we must accede to Rosa's premise and follow his "what if?" to its logical conclusion.

But how can *logic* have a place in a narration of "what could not possibly happen"? One of the ways in which this story, or any piece of fiction with an imagined fantastic or unlikely premise, works is by surrounding the "impossible" conjecture with recognizable human behaviors; thus it lures its readers into suspending their disbelief, as Rosa does here.

In titling his story "The Third Bank of the River," Rosa immediately suggests its concern with material beyond the entirely literal. He challenges the reader to wonder where such a "third" bank of a river could be and what its import might be in the story. We are hooked before the narration has even begun.

The story's opening paragraph, though, is, like the narrator's father, deceptively straightforward—the family depicted is immediately recognizable for its very ordinariness, even, perhaps, for its matriarchal power structure. The "But" that begins the last sentence here, however, signals the beginning of something out of the ordinary. Had Rosa written "*And* it happened one day that father ordered a boat," we might have envisioned the story's going on to recount some waterborne family adventure. As it is, we are made to recognize that the advent of the boat is somehow a contrast to the regular ongoing pattern of this family's life.

The details that follow emphasize the potential strangeness of the father's interest in this boat—he has had it built to last for many years and able to carry only one person; it is hardly meant for weekend outings with wife and children. As though to root these odd circumstances even more strongly in a shared, and thus believable, world, Rosa here begins a design in which, throughout the story, its characters' questions echo our own. The wife asks, just as the reader does, if her husband is "going to become a fisherman all of a sudden? Or a hunter?" We align ourselves with this family, which is as puzzled as we are.

Like them, faced with the seemingly inexplicable, here imaged by the father's decision to spend his life out on the river, where "he just rowed and floated across and around," we first reach for rational explanations. Thus the townspeople propose insanity, a religious vow, or a dread disease to explain why the father has so embarrassingly taken to the water. And even as we dismiss these hypotheses as too simple, we tend to come up with our own: Perhaps the father wants to escape his wife's domination, perhaps he is fed up with home and children, perhaps he is suffering a midlife personality crisis.

Rosa shows, though, that even such "answers" cannot provide a satisfactory explanation. The scolding, angry wife is revealed to have "a lot of feelings she didn't show" in her silent help in feeding her husband; the father's gentle care for his son is apparent in his blessing the boy; and his departure—quiet, unemotional, and carefully planned—is shown to be consistent with his lifelong behavior as a "dutiful, orderly, straightforward man."

Unable to determine the father's motivation, therefore, we, like his family, must come to accept his choice of life on the river as an essentially inexplicable given; we must accede to Rosa's "what if?" As the narrator reminds us, "nobody is crazy. Or maybe everybody." In this light, we can join the narrator, who, although he cannot know *why* his father travels the river, nonetheless "understood to some degree what [he] wanted and what he did not want."

What the father does not want is any part of the company gathered to deal with the emergency of his bizarre embarkation or of the larger social context it images through brother-in-law, schoolteacher, priest, soldiers, and the press. He does not want to be saved from the river and its hardships; what he does want is to be "safe" in its free-flowing currents. Even the tangles of river marshes do not daunt him—he has abandoned social complexity for his own "private maze."

Because Rosa has not provided reasons why the father has made this choice, the story asks us to concentrate instead on its effects on his family, particularly his son, the narrator. The interest, after all, that a "what if?" premise holds for fiction writers is its results—if this, then what? In investigating what these results might be, their fiction can allow the reader to understand something about human possibilities even while depicting what, in all likelihood, "could not possibly happen."

Thus, in "The Third Bank of the River" Rosa presents the effects of the father's choice as a paradigm of the ways any inexplicable absence of a loved one, by death or departure, can become a continuing presence to those left standing on the shore. Here the father, who after his leaving "never lit a fire" or "set foot on earth or grass" or "talked to a living soul," has literally abandoned the activities that we equate with living in this world. Like the dead, he "did not come back. Nor did he go anywhere, really."

His family responds to his absence in ways that we recognize as mirroring response to any unfathomable loss; if momentarily they can forget their father rowing about in the unknown, again and again they awaken into that terrible reality. It is this constant awareness of his father's absence and its probable trials that taints the narrator's enjoyment of the things of this world that he had hitherto taken for granted, its "tasty food" and "cozy beds."

Absent, the father asserts a stronger presence in his son's imagination than he did in their real life together. Indeed, the narrator visualizes his departed father with such clarity that he—and the reader—can witness the man's altered state as if experiencing it. It is as though the narrator himself were following a fictional "what if?" much as Rosa has done. Asking himself the same kinds of rhetorical questions ("What could the state of his health have been?") that the writer of such a fiction, as well as its reader, might well ask, the narrator begins an image-making process that creates a version of his father as real and immediate to the reader as to him: "I pictured him thin and sickly, black with hair and sunburn, and almost naked despite the articles of clothing I occasionally left for him." In this way the son forms an empathetic connection with his father that, though imagined, is more profound than simply providing him with clothes or food. The narrator's circumstance reminds us of the fictive capability of men and women and its inherent power. With our imaginations we can make a world as tangible and concrete as the "real" world we inhabit.

Thus, although time passes and the rest of the family move away with their lives, the narrator remains behind, unable to marry, alone with "the impedimenta of [his] life," the vivid, ageless, continual presence of his absent father. It is his sense of responsibility to this presence that robs him of a functional life of his own. Again Rosa investigates issues of consequence through the story's conjectural premise. Much as the dead or missing who remain with us only as long as there are those who remember them, the father "needs" his son, who, almost Jesus-like, sacrifices his own independent life to keeping his father's presence alive.

Despite this sacrifice, however, the aging narrator continues to suffer the guilt of the survivor: "He was out there and I was forever robbed of my peace. I am guilty of I know not what . . ." As much as he has tried to relieve the guilt of being left alive in this world by negating his possibilities for a meaningful life in it, the narrator remains in pain. By shifting in and out of present tense in its last paragraphs, the son's narration emphasizes his ongoing and intensifying torment.

"I have only sad things to say," he confesses, and the direct immediacy of that statement reminds us that the events of the story are, in fact, being told rather than shown to us. Rosa's choice of this often maligned narrative approach seems purposeful; by relying on summary rather than scene he further focuses the reader's attention on the effect of the "what if?" events rather than on these events themselves. In this way the entire story is like a reaction shot in cinematography—we never see the father directly; his equivocal departure serves to evoke those reactive responses in the narrator that are Rosa's primary concern and that the summarizing narration reveals directly.

In his ongoing struggle somehow to heal the "open wound" that his life has become, the narrator continues to ask questions: "What bad had I done . . . ?" he wonders, turning the responsibility for what has occurred against himself much as a child might do with a "father always away and his absence always with me." But the narrator is now an old man, and the pain has not stopped. Finally he posits his own ultimate "what if?"; by setting out on the river himself in his father's place, he may come to know the answers to the many questions that are torturing him and make some sense out of his life.

In the story's climactic moment, however, the son is unable to make this last sacrifice and flees in terror from the father who "seemed to come from another world" to accept his offer. Thus rejected, his father *really* disappears, for from that moment "Nobody ever saw or heard about him again." The narrator's final guilty question, "Am I a man, after such a failure?" remains, like many others in the story, unanswered. Are we to see his failure of will as a moral defeat or as a victory of life over the pull of death?

It is here that the symbolic import of the river itself may be significant. In this story, water, often a symbol of the life force, is the element on which the father effects his own metaphoric death to the world and his family. Yet, as Rosa makes clear, the old man remains preternaturally alive to his son while on the river, "always the river, perpetually renewing itself. The river, always." The river, then, does suggest a kind of continuing life, and the images of drought and desiccation with which the narrator describes his circumstances after his inability to trade places with his father seem important. "I must," he says, "stay in the deserts and unmarked plains of my life," suffering a kind of death in life as his father had metaphorically sustained a kind of life in his "death" on the water.

When, therefore, the narrator relates his final wish that when he dies he be "put in a little boat in this perpetual water between the shores," we may understand it as a desire to be in death what he could not be in life, a part of the going on of everything, as his father had been. "Inside the river," where he longs to be, he might be drawn down to its "third bank" and peace. The questions raised by the story's title are now approachable as its "what if?" has played itself out to a conclusion that seems emotionally and psychologically, if not intellectually, logical.

Although it might be tempting to assign a kind of intellectual logic to the story by reading it in heavily symbolic ways, perhaps even as Christian allegory, Rosa's approach suggests that an attempt to find neat symbolic or allegorical equations here would be reductive. Rich with rhetorical questions, repetitions, and imagined images, "The Third Bank of the River" even ends with an ellipsis. The story's elliptical nature, though, arising as it does from its evocative "what if?" premise, does not keep us from finding in it that exploration of central human concerns to which the premise has led: the mysterious ways we bind, separate from, and connect with others, and our responsibilities to them and to ourselves. Rosa, "like Noah," the narrator, and the narrator's father, here tests the possibilities for survival and continuity in the face of the inexplicable.

As this story shows, positing an impossible, or at least improbable, "what if?" and following where it can lead need not take fiction writers away from recognizable human experience; it can free them to explore it in new ways. What if a man chose to starve himself and be exhibited in a circus as a caged "hunger artist"? See Kafka's story, which follows.

ABOUT   Franz Kafka

Franz Kafka was born in Prague, Czechoslovakia, in 1883, took a law degree from the German University, and worked for most of his life as a civil servant in that city. After his death from tuberculosis in 1924, Kafka was buried in Prague. Passionately committed to his writing, he nevertheless published little during his lifetime. His friend Max Brod was responsible for the posthumous publication of three of Kafka's unfinished novels, *The Trial, The Castle,* and *Amerika.* Today Kafka is considered among the most significant Modernist fiction writers.

A Hunger Artist

Franz Kafka

During these last decades the interest in professional fasting has markedly diminished. It used to pay very well to stage such performances under one's own management, but today that is quite impossible. We live in a different world now. At one time the whole town took a lively interest in the hunger artist; from day to day of his fast the excitement mounted; everybody wanted to see him at least once a day; there were people who bought season tickets for the last few days and sat from morning till night in front of his small barred cage; even in the nighttime there were visiting hours, when the whole effect was heightened by torch flares; on fine days the cage was set out in the open air, and then it was the children's special treat to see the hunger artist; for their elders he was often just a joke that happened to be in fashion, but the children stood open-mouthed, holding each other's hands for greater security, marveling at him as he sat there pallid in black tights, with his ribs sticking out so prominently, not even on a seat but down among straw on the ground, sometimes giving a courteous nod, answering questions with a constrained smile, or perhaps stretching an arm through the bars so that one might feel how thin it was, and then again withdrawing deep into himself, paying no attention to anyone or anything, not even to the all-important striking of the clock that was the only piece of furniture in his cage, but merely staring into vacancy with half-shut eyes, now and then taking a sip from a tiny glass of water to moisten his lips.

Besides casual onlookers there were also relays of permanent watchers selected by the public, usually butchers, strangely enough, and it was their task to watch the hunger artist day and night, three of them at a time, in case he should have some secret recourse to nourishment. This was nothing but a formality, instituted to reassure the masses, for the initiates knew well enough that during his fast the artist would never in any circumstances, not even under forcible compulsion, swallow the smallest morsel of food; the honor of his profession forbade it. Not every watcher, of course, was capable of understanding this, there were often groups of night watchers who were very lax in carrying out their duties and deliberately huddled together in a retired corner to play cards with great absorption, obviously intending to give the hunger artist the chance of a little refreshment, which they supposed he could draw from some private hoard. Nothing annoyed the artist more than such watchers; they made him miserable; they made his fast seem unendurable; sometimes he mastered his feebleness sufficiently to sing during their watch for as long as he could keep going, to show them how unjust their suspicions were. But that was of little use; they only wondered at his cleverness in being able to fill his mouth even while singing. Much more to his taste were the watchers who sat close up to the bars, who were not content with the dim lighting of the hall but focused him in the full glare of the electric pocket torch given them by the impresario. The harsh light did not trouble him at all. In any case he could never sleep properly, and he could always drowse a little, whatever the light, at any hour, even when the hall was thronged with noisy onlookers. He was quite happy at the prospect of spending a sleepless night with such watchers; he was ready to exchange jokes with them, to tell them stories out of his nomadic life, anything at all to keep them awake and demonstrate to them again that he had no eatables in his cage and that he was fasting as not one of them could fast. But his happiest moment was when the morning came and an enormous breakfast was brought them, at his expense, on which they flung themselves with the keen appetite of healthy men after a weary night of wakefulness. Of course there were people who argued that this breakfast was an unfair attempt to bribe the watchers, but that was going rather too far, and when they were invited to take on a night's vigil without a breakfast, merely for the sake of the cause, they made themselves scarce, although they stuck stubbornly to their suspicions.

Such suspicions, anyhow, were a necessary accompaniment to the profession of fasting. No one could possibly watch the hunger artist continuously, day and night, and so no one could produce first-hand evidence that the fast had really been rigorous and continuous; only the artist himself could know that; he was therefore bound to be the sole completely satisfied spectator of his own fast. Yet for other reasons he was never satisfied; it was not perhaps mere fasting that had brought him to such skeleton thinness that many people had regretfully to keep away from his exhibitions, because the sight of him was too much for them, perhaps it was dissatisfaction with himself that had worn him down. For he alone knew, what no other initiate knew, how easy it was to fast. It was the easiest thing in the world. He made no secret of this, yet people did not believe him; at the best they set him down as modest; most of them, however, thought he was out for publicity or else was some kind of cheat who found it easy to fast because he had discovered a way of making it easy, and then had the impudence to admit the fact, more or less. He had to put up with all that, and in the course of time had got used to it, but his inner dissatisfaction always rankled, and never yet, after any term of fasting—this must be granted to his credit—had he left the cage of his own free will. The longest period of fasting was fixed by his impresario at forty days, beyond that term he was not allowed to go, not even in great cities, and there was good reason for it, too. Experience had proved that for about forty days the interest of the public could be stimulated by a steadily increasing pressure of advertisement, but after that the town began to lose interest, sympathetic support began notably to fall off; there were of course local variations as between one town and another or one country and another, but as a general rule forty days marked the limit. So on the fortieth day the flower-bedecked cage was opened, enthusiastic spectators filled the hall, a military band played, two doctors entered the cage to measure the results of the fast, which were announced through a megaphone, and finally two young ladies appeared, blissful at having been selected for the honor, to help the hunger artist down the few steps leading to a small table on which was spread a carefully chosen invalid repast. And at this very moment the artist always turned stubborn. True, he would entrust his bony arms to the outstretched helping hands of the ladies bending over him, but stand up he would not. Why stop fasting at this particular moment, after forty days of it? He had held out for a long time, an illimitably long time; why stop now, when he was in his best fasting form, or rather, not yet quite in his best fasting form? Why should he be cheated of the fame he would get for fasting longer, for being not only the record hunger artist of all time, which presumably he was already, but for beating his own record by a performance beyond human imagination, since he felt that there were no limits to his capacity for fasting? His public pretended to admire him so much, why should it have so little patience with him; if he could endure fasting longer, why shouldn't the public endure it? Besides, he was tired, he was comfortable sitting in the straw, and now he was supposed to lift himself to his full height and go down to a meal the very thought of which gave him a nausea that only the presence of the ladies kept him from betraying, and even that with an effort. And he looked up into the eyes of the ladies who were apparently so friendly and in reality so cruel, and shook his head, which felt too heavy on its strengthless neck. But then there happened yet again what always happened. The impresario came forward, without a word—for the band made speech impossible—lifted his arms in the air above the artist, as if inviting Heaven to look down upon its creature here in the straw, this suffering martyr, which indeed he was, although in quite another sense; grasped him around the emaciated waist, with exaggerated caution, so that the frail condition he was in might be appreciated; and committed him to the care of the blenching ladies, not without secretly giving him a shaking so that his legs and body tottered and swayed. The artist now submitted completely; his head rolled on his breast as if it had landed there by chance; his body was hollowed out; his legs in a spasm of self-preservation clung close to each other at the knees, yet scraped on the ground as if it were not really solid ground, as if they were only trying to find solid ground; and the whole weight of his body, a featherweight after all, relapsed onto one of the ladies, who, looking round for help and panting a little—this post of honor was not at all what she had expected it to be—first stretched her neck as far as she could to keep her face at least free from contact with the artist, then finding this impossible, and her more fortunate companion not coming to her aid but merely holding extended on her own trembling hand the little bunch of knucklebones that was the artist's, to the great delight of the spectators burst into tears and had to be replaced by an attendant who had long been stationed in readiness. Then came the food, a little of which the impresario managed to get between the artist's lips, while he sat in a kind of half-fainting trance, to the accompaniment of cheerful patter designed to distract the public's attention from the artist's condition; after that, a toast was drunk to the public, supposedly prompted by a whisper from the artist in the impresario's ear; the band confirmed it with a mighty flourish, the spectators melted away, and no one had any cause to be dissatisfied with the proceedings, no one except the hunger artist himself, he only, as always.

So he lived for many years, with small regular intervals of recuperation, in visible glory, honored by the world, yet in spite of that troubled in spirit, and all the more troubled because no one would take his trouble seriously. What comfort could he possibly need? What more could he possibly wish for? And if some good-natured person, feeling sorry for him, tried to console him by pointing out that his melancholy was probably caused by fasting, it could happen, especially when he had been fasting for some time, that he reacted with an outburst of fury and to the general alarm began to shake the bars of his cage like a wild animal. Yet the impresario had a way of punishing these outbreaks which he rather enjoyed putting into operation. He would apologize publicly for the artist's behavior, which was only to be excused, he admitted, because of the irritability caused by fasting; a condition hardly to be understood by well-fed people; then by natural transition he went on to mention the artist's equally incomprehensible boast that he could fast for much longer than he was doing; he praised the high ambition, the good will, the great self-denial undoubtedly implicit in such a statement; and then quite simply countered it by bringing out photographs, which were also on sale to the public, showing the artist on the fortieth day of a fast lying in bed almost dead from exhaustion. This perversion of the truth, familiar to the artist though it was, always unnerved him afresh and proved too much for him. What was a consequence of the premature ending of his fast was here presented as the cause of it! To fight against this lack of understanding, against a whole world of non-understanding, was impossible. Time and again in good faith he stood by the bars listening to the impresario, but as soon as the photographs appeared he always let go and sank with a groan back on to his straw, and the reassured public could once more come close and gaze at him.

A few years later when the witnesses of such scenes called them to mind, they often failed to understand themselves at all. For meanwhile the aforemen-tioned change in public interest had set in; it seemed to happen almost overnight; there may have been profound causes for it, but who was going to bother about that; at any rate the pampered hunger artist suddenly found him-self deserted one fine day by the amusement seekers, who went streaming past him to other more favored attractions. For the last time the impresario hurried him over half Europe to discover whether the old interest might still survive here and there; all in vain; everywhere, as if by secret agreement, a positive re-vulsion from professional fasting was in evidence. Of course it could not really have sprung up so suddenly as all that, and many premonitory symptoms which had not been sufficiently remarked or suppressed during the rush and glitter of success now came retrospectively to mind, but it was now too late to take any countermeasures. Fasting would surely come into fashion again at some future date, yet that was no comfort for those living in the present. What, then, was the hunger artist to do? He had been applauded by thousands in his time and could hardly come down to showing himself in a street booth at vil-lage fairs, and as for adopting another profession, he was not only too old for that but too fanatically devoted to fasting. So he took leave of the impresario, his partner in an unparalleled career, and hired himself to a large circus; in order to spare his own feelings he avoided reading the conditions of his con-tract.

A large circus with its enormous traffic in replacing and recruiting men, animals and apparatus can always find a use for people at any time, even for a hunger artist, provided of course that he does not ask too much, and in this particular case anyhow it was not only the artist who was taken on but his fa-mous and long-known name as well; indeed considering the peculiar nature of his performance, which was not impaired by advancing age, it could not be ob-jected that here was an artist past his prime, no longer at the height of his pro-fessional skill, seeking a refuge in some quiet corner of a circus; on the con-trary, the hunger artist averred that he could fast as well as ever, which was entirely credible; he even alleged that if he were allowed to fast as he liked, and this was at once promised him without more ado, he could astound the world by establishing a record never yet achieved, a statement which certainly pro-voked a smile among the other professionals, since it left out of account the change in public opinion, which the hunger artist in his zeal conveniently for-got.

He had not, however, actually lost his sense of the real situation and took it as a matter of course that he and his cage should be stationed, not in the mid-dle of the ring as a main attraction, but outside, near the animal cages, on a site that was after all easily accessible. Large and gaily painted placards made a frame for the cage and announced what was to be seen inside it. When the pub-lic came thronging out in the intervals to see the animals, they could hardly avoid passing the hunger artist's cage and stopping there for a moment; per-haps they might even have stayed longer had not those pressing behind them in the narrow gangway, who did not understand why they should be held up on their way towards the excitements of the menagerie, made it impossible for anyone to stand gazing quietly for any length of time. And that was the reason why the hunger artist, who had of course been looking forward to these visiting hours as the main achievement of his life, began instead to shrink from them. At first he could hardly wait for the intervals; it was exhilarating to watch the crowds come streaming his way, until only too soon—not even the most obstinate self-deception, clung to almost consciously, could hold out against the fact—the conviction was borne in upon him that these people, most of them, to judge from their actions, again and again, without exception, were all on their way to the menagerie. And the first sight of them from the distance remained the best. For when they reached his cage he was at once deafened by the storm of shouting and abuse that arose from the two contending factions, which renewed themselves continuously, of those who wanted to stop and stare at him—he soon began to dislike them more than the others—not out of real interest but only out of obstinate self-assertiveness, and those who wanted to go straight on to the animals. When the first great rush was past, the stragglers came along, and these, whom nothing could have prevented from stopping to look at him as long as they had breath, raced past with long strides, hardly even glancing at him, in their haste to get to the menagerie in time. And all too rarely did it happen that he had a stroke of luck, when some father of a family fetched up before him with his children, pointed a finger at the hunger artist and explained at length what the phenomenon meant, telling stories of earlier years when he himself had watched similar but much more thrilling performances, and the children, still rather uncomprehending, since neither inside nor outside school had they been sufficiently prepared for this lesson—what did they care about fasting?—yet showed by the brightness of their intent eyes that new and better times might be coming. Perhaps, said the hunger artist to himself many a time, things would be a little better if his cage were set not quite so near the menagerie. That made it too easy for people to make their choice, to say nothing of what he suffered from the stench of the menagerie, the animals' restlessness by night, the carrying past of raw lumps of flesh for the beasts of prey, the roaring at feeding times, which depressed him continually. But he did not dare to lodge a complaint with the management; after all, he had the animals to thank for the troops of people who passed his cage, among whom there might always be one here and there to take an interest in him, and who could tell where they might seclude him if he called attention to his existence and thereby to the fact that, strictly speaking, he was only an impediment on the way to the menagerie.

A-small impediment, to be sure, one that grew steadily less. People grew familiar with the strange idea that they could be expected, in times like these, to take an interest in a hunger artist, and with this familiarity the verdict went out against him. He might fast as much as he could, and he did so; but nothing could save him now, people passed him by. Just try to explain to anyone the art of fasting! Anyone who has no feeling for it cannot be made to understand it.

The fine placards grew dirty and illegible, they were torn down; the little notice board telling the number of fast days achieved, which at first was changed carefully every day, had long stayed at the same figure, for after the first few weeks even this small task seemed pointless to the staff; and so the artist simply fasted on and on, as he had once dreamed of doing, and it was no trouble to him, just as he had always foretold, but no one counted the days, no one, not even the artist himself, knew what records he was already breaking, and his heart grew heavy. And when once in a time some leisurely passer-by stopped, made merry over the old figure on the board and spoke of swindling, that was in its way the stupidest lie ever invented by indifference and inborn malice, since it was not the hunger artist who was cheating; he was working honestly, but the world was cheating him of his reward.

Many more days went by, however, and that too came to an end. An overseer's eye fell on the cage one day and he asked the attendants why this perfectly good cage should be left standing there unused with dirty straw inside it; nobody knew, until one man, helped out by the notice board, remembered about the hunger artist. They poked into the straw with sticks and found him in it. "Are you still fasting?" asked the overseer. "When on earth do you mean to stop?" "Forgive me, everybody," whispered the hunger artist; only the overseer, who had his ear to the bars, understood him. "Of course," said the overseer, and tapped his forehead with a finger to let the attendants know what state the man was in, "we forgive you." "I always wanted you to admire my fasting," said the hunger artist. "We do admire it," said the overseer, affably. "But you shouldn't admire it," said the hunger artist. "Well, then we don't admire it," said the overseer, "but why shouldn't we admire it?" "Because I have to fast, I can't help it," said the hunger artist. "What a fellow you are," said the overseer; "and why can't you help it?" "Because," said the hunger artist, lifting his head a little and speaking, with his lips pursed, as if for a kiss, right into the overseer's ear, so that no syllable might be lost, "because I couldn't find the food I liked. If I had found it, believe me, I should have made no fuss and stuffed myself like you or anyone else." These were his last words, but in his dimming eyes remained the firm though no longer proud persuasion that he was still continuing to fast.

"Well, clear this out now!" said the overseer, and they buried the hunger artist, straw and all. Into the cage they put a young panther. Even the most insensitive felt it refreshing to see this wild creature leaping around the cage that had so long been dreary. The panther was all right. The food he liked was brought him without hesitation by the attendants; he seemed not even to miss his freedom; his noble body, furnished almost to the bursting point with all that it needed, seemed to carry freedom around with it too; somewhere in his jaws it seemed to lurk; and the joy of life streamed with such ardent passion from his throat that for the onlookers it was not easy to stand the shock of it. But they braced themselves, crowded round the cage, and did not want ever to move away.

An Interview with a Hunger Artist

David Huddle

Us: Sir, we're delighted to have encountered you, alive and well, so to speak, here in Nice, France, and we're honored by your granting us this interview. Could you first tell us why you have agreed to step forward, to go public, as it were, and to reveal your identity to the world?

A Hunger Artist: Thank you, thank you. Yes, a very good question. This stupid desire has been my affliction from the beginning: I wish to be known. I still wish to be known, though I am no longer a practicing artist. But you see, that was always the way of it. I was never a flashy person. In games at school, I was always the one who hung back, who really didn't want to play. When called upon in school, I experienced stage fright. I begged my mother to stop giving birthday parties for me because I didn't want to be the center of attention. And yet I have always wanted to be publicly recognized for something. A terrible curse. When I discovered my gift for fasting, then my desire for public acknowledgment suddenly made sense. I had a claim. As you know, for a number of years I was internationally famous. Never famous enough to suit me, mind you—and that is a part of the curse, that no matter how much fame one has, one nevertheless wants more. But famous. And of course you know what happened to me: With a swatch of old straw, I was swept out of my filthy circus cage; I literally disappeared from sight. I was replaced with a jungle animal. A fitting end for one whose yearning for fame enabled him to reach a state of unparalleled discipline, don't you think? Consigned to oblivion. Ha, ha.

Us: By the way, why *did* they replace you with a panther, sir?

A Hunger Artist: Obviously I'm the wrong person to ask that question, don't you think? Ha, ha. Actually I think it was because the panther was incapable either of yearning for fame or of disciplining itself not to eat. But I've never held it against the animal. As a matter of fact, it was seeing that panther that inspired me to begin eating again. Even now, when I think of that magnificent animal, I feel a reinvigoration of my appetite. But of course, nowadays no one cares whether I'm hungry or not.

Us: Well, sir, we find you more than famous enough for us. After all, people have been reading your story for what now, almost a hundred years?

A Hunger Artist: Oh, no, no, no. Do I look that old? I'm barely in my seventies, you know. I was born in February 1922, they tell me—one of my creator's "late works." Better late than never, don't you think? Ha, ha. And you must remember that almost no one read my story in the beginning. My creator, Mr. Kafka (speaking of modest men), lived only until 1924, and during his lifetime he allowed only a few people to read "A Hunger Artist." Even so, there is some evidence that he honored me among his various creations. As you perhaps know, Mr. Kafka requested that all his manuscripts be burned after his death. But in his final months, he revised his will and exempted my story, along with a few other pieces of writing, from being burned. If I feel somewhat "special," I do so with good reason. But it was touch-and-go there for a while—ha, ha. In those early years, the pages on which my life depended lay in almost constant darkness. Those were very difficult times for me.

Us: Sir, have you read the essays and books that students and professors have written about you?

A Hunger Artist: I've glanced at a few academic papers over the years. I'm always shocked at how conventional they are. I would assume that someone who truly appreciated my story would try a new approach to writing about it. If nothing else, my story should inspire a reader to question the conventional thinking about artists and the ways that art is "consumed." (Forgive me.)

Us: Pardon us for asking you a conventional question, sir, but do you mind telling us how much you weigh?

A Hunger Artist: Not at all. This morning I tipped the scales at 307 pounds. Remarkable, don't you think? And I feel terrific!

Us: You have a great tan, too, if you don't mind our saying so. Would you mind commenting on your—how shall we put it?—your current size?

A Hunger Artist: Not at all. I'm quite proud of my size, as you put it. You see, my origins were in fasting. I was originally conceived—ha, ha—as someone who did not eat. Rather than being named like any normal character, I was given a *designation*, which completely restricted my identity. I was merely the one who did not eat; I was allowed no family, no private life, no hobbies, no childhood, no romance, no time off. Talk about the ultimate diet—that's my story. Ironically enough, my creator, Mr. Kafka, died of starvation. This is a little-known fact because tuberculosis was the official designation of the disease that killed him. But the tuberculosis caused lesions in his throat that prevented him from eating or drinking. Don't you find that fascinating? The further irony is that among his last acts, at Kierling Sanatorium, near Vienna, where he died, was proofreading the little volume of his stories that was about to be published—*A Hunger Artist*. Mine was the title story of that volume. When he finished the task of proofreading, he wept. It is reported that his "tears kept flowing for a long time" and that it was the first time my creator had ever been seen "overtly expressing his emotions." Among his small circle of friends, Mr. Kafka had a reputation of showing "an almost superhuman self-control."

But as to your original question: What you really mean to ask me, I think, is why I eat so much nowadays, I who ate so little in your original acquaintance with me. Well, there you have the answer, too, don't you? I eat so much now because in the past I ate so little. I have a lot of eating to make up for, don't you think?—ha, ha. No, seriously, it is all the same, eating and not eating, there isn't a great deal of difference. It all comes out of the same impulse, a pursuit of something that resides within one's inner being. One wants to eat; one wants not to eat: two sides of a coin.

Although I found not eating somewhat painful—spiritually, I mean; the physiological discomfort was never much to complain about—there was nevertheless an excitement about fasting that I still miss occasionally. But here is what may astonish you: Eating with the aim of enlarging oneself is the more difficult task. It is so tiresome after a while, because, you see, food loses its integrity, its distinctive qualities. Try eating in rapid sequence four pieces of chocolate cake, and you will see exactly what I mean. Of course there are also the social side effects: Those who are thin are admired, even if begrudgingly, whereas the obese are scorned, pitied, mocked. In restaurants, I have been tempted to lecture people who look at me in that certain way. I could tell them a thing or two.

Us: Tell me, sir. Can you account for the strangeness of your—how should we say it?—your career, or perhaps your former career?

A Hunger Artist: Strangeness is in the eye of the beholder, don't you think? Ha, ha. No, seriously, I never thought that what I was doing—public fasting— was all that strange. It seemed to me that people came to see me not so much because of the spectacle as because I represented a version of themselves they could envision all too easily. The truly strange—that which is entirely beyond our imagining—would probably not interest people nearly so much as that which is only a slight mutation of themselves. As a matter of fact, contemporary fashion is very much informed by public fasting. Surely you've heard of "hunger strikes," fasting as a political statement? And what about these successful fashion models we're seeing so much of these days? Are they not, like myself seventy years ago, unable to find the food they like, and do they not present themselves to be gazed at by millions of spectators? They are celebrities of the present day as I was in mine. I also hear that women attending American high schools and colleges are afflicted with what is currently termed "eating disorders." Perhaps you should ask one of those young women if she finds "A Hunger Artist" a truly strange story.

Us: Speaking of the opposite sex, sir, could you say a few words about your attitude toward women? As you know, the only female characters in your story are presented in heavily biased terms. If I may quote from the text of your story: "the ladies who were apparently so friendly and in reality so cruel."

A Hunger Artist: I was always at odds with my creator over that issue. I begged for changes in my story that would have allowed me some female companionship. I begged for the presence of a woman with positive qualities. Mr. Kafka insisted that in the world of "A Hunger Artist" there was no room for even the possibility of nourishment, gastronomic, psychological, or otherwise. As you may know, his own relationships with the opposite sex were extremely problematic—he kept breaking off his engagement to Miss Bauer—a maddening, brilliant, pitiful man, really. I felt sorry for him, but I tried to tell him—as diplomatically as possible—that he didn't have to intrude his personal psychosexual difficulties into my world. He insisted that his personal problems were not relevant to his artistic creations. I kept pointing out to him that perhaps it wasn't an accident that he allowed me no positive contact with the opposite sex when he himself . . . blah, blah, blah. You can imagine for yourself how these dialogues proceeded. The point is that Mr. Kafka was single-minded—if you get my drift, ha, ha. He was not to be persuaded.

All that is behind me, thank goodness. I have a new life here in Nice. I have many friends of diverse backgrounds, interests, and inclinations. For instance, one of my friends is a lovely young Swiss woman who has most considerately agreed to wake me from my customary afternoon siesta on the beach so that I may change my position and tan evenly, front and back. Many of my friends come to sit with me on the beach through the later hours of the afternoon; they never fail to bring me an ice cream or a sweet of some sort. "Omigod, I can't believe I'm feeding a hunger artist," one of my young American friends says every afternoon. "A *recovering* hunger artist," I correct him. After all, none of us is really *stuck* with who we were to begin with. These are the 1990s. Mr. Kafka wouldn't have believed the world we live in now. One can be whoever one wishes. If one wants to, one can make oneself up completely. That is my mission nowadays. I am making myself up. Ha, ha.

Us: I hope you don't mind if we go on reading your story.

A Hunger Artist: Oh, certainly not. After all, those royalties are paying my hotel bills here on the Riviera. Ha, ha. But, as they say in school, everyone should be informed about the way things were back then. Or the way Mr. Kafka imagined they were. Poor fellow. Ha, ha. If you'd like more information about him, I recommend Ernst Pawel's *The Nightmare of Reason,* published in 1984 by Farrar, Straus, Giroux, of New York. It's somewhat dated, of course, but there are fascinating photographs and some excellent quotations.

Us: Sir, what, if anything, do you, as a hunger artist, have in common with a fiction writer?

A Hunger Artist: Would you ask a glass of milk what it has in common with a cow? Would you ask an egg what it has in common with a chicken? Everything. Nothing.

Us: Thank you very much for your time and attention, sir. Good luck with your new life.

A Hunger Artist: You're very welcome. And thanks for the double order of french fries.

Louise Erdrich

Louise Erdrich, born in 1956, is a Native American short story writer, novelist, and poet; she grew up near the Turtle Mountain Chippewa Reservation in North Dakota. Erdrich teaches at Dartmouth College and has published four novels, *Love Medicine* (1984), *The Beet Queen* (1986), *Tracks* (1988), and *The Bingo Palace* (1994).

Fleur

Louise Erdrich

The first time she drowned in the cold and glassy waters of Lake Turcot, Fleur Pillager was only a girl. Two men saw the boat tip, saw her struggle in the waves. They rowed over to the place she went down, and jumped in. When they dragged her over the gunwales, she was cold to the touch and stiff, so they slapped her face, shook her by the heels, worked her arms back and forth, and pounded her back until she coughed up lake water. She shivered all over like a dog, then took a breath. But it wasn't long afterward that those two men disappeared. The first wandered off, and the other, Jean Hat, got himself run over by a cart.

It went to show, my grandma said. It figured to her, all right. By saving Fleur Pillager, those two men had lost themselves.

The next time she fell in the lake, Fleur Pillager was twenty years old and no one touched her. She washed ashore, her skin a dull dead gray, but when George Many Women bent to look closer, he saw her chest move. Then her eyes spun open, sharp black riprock, and she looked at him. "You'll take my place," she hissed. Everybody scattered and left her there, so no one knows how she dragged herself home. Soon after that we noticed Many Women changed, grew afraid, wouldn't leave his house, and would not be forced to go near water. For his caution, he lived until the day that his sons brought him a new tin bathtub. Then the first time he used the tub he slipped, got knocked out, and breathed water while his wife stood in the other room frying breakfast.

Men stayed clear of Fleur Pillager after the second drowning. Even though she was good-looking, nobody dared to court her because it was clear that Misshepeshu, the waterman, the monster, wanted her for himself. He's a devil, that one, love-hungry with desire and maddened for the touch of young girls, the strong and daring especially, the ones like Fleur.

Our mothers warn us that we'll think he's handsome, for he appears with green eyes, copper skin, a mouth tender as a child's. But if you fall into his arms, he sprouts horns, fangs, claws, fins. His feet are joined as one and his skin, brass scales, rings to the touch. You're fascinated, cannot move. He casts a shell necklace at your feet, weeps gleaming chips that harden into mica on your breasts. He holds you under. Then he takes the body of a lion or a fat brown worm. He's made of gold. He's made of beach moss. He's a thing of dry foam, a thing of death by drowning, the death a Chippewa cannot survive.

Unless you are Fleur Pillager. We all knew she couldn't swim. After the first time, we thought she'd never go back to Lake Turcot. We thought she'd keep to herself, live quiet, stop killing men off by drowning in the lake. After the first time, we thought she'd keep the good ways. But then, after the second drowning, we knew that we were dealing with something much more serious. She was haywire, out of control. She messed with evil, laughed at the old women's advice, and dressed like a man. She got herself into some half-forgotten medicine, studied ways we shouldn't talk about. Some say she kept the finger of a child in her pocket and a powder of unborn rabbits in a leather thong around her neck. She laid the heart of an owl on her tongue so she could see at night, and went out, hunting, not even in her own body. We know for sure because the next morning, in the snow or dust, we followed the tracks of her bare feet and saw where they changed, where the claws sprang out, the pad broadened and pressed into the dirt. By night we heard her chuffing cough, the bear cough. By day her silence and the wide grin she threw to bring down our guard made us frightened. Some thought that Fleur Pillager should be driven off the reservation, but not a single person who spoke like this had the nerve. And finally, when people were just about to get together and throw her out, she left on her own and didn't come back all summer. That's what this story is about.

During that summer, when she lived a few miles south in Argus, things happened. She almost destroyed that town.

When she got down to Argus in the year of 1920, it was just a small grid of six streets on either side of the railroad depot. There were two elevators, one central, the other a few miles west. Two stores competed for the trade of the three hundred citizens, and three churches quarreled with one another for their souls. There was a frame building for Lutherans, a heavy brick one for Episcopalians, and a long narrow shingled Catholic church. This last had a tall slender steeple, twice as high as any building or tree.

No doubt, across the low, flat wheat, watching from the road as she came near Argus on foot, Fleur saw that steeple rise, a shadow thin as a needle. Maybe in that raw space it drew her the way a lone tree draws lightning. Maybe, in the end, the Catholics are to blame. For if she hadn't seen that sign of pride, that slim prayer, that marker, maybe she would have kept walking.

But Fleur Pillager turned, and the first place she went once she came into town was to the back door of the priest's residence attached to the landmark church. She didn't go there for a handout, although she got that, but to ask for work. She got that too, or the town got her. It's hard to tell which came out worse, her or the men or the town, although the upshot of it all was that Fleur lived.

The four men who worked at the butcher's had carved up about a thousand carcasses between them, maybe half of that steers and the other half pigs, sheep, and game animals like deer, elk, and bear. That's not even mentioning the chickens, which were beyond counting. Pete Kozka owned the place, and employed Lily Veddar, Tor Grunewald, and my stepfather, Dutch James, who had brought my mother down from the reservation the year before she disappointed him by dying. Dutch took me out of school to take her place. I kept house half the time and worked the other in the butcher shop, sweeping floors, putting sawdust down, running a hambone across the street to a customer's bean pot or a package of sausage to the corner. I was a good one to have around because until they needed me, I was invisible. I blended into the stained brown walls, a skinny, big-nosed girl with staring eyes. Because I could fade into a corner or squeeze beneath a shelf, I knew everything, what the men said when no one was around, and what they did to Fleur.

Kozka's Meats served farmers for a fifty-mile area, both to slaughter, for it had a stock pen and a chute, and to cure the meat by smoking it or spicing it in sausage. The storage locker was a marvel, made of many thicknesses of brick, earth insulation, and Minnesota timber, lined inside with sawdust and vast blocks of ice out from Lake Turcot, hauled down from home each winter by horse and sledge.

A ramshackle board building, part slaughterhouse, part store, was fixed to the low, thick square of the lockers. That's where Fleur worked. Kozka hired her for her strength. She could lift a haunch or carry a pole of sausages without stumbling, and she soon learned cutting from Pete's wife, a string-thin blonde who chain-smoked and handled the razor-sharp knives with nerveless precision, slicing close to her stained fingers. Fleur and Fritzie Kozka worked afternoons, wrapping their cuts in paper, and Fleur hauled the packages to the lockers. The meat was left outside the heavy oak doors that were only opened at 5:00 each afternoon, before the men ate supper.

Sometimes Dutch, Tor, and Lily ate at the lockers, and when they did I stayed too, cleaned floors, restoked the fires in the front smokehouses, while the men sat around the squat cast-iron stove spearing slats of herring onto hardtack bread. They played long games of poker or cribbage on a board made from the planed end of a salt crate. They talked and I listened, although there wasn't much to hear since almost nothing ever happened in Argus. Tor was married, Dutch had lost my mother, and Lily read circulars. They mainly discussed about the auctions to come, equipment, or women.

Every so often, Pete Kozka came out front to make a whist, leaving Fritzie to smoke cigarettes and fry raised doughnuts in the back room. He sat and played a few rounds but kept his thoughts to himself. Fritzie did not tolerate him talking behind her back, and the one book he read was the New Testament. If he said something, it concerned weather or a surplus of sheep stomachs, a ham that smoked green or the markets for corn and wheat. He had a good-luck talisman, the opal-white lens of a cow's eye. Playing cards, he rubbed it between his fingers. That soft sound and the slap of cards was about the only conversation.

Fleur finally gave them a subject.

Her cheeks were wide and flat, her hands large, chapped, muscular.

Fleur's shoulders were broad as beams, her hips fishlike, slippery, narrow. An old green dress clung to her waist, worn thin where she sat. Her braids were thick like the tails of animals, and swung against her when she moved, deliberately, slowly in her work, held in and half-tamed, but only half. I could tell, but the others never saw. They never looked into her sly brown eyes or noticed her teeth, strong and curved and very white. Her legs were bare, and since she padded around in beadwork moccasins they never saw that her fifth toes were missing. They never knew she'd drowned. They were blinded, they were stupid, they only saw her in the flesh.

And yet it wasn't just that she was a Chippewa, or even that she was a woman, it wasn't that she was good-looking or even that she was alone that made their brains hum. It was how she played cards.

Women didn't usually play with men, so the evening that Fleur drew a chair up to the men's table without being so much as asked, there was a shock of surprise.

"What's this," said Lily. He was fat, with a snake's cold pale eyes and precious skin, smooth and lily-white, which is how he got his name. Lily had a dog, a stumpy mean little bull of a thing with a belly drum-tight from eating pork rinds. The dog liked to play cards just like Lily, and straddled his barrel thighs through games of stud, rum poker, vingt-un. The dog snapped at Fleur's arm that first night, but cringed back, its snarl frozen, when she took her place.

"I thought," she said, her voice soft and stroking, "you might deal me in."

There was a space between the heavy bin of spiced flour and the wall where I just fit. I hunkered down there, kept my eyes open, saw her black hair swing over the chair, her feet solid on the wood floor. I couldn't see up on the table where the cards slapped down, so after they were deep in their game I raised myself up in the shadows, and crouched on a sill of wood.

I watched Fleur's hands stack and ruffle, divide the cards, spill them to each player in a blur, rake them up and shuffle again. Tor, short and scrappy, shut one eye and squinted the other at Fleur. Dutch screwed his lips around a wet cigar.

"Gotta see a man," he mumbled, getting up to go out back to the privy. The others broke, put their cards down, and Fleur sat alone in the lamplight that glowed in a sheen across the push of her breasts. I watched her closely, then she paid me a beam of notice for the first time. She turned, looked straight at me, and grinned the white wolf grin a Pillager turns on its victims, except that she wasn't after me.

"Pauline there," she said, "how much money you got?"

We'd all been paid for the week that day. Eight cents was in my pocket.

"Stake me," she said, holding out her long fingers. I put the coins in her palm and then I melted back to nothing, part of the walls and tables. It was a long time before I understood that the men would not have seen me no matter what I did, how I moved. I wasn't anything like Fleur. My dress hung loose and my back was already curved, an old woman's. Work had roughened me, reading made my eyes sore, caring for my mother before she died had hardened my face. I was not much to look at, so they never saw me.

When the men came back and sat around the table, they had drawn together. They shot each other small glances, stuck their tongues in their cheeks,
burst out laughing at odd moments, to rattle Fleur. But she never minded.
They played their vingt-un, staying even as Fleur slowly gained. Those pen-
nies I had given her drew nickels and attracted dimes until there was a small
pile in front of her.

Then she hooked them with five-card draw, nothing wild. She dealt, discarded, drew, and then she sighed and her cards gave a little shiver. Tor's eye
gleamed, and Dutch straightened in his seat.

"I'll pay to see that hand," said Lily Veddar.

Fleur showed, and she had nothing there, nothing at all.

Tor's thin smile cracked open, and he threw his hand in too.

"Well, we know one thing," he said, leaning back in his chair, "the squaw
can't bluff!"

With that I lowered myself into a mound of swept sawdust and slept. I
woke up during the night, but none of them had moved yet, so I couldn't either. Still later, the men must have gone out again, or Fritzie come out to break
the game, because I was lifted, soothed, cradled in a woman's arms and rocked
so quiet that I kept my eyes shut while Fleur rolled me into a closet of grimy
ledgers, oiled paper, balls of string, and thick files that fit beneath me like a
mattress.

The game went on after work the next evening. I got my eight cents back
five times over, and Fleur kept the rest of the dollar she'd won for a stake. This
time they didn't play so late, but they played regular, and then kept going at it
night after night. They played poker now, or variations, for one week straight,
and each time Fleur won exactly one dollar, no more and no less, too consistent
for luck.

By this time, Lily and the other men were so lit with suspense that they got
Pete to join the game with them. They concentrated, the fat dog sitting tense in
Lily Veddar's lap, Tor suspicious, Dutch stroking his huge square brow, Pete
steady. It wasn't that Fleur won that hooked them in so, because she lost hands
too. It was rather that she never had a freak hand or even anything above a
straight. She only took on her low cards, which didn't sit right. By chance,
Fleur should have gotten a full or flush by now. The irritating thing was she
beat with pairs and never bluffed, because she couldn't, and still she ended up
each night with exactly one dollar. Lily couldn't believe, first of all, that a
woman could be smart enough to play cards, but even if she was, that she
would then be stupid enough to cheat for a dollar a night. By day I watched
him turn the problem over, his hard white face dull, small fingers probing at
his knuckles, until he finally thought he had Fleur figured out as a bit-time
player, caution her game. Raising the stakes would throw her.

More than anything now, he wanted Fleur to come away with something
but a dollar. Two bits less or ten more, the sum didn't matter, just so he broke
her streak.

Night after night she played, won her dollar, and left to stay in a place that
just Fritzie and I knew about. Fleur bathed in the slaughtering tub, then slept in

the unused brick smokehouse behind the lockers, a windowless place tarred on the inside with scorched fats. When I brushed against her skin I noticed that she smelled of the walls, rich and woody, slightly burnt. Since that night she put me in the closet I was no longer afraid of her, but followed her close, stayed with her, became her moving shadow that the men never noticed, the shadow that could have saved her.

August, the month that bears fruit, closed around the shop, and Pete and Fritzie left for Minnesota to escape the heat. Night by night, running, Fleur had won thirty dollars, and only Pete's presence had kept Lily at bay. But Pete was gone now, and one payday, with the heat so bad no one could move but Fleur, the men sat and played and waited while she finished work. The cards sweat, limp in their fingers, the table was slick with grease, and even the walls were warm to the touch. The air was motionless. Fleur was in the next room boiling heads.

Her green dress, drenched, wrapped her like a transparent sheet. A skin of lakeweed. Black snarls of veining clung to her arms. Her braids were loose, half-unraveled, tied behind her neck in a thick loop. She stood in steam, turning skulls through a vat with a wooden paddle. When scraps boiled to the surface, she bent with a round tin sieve and scooped them out. She'd filled two dishpans.

"Ain't that enough now?" called Lily. "We're waiting." The stump of a dog trembled in his lap, alive with rage. It never smelled me or noticed me above Fleur's smoky skin. The air was heavy in my corner, and pressed me down. Fleur sat with them.

"Now what do you say?" Lily asked the dog. It barked. That was the signal for the real game to start.

"Let's up the ante," said Lily, who had been stalking this night all month. He had a roll of money in his pocket. Fleur had five bills in her dress. The men had each saved their full pay.

"Ante a dollar then," said Fleur, and pitched hers in. She lost, but they let her scrape along, cent by cent. And then she won some. She played unevenly, as if chance was all she had. She reeled them in. The game went on. The dog was stiff now, poised on Lily's knees, a ball of vicious muscle with its yellow eyes slit in concentration. It gave advice, seemed to sniff the lay of Fleur's cards, twitched and nudged. Fleur was up, then down, saved by a scratch. Tor dealt seven cards, three down. The pot grew, round by round, until it held all the money. Nobody folded. Then it all rode on one last card and they went silent. Fleur picked hers up and blew a long breath. The heat lowered like a bell. Her card shook, but she stayed in.

Lily smiled and took the dog's head tenderly between his palms.

"Say, Fatso," he said, crooning the words, "you reckon that girl's bluffing?"

The dog whined and Lily laughed. "Me, too," he said, "let's show." He swept his bills and coins into the pot and then they turned their cards over.

Lily looked once, looked again, then he squeezed the dog up like a fist of dough and slammed it on the table.

Fleur threw her arms out and drew the money over, grinning that same wolf grin that she'd used on me, the grin that had them. She jammed the bills in her dress, scooped the coins up in waxed white paper that she tied with string.

"Let's go another round," said Lily, his voice choked with burrs. But Fleur opened her mouth and yawned, then walked out back to gather slops for the one big hog that was waiting in the stock pen to be killed.

The men sat still as rocks, their hands spread on the oiled wood table. Dutch had chewed his cigar to damp shreds, Tor's eye was dull. Lily's gaze was the only one to follow Fleur. I didn't move. I felt them gathering, saw my stepfather's veins, the ones in his forehead that stood out in anger. The dog had rolled off the table and curled in a knot below the counter, where none of the men could touch it.

Lily rose and stepped out back to the closet of ledgers where Pete kept his private stock. He brought back a bottle, uncorked and tipped it between his fingers. The lump in his throat moved, then he passed it on. They drank, quickly felt the whiskey's fire, and planned with their eyes things they couldn't say out loud.

When they left, I followed. I hid out back in the clutter of broken boards and chicken crates beside the stock pen, where they waited. Fleur could not be seen at first, and then the moon broke and showed her, slipping cautiously along the rough board chute with a bucket in her hand. Her hair fell, wild and coarse, to her waist, and her dress was a floating patch in the dark. She made a pig-calling sound, rang the tin pail lightly against the wood, froze suspiciously. But too late. In the sound of the ring Lily moved, fat and nimble, stepped right behind Fleur and put out his creamy hands. At his first touch, she whirled and doused him with the bucket of sour slops. He pushed her against the big fence and the package of coins split, went clinking and jumping, winked against the wood. Fleur rolled over once and vanished in the yard.

The moon fell behind a curtain of ragged clouds, and Lily followed into the dark muck. But he tripped, pitched over the huge flank of the pig, who lay mired to the snout, heavily snoring. I sprang out of the weeds and climbed the side of the pen, stuck like glue. I saw the sow rise to her neat, knobby knees, gain her balance, and sway, curious, as Lily stumbled forward. Fleur had backed into the angle of rough wood just beyond, and when Lily tried to jostle past, the sow tipped up on her hind legs and struck, quick and hard as a snake. She plunged her head into Lily's thick side and snatched a mouthful of his shirt. She lunged again, caught him lower, so that he grunted in pained surprise. He seemed to ponder, breathing deep. Then he launched his huge body in a swimmer's dive.

The sow screamed as his body smacked over hers. She rolled, striking out with her knife-sharp hooves, and Lily gathered himself upon her, took her foot-long face by the ears and scraped her snout and cheeks against the trestles of the pen. He hurled the sow's tight skull against an iron post, but instead of knocking her dead, he merely woke her from her dream.

She reared, shrieked, drew him with her so that they posed standing upright. They bowed jerkily to each other, as if to begin. Then his arms swung and flailed. She sank her black fangs into his shoulder, clasping him, dancing him forward and backward through the pen. Their steps picked up pace, went wild. The two dipped as one, box-stepped, tripped each other. She ran her split foot through his hair. He grabbed her kinked tail. They went down and came up, the same shape and then the same color, until the men couldn't tell one from the other in that light and Fleur was able to launch herself over the gates, swing down, hit gravel.

The men saw, yelled, and chased her at a dead run to the smokehouse. And Lily too, once the sow gave up in disgust and freed him. That is where I should have gone to Fleur, saved her, thrown myself on Dutch. But I went stiff with fear and couldn't unlatch myself from the trestles or move at all. I closed my eyes and put my head in my arms, tried to hide, so there is nothing to describe but what I couldn't block out, Fleur's hoarse breath, so loud it filled me, her cry in the old language, and my name repeated over and over among the words.

The heat was still dense the next morning when I came back to work. Fleur was gone but the men were there, slack-faced, hung over. Lily was paler and softer than ever, as if his flesh had steamed on his bones. They smoked, took pulls off a bottle. It wasn't noon yet. I worked awhile, waiting shop and sharpening steel. But I was sick, I was smothered, I was sweating so hard that my hands slipped on the knives, and I wiped my fingers clear of the greasy touch of the customers' coins. Lily opened his mouth and roared once, not in anger. There was no meaning to the sound. His boxer dog, sprawled limp beside his foot, never lifted its head. Nor did the other men.

They didn't notice when I stepped outside, hoping for a clear breath. And then I forgot them because I knew that we were all balanced, ready to tip, to fly, to be crushed as soon as the weather broke. The sky was so low that I felt the weight of it like a yoke. Clouds hung down, witch teats, a tornado's green-brown cones, and as I watched one flicked out and became a delicate probing thumb. Even as I picked up my heels and ran back inside, the wind blew suddenly, cold, and then came rain.

Inside, the men had disappeared already and the whole place was trembling as if a huge hand was pinched at the rafters, shaking it. I ran straight through, screaming for Dutch or for any of them, and then I stopped at the heavy doors of the lockers, where they had surely taken shelter. I stood there a moment. Everything went still. Then I heard a cry building in the wind, faint at first, a whistle and then a shrill scream that tore through the walls and gathered around me, spoke plain so I understood that I should move, put my arms out, and slam down the great iron bar that fit across the hasp and lock.

Outside, the wind was stronger, like a hand held against me. I struggled forward. The bushes tossed, the awnings flapped off storefronts, the rails of porches rattled. The odd cloud became a fat snout that nosed along the earth and sniffed, jabbed, picked at things, sucked them up, blew them apart, rooted around as if it was following a certain scent, then stopped behind me at the butcher shop and bored down like a drill.

I went flying, landed somewhere in a ball. When I opened my eyes and looked, stranger things were happening.

A herd of cattle flew through the air like giant birds, dropping dung, their mouths opened in stunned bellows. A candle, still lighted, blew past, and tables, napkins, garden tools, a whole school of drifting eyeglasses, jackets on hangers, hams, a checkerboard, a lampshade, and at last the sow from behind the lockers, on the run, her hooves a blur, set free, swooping, diving, screaming as everything in Argus fell apart and got turned upside down, smashed, and thoroughly wrecked.

Days passed before the town went looking for the men. They were bachelors, after all, except for Tor, whose wife had suffered a blow to the head that made her forgetful. Everyone was occupied with digging out, in high relief because even though the Catholic steeple had been torn off like a peaked cap and sent across five fields, those huddled in the cellar were unhurt. Walls had fallen, windows were demolished, but the stores were intact and so were the bankers and shop owners who had taken refuge in their safes or beneath their cash registers. It was a fair-minded disaster, no one could be said to have suffered much more than the next, at least not until Fritzie and Pete came home.

Of all the businesses in Argus, Kozka's Meats had suffered worst. The boards of the front building had been split to kindling, piled in a huge pyramid, and the shop equipment was blasted far and wide. Pete paced off the distance the iron bathtub had been flung—a hundred feet. The glass candy case went fifty, and landed without so much as a cracked pane. There were other surprises as well, for the back rooms where Fritzie and Pete lived were undisturbed. Fritzie said the dust still coated her china figures, and upon her kitchen table, in the ashtray, perched the last cigarette she'd put out in haste. She lit it up and finished it, looking through the window. From there, she could see that the old smokehouse Fleur had slept in was crushed to a reddish sand and the stockpens were completely torn apart, the rails stacked helter-skelter. Fritzie asked for Fleur. People shrugged. Then she asked about the others and, suddenly, the town understood that three men were missing.

There was a rally of help, a gathering of shovels and volunteers. We passed boards from hand to hand, stacked them, uncovered what lay beneath the pile of jagged splinters. The lockers, full of the meat that was Pete and Fritzie's investment, slowly came into sight, still intact. When enough room was made for a man to stand on the roof, there were calls, a general urge to hack through and see what lay below. But Fritzie shouted that she wouldn't allow it because the meat would spoil. And so the work continued, board by board, until at last the heavy oak doors of the freezer were revealed and people pressed to the entry. Everyone wanted to be the first, but since it was my stepfather lost, I was let go in when Pete and Fritzie wedged through into the sudden icy air.

Pete scraped a match on his boot, lit the lamp Fritzie held, and then the three of us stood still in its circle. Light glared off the skinned and hanging carcasses, the crates of wrapped sausages, the bright and cloudy blocks of lake ice, pure as winter. The cold bit into us, pleasant at first, then numbing. We must have stood there a couple of minutes before we saw the men, or more rightly, the humps of fur, the iced and shaggy hides they wore, the bearskins they had taken down and wrapped around themselves. We stepped closer and tilted the lantern beneath the flaps of fur into their faces. The dog was there, perched among them, heavy as a doorstop. The three had hunched around a barrel where the game was still laid out, and a dead lantern and an empty bottle, too. But they had thrown down their last hands and hunkered tight, clutching one another, knuckles raw from beating at the door they had also attacked with hooks. Frost stars gleamed off their eyelashes and the stubble of their beards. Their faces were set in concentration, mouths open as if to speak some careful thought, some agreement they'd come to in each other's arms.

Power travels in the bloodlines, handed out before birth. It comes down through the hands, which in the Pillagers were strong and knotted, big, spidery, and rough, with sensitive fingertips good at dealing cards. It comes through the eyes, too, belligerent, darkest brown, the eyes of those in the bear clan, impolite as they gaze directly at a person.

In my dreams, I look straight back at Fleur, at the men. I am no longer the watcher on the dark sill, the skinny girl.

The blood draws us back, as if it runs through a vein of earth. I've come home and, except for talking to my cousins, live a quiet life. Fleur lives quiet too, down on Lake Turcot with her boat. Some say she's married to the waterman, Misshepeshu, or that she's living in shame with white men or windigos, or that she's killed them all. I'm about the only one here who ever goes to visit her. Last winter, I went to help out in her cabin when she bore the child, whose green eyes and skin the color of an old penny made more talk, as no one could decide if the child was mixed blood or what, fathered in a smokehouse, or by a man with brass scales, or by the lake. The girl is bold, smiling in her sleep, as if she knows that people wonder, as if she hears the old men talk, turning the story over. It comes up different every time and has no ending, no beginning. They get the middle wrong too. They only know that they don't know anything.

Fantasy and Violence in Louise Erdrich's "Fleur"

Allen Shepherd

Every year since 1966, at 7:30 on the last Saturday evening in January and the first two in February, I have gone to the Golden Gloves boxing tournament at Memorial Auditorium, which a number of my friends and acquaintances seem to find almost as odd, even mysterious, as the fact that I'm a Republican. Indeed, perhaps they make a connection. How can an apparently decent person (resembling themselves) take pleasure in others' pain, or have voted, the first time (1988), for George Bush? I tell them that they should know at least one Republican and one person who is devoted to boxing; in me they get two for one.

My Republicanism is clearly too arcane a topic for consideration here, but by way of approaching Louise Erdrich's "Fleur," it ought to be possible to examine how a viewer's (or reader's) response to violence may be conditioned or directed. As it happens, years ago while still an undergraduate I had three amateur bouts, of which I lost the third very one-sidedly. Even as I was losing, however, I was aware that the person to whom I was losing was not really very good. And even though I wasn't skillful enough to counter him successfully, I knew that it could be done, fairly easily. Just a matter of being able to perform physically what you understand intellectually. Thus I know what I'm seeing at Golden Gloves, know the rush of adrenaline, but I also know how hard it is even to keep your hands up for two or three minutes at a time, let alone outmaneuver an opponent. All of this is to say that I take with some seriousness even the inept performances in the ring, although they are frequently comic.

Let me illustrate with a brief anecdote. One year, perhaps a month before the Golden Gloves finals, a local sports announcer of many years' service had died and it was thought fitting that immediately before the first fight his memory be honored by a tolling of the bell ten times, signifying that although he was down for the count he had not been forgotten. Members of the audience were asked to rise in silent tribute. No one, however, had thought to communicate these ceremonial plans to the first two boxers on the card. Thus when after waiting nervously in their corners through "The Star-Spangled Banner," they at last heard the bell, they attacked furiously. Then not only did the bell *keep* tolling, but remarkably everyone in the audience was on their feet watching, but not making a sound, which produced (as you can imagine) a truly prodigious effort—double hooks, triple jabs, quadruple uppercuts. Nobody was hurt, but a number (excluding the combatants) were vastly entertained.

As regards Erdrich's "Fleur," selected incidents from my career as a devotee of boxing seem to suggest that ordinary life, even as lived by a Republican, may present experiences that are every bit as strange as what a reader encounters in the most fantastic of short stories. That's to say we all have our resources, interpretive and creative.

Consider now the opening line of "Fleur": "The *first time* [my emphasis] she drowned in the cold and glassy waters of Lake Turcot, Fleur Pillager was only a girl." Erdrich here puts us on notice that the sort of violence which this story features, to include the deaths of six named men and one dog, not to mention anonymous others, is not to be taken in the same way as, for example, a realistic reportorial account of a bloody civil war in Eastern Europe, complete with "ethnic cleansing," or—to focus on the performer's perspective—a chilling prison interview with, for instance, Jeffrey Dahmer, in which he recalls at some length, in considerable and vivid detail, how he waylaid his many victims and then assaulted, tortured, and killed them, then preserved and ate parts of some of them. In conclusion, he remarks that he still feels the urge sometimes.

"Fleur" is a different kind of narrative. Anyone who twice survives drowning, as Fleur does, has a substantial edge over the rest of us; anyone who crosses her had best be very careful. By the end of the first paragraph, in fact, the two Indian men unwise enough to save her have disappeared and within a page the pattern has been repeated: Another man, the ironically named George Many Women, has interposed himself and paid the price. Fleur Pillager lives up to her oxymoronic name: She is both exotically attractive and, if interfered with, a fearful despoiler of merely human beings.

Consider the violence she is responsible for, how it is performed, to whom, and with what results. Immediately after the two men have completed their rescue, such as would earn them medals in other narratives, we read: "But it wasn't long afterward that those two men disappeared." Cause and effect are implied, not stated; if Fleur is responsible for the disappearances, it is through the operation of her own or another's supernatural powers. More specifically, in the next sentence, we're told: "The first wandered off, and the other, Jean Hat, got himself run over by a cart." For whatever happened, the men are made to seem responsible, as even the locution "got himself run over" suggests.

Then in the next paragraph the men's fate is further recast, as it is made metaphorical: "By saving Fleur Pillager, those two men had lost themselves." George Many Women, the next victim, was very careful, didn't lay a hand on Fleur, just looked. But he died by water just the same, accidentally, it seems, in his own bathtub. One man wanders away, another is run over, the third drowns; all die from Fleur's bad intentions, but it's they who are guilty.

Thus, when the poker games begin in Argus, we have little doubt as to the fate of the three besotted men who imagine they can outplay her and then, when this fails, undertake to assault her. That they should do so makes perfect sense, however, for she has, literally and metaphorically, beat them at what they consider their own game. Fleur's limiting her winnings to exactly a dollar a night constitutes a further affront to their masculine pride, indicating as it does the measure of control she exerts over the proceedings. We cannot be surprised at the three men's subsequent deaths in the freezing storage locker, both because Pauline locks them in (though one of them is her stepfather) and because it is filled with ice from Lake Turcot, the home of Misshepeshu, thought to be Fleur's demon lover. And these three men, of course, recall the first three who died.

What characters look like substantially affects our response to them and how we regard violence done to them. For example, consider how Fleur is described—that her "shoulders were broad as beams, her hips fishlike, slippery, narrow," or that she is missing the fifth toe on each foot, or that her "braids were thick like the tails of animals," or, finally, that the men at Kozka's Meats "never looked into her sly brown eyes or noticed her teeth, strong and curved and very white." She is as much animal or fish as conventionally human; we are not surprised to learn that she is adept at shape shifting, that at night she is said to hunt in the form of a bear. The men at Kozka's, however, were "blinded, they were stupid, they only saw her in the flesh."

Consider now what these men look like and how it affects our response to their deaths. Lily, for example, is "fat, with a snake's cold pale eyes and precious skin, smooth and lily-white." Lily's dog is "a stumpy mean little bull of a thing with a belly drum-tight from eating pork rinds." When these two are frozen solid, there can't be many mourners. If, by unlikely contrast, one of Fleur's poker opponents were a handsome young man, happily married, with two delightful small children, we would feel different about his demise, assuming that he hadn't participated in the assault upon her.

Erdrich employs the same kind of readily accessible symbolism in chronicling the violence wrought in Argus by the (apparently) supernaturally raised tornado. Performing retributive justice, the storm rips off the steeple of the Catholic church, emblematic of white religion and male dominance. It was this very steeple which drew Fleur to Argus in the first place, when she was perhaps looking for men who would not try to save her. "Of all the businesses in Argus," we're told, "Kozka's Meats had suffered worst," yet "the back rooms where Fritzie and Pete lived were undisturbed." Mr. and Mrs. Kozka, then, who had done no evil to Fleur, were exempt from harm.

"Fleur" features violence aplenty, but we always know how to take it. The violence is induced by the male victims, who seem to deserve it; it is not raw and bloody, but metaphorical and fantastic. Pauline, the narrator, hears a voice in the tornado, which "spoke plain so [she] understood" that she was to lock the three men in the freezer, even as a "herd of cattle flew through the air like giant birds, dropping dung, their mouths opened in stunned bellows." A voice out of the storm (which puts one in mind of biblical passages), airborne cattle passing overheard (which makes one think of a cartoon), and, below ground, three men and a dog, frozen solid (which, depicted as they are, makes them appear surreal): This is Erdrich's vision.

To some readers, "Fleur" has proved a puzzling and intimidating story, balancing as it does the magical and the mundane, and, as a classic instance of the open-ended narrative, yielding no resolution. As Pauline tells us, "It comes up different every time and has no ending, no beginning." Perhaps not, but the essence of the narrative is clear enough. Fleur is "out of control." "She messed with evil, laughed at the old women's advice, and dressed like a man. She got herself into some half-forgotten medicine, studied ways we shouldn't talk about." At one time she would have been punished as a witch; in some circles today, perhaps, decried as a radical feminist.

No merely human male seems adequate as Fleur's consort; thus the introduction of Misshepeshu, who is perhaps the father of her child and to whom "some say she's married." Other rumors suggest "that she's living in shame with white men or windigos, or that she's killed them all." Fatal Fleur, consorting with the enemy or cohabitating with fiends. Windigos, by the way, are evil demons, in Algonquian mythology; they are also, alternatively, a mythical tribe of cannibals believed to inhabit an island in Hudson Bay.

Variations on a theme are embodied in the violent conflict between Fleur and a number of male antagonists. Contrasted with this battle is the evolving alliance between Fleur and Pauline, who, we hear in the story's last paragraph, is "about the only one here who ever goes to visit her." And it was Pauline who "went to help out in her cabin when she bore the child." We are offered two perspectives on their developing relationship, one apparent in the evolution of plot, the other in the management of point of view.

As regards plot, Fleur asks Pauline to stake her in the poker game, then, many hours later, in almost maternal fashion, lifts, soothes, and cradles Pauline before putting her to sleep. The next day Fleur repays the loan five times over, after which, no longer afraid of her, Pauline follows Fleur, "stayed with her, became her moving shadow that the men never noticed, the shadow that could have saved her." Out of fear Pauline fails Fleur, however, when Fleur is assaulted, presumably gang-raped, in the smokehouse. Afterward, directed by a voice in the wind, Pauline locks the three men in the meat freezer, thereby perhaps redeeming herself. As the story ends, we hear that "[p]ower travels in the bloodlines" and are given reason to believe that Pauline shares some of that sisterly power with Fleur.

Erdrich's management of point of view also exemplifies their evolving relationship and is perhaps the most interesting technical aspect of the story. Although Pauline is throughout "Fleur" the first-person narrator, Erdrich achieves some of the effects of third-person narrative as her purposes dictate. Pauline preceded Fleur to Argus; working part-time at Kozka's Meats, she is strategically situated to observe Fleur's triumphs and travails. Almost as if addressing the issue of point of view, how first may yield to third, Pauline says,

> I was a good one to have around because until they needed me, I was invisible.
> . . . Because I could fade into a corner or squeeze beneath a shelf, I knew everything, what the men said when no one was around, and what they did to Fleur.

From this point on, Erdrich is no longer obligated formally to account for Pauline's presence. At story's end, Pauline resumes her role as communal observer, now possessing, however, the authority of one who was there unseen, who knows what others do not know.

My own experience with fantasy and violence, as a writer, leads me to conclude that George Many Women had it about right—that in such an alien environment, in the presence of such powers, one has to be very careful. He met a faintly ridiculous fate, you remember, while his wife was fixing breakfast in the kitchen. Given my choice, I would prefer to be having a cup of coffee with her.

Now that may just be the Republican in me speaking. Toll the bell for *me*, however, and Misshepeshu had better watch himself.

ABOUT _____ James Joyce

James Joyce, born in Dublin in 1882, left Ireland at twenty. Although he spent the rest of his life in Europe, the city of his birth was always at the center of his fiction—*Dubliners* (1914), short stories, and the novels *Portrait of the Artist as a Young Man* (1916), *Ulysses* (1922), and *Finnegans Wake* (1939). Best known for his innovative fiction, Joyce also published poetry and *Exiles,* a play. He died in Zurich in 1941 and is buried there.

Eveline

James Joyce

She sat at the window watching the evening invade the avenue. Her head was leaned against the window curtains and in her nostrils was the odour of dusty cretonne. She was tired.

Few people passed. The man out of the last house passed on his way home; she heard his footsteps clacking along the concrete pavement and afterwards crunching on the cinder path before the new red houses. One time there used to be a field there in which they used to play every evening with other people's children. Then a man from Belfast bought the field and built houses in it—not like their little brown houses but bright brick houses with shining roofs. The children of the avenue used to play together in that field—the Devines, the Waters, the Dunns, little Keogh the cripple, she and her brothers and sisters. Ernest, however, never played: he was too grown up. Her father used often to hunt them in out of the field with his blackthorn stick; but usually little Keogh used to keep *nix* and call out when he saw her father coming. Still they seemed to have been rather happy then. Her father was not so bad then; and besides, her mother was alive. That was a long time ago; she and her brothers and sisters were all grown up; her mother was dead. Tizzie Dunn was dead, too, and the Waters had gone back to England. Everything changes. Now she was going to go away like the others, to leave her home.

Home! She looked around the room, reviewing all its familiar objects which she had dusted once a week for so many years, wondering where on earth all the dust came from. Perhaps she would never see again those familiar objects from which she had never dreamed of being divided. And yet during all those years she had never found out the name of the priest whose yellowing photograph hung on the wall above the broken harmonium beside the coloured print of the promises made to Blessed Margaret Mary Alacoque. He had been a school friend of her father. Whenever he showed the photograph to a visitor her father used to pass it with a casual word:

—He is in Melbourne now.

She had consented to go away, to leave her home. Was that wise? She tried to weigh each side of the question. In her home anyway she had shelter and food; she had those whom she had known all her life about her. Of course she had to work hard both in the house and at business. What would they say of her in the Stores when they found out that she had run away with a fellow? Say she was a fool, perhaps; and her place would be filled up by advertisement. Miss Gavan would be glad. She had always had an edge on her, especially whenever there were people listening.

—Miss Hill, don't you see these ladies are waiting?

—Look lively, Miss Hill, please.

She would not cry many tears at leaving the Stores.

But in her new home, in a distant unknown country, it would not be like that. Then she would be married—she, Eveline. People would treat her with respect then. She would not be treated as her mother had been. Even now, though she was over nineteen, she sometimes felt herself in danger of her father's violence. She knew it was that that had given her the palpitations. When they were growing up he had never gone for her, like he used to go for Harry and Ernest, because she was a girl; but latterly he had begun to threaten her and say what he would do to her only for her dead mother's sake. And now she had nobody to protect her. Ernest was dead and Harry, who was in the church decorating business, was nearly always down somewhere in the country. Besides, the invariable squabble for money on Saturday nights had begun to weary her unspeakably. She always gave her entire wages—seven shillings—and Harry always sent up what he could but the trouble was to get any money from her father. He said she used to squander the money, that she had no head, that he wasn't going to give her his hard-earned money to throw about the streets, and much more, for he was usually fairly bad of a Saturday night. In the end he would give her the money and ask her had she any intention of buying Sunday's dinner. Then she had to rush out as quickly as she could and do her marketing, holding her black leather purse tightly in her hand as she elbowed her way through the crowds and returning home late under her load of provisions. She had hard work to keep the house together and to see that the two young children who had been left to her charge went to school regularly and got their meals regularly. It was hard work—a hard life—but now that she was about to leave it she did not find it a wholly undesirable life.

She was about to explore another life with Frank. Frank was very kind, manly, open-hearted. She was to go away with him by the night-boat to be his wife and to live with him in Buenos Ayres where he had a home waiting for her. How well she remembered the first time she had seen him; he was lodging in a house on the main road where she used to visit. It seemed a few weeks ago. He was standing at the gate, his peaked cap pushed back on his head and his hair tumbled forward over a face of bronze. Then they had come to know each other. He used to meet her outside the Stores every evening and see her home. He took her to see *The Bohemian Girl* and she felt elated as she sat in an unaccustomed part of the theatre with him. He was awfully fond of music and sang a little. People knew that they were courting and, when he sang about the lass that loves a sailor, she always felt pleasantly confused. He used to call her Poppens out of fun. First of all it had been an excitement for her to have a fellow and then she had begun to like him. He had tales of distant countries. He had started as a deck boy at a pound a month on a ship of the Allan Line going out to Canada. He told her the names of the ships he had been on and the names of the different services. He had sailed through the Straits of Magellan and he told her stories of the terrible Patagonians. He had fallen on his feet in Buenos Ayres, he said, and had come over to the old country just for a holiday. Of course, her father had found out the affair and had forbidden her to have anything to say to him.

—I know these sailor chaps, he said.

One day he had quarrelled with Frank and after that she had to meet her lover secretly.

The evening deepened in the avenue. The white of two letters in her lap grew indistinct. One was to Harry; the other was to her father. Ernest had been her favourite but she liked Harry too. Her father was becoming old lately, she noticed; he would miss her. Sometimes he could be very nice. Not long before, when she had been laid up for a day, he had read her out a ghost story and made toast for her at the fire. Another day, when their mother was alive, they had all gone for a picnic to the Hill of Howth. She remembered her father putting on her mother's bonnet to make the children laugh.

Her time was running out but she continued to sit by the window, leaning her head against the window curtain, inhaling the odour of dusty cretonne. Down far in the avenue she could hear a street organ playing. She knew the air. Strange that it should come that very night to remind her of the promise to her mother, her promise to keep the home together as long as she could. She remembered the last night of her mother's illness; she was again in the close dark room at the other side of the hall and outside she heard a melancholy air of Italy. The organ-player had been ordered to go away and given sixpence. She remembered her father strutting back into the sickroom saying:

—Damned Italians! coming over here!

As she mused the pitiful vision of her mother's life laid its spell on the very quick of her being—that life of common place sacrifices closing in final craziness. She trembled as she heard again her mother's voice saying constantly with foolish insistence:

—Derevaun Seraun! Derevaun Seraun!

She stood up in a sudden impulse of terror. Escape! She must escape! Frank would save her. He would give her life, perhaps love, too. But she wanted to live. Why should she be unhappy? She had a right to happiness. Frank would take her in his arms, fold her in his arms. He would save her.

She stood among the swaying crowd in the station at the North Wall. He held her hand and she knew that he was speaking to her, saying something about the passage over and over again. The station was full of soldiers with brown baggages. Through the wide doors of the sheds she caught a glimpse of the black mass of the boat, lying in beside the quay wall, with illumined portholes. She answered nothing. She felt her cheek pale and cold and, out of a maze of distress, she prayed to God to direct her, to show her what was her duty. The boat blew a long mournful whistle into the mist. If she went, to-morrow she would be on the sea with Frank, steaming towards Buenos Ayres. Their passage had been booked. Could she still draw back after all he had done for her? Her distress awoke a nausea in her body and she kept moving her lips in silent fervent prayer.

A bell clanged upon her heart. She felt him seize her hand:

—Come!

All the seas of the world tumbled about her heart. He was drawing her into them: he would drown her. She gripped with both hands at the iron railing.

—Come!

No! No! No! It was impossible. Her hands clutched the iron in frenzy. Amid the seas she sent a cry of anguish!

—Eveline! Evvy!

He rushed beyond the barrier and called to her to follow. He was shouted at to go on but he still called to her. She set her white face to him, passive, like a helpless animal. Her eyes gave him no sign of love or farewell or recognition.

Conflict and Plot in James Joyce's "Eveline"

Ghita Orth

In life, trouble is the last thing we need; in fiction, it's the first. If the word processor loses your term paper file or the bus breaks down on your way to work, you have trouble, but since you now can say, "Wait till you hear what happened today!" you also have the beginning of a story. "What happens" in a piece of fiction is its plot; what sets that plot in motion is a problematic situation, usually involving some kind of tension or conflict—in other words, trouble.

Our sense of fictional conflict, nurtured in movie theaters or in front of television screens, might seem to demand the high drama of physical confrontation and multiple suspenseful events, as in "Fleur." In "Eveline," only a few pages long, James Joyce proves, however, that trouble in fiction doesn't have to be grand in scale to capture the reader's attention or involvement.

Nothing "happens" in this recounting of Eveline's evening until the last terrible moments at dockside; that final scene could seem just a gimmick, a gratuitously surprising reversal of our, and Eveline's, expectations, until we recognize that this seemingly plotless narrative *does* move, logically, inexorably, to the foregone resolution of its central conflict.

Contrary to cinematic expectations, there are no speaking voices to be heard in most of the story, and someone watching for "action" would not see any. Eveline simply sits thinking at her window; she does not do anything, nor does she say anything aloud. This externally static scene, though, one that would put movie audiences to sleep, is not without tension and conflict. In "Eveline," Joyce demonstrates the ways in which trouble, seen as *inner* conflict and *psychological* tension, can, in fiction, be rendered as powerful as any shouting match or fistfight.

The internal conflict on which the plot of the story turns is clear. The pull of habit and conformity, suggested by Eveline's relationship with her father, her dead-end job, and her promise to her dying mother, is opposed by the lure of love, freedom, and new life exemplified by Frank, the wandering sailor. The fact that Eveline never even moves until she stands in terror at the end of the first section suggests the paralyzing effect of these opposing claims. Each pulls on her with seemingly equal force; while at the fulcrum of this conflict, she is literally immobilized.

And yet the story itself does move. As with any fictional plot, it leads us to a denouement that, while surprising, also seems on reflection to be the inevitable result of the "events" that preceded it. If the issue central to the story's suspense is "Will she really leave?" Joyce's narrative approach resolves it as certainly as if we watched Eveline involved in a sequence of dramatic actions. What can substitute for such actions to lead a story along toward some resolution of its conflict? Perhaps a different definition of action—one in which language, detail, and image take center stage.

We are introduced to Eveline simply "watching" the world outside her window. She sees the evening actively "invade" the street, but Joyce describes her own behavior in passive constructions: "Her head was leaned against the window and in her nostrils was the odour of dusty cretonne." By the story's second sentence, then, even before the narration provides access to Eveline's thoughts, we have been made to notice her passivity; we begin to wonder if her lack of energy is its cause or its result. Her inaction has begun the story's "action."

With the story's second paragraph, Joyce provides the necessary exposition that locates Eveline for us in the circumstances of her life, circumstances that may help explain her enervation. She has been left by the passage of years to live in a claustrophobic "little brown house," with a dominating father and memories of a dead mother and a lost and happier childhood. As the details that delineate Eveline's situation at home accumulate, we recognize its oppressive limitations—her lack of financial independence, her responsibility for two small children, her fear of her father's drunken violence.

Like Eveline, we acknowledge hers as "a hard life." Seeing what is wrong with its patterns of repression, we know the unlikelihood of her ever being able to breathe freely within its confines, and we understand her seeming commitment to "go away." What is harder to understand, though, is why Eveline calls such a life a not "wholly undesirable" one. Joyce, however, has built into the story's language evidence of Eveline's fear of the unknown and her dependence on what, though repressive and constricting, is at least familiar.

Revelatory as any dialogue, Eveline's unspoken words serve to foreshadow and explain the final resolution of her conflict. Although told by a third-person narrator, the story presents Eveline's thoughts in her own language of vulnerability. Joyce's careful fidelity to the diction of Eveline's mental processes clarifies her motivations and allows him indirectly to reveal truths of which she remains consciously unaware. The way characters think—their habits of mind—can reveal a lot about them to a reader.

Eveline's thoughts are marked, for example, by recurrent conditionals ("People would treat her with respect then"), qualifiers ("she did not find it a wholly undesirable life"), rhetorical questions ("Was that wise?"), and repetitions of the word "home." Thus, even though Eveline avers at the end of the second paragraph that she is going "to leave her home," these verbal characteristics emphasize her tenuous hold on the decision she has ostensibly made. Eveline may think she has no trouble, just as the reader might think the narrative consequently has no plot, but her conflict has yet to play itself out in the drama of her silent inner monologue.

Significantly, in that monologue the present virtually disappears, although in the story's time frame all the "action" takes place in one evening, with a space to indicate the brief passage of time before Eveline's appearance at the North Wall. Yet during the present time of the story Eveline's thoughts constantly shift back into the past, about which she concludes "Everything changes," and forward into the future, about which she can only conditionally hope "all would be well." Her considerations of this unknown and unreal future with Frank inevitably lead back to memories of the lost past and its "familiar objects from which she had never dreamed of being divided." The present, for Eveline, seems as much an "unaccustomed" place as the part of the theater in which she sat with Frank to see *The Bohemian Girl*, yet it is in the present that she must act if she is to leave the past, in which she "*seemed* to have been *rather* happy" (emphasis mine), and move into the future with Frank.

Eveline's thoughts, like her immobility, thus reveal a potentially paralyzing incapacity for decisive present action that foreshadows the story's outcome. So too, as in a more overtly plotted work, her relation to other characters in her life helps us to understand the denouement toward which the narrative is moving. Although ostensibly a one-character story, "Eveline" is richly peopled. Characters need not appear in the flesh in a piece of fiction to have an effect on its protagonist and on the reader.

Frank, the complicating agent in the plot as in Eveline's life, is associated throughout with romantic escape. He woos her, Othello-like, with exotic "tales of distant countries" far from the confines of her narrow window on the world, takes her to an opera about the freedom of Gypsy life, and sings of "the lass that loves a sailor." The seagoing Frank engenders confusion in housebound Eveline, but she feels it "pleasantly." The refrain of his song,

> But the standing toast that pleas'd the most
> Was the wind that blows,
> The ship that goes,
> And the lass that loves a sailor,

implies a world of love, freedom of movement, and possibility that she has not known before. It is to "Buenos Ayres" that Frank would take her on the ship, a city of *good air*, free of the dust that hovers around her enclosed Dublin home. We readily assent to Eveline's assertions at the end of the story's first section: "She must escape! Frank would save her."

But does *she* really assent? If so, her change of mind at story's end can only seem inexplicable and unmotivated. Like her thought patterns, however, Eveline's relation to other characters in the story can help clarify her later behavior. As dashing as "kind, manly, open-hearted" Frank seems, he must compete with ghosts, dead or alive, from Eveline's past. Some of these ghosts also suggest "the ship that goes"; they have managed their own escapes through independent adulthood, emigration, or death. Even the priest whose presence in the musty house is reduced to an aging "yellowing photograph" has himself been liberated to Australia.

The Italians who have dared to choose a new land, however, are "damned" in Eveline's father's eyes, and in contrast to those characters who are images of potential freedom are those who are antithetical emblems of entrapment. The print of Blessed Margaret Mary Alacoque, for example, honors a saint whose childhood paralysis, self-inflicted tortures, and mortifications of the flesh were rewarded by revelations indicating she had been chosen to be martyred for the sins and weaknesses of others.

Eveline's father embodies such human failings. Both physically and psychologically threatening, he has locked Eveline into a martyrlike pattern of dependency that she accepts as inevitable, as somehow her due—"of course" when he learns about Frank he forbids her to see him. Eveline's willingness to continue to meet the magnetic Frank in secret suggests some measure of self-assertion, but her inability to acknowledge her father's oppression as oppression, rather than simply his prerogative as a father, is clear when she dutifully concedes he sometimes "could be very nice" and finds ways of rehabilitating him in her memories.

In those memories the "pitiful vision" of Eveline's mother, who patiently bore her husband's violence and "that life of commonplace sacrifices" that Eveline herself knows too well, could serve as an object lesson of how not to live one's life. Instead, however, it seems to emphasize the ongoing pattern of repression and passivity in which Eveline's role, one she promised her mother to continue, has become nearly habitual. Eveline's own "palpitations" of fear may even mirror the tremulous beginnings of her mother's descent into "final craziness." Her mother's garbled final words have been variously interpreted;

they may be merely lunatic ravings, or, as one critic has suggested, "Derevaun Seraun" may be corrupt Gaelic for "the end of pleasure is pain," a grimly prophetic warning to anyone who might think of reaching for a better, happier life.

Even though Eveline consciously does not want to be "treated as her mother had been," through these inhibiting characters and Eveline's relation to them, Joyce makes clear the pull of the familiar pattern of self-sacrifice and entrapment that, coupled with Eveline's innate passivity (even at work she is told to "Look lively"), may keep her from the man who "would give her life" if she could give herself to that possibility.

Thus, although nothing seems to have happened to advance the story's narrative while Eveline sits silent at the window, Joyce has clearly revealed the nature of Eveline's "trouble" and, through the focus and texture of her thoughts alone, has provided the exposition, suspense, foreshadowing, and character interactions that traditionally constitute the rising action of a plot. When, in her first visible action, Eveline leaps to her feet at the end of the story's first section, her "terror" seems less a fear of leaving than of being unable to leave. Its intensity is a measure of the strength of the pull toward stasis and paralysis which, Joyce has shown, she will have to counteract if she is to escape.

That she is, ultimately, unable to do so has been prepared for by what has gone before, even in her final moments at home, when we might expect her happily to count the minutes until her flight to freedom, she thinks, in the language of a condemned criminal whose execution is approaching, that "Her time was running out." The story's final scene, in which Eveline's time does run out, functions as the climax of the plot—the point of no return, when the shifting balance of conflicting forces in a story irrevocably tips in one direction or the other.

Because of the direction in which this story has been moving, it is shocking but not really surprising that at the climactic moment when Eveline must make an immediate, crucial decision, she is paralyzed, incapable of seizing the present. Many critics have looked closely at the language of this section, noting the possible implications of the "black mass" of the boat and the "seas of the world," which could be a life-giving source of vitality but which threaten Eveline with drowning in an unknown element.

One need not read these passages symbolically, though, to recognize their import—suddenly almost unhearing, unspeaking, physically nauseated, Eveline is reduced to "silent fervent prayer." She can ask for a sign, she cannot make one. Even her pain is presented in an image of entrapment; unable to find her way "out of a maze of distress," Eveline prays for direction from God. She is simply and entirely incapable of freeing herself, of taking charge of her own life. The final image of Eveline gripping the "iron railing" that surrounds her is that of a caged, insensible, "passive . . . helpless animal." Dehumanized, her emotionless eyes are vacant; she seems to be irrevocably locked in a "close dark room" like the one in which she sat as the story began and the one in which her mother died.

It would seem, then, that Eveline's potential for animated life has not been lost to her only because of one moment's failure of will. As the story implies, that potential has been leached out of her by all the moments of static impotence that have characterized her life and conditioned her thinking. From the story's first sentence we have watched and listened to a young woman unable to break the enervating bonds of emotional passivity. It is understandable that Eveline's one crucial action in the story is a commitment to *in*action.

The assumption that Eveline has a conscious decision before her has thus been an illusion from the beginning. Even as she attempts "to weigh each side of the question," Joyce makes clear through the story's plot that she has no real choice. It is not her choosing noble "duty" to home and family that finally negates Eveline's possibility of leaving; rather, she is doomed by the ingrown weakness of will and spirit that Joyce's narrative approach has revealed. When this seemingly plotless story has drawn to its inevitable conclusion, we may be disturbed by that conclusion and wish it otherwise, but we have been convinced by language, detail, and image that Eveline's conflict has been resolved in the only way possible for her. The only thing she can do is not do anything.

In its brief span, "Eveline" thus demonstrates some of the ways in which fiction can speak in whispers rather than shouts, move in barely visible increments rather than leaps. When you whisper, people have to listen carefully; when you move stealthily, they have to observe closely. The audience of this kind of story can't just sit back and watch, the way it might a wide-screen extravaganza. Reading stories like "Eveline," you become involved in the meaning-making process; writing them, you compel the reader's attention to, and participation in, their progressing action. And "Eveline" does progress. Joyce has managed to resolve one of fiction's paradoxes—he has written about stasis in a story that is not itself static. It is possible, then, to write about boredom without being boring, to convey lethargy without putting your reader to sleep, to create dramatic conflict and action without high drama.

The potential for trouble exists in even the smallest of circumstances. This fact may not make our lives any easier, but it makes our stories possible.

James Alan McPherson

James Alan McPherson was born in 1943 in Savannah, Georgia.
He is a graduate of Harvard Law School and the University of
Iowa Writers' Workshop. McPherson has held jobs as a paper-
boy, a dining car waiter, a janitor, a community organizer, a research assistant, and a newspaper reporter. His first collection of
stories, *Hue and Cry,* was published in 1969. For his second,
Elbow Room (1977), he won the Pulitzer Prize. McPherson has
taught at the University of Virginia and the University of Iowa.

The Story of a Dead Man

James Alan McPherson

It is not true that Billy Renfro was killed during that trouble in Houston. The
man is an accomplished liar and likes to keep his enemies nervous. It was he
who spread this madness. The truth of what happened, he told me in Chicago,
was this: After tracking the debtor to a rented room, Billy Renfro's common
sense was overwhelmed by the romantic aspects of the adventure. That was
why he kicked open the door, charged boldly into the room, and shouted,
"Monroe Ellis, give *up* Mr. Floyd's Cadillac that you done miss nine payments
on!" Unhappily for Billy, neither Monroe Ellis nor the woman with him was in
the giving-up mood. The woman fired first, aiming from underneath Ellis on
the bed. Contrary to most reports, that bullet only wounded Billy's arm. It was
one of the subsequent blasts from Monroe's .38 that entered Billy's side. But
this wound did not slow Billy's retreat from the room, the rooming house, or
the city of Houston. He was alive and fully recovered when I saw him in
Chicago, on his way back from Harvey after reclaiming a defaulted Chevy.

Neither is it true, as certain of his enemies have maintained, that Billy's left
eye was lost during a rumble with that red-neck storekeep outside Limehouse,
South Carolina. That eye, I now have reason to believe, was lost during domestic troubles. That is quite another story. But I have this full account of the
Limehouse difficulty: Billy had stopped off there en route to Charleston to re-
possess another defaulting car for this same Mr. Floyd Dillingham. He entered
the general store with the sole intention of buying a big orange soda. However,
the owner of the joint, a die-hard white supremacist, refused to execute the
transaction. Being naturally suspicious of governmental intervention, Billy fell

59

back on his own resources: He reached for the .22 he carried under his shirt for just such dalliances. But the storekeep was too swift. While Billy's right hand was still moving cloth, the red-neck was caressing the trigger of his Springfield and looking joyous: "Private club, *Mr.* Nigger!" the red-neck sang. Though he is a liar and a madman, my cousin Billy Renfro is no fool. He allowed himself to be two-stepped and back-backed out of the place, the storekeep, of course, making all the leading moves. As Billy sped off, the red-neck fired several rounds into the air and gave a hungry rebel yell. Billy did not respond.

On his return from Charleston, however, the defaulted car reclaimed, he experienced an overpowering thirst for a big orange soda. This thirst became obsessive as he neared Limehouse. It was a hot, sleepy day, nearing sunset, and his arrival at the general store went unnoticed. Billy was at the counter blowing gently on his .22 before the storekeep could resurface from the reveries he enjoyed, dozing in his wicker rocking chair. "*Two* big orange sodas and a dill pickle!" my cousin ordered. Liar that he is, he told me in Chicago that he belched nonchalantly before departing from the store. I do not believe this, but I believe him when he said he shot off five rounds, and gave a swamp cry, when he was in his car and pointed toward Atlanta. Ah, Billy! It is part of his style to add such touches.

I bother to refute these rumors because the man is my cousin, and I am honor-bound to love him as I know he really is. He and I are one with the same ancestors, and whatever fires rage in him I must look to find smolderings of within myself. Recognizing this obligation, I here attempt to deflate mean rumors circulated by his enemies, cut through the fat of Billy's own lies, and lay bare the muscles of his life. From youth onward, he has possessed a warm heart and a certain tolerance of misfortune; and he is as likely, for a friend, to strip the shirt from his back as he is to murder. That he contains such broad extremes speaks favorably of his eventual reform.

I myself have contributed considerable energy toward this goal. In Chicago, when we drank together in that dive on Halstead, I offered my best advice for whatever it was worth to him. "We are no longer young men," I said. "The foam has settled down into the beer. I, myself, no longer chase women, speak hotly, challenge opinions too far different from my own. I have learned it is to my advantage to get along. Chelseia, the woman I plan to marry, you will meet in a few hours. She is steady and refined, and will bear me sturdy children. In short, Billy, in my manhood I have become aware of complexity. You owe it to the family, and to the memory of your mother, to do the same."

Billy swished his Scotch and drank it down, then rapped the glass on the table to alert the barmaid. When she looked, he pointed two fingers downward toward our glasses and kissed at her. Then, turning to focus his single, red-rimmed eye on my face, he said, "Bullshit!"

He was dressed in the black gabardine suit of an undertaker. Dried purple-black blood streaked his coat sleeves, his black string tie, and the collar of the dirty white shirt he wore.

"People change, Billy," I said.

"Bullshit!" Billy Renfro said.

I looked closely at him and saw a gangster. He was not the kind of man I wanted to meet my family. I glanced at my watch and sipped my drink. I listened to his stories.

Billy spun his usual lies.

This meeting in Chicago took place three years after he began work for this Mr. Dillingham, seven years after his mother's death, and thirteen years after Billy, at seventeen, went to prison for life. But I will speak here of his life before he went to prison, for insights into what he might have become. His mother was my father's sister, and both gave their first-born males the same treasured family name. Both my cousin and I were named "William" after our paternal grandfather, Willie Joe Warner, a jackleg Baptist preacher. But because her child was somewhat older, Billy's mother claimed for him the more affectionate nickname "Billy." I will not speak here of the grandfather in whose shadow we both lived, but I have heard it mentioned in the family that he favored, in his old age, the name "William" over the more secular "Billy." I would not swear to this, however, because my father winked when he told it to me. And Billy's mother, whom we nicknamed "Mama Love," laughed loudly when I asked her confirmation. I accepted my name. Billy gloried in his, draining from it as much territory as the world would concede.

He outgrew me from the start, perhaps because his father succumbed to alcohol before Billy was ten. And his mother, soon afterward made invalid by a stroke, let her son roam freely. Evenings at his house, playing in his room, Billy taught me the dozens, chanted bawdy songs, drilled me on how to eyeball a girl with maximum style. I followed as much of his advice, given the stricter circumstances of my home, as was discreet. I loved him, but I loved his mother more. Billy loved only the streets. And since Mama Love could not contain his wanderings, she gave up finally and developed a defensive sense of humor. While Billy gallivanted, I would go and sit with her and listen to her spin raucous anecdotes about her wayward son. She loved him deeply. This was witnessed in the contrast between her merry, mysterious eyes and her unhappy face whenever she shook her head and sighed, and said, "Ah, Billy! He just won't *do*!"

I suffered with Mama Love when Billy, at sixteen, threw away his youth. Here, as I recall, is how it happened: Always one to embrace completely any adventure, Billy ran wild with a crowd of older boys whose imagination lacked the brakes of self-restraint. Following their tottering lead, Billy was dared to test the first full wetness of his manhood in the arms of a much experienced girl. This girl, I have reason to believe, knew better than he how unerringly passion can boomerang, especially when heated by the trusting flame of innocence. I believe that Billy was unaware. At least this was his defense to the girl's father, and also the female judge notorious in our city for curbing wayward boys, and protecting the coffers of the state, with one stiff dose of justice.

"You feed that baby," Judge Gladys Moon told him.

I was with him in court that day and heard Billy's plea. He said, "Judge, that baby don't even *look* like me."

Judge Moon sat stone-faced and sober. "You feed it anyway," she told Billy, "and it might look like you. Feed it for twenty-one years, and if it don't look like you after twenty-one years, you don't have to feed it no more."

While I completed school, he worked as the relay man on a garbage truck. While I attended church and learned social graces, he became more a loner, grew sullen, worked a tentative cynicism into his voice. The whites of his eyes reddened. He cultivated a process, dressed flashily, began socializing on a certain street corner sanctified by a tree that had once stood there. These developments cracked his mother's heart. She believed with Judge Gladys Moon that it was Billy's baby. He protested this violently, expressing bitterness that of all the boys who had known the girl, he alone had had to pay. And because Mama Love could not bear to fight him, she ordered him finally out of her home. Yet she still loved her son, and often sent messages and food to him by me. But during this time I began avoiding most social contacts with Billy, because I too believed that he was guilty. Besides, our vocabularies were growing rapidly apart. He moved into a rented room with his common-law wife and child, a room in a section of the city I dreaded to enter. The year I finished high school and won a church scholarship to college, Billy stabbed during a dice game a man who had questioned the honor of Billy's common-law wife. But to Billy's credit it must be said that he waited until the man, who was winning, had lost back to the others in the game as much as they had lost to him. The code required such graciousness, even before a deadly act. This man died, and Billy's life was finished.

As a favor to his mother, who could not go herself, I took off from college and went by bus to Harper's Farm, where, in those days, black men were stocked for the road gangs. I waited for Billy in the moist, chicken-wired reception room. Around me sat weeping mothers, sportily dressed sweethearts, somber wives. The pungent smells of overripe peaches, sweat, potato salad, toilet water and fried chicken assaulted my nose. Over in a corner, on a wooden bench, a sun-whipped trustee, with his eyes closed and his face turned upward toward the ceiling, was singing:

> *They 'cuse me of* mur-der,
> *Never harm a man.*
> *Never harm a man.*
> *I say, "Wake up, old* Dead Man
> *Help me ca'ry my load*
> *Help me ca'ry my load! . . ."*

I did not want to be in such a place.

When Billy came out and took his seat, I studied him through the chicken wire. This was long before he lost the eye, and there was the beginning of a rough handsomeness about his face. His hair, processed heavily now in the style of Nat King Cole, was protected from the flies and red dust by a blue and yellow cloth bandanna. He wore prison-issue blues, the worn paleness of which contrasted favorably with his sun-glossed skin. He chewed gum rapidly. Behind him, coming in the door from the prison section, I could see gelded young men walking with legs jangling loosely. Caged, they seemed bent on proving, to watching wives and sweethearts, that their manhood was still intact.

"Billy," I said through the dirty wire, "why do you insist on breaking your mama's heart? She suffers because she cannot be here. Yet she would suffer even more if she could see you here in this death-infected place. Look around you at these wasted men," I urged him, "then look me in the eye and tell me you like the future you have set for yourself."

But he would not look me in the eye. Nor would he respond to my pleadings. Instead, he chewed arrogantly. Then he smiled. In that smile was a mysterious humor that I had not, before this meeting, observed in his manner. Billy looked past me, perhaps at the waiting women seated on the benches against the walls, perhaps at the humming trustee. He tossed his head and said, "Me, I'm a dead man."

I drew my chair up closer to the wire. "It does not have to end that way," I told him.

"What you doin' with your life?" he asked me.

"Making something of it," I answered.

"That's good," Billy said.

Over in the corner, the trustee stopped humming and sang:

> *Well, the load so* hea-vy
> *I can* hardly *go*
> *I can* hardly *go . . .*

I talked awhile about college. Billy chewed in a relaxed way and listened. I tried my best to communicate to him some sense of the broader options available to the man in possession of salable knowledge. I mapped out my future in blocks of years, stepladders of subgoals, ending with an affirmation of my ultimate ambition to settle into the good life in Los Angeles.

Billy smiled and gave several agreeable nods. But when my conversation came to dwell on the wonders of Los Angeles, he interrupted suddenly. "Looka here," he said. "How 'bout runnin' cross the road and get me a hot sausage sandwich, heavy on the mustard, and a big orange soda."

I looked hard at him and wanted to weep. "Is that *all* you want?" I asked.

Billy chewed steadily. "No," he answered, looking out over the crowded room. "Bring me a side of fries, hold the salt."

Then he laughed, a strange, uncaring demon laughter. The sound bragged of his urge to self-destruct. Ah, Billy! He just would not *do*! He listened only to the beating of his own heart.

The last time I saw him, before we drank together in Chicago, was when he was furloughed from Harper's Farm to attend Mama Love's funeral. She died, I believe, from a broken heart and loneliness, although the doctor claimed it was the predictable second stroke. I returned home from college to gather with the family. And after the burial, while the others ate, Billy and I drank heavily together in the back room of his mother's rented house. All day he had smiled broadly at the grief and embarrassment of the family. Now he sat on his old bed, drinking with absolute detachment. I sat near him on a hard-back chair, talking aimlessly of college, of the admirable habits of girls met there, of my ambition to find, in a year or so, permanent employment in Los Angeles. Billy said nothing. But toward midnight, after the other members of the family had left and I grew tearful in recollecting the martyred life of Mama Love, Billy turned to face me. "What *you* cryin' for, *motherfucker*?" he said. "It's *my* mama!" Just then the prison guard, who had escorted him home, came in the room and touched Billy on the shoulder. My cousin rose slowly from the bed, and laughing with that same clucking sound in his chest, he sang:

> *I'm Wild Nigger Bill*
> *From Red Pepper Hill;*
> *I never did die, and I never will . . .*

He chanted his song with such complete absorption, and laughed so menacingly, that I shuddered, and covered my face, and knew with his mother that Billy was doomed.

Seven years later, following his parole, Billy Renfro began work for Mr. Floyd Dillingham of Atlanta's Dillingham Automotives, Inc. A liberal man, Mr. Dillingham had negotiated with the state for Billy's release. The job was to track down Negroes who had defaulted on their car payments. No white man would even consider such employment. I do believe that Dillingham wanted a Negro with a reputation for ruthlessness sufficient to strike fear into the hearts of the deadbeats. In the inevitable tug between desire and justice, some of Dillingham's clients had been known to kill. Paid agents do not grow old in such an enterprise. Had I seen Billy Renfro I would have advised him of this, but I did not see him after the funeral for almost ten years. However, word-of-mouth reports from members of the family, bits of gossip from home folk passing through, placed him now in New York, now in California, one month wounded in a Detroit hospital, another month married to a woman romanced during a repossession mission outside Baton Rouge.

In contrast to him, I moved westward, but only as far as Chicago, and settled in against this city's soul-killing winter winds. I purged from my speech all traces of the South and warmed myself by the fire of my thirty-year plan. Employment was available in the credit reference section of the Melrose Department Store, and there I established, though slowly, a reputation for efficiency and tact. Because I got along, I began moving up. In my second year in Chicago, I found and courted Chelseia Raymond, a family-backed, efficiency-minded girl. She was the kind of woman I needed to make my children safe. Her family loved me, and had the grace to overlook the fact that I had once been a poor migrant from the South. Third-generation Chicagoans, they nonetheless opened their hearts and home to me as if I had been native to their city. With their backing, I settled into this rough-and-tumble city and learned to dodge all events detracting attention from the direction in which I had determined to move. From time to time, trudging through the winter slush on Michigan, I would pause to explore a reflection of myself in a store window. By my fifth year in Chicago, I became satisfied that no one could have mistaken me for a refugee from the South.

This was my situation when Billy Renfro came to visit.

But it is certainly not true, as Billy has gossiped among the family, that when he arrived I refused to see him at my office. I do not call the man a liar, but I do say his imagination is sometimes a stranger to the truth. For the sake of accuracy, here is the truth of what happened: It was not my fault that Billy got only as far into our office as the receptionist's desk. It may be he was not dressed properly for the occasion. I know that I received his card from Mrs. Mohr only *after* he had left the building, when I was going out to lunch. She told me, with a nervousness I could not at first understand, "The gentleman said he's related to you." On my honor as a member of the family, I did not deny the bond. I accepted his card. Its face was embossed in elegant script:

RED PEPPER COLLECTION AGENCY
"We Bring Back the Goods"
B. J. Renfro, Pres.

On the back of the card Billy had scribbled: "Got me a turkee over in Harvey. Call soon. Yours truly, Billy Joe."

We met, as I have said, in the late afternoon of the following day at a bar over on Halstead. At first I did not recognize Billy. The years had treated him so unkindly. A single red eye inspected me as I approached the booth where he sat drinking. His left eye socket was hollow, no more than a shriveled piece of flesh pressed grimly against skull. His outfit—the black gabardine suit, the dirty white shirt, the black string tie—brought to my mind the image of an undertaker. Dried blood and dirt smeared the fabric of his sleeve, looking eerily green in the blue-smoked light. We shook hands awkwardly, and I slid into the booth across from him. I looked closely at his face and saw death walking.

Billy grinned foolishly.

"I have heard," I began with much politeness, "that at the point of death your whole life passes in review before your eyes. Knowing this, I wonder about the agony you will suffer with only one eye in service. Won't it take twice as long, and prolong your pains, before your full life passes and goes away?"

Billy looked hurt. He insisted the eye had been lost during domestic troubles with a woman. I did not believe this, and he began embellishing the statement with extravagant lies. He drained his glass, leaned forward across the table, and said, "It was a hard-hearted woman down in Eufaula, Alabama, that done it, a widow-woman name of Miss Ruby Watson. I was laid up at her place, tired of runnin' the road for Mr. Floyd. She done root work, said she was gonna make me smart and set me up in business, if I done right by her. It didn't make no nevermind to me. I just laid on in the cut and took these white pills she give me. But I didn't feel no smarter. Mr. Floyd, he sent a telegram over there. He said, 'Billy Joe, *son,* come on *home,* these niggers just *a-stealin'* my cars!'" Billy laughed loudly, using the sound to catch the attention of the barmaid. When she looked, he held up two rough brown fingers. She brought the drinks over and Billy tried to feel her rump. The woman jostled playfully against his arm. He rinsed his mouth with the Scotch and continued.

"I said, '*Motherfuck a Mr. Floyd!* I'm livin' my life *right here!*' I kept takin' them pills, layin' steady in the cut, but I didn't feel no smarter. Then one day I seed her go out to the fields. I seed her pickin' up *jackrabbit* shit. I didn't say nothin'. I just snuck on back to the house and got in bed with my twenty-two. She come in and go to give me the stuff. I sit up and say, 'Miss Ruby, all this time I been wastin' round here, and all you been givin' me is jackrabbit shit!' She was a old widow-woman, Ruby, and I guess they just crafty that way. She just laugh at me and stood over the bed and say, '*Now* you gettin' *smart.*' Well, that's when I whip my twenty-two under her nose. But she just keep laughin' and say, 'Them bullets *dead* by now. Don't you know them bullets dead?' She had me. She knowed it. I knowed it. She sat down on the bed and commence to stroke my chest. She say, 'Now ain't *you* a sight? Don't even know whichaway is up. But you *my* sweetmeat now, and there ain't a damn thing you can do about it.'"

Billy looked calmly around the barroom, like a priest about to say Mass. And yet beneath his cool exterior I thought I sensed, in the broad sweep of his red eye, the hint of a certain rough pride. "When she said that," he went on, "I *knowed* what I had to do. I gived the gun to her. I made her point it at my head. I told Miss Ruby, 'Me, I'm just dumb enough to believe it ain't even loaded. And if it is, it won't be the first time I been dead.' Then I ram my fist in her jaw."

I waited. The clink of glasses and the noisy blend of barroom voices teased my anticipating ear. Billy was a master of suspense. Finally, I said, "So you called her bluff, got your eye shot out, but proved you were a man."

Billy laughed, his demon thumping triumphantly in his chest. "Naw," he said. "She pulled the trigger and *killed* me. That's how come I'm back on the road for Mr. Floyd today."

Such were his lies that evening in that bar on Halstead.

While the purple and red jukebox belted accommodating rhythms, and while a couple slow-dragged, Billy spun yarns about his adventures. He told magnificent lies. He spoke of the chain gang, of buddies still anchored there, and hummed snatches of songs, remembered from that time, which still sustained him. He assessed his errors in the Houston incident, and as an aside contrasted the pungency of Mexican cuisine in joints as far apart as Brownsville, Oakland, Tempe, Arizona. Billy pantomimed, while standing, his one eye fixed on the barmaid, the body movements of black men in Savannah and San Francisco, and speculated how the spirit of a region informed the rhythms of a man's fucking. From this he moved to assessments of women in Buffalo, Cleveland, Hartford, Newark, and East Saint Louis, offering details about liaisons in these cities that convinced him, should he ever marry, that Southern women provide the safest, strongest havens. He spoke of Limehouse, South Carolina, but only in passing on his way to recollections of a Newark house-rent party, the highlights of a fish fry in Baltimore, the economics of picking beans in New Jersey if one is ever stranded there, in August, without cash. Billy recited his contributions to bus-depot graffiti inscribed in stalls in Memphis, Little Rock, Phoenix, and Los Angeles, and observed that practitioners of this art became more assertive, sexually and politically, the farther west one went. I heard his accounts of fights, poker games, epic bouts of wrestling, with recalcitrant claimers of defaulted cars. Billy conveyed the flow of his emotions while contracting an assignation, on a lonely highway driving southward from Denver, when he and the woman driver of a car licensed in Maine sped sexual brags for three hundred miles before ending, in silent completion, in a wet cornfield just west of Kansas City.

While he was still reciting, I went quickly to the telephone and called Chelseia.

It is certainly not true, though Billy maintains otherwise, that my in-laws and Chelseia ordered him out of their home. What happened that evening with the Raymonds is still fresh in my mind. They were civil to Billy, though a little bit wary about why he wore blue sunshades. I had advised him to take this precaution while at my apartment, where Billy had bathed and shaved and changed into one of my better suits. Before visiting the Raymonds he had been completely transformed. His muscles rippled in the close embrace of my gray pinstripe; his face, clean shaven now, was set off favorably by one of my sky blue shirts; my very best red and white polka-dot tie swept deftly into the V of my chest-hugging vest. Even Billy's scuffed shoes had been spit-polished and shone like hot tar. This outfit, together with my blue sunshades shielding his eyesocket from inspection, gave Billy the appearance of a publicity-shy banker.

Mr. and Mrs. Raymond were enormously impressed.

"What business are you in, Mr. Renfro?" Mrs. Raymond asked, while her husband passed around the cheese board.

Conforming to my warnings, Billy spoke briefly. "Automotives," he answered.

Chelseia, seated next to me on the sofa, said nothing. But she watched Billy very closely.

"Selling?" Mrs. Raymond asked. She was a round, self-possessed woman who called me "darling" and winked reassuringly whenever we drank more than two glasses of sherry. She had already given me the understanding that Chelseia was mine. "You have a dealership, then?" she asked Billy.

He sat on a purple settee, his legs crossed elegantly, a glass of sherry posed in his hand. He pretended he had not heard Mrs. Raymond.

I had not anticipated that Chelseia's parents would be at home. Usually on

Thursday evenings they played canasta with a church group. But, being self-less people, they had canceled their engagement when they heard from Chelseia that my cousin was in town. Mr. Raymond himself had prepared the dinner. I wanted things to go smoothly. "Billy is more a traveling salesman," I answered for my cousin. "His business takes him around the country."

Mr. Raymond sighed and stroked the top of his head. He was completely bald. He said, "It does my heart good to see the younger generation getting a few breaks. Why, in my day, with two degrees, all I could get was being a red-cap down at the Union Station."

"Of course you've been out to California?" Mrs. Raymond said quickly. Both she and her husband had worked very hard to achieve the good life, and she did not like to hear him reminisce.

"Yes, m'am," Billy answered.

"We've got relatives out in Culver City," Chelseia volunteered. She had sensed my tension, and had not asked why Billy was wearing a suit she had se-lected for me at Marshall Fields. But she stared long and hard at the blue-tinted sunshades, familiar to her from our long summer walks along the lakeshore.

"Is it true what they say about those movie stars?" Mr. Raymond asked Billy.

Such was the flow of conversation during dinner.

For well over an hour, Billy successfully maintained his cloud of mystery. And at such moments when it seemed about to break apart in the breeze of chitchat, I puffed it back into place with a swift retort. We were relaxed until after dinner, when Mr. Raymond, still rummaging in the storehouses of his youth, lit up a cigar and became expansive. He loosened his tie and began telling anecdotes about his escapades as a redcap. Chelseia, her eyes flitting nervously, kept saying, "Please, don't get naughty now, Daddy." But her words were of no avail. Billy, puffing fiercely on a cigar, laughed and egged him on. Mrs. Raymond smiled painfully. Several times Chelseia knocked her knee against my leg beneath the table. Toward ten-thirty Mr. Raymond brought out a bottle of bourbon. He said, "How about a little snort, Mr. Renfro," and winked at Billy. My cousin willfully ignored the suggestion in my stare. "Call me Billy," he said to Mr. Raymond, draining his water glass.

In less than half an hour, drunk now, Billy was offering tales about his own exploits on the Coast. Mr. Raymond kept laughing, shaking his head wistfully, and saying, "I *knew* it was true what they say about them stars." And while Billy dived for more details on this point, Mr. Raymond regaled us with anec-dotes drawn from his days as a bellhop at the Palmer House. When he men-tioned the adventures of a hustling bellhop named "Swifty," Billy leaned for-ward, pounded the table, and shouted, "Damn if I don't *know* that nigger. He in *Dee*troit now, still *just as crazy as a bedbug!*"

Mrs. Raymond coughed violently and left the room.

From this point onward the evening deteriorated. Chelseia sat with a cold and distant expression on her face. From time to time she kicked my foot be-neath the table. I flashed signals to Billy, tried to head off his speech when I perceived where it was leading, suggested many times that we should go. But none of it was of any use. Billy seemed to have induced some unhealthy chemical reaction in Mr. Raymond. He and Billy seemed locked in some unholy union. He laughed, giggled, and hooted as he talked. Even when Mrs. Raymond returned to the room in a housecoat, her husband did not lower his voice. When Mr. Raymond, on his fourth bourbon, started to recite a salacious jingle, Billy jumped up and overruled it with a more earthy variant. But in the rush of excitement while reciting the punch line, he laughed lustily, screeched, and tore off his glasses. This one gesture destroyed all his mystery. His single eye, red-rimmed and watery, flashed horribly in the soft glow of the green and red Tiffany lamp.

Chelseia gasped.

"Why, Mr. Renfro," said Mrs. Raymond, the back of her hand drawn to her mouth, "whatever happened to your eye?"

"Nothing but a knife fight," Chelseia muttered.

"Let it go," called Mr. Raymond across the littered dining table. "It's not our business." He was drunk, but there was an extreme soberness in his voice. He said to all of us, "Let it go."

Mrs. Raymond acted on this cue. "When you get back South," she said to Billy, "tell the family that William is a very nice young man." She rounded the table with her right arm outstretched. She grasped and wagged Billy's limp right hand. "What did you say your business was?"

Billy looked confused. "Automotives, ma'am," he told her.

"Washing or pumping gas?" Chelseia said. It was not a question, and the tone of her voice I had heard before in the chill of the winter winds off Lake Michigan. When I looked at Chelseia I saw in her face a vengeful twist I had not before then, and have never since, seen in her store of expressions. Mrs. Raymond had this very same look.

Billy stiffened. He jerked his hand away from Mrs. Raymond. He looked enraged.

The rest of the evening has been clouded by his lies.

But it is certainly true that I tried hard to save the situation, although Billy has maintained that I turned on him. The man is a notorious liar, and likes to keep the family jumpy. Here is the truth of what happened: I moved quickly to Billy's side. I put my hand on his shoulder. I faced the Raymonds for the two of us. I said, "Thank you for a splendid evening." But all my tact was introduced too late. With a purposeful shrug, Billy separated his shoulder from my hand. All our eyes were on him. Only Mr. Raymond, sitting drooped and still in his chair, seemed distracted by thoughts of other matters.

Someone had to take control. I took it as best I could. "A red-neck down in South Carolina shot out Billy's eye," I said. "Billy is too proud to speak of it."

"*Bull*shit!" Billy said.

By this one word, and through his subsequent actions, Billy himself completely severed what was left of our family bond.

He stripped off my coat, my vest, my polka-dot tie. These he flung on the purple settee. My sky blue shirt he let fall to the floor. Billy stood broad-shouldered and brown in a ragged, yellowed undershirt. He directed all our eyes to weltlike scars on his arms and neck. "These here come from runnin' round the country," he grinned. "And I'm *keep* runnin' till the pork chops get thicker and they give me two dollars more."

"Please, Billy," I pleaded. "Please, Billy, tell the truth now."

He laughed wickedly, his teeth clamped tight. His eyes darted from me, to Chelseia, to Mrs. Raymond standing by the table with her right hand clutching her chest.

But Billy did not tell the truth. His story to me in the bar on Halstead vanished like a summer cloud. He pointed to his empty eye socket and said, "I lost this over in Harvey several years ago. Mr. Floyd Dillingham, my boss, was the one that sent me up here. He had this here turkey that flew the coop with a fistful of notes due on his Impala. Nigger's name was Wilfred 'Inner City' Jones, and he had balls enough to cruise pass Mr. Floyd's lot and honk when he was leavin' town. People on the corner saw him frontin' off Mr. Floyd. It looked bad. Mr. Floyd called me in and give me my runnin' orders. He say, '*Fuck* the *money*, Billy. What he done is bad for *business*! Now bring me back my *car* or that nigger's *ass*!'" He pounded the table twice, with great seriousness in his face, as if still hearing the beat of his boss's voice. Mrs. Raymond and Chelseia jumped each time he pounded. But Mr. Raymond remained seated in his chair, his head bowed, his eyes closed. Billy smiled slightly. "I put out word I was lookin' for Inner City. He put out word he was lookin' for me to come lookin' for him. Said I would find him waitin' for me over in Birmingham, if I came lookin' that far. But I knowed that Earline, his old lady, was up here in Harvey and he only felt safe with his head up under her dress. So I bought me a one-way bus ticket." Billy moved to the table, swished the last of the bourbon in his glass and drank it down. Then he set the glass on the white tablecloth and arranged soiled knives and forks around it, setting the scene. "He must have been layin' for me," he went on, "cause when I knock on the door people commence to scuffle round inside. Then Earline sing out, 'What you want?' I holler back, 'Them keys to that Impala park outside or a piece of Inner City's ass, it don't matter to me which one!' They was quiet for a minute, then Inner City holler, 'Come on in, *motherfucker*, and take your choice!' I went on in."

His single eye, though red-rimmed and watery, sparkled dimly with pride. I sensed that he was enjoying himself, though Mrs. Raymond was almost in a swoon. She was dabbing excitedly at her forehead with a dinner napkin. I saw Billy watching her. I saw him smile. I thought I saw him lick his lips. "Inner City was shootin' wild from behind the bed," he continued. "Though he is in bad with Mr. Floyd, I won't bad-talk his reputation by sayin' where them bullets hit. But I stood in the middle of the room and shout, 'Missed me, *sapsucker*!' Then I opened up with my thirty-eight, whistlin' whilst I worked. My habit is to aim high when ladies is present, cause a scared woman can talk quick sense to a hard-headed man. Pretty soon Inner City yell out, 'Hey Billy, let's be *gentlemens* and do this without no heat!' He slide his gun out from under the bed. I throwed mine on the sheets and wait. Then Earline yell, 'Hey Billy, what about that twenty-two you keeps strap to your spine?' They was quiet for a minute. Me, I didn't move. Then I heard Inner City pop Earline in the jaw. While she was still hollerin' he rise up from under the bed, limber as a bear. His eyes was steamin' and his jaws was tight. He wolf, 'I'ma *keep* that Impala, Billy, but first I'ma do me some business on your *ass*!'"

By now Billy had moved the gravy-stained knife closer to the glass. He leaned over the table like a magician about to pluck a pigeon from thin air. But suddenly his body relaxed. He straightened and reached one hand into his pocket. "Now I ain't sayin' it was *easy*," he said, looking directly at Chelseia, "but I *do* say I just ain't *use* to buyin' no bus ticket and ridin' with a sore ass and a bleedin' eye all the way home." He tossed a set of car keys onto the table. Tiny flecks of dried blood flew from the keys as they clinked against the glass. Then Billy laughed loud and confidently. It was an even, bass-filled laughter that sounded the image of a persistent demon pounding happily against a friendly door. "One of us knowed he had to die," he announced calmly. "Next time, it might be *me*."

"You common *street nigger*!" Chelseia shouted.

Billy held his naked arm toward me as if he were a ringmaster introducing an act. "And this here's my cousin William," he told Chelseia.

Mrs. Raymond shuddered and rushed from the room.

And then there came a burst of wild, almost hysterical laughter. But this was not Billy. I turned and saw Mr. Raymond. His bald head was bent almost into his empty plate. He seemed to be shedding tears.

"Billy!" I pleaded. "Tell the truth. Sometimes, Billy, please tell the *truth*!"

But he ignored me. Instead, he joined with Mr. Raymond in this wild, uncaring laughter.

"Gangster!" Chelseia shouted.

"God bless Mr. Floyd!" Billy yelled.

Someone had to keep order. I assumed that responsibility. I was the one who asked Billy out.

But it is not true, contrary to rumors circulating in my family, that Billy Renfro is unwelcome in my home. His own lying stories spread this madness, and both he and I know the truth of where I stand. As far as I am concerned, he is welcome here at any time. Chelseia is another matter, but even she has said she would not interfere if Billy chose to come again. She would even let me prepare dinner for him. Whenever I am confronted by members of the family with one of his lies, I say this in response. For whatever it is worth to them, or to Billy. The man is, after all, my cousin. It is a point of family pride. Chelseia agrees, and says our family unit will likely be the place where Billy finds ultimate reconstruction, once he has put aside his wanderings. I say it is just a matter of time. We are, after all, the same age. Yet I have already charted my course. I have settled into Chicago, against the winter whippings of this city's winds. He can do the same. But as things stand now, he is still someplace out there, with a single eye flickering over open roadways, in his careless search for an exciting death. Ah, *Billy!*

Symmetry and Subversion in James Alan McPherson's "The Story of a Dead Man"

David Huddle

A short story's most distinctive qualities are often produced somewhat incidentally, without the author's paying a great deal of attention to them. For instance, the music of a story—the way it sounds to the ear when read aloud or the way it sounds to the inner ear when read silently—is not the primary concern of most story writers, though it may be the first aspect of a story that a reader notices. Or the length of a story, especially when it is very long or extremely short, may be a mere by-product of a larger concern of the author, though "how long it is" is quite often the characteristic of a story that a reader checks out before even reading its first sentence!

As short story technique has developed over the past hundred and fifty years or so, more writers have begun paying more attention to these fundamental aspects of the story. The music of "Love Too Long" (p. 199) may be the quality to which Barry Hannah gave the most attention in its composition. The economy of "The Third Bank of the River" might have been the feature João Guimarães Rosa worked hardest on in writing that story.

Symmetry—or *balance*, or *harmony*—is another of those qualities, present to some extent in all short stories but seldom the primary *conscious* concern of an author. In James Alan McPherson's "The Story of a Dead Man," however, symmetry becomes such a central element of the story that we must assume the author paid a great deal of attention to its role in his composition. Indeed, to understand the story at all, we readers must consider the ways in which McPherson has balanced its contrasting elements.

Before we even become acquainted with the characters in "The Story of a Dead Man" in the opening paragraph, we begin hearing two distinctive voices, the first of which is the narrator's very proper, and somewhat wordy, standard English:

> After tracking the debtor to a rented room, Billy Renfro's common sense was overwhelmed by the romantic aspects of the adventure.

The second voice is Billy Renfro's, which we might describe as "street language," a very colloquial and crude version of black English:

> "Monroe Ellis, give *up* Mr. Floyd's Cadillac that you done miss nine payments on!"

That these voices contrast so sharply, so immediately, and so consistently throughout the story is no accident: McPherson's design is one that depends on a reader's quickly forming contrasting and balancing impressions of each of these characters. Listening to the way people talk is one of the most instinctive ways we have of making positive and/or negative judgments of people.

A thoughtful reading of "The Story of a Dead Man" will lead us to one of its primary thematic concerns, the connection between racial prejudice and language. This story is not merely *about* the connection between prejudice and language; it also *demonstrates* this connection as it informs the attitudes of its reader.

Because we are more likely to be educated than not, we readers of "The Story of a Dead Man," regardless of our ethnic background, are likely to have more in common with the standard-English-speaking narrator of the story, William, than with the street-language-rapping Billy Renfro. Thus most readers enter this story with a bias in favor of William and against Billy.

That these two characters are named similarly (or very nearly *identically*) is an obvious element of McPherson's design. Their personalities, however, like their voices, are utterly dissimilar. William is success oriented, conventionally responsible (and thinking); whereas Billy is self-destructive, deeply rebellious, and so independent minded as to be dangerous to anyone he encounters (especially in his business dealings) as well as to himself. Whereas William is obsessed with his image—with how he is seen by the eyes of the world—Billy seems unavoidably stuck with being himself, regardless of the situation. In the story's climactic scene, the two of them are revealed in their metaphorical essences:

> I moved quickly to Billy's side. I put my hand on his shoulder. I faced the Raymonds for the two of us. I said, "Thank you for a splendid evening." But all my tact was introduced too late. With a purposeful shrug, Billy separated his shoulder from my hand. All our eyes were on him. . . .
>
> He stripped off my coat, my vest, my polka-dot tie. These he flung on the purple settee. My sky blue shirt he let fall to the floor. Billy stood broad-shouldered and brown in a ragged, yellowed undershirt. He directed all our eyes to weltlike scars on his arms and neck. "These here come from runnin' round the country," he grinned. "And I'm *keep* runnin' till the pork chops get thicker and they give me two dollars more."
>
> . . .
>
> "You common *street nigger!*" Chelseia shouted.
>
> Billy held his naked arm toward me as if he were a ringmaster introducing an act. "And this here's my cousin William," he told Chelseia.
>
> . . .
>
> Someone had to keep order. I assumed that responsibility. I was the one who asked Billy out.

"The Story of a Dead Man" is subversive in its design—it is intended to disturb a reader's sense of the conventions of behavior and speech. The success of its subversion depends on the way it balances these two characters and their ways of behaving and speaking. The narrator's very first words are "It is not true," and the final paragraph carries on William's insistence on the matter of truth: "[Billy's] own lying stories spread this madness, and both he and I know the truth of where I stand." By the end of the story we have been invited so many times to consider what is true and what is not true that we can hardly help giving uncommon attention to the question of what is the truth of these matters.

If we readers were to envision William and Billy on a seesaw of truth telling, we would begin by seeing William on the high end, with truth on his side. We would see it that way because we have the most in common with William, especially in terms of his language but also in terms of his "life story." Again regardless of ethnic background, if we are story readers, we are much more likely to be living a life that resembles William's than one that resembles Billy's. The very fact that we're reading a short story is testimony to our own success-oriented life story. Though William the narrator may very well read short stories in his spare time to improve his cultural background, Billy Renfro, if advised to read a story, even one in which he himself plays a starring role, would most likely respond by laughing and shouting, "Bullshit!"

If the story works on us readers as it is designed to work, what we think when we finish the story is the opposite of what we thought when we began it. Though our prejudged views of William and Billy are unavoidable at the beginning the story, we also can't help comparing the two of them as the story proceeds according to its symmetrical design:

- Billy "dared to test the first full wetness of his manhood in the arms of a much experienced girl"—and pays for this testing by being brought to court in a paternity suit. William "found and courted Chelseia Raymond, a family-backed, efficiency-minded girl . . . the kind of women I needed to make my children safe."
- Billy openly flaunts his rural origins. William constructs his image to make sure "that no one could have mistaken me for a refugee from the South."
- William seems to have no stories of his own. Billy is full of stories that, even if they are the lies that William claims them to be, are mightily entertaining. Even though he claims they are all lies, William obviously prefers telling Billy's stories to telling ones of his own. For the lack of having any of his own, William seems to *need* Billy's stories.
- William is determined to live a life of security and safety. Billy is "still someplace out there, with a single eye flickering over open roadways, in his careless search for an exciting death."

Although our alliance with William remains intact from the beginning to the end of "The Story of a Dead Man," we can't help changing our view of both him and Billy. Gradually we have to see that William has sacrificed his integrity—indeed, his identity—for the sake of success and safety. The only lively element in his life is his cousin and his cousin's stories. If the rest of Billy's days seem fraught with uncertainty, danger, and the likelihood of a violent death, William's future looks as dull and gray as a flannel suit. At the end, we can't help asking ourselves which one of these characters is more true to himself, which one of them is more truly alive. And the answer to both questions is most likely to be *Billy*.

Ah ha!, we readers are likely to say to ourselves, *I see what's going on here: The real "dead man" of this story is actually William, whereas at the beginning I thought it was Billy.*

But that insight can't be the end of our consideration of "The Story of a Dead Man." McPherson's design—of these two characters being pitted against each other—is just too carefully balanced to let us off with arriving at such an easy conclusion. We are forced to ask ourselves which character has chosen a life we would prefer to live. Or which character has a future that most resembles our own. The answer to both these questions is likely to be *William*.

So at this point in a reader's involvement with "The Story of a Dead Man," McPherson manages something quite remarkable in esthetic terms: He moves the moral question of his story into the reader's consideration of his or her own life. We readers can't help acknowledging the prejudice with which we entered the story and can't help acknowledging how much we have in common with William—as opposed to Billy. And we readers can't help seeing that because of that very prejudice, the characters in the story have had to choose between two very unattractive alternatives. Choose William's way, and give up your integrity; choose Billy's way, and give up any possibility of safety or lasting comfort.

Elbow Room, McPherson's collection of short stories that includes "The Story of a Dead Man," addresses this very dilemma: How does a black man go about making some "elbow room" for himself? McPherson asks his readers to consider how little middle ground is available to male African Americans, who may see success as selling out (*à la* William) and maintaining integrity as dooming them to a life of failure (*à la* Billy).

Presenting the dilemma in these abstract terms would allow us to nod approvingly and then forget it. But McPherson's moving that dilemma into the value system of his readers makes us feel it, view it in personal terms, and even understand our individual participation in it, holding, as we know we do, the unavoidable bias with which we entered the story.

We readers of "The Story of a Dead Man" become more and more aware that this bias is located in language: We speak as the narrator speaks, not as Billy Renfro speaks; therefore, our values are much closer to William's than to Billy's. At the same time, the story makes us question William's values—which are our own values. Thus, McPherson produces a disturbance within the consciousness of a reader. Through a story that is exuberantly entertaining in its language, the author demonstrates the sobering idea that language can be imprisoning: Because of the way he talks, Billy Renfro's life is severely restricted. But the narrator is more subtly imprisoned within the language he has chosen to speak—a language that denies his true identity, a language that denies him stories of his own, a language that sentences him to a life of "faking it," of falsehood.

And because the story has required us to be forming and re-forming our opinions of these characters—balancing and rebalancing our views of them—it has also required us to take a look at our own lives, our own language. Are we not also imprisoned within the language bias that originally had us seeing William as the admirably responsible person and Billy as the reprobate of this story?

Finally, we must look deeply into ourselves to try to fathom the moral

What sort of man was Wakefield? We are free to shape out our own idea, and call it by his name. He was now in the meridian of life; his matrimonial affections, never violent, were sobered in a calm, habitual sentiment; of all husbands, he was likely to be the most constant, because a certain sluggishness would keep his heart at rest, wherever it might be placed. He was intellectual, but not actively so; his mind occupied itself in long and lazy musings, that tended to no purpose, or had not vigor to attain it; his thoughts were seldom so energetic as to seize hold of words. Imagination, in the proper meaning of the term, made no part of Wakefield's gifts. With a cold, but not depraved nor wandering heart, and a mind never feverish with riotous thoughts, nor perplexed with originality, who could have anticipated, that our friend would entitle himself to a foremost place among the doers of eccentric deeds? Had his acquaintances been asked, who was the man in London, the surest to perform nothing to-day which should be remembered on the morrow, they would have thought of Wakefield. Only the wife of his bosom might have hesitated. She, without having analyzed his character, was partly aware of a quiet selfishness, that had rusted into his inactive mind—of a peculiar sort of vanity, the most uneasy attribute about him—of a disposition to craft, which had seldom produced more positive effects than the keeping of petty secrets, hardly worth revealing—and, lastly, of what she called a little strangeness, sometimes, in the good man. This latter quality is indefinable, and perhaps nonexistent.

Let us now imagine Wakefield bidding adieu to his wife. It is the dusk of an October evening. His equipment is a drab great-coat, a hat covered with an oil-cloth, top-boots, an umbrella in one hand and a small portmanteau in the other. He has informed Mrs. Wakefield that he is to take the night-coach into the country. She would fain inquire the length of his journey, its object, and the probable time of his return; but, indulgent to his harmless love of mystery, interrogates him only by a look. He tells her not to expect him positively by the return coach, nor to be alarmed should he tarry three or four days; but, at all events, to look for him at supper on Friday evening. Wakefield himself, be it considered, has no suspicion of what is before him. He holds out his hand; she gives her own, and meets his parting kiss, in the matter-of-course way of a ten years' matrimony; and forth goes the middle-aged Mr. Wakefield, almost resolved to perplex his good lady by a whole week's absence. After the door has closed behind him, she perceives it thrust partly open, and a vision of her husband's face, through the aperture, smiling on her, and gone in a moment. For the time, this little incident is dismissed without a thought. But, long afterwards, when she has been more years a widow than a wife, that smile recurs, and flickers across all her reminiscences of Wakefield's visage. In her many musings, she surrounds the original smile with a multitude of fantasies, which make it strange and awful; as, for instance, if she imagines him in a coffin, that parting look is frozen on his pale features; or, if she dreams of him in Heaven, still his blessed spirit wears a quiet and crafty smile. Yet, for its sake, when all others have given him up for dead, she sometimes doubts whether she is a widow.

But, our business is with the husband. We must hurry after him, along the street, ere he lose his individuality, and melt into the great mass of London life.

It would be vain searching for him there. Let us follow close at his heels, there-fore, until, after several superfluous turns and doublings, we find him com-fortably established by the fireside of a small apartment, previously bespoken. He is in the next street to his own, and at his journey's end. He can scarcely trust his good fortune, in having got thither unperceived—recollecting that, at one time, he was delayed by the throng, in the very focus of a lighted lantern; and, again, there were footsteps, that seemed to tread behind his own, distinct from the multitudinous tramp around him; and, anon, he heard a voice shout-ing afar, and fancied that it called his name. Doubtless, a dozen busy-bodies had been watching him, and told his wife the whole affair. Poor Wakefield! Little knowest thou thine own insignificance in this great world! No mortal eye but mine has traced thee. Go quietly to thy bed, foolish man; and, on the mor-row, if thou wilt be wise, get thee home to good Mrs. Wakefield, and tell her the truth. Remove not thyself, even for a little week, from thy place in her chaste bosom. Were she, for a single moment, to deem thee dead, or lost, or lastingly divided from her, thou wouldst be woefully conscious of a change in thy true wife, forever after. It is perilous to make a chasm in human affections; not that they gape so long and wide—but so quickly close again!

Almost repenting of his frolic, or whatever it may be termed, Wakefield lies down betimes, and starting from his first nap, spreads forth his arms into the wide and solitary waste of the unaccustomed bed. "No"—thinks he, gathering the bed-clothes about him—"I will not sleep alone another night."

In the morning, he rises earlier than usual, and sets himself to consider what he really means to do. Such are his loose and rambling modes of thought, that he has taken this very singular step, with the consciousness of a purpose, indeed, but without being able to define it sufficiently for his own contempla-tion. The vagueness of the project, and the convulsive effort with which he plunges into the execution of it, are equally characteristic of a feeble-minded man. Wakefield sifts his ideas, however, as minutely as he may, and finds him-self curious to know the progress of matters at home—how his exemplary wife will endure her widowhood, of a week; and, briefly, how the little sphere of creatures and circumstances, in which he was a central object, will be affected by his removal. A morbid vanity, therefore, lies nearest the bottom of the affair. But, how is he to attain his ends? Not, certainly, by keeping close in this com-fortable lodging, where, though he slept and awoke in the next street to his home, he is as effectually abroad, as if the stage-coach had been whirling him away all night. Yet, should he reappear, the whole project is knocked in the head. His poor brains being hopelessly puzzled with this dilemma, he at length ventures out, partly resolving to cross the head of the street, and send one hasty glance towards his forsaken domicile. Habit—for he is a man of habits—takes him by the hand, and guides him, wholly unaware, to his own door, where, just at the critical moment, he is aroused by the scraping of his foot upon the step. Wakefield! whither are you going?

At that instant, his fate was turning on the pivot. Little dreaming of the doom to which his first backward step devotes him, he hurries away, breath-less with agitation hitherto unfelt, and hardly dares turn his head, at the distant corner. Can it be, that nobody caught sight of him? Will not the whole house-hold—the decent Mrs. Wakefield, the smart maid-servant, and the dirty little foot-boy—raise a hue-and-cry, through London streets, in pursuit of their fugi-tive lord and master? Wonderful escape! He gathers courage to pause and look homeward, but is perplexed with a sense of change about the familiar edifice, such as affects us all, when, after a separation of months or years, we again see some hill or lake, or work of art, with which we were friends, of old. In ordi-nary cases, this indescribable impression is caused by the comparison and con-trast between our imperfect reminiscences and the reality. In Wakefield, the magic of a single night has wrought a similar transformation, because, in that brief period, a great moral change has been effected. But this is a secret from himself. Before leaving the spot, he catches a far and momentary glimpse of his wife, passing athwart the front window, with her face turned towards the head of the street. The crafty nincompoop takes to his heels, scared with the idea, that, among a thousand such atoms of mortality, her eye must have detected him. Right glad is his heart, though his brain be somewhat dizzy, when he finds himself by the coal-fire of his lodgings.

So much for the commencement of this long whim-wham. After the initial conception, and the stirring up of the man's sluggish temperament to put it in practice, the whole matter evolves itself in a natural train. We may suppose him, as the result of deep deliberation, buying a new wig, of reddish hair, and selecting sundry garments, in a fashion unlike his customary suit of brown, from a Jew's old-clothes bag. It is accomplished. Wakefield is another man. The new system being now established, a retrograde movement to the old would be almost as difficult as the step that placed him in his unparalleled position. Furthermore, he is rendered obstinate by a sulkiness, occasionally incident to his temper, and brought on, at present, by the inadequate sensation which he conceives to have been produced in the bosom of Mrs. Wakefield. He will not go back until she be frightened half to death. Well, twice or thrice has she passed before his sight, each time with a heavier step, a paler cheek, and more anxious brow; and, in the third week of his non-appearance, he detects a por-tent of evil entering the house, in the guise of an apothecary. Next day, the knocker is muffled. Towards night-fall, comes the chariot of a physician, and deposits its big-wigged and solemn burthen at Wakefield's door, whence, after a quarter of an hour's visit, he emerges, perchance the herald of a funeral. Dear woman! Will she die? By this time, Wakefield is excited to something like en-ergy of feeling, but still lingers away from his wife's bedside, pleading with his conscience, that she must not be disturbed at such a juncture. If aught else re-strains him, he does not know it. In the course of a few weeks, she gradually re-covers; the crisis is over; her heart is sad, perhaps, but quiet; and, let him return soon or late, it will never be feverish for him again. Such ideas glimmer through the mist of Wakefield's mind, and render him indistinctly conscious, that an almost impassable gulf divides his hired apartment from his former home. "It is but in the next street!" he sometimes says. Fool! it is in another world. Hitherto, he has put off his return from one particular day to another;

henceforward, he leaves the precise time undetermined. Not to-morrow—probably next week—pretty soon. Poor man! The dead have nearly as much chance of re-visiting their earthly homes, as the self-banished Wakefield.

Would that I had a folio to write, instead of an article of a dozen pages! Then might I exemplify how an influence, beyond our control, lays its strong hand on every deed which we do, and weaves its consequences into an iron tissue of necessity. Wakefield is spell-bound. We must leave him, for ten years or so, to haunt around his house, without once crossing the threshold, and to be faithful to his wife, with all the affection of which his heart is capable, while he is slowly fading out of hers. Long since, it must be remarked, he has lost the perception of singularity in his conduct.

Now for a scene! Amid the throng of a London street, we distinguish a man, now waxing elderly, with few characteristics to attract careless observers, yet bearing, in his whole aspect, the hand-writing of no common fate, for such as have the skill to read it. He is meagre; his low and narrow forehead is deeply wrinkled; his eyes, small and lustreless, sometimes wander apprehensively about him, but oftener seem to look inward. He bends his head, but moves with an indescribable obliquity of gait, as if unwilling to display his full front to the world. Watch him long enough to see what we have described, and you will allow that circumstances—which often produce remarkable men from nature's ordinary handiwork—have produced one such here. Next, leaving him to sidle along the foot-walk, cast your eyes in the opposite direction, where a portly female, considerably in the wane of life, with a prayer-book in her hand, is proceeding to yonder church. She has the placid mien of settled widowhood. Her regrets have either died away, or have become so essential to her heart, that they would be poorly exchanged for joy. Just as the lean man and well conditioned woman are passing, a slight obstruction occurs, and brings these two figures directly in contact. Their hands touch; the pressure of the crowd forces her bosom against his shoulder; they stand, face to face, staring into each other's eyes. After a ten years' separation, thus Wakefield meets his wife!

The throng eddies away, and carries them asunder. The sober widow, resuming her former pace, proceeds to church, but pauses in the portal, and throws a perplexed glance along the street. She passes in, however, opening her prayer-book as she goes. And the man? With so wild a face, that busy and selfish London stands to gaze after him, he hurries to his lodgings, bolts the door, and throws himself upon the bed. The latent feelings of years break out; his feeble mind acquires a brief energy from their strength; all the miserable strangeness of his life is revealed to him at a glance; and he cries out, passionately—"Wakefield! Wakefield! You are mad!"

Perhaps he was so. The singularity of his situation must have so moulded him to itself, that, considered in regard to his fellow-creatures and the business of life, he could not be said to possess his right mind. He had contrived, or rather he had happened, to dissever himself from the world—to vanish—to give up his place and privileges with living men, without being admitted among the dead. The life of a hermit is nowise parallel to his. He was in the bustle of the city, as of old; but the crowd swept by, and saw him not; he was, we may figuratively say, always beside his wife, and at his hearth, yet must never feel the warmth of one, nor the affection of the other. It was Wakefield's unprecedented fate, to retain his original share of human sympathies, and to be still involved in human interests, while he had lost his reciprocal influence on them. It would be a most curious speculation, to trace out the effect of such circumstances on his heart and intellect, separately, and in unison. Yet, changed as he was, he would seldom be conscious of it, but deem himself the same man as ever; glimpses of the truth, indeed, would come, but only for the moment; and still he would keep saying—"I shall soon go back."—nor reflect, that he had been saying so for twenty years.

I conceive, also, that these twenty years would appear, in the retrospect, scarcely longer than the week to which Wakefield had at first limited his absence. He would look on the affair as no more than an interlude in the main business of his life. When, after a little while more, he should deem it time to re-enter his parlor, his wife would clap her hands for joy, on beholding the middle-aged Mr. Wakefield. Alas, what a mistake! Would Time but await the close of our favorite follies, we should be young men, all of us, and till Doom's Day.

One evening, in the twentieth year since he vanished, Wakefield is taking his customary walk towards the dwelling which he still calls his own. It is a gusty night of autumn, with frequent showers, that patter down upon the pavement, and are gone, before a man can put up his umbrella. Pausing near the house, Wakefield discerns, through the parlor-windows of the second floor, the red glow, and the glimmer and fitful flash, of a comfortable fire. On the ceiling, appears a grotesque shadow of good Mrs. Wakefield. The cap, the nose and chin, and the broad waist, form an admirable caricature, which dances, moreover, with the up-flickering and down-sinking blaze, almost too merrily for the shade of an elderly widow. At this instant, a shower chances to fall, and is driven, by the unmannerly gust, full into Wakefield's face and bosom. He is quite penetrated with its autumnal chill. Shall he stand, wet and shivering here, when his own hearth has a good fire to warm him, and his own wife will run to fetch the gray coat and small-clothes, which, doubtless, she has kept carefully in the closet of their bed-chamber? No! Wakefield is no such fool. He ascends the steps—heavily!—for twenty years have stiffened his legs, since he came down—but he knows it not. Stay, Wakefield! Would you go to the sole home that is left you? Then step into your grave! The door opens. As he passes in, we have a parting glimpse of his visage, and recognize the crafty smile, which was the precursor of the little joke, that he has ever since been playing off at his wife's expense. How unmercifully has he quizzed the poor woman! Well, a good night's rest to Wakefield!

This happy event—supposing it to be such—could only have occurred at an unpremeditated moment. We will not follow our friend across the threshold. He has left us much food for thought, a portion of which shall lend its wisdom to a moral, and be shaped into a figure. Amid the seeming confusion of our mysterious world, individuals are so nicely adjusted to a system, and systems to one another, and to a whole, that, by stepping aside for a moment, a man exposes himself to a fearful risk of losing his place forever. Like Wakefield, he may become, as it were, the Outcast of the Universe.

Point of View in Hawthorne's "Wakefield"

Allen Shepherd

Only after having known and talked about the story for years have I come really to understand Hawthorne's "Wakefield" (1835): if not *really* understand (in the sense of really and truly and definitively), then at least differently and usably. This is to say that I have appropriated the story, that I have converted it to my own fictional use, which is another thing altogether from discussing it, however thoroughly and insightfully, in a literature course. In 1835 or thereabouts Hawthorne accomplished with considerable skill and sophistication (and accessibility, as I finally realized) several things that I had for some time been half consciously and haphazardly working toward in my own writing, one story in particular.

It might be argued that my using Hawthorne in this fashion is to interpret his story not objectively but in the dim light of my own compositional problems, to which I would respond yes, indeed, and insist that nobody's insights, however derived, are really and truly objective. I would urge the general importance, even the practical usefulness, of reading for writers and would further assert that since levying upon our literary forebears is what we all do anyway, knowingly or not, we ought thus to do it with full consciousness and to our own best advantage. Hawthorne's reputation will not suffer from such use, any more than it will from the (generally benighted) opinion of a recent critic who complained that "Hawthorne is so dated and quaint."

I do in fact know what she means; Hawthorne is in many respects a writer of his time, not ours, and of course nobody writes the way he did anymore. Nonetheless he's been for me and I expect will remain a major resource. We should be clear that the issue is not the conventionally determined literary merit of our sources and inspirations and instructive examples, although Hawthorne remains clearly canonical. The issue is rather what we do with what we find, through whatever unlikely connections we make. Harry Crews, a present-day American novelist, for example, recalls that he learned important things about writing—matters of style and syntax—by copying out long passages of Graham Greene, whose work is as different from Crews's as could be imagined. And Barry Hannah, another contemporary author, confesses, "I am still stealing from *me*." The operative motto: Whatever works. To return to me and my resource, no one on reading my story would think of Hawthorne, yet I am certainly in his debt, principally because thinking about and then rereading his story enabled me to reconceive my own fictional possibilities, to revise and improve my work.

This is, then, a case study of sorts, exemplifying both my interpretation of Hawthorne's story and, to a limited extent, my use of Hawthorne. I need now to sketch the story I have been rewriting. It features Fred (my working name for any male character), a divorced man in his forties who is making a very hesitant romantic approach to Kay, a generally receptive widow. Kay has two children, a son, Randy, and a daughter, Tish. At her invitation, Fred accompanies Kay to Randy's graduation from a school for athletically gifted, well-financed academic underachievers. By several people there Fred is mistaken for Kay's husband (and Randy's father), but although he rather likes such incorporation, which Kay realizes and emphasizes, the story's unrevised penultimate sentence sees him at evening's end sitting "in the cool dark on Kay's living room sofa waiting for her" and wondering "how he would live." Those last four words seem to me now more than a little pretentious, but they were meant to suggest that the man was unhappy, uncertain, and probably about to withdraw.

The story was originally narrated in the third person, which seemed the natural and was certainly the easiest way to tell it. The story's principal shortcoming, I think, was that it was virtually indistinguishable from scores (perhaps hundreds) of other narratives about end-of-century divorced, middle-aged American men and their romantic impasses. How to elevate Fred's angst above the status of pop sociological cliché? How to get out from under John Updike? How to escape from the trap of copious observed detail, however authentic and evocative? How to engage the reader in a collaborative creative-interpretive effort? Calling Dr. Hawthorne.

The first complete draft of my story, as I mentioned, was cast in the limited omniscient (third-person) point of view, well suited to convey detachment, authority, coherence, and comprehension on the part of the narrator. But these, as eventually became clear to me when I read it over for the third time, were precisely the tonal qualities I wanted to avoid. My man was engaged in an ongoing process of (self-)discovery; he was not so much marching purposefully forward as he was circling anxiously while trying to pick up a trail.

So what other points of view would work better? How about first person—Fred himself or perhaps Kay or even Randy telling the story? I wanted less introversion than Fred would provide. Also, he knew too much. Kay as first-person narrator interested me, but that would change the focus of the story; it would become hers, not his. Randy simply couldn't know enough, would not be present when he needed to be. But how about another, different first-person narrator—one who (like Hawthorne's narrator) isn't intimately familiar with all the protagonist's circumstances and who will thus speculate and hypothesize and construct? One who might seem, as the story continues, to come to know more? Will the identity of this narrator be an issue? Who is he, how does he know these things, why does he talk about them, why is he interested? Not to worry—see how it works. It worked, I thought, pretty well. As the story proceeded in revision, the narrator (like the reader) came to understand Fred better. One might even have imagined, at times, that the narrator *was* Fred, or his alter ego. The judgments passed on Fred—on his history, his failings, his feelings—became self-appraisals.

Before offering a brief excerpt of my story revised, I should point out that Hawthorne is not by any means the only source of such instruction regarding point of view. Henry James, in fact, would probably occur to many people as a more likely person to turn to. As it happens, however, I know and like Hawthorne's work better.

"Before they at last left the interstate, Kay also told him [Fred] that she was lonely, that she had started to smoke again, that Tish wasn't speaking to her, that she had mailed Randy a packet of condoms at the school, and that she hadn't seen or heard from Ann [Fred's ex-wife] for months. But they had never been very close.

"Fred is a very attentive listener; I expect he would have made a good lawyer—cool, reasonable seeming, fairly articulate. What to make of these confessions? 'Lonely' was easy—of course she would be. He had probably never smoked himself but could believe it would be hard to stop. Your daughter not talking to you: a bad sign. Fred, being an only child himself and not having any children of his own, would defer judgment. The business of the condoms I am sure would make him uneasy, though he could imagine most of the arguments pro and con. He didn't like to hear about Ann. Who would?"

The first of the two preceding paragraphs is essentially a summary of what Kay said, an account that closely approaches indirect discourse, that is, "She said that . . ." The second paragraph opens with a first-person observation, followed by informed speculation, which turns into reflection on each of Kay's presumably true confessions. By the last sentence the speaker and Fred seem to be of one mind and to expect the reader both to understand and probably to agree.

Let me return now to my source of instruction, to "Wakefield." I see Hawthorne's story as a three-party narrative. There is the title figure, an inscrutable loner, not by usual criteria a particularly engaging character. Second, there is the first-person narrator, who early makes clear that his knowledge of the narrative is limited. "This outline," he tells us, "is all that I remember." From this circumstance derives a certain ambiguity of character motivation, the consequent necessity of speculation and informed inference, and finally the substantial involvement of the reader (the third party) in the interpretive process. Of this process the end result, to put it succinctly, is that character and narrator become virtually doubles while the involved reader figures finally as a kind of contributing editor and even perhaps, self-judged, as a kind of unindicted coconspirator. Perhaps that's overly dramatic; better maybe to say that the reader realizes that the potential to behave out of motives similar to the protagonist's is not uncommon.

It was, I think, certain ostensible similarities of characterization and theme between my own and Hawthorne's story which first suggested that I might convert some of his narrative techniques. Wakefield throughout displays a "quiet selfishness," a rather cold self-possession; he conducts a sort of bloodless experiment. During the whole of his twenty-year absence, he retains the freedom to renew the comfort and possibly the happiness of his married life at any time.

There is something enormously appealing in the idea of setting one persona aside and constructing a second to take its place. The notion of reinventing oneself is invigorating. But this is not what Wakefield does; instead, he camps around the corner, becoming a sort of asexual voyeur, almost in residence.

Fred, however, does not have the option to return to his ex-wife. Today Mrs. Wakefield would not, I expect, remain twenty years faithfully unmarried. But Fred does encounter another woman, Kay, much like his ex-spouse (she's described as taller and blonder), complete with ready-made family, and by story's (revised) end seems to have made up his mind. Thus, altered, the last paragraph reads:

> As he sat in the cool dark on Kay's living room sofa waiting for her, Fred thought he had decided. "I have a question I'd like to ask you," he called to her.

Let me leave Fred to ask his question and attend for a time to Wakefield, who has been waiting patiently. I do wonder, however, what Fred will do if he is turned down. Wakefield is described, unattractively, as sluggish, passably intellectual, unimaginative, cold hearted, selfish and vain and crafty and strange. Furthermore, he is not a man motivated by high principle or driven by invincible monomania, as may be said of the withdrawn and isolated protagonists of a number of Hawthorne's other celebrated tales, for instance, "The Minister's Black Veil" or "Ethan Brand." In "Wakefield," an eighteenth-century London husband disappears, or pretends to, his principal motive at first being curiosity to see how his wife will take it. He suffers, it seems, from a kind of morbid vanity in wanting to see how his world will be affected by his sudden removal. It is out of similar motives, perhaps, that people fantasize about attending their own funerals, as Tom Sawyer does. Mrs. Wakefield is decently distressed but soon enough recovers. Whether Wakefield does or can recover is the question. The world, not very surprisingly, is unaffected by Wakefield's change of address. By "stepping aside for a moment," the narrator remarks, "a man exposes himself to a fearful risk of losing his place forever."

As regards character, then, Hawthorne seems not to offer us in the Wakefields either notable profundity or complexity or even attractiveness. And of course not very much happens in "Wakefield." Indeed, the plotting seems almost perfunctory. Much commonplace, lifelike detail is deliberately omitted; we aren't told, for instance, how Wakefield spends his time, whether he has children, how he is employed. Overall the story seems to be rather abstract in conception.

"Wakefield" differs from much twentieth-century short fiction in that it resembles neither play nor poem but instead a familiar essay, in the creation of which we as readers are invited to join. This is to say that from our perspective a principal distinction of the story is Hawthorne's management of point of view; the narrator seems to invent the story before our eyes and with our collaboration. As early as the second paragraph, he invites us inside. "We know, each for himself, that none of us would perpetrate such a folly, yet feel as if some other might."

Much of the narrative is frankly hypothetical. The storyteller wonders, "What sort of a man was Wakefield? We are free to shape out our own idea, and call it by his name." Hawthorne might almost have written, "and call it by our name," for we are, even at this early point in the story, involved, even implicated.

What do we find in this self-portrait? How to describe this story's thematic concerns? We are cautioned not to break "the magnetic chain of humanity," as does Ethan Brand in the story of that name. In a way, perhaps, this story is even more frightening because Wakefield severs his connection not out of pride or passion but almost by chance. We can say, "I'd never be Ethan Brand, not such a monster" and feel safe, but can we say, as easily, "I'd never get involved in a 'whim-wham,' something foolish and irrational"? We learn that although they may at first be easily achieved, withdrawal, independence, or isolation may prove very costly in the end. We see that our lives are only partially under our control, much less than we would prefer to think. As Wakefield leaves his wife, Hawthorne writes, "So much for the commencement of this long whim-wham." "Whim-wham" means whim or caprice, and Hawthorne, ever the ironist, uses the term because it is comic in tone (like mish-mash or wiggle-waggle) and suggests the inconsequential. Whim-wham it may be, but an act illustrative of how readily, imperceptibly, and irreversibly our comfortable, conventional lives may be radically altered, may in fact disintegrate before our astonished eyes, while we, victims of inertia, are helpless to resist.

Shortly Hawthorne writes, "It is accomplished. Wakefield is another man." What he means is that Wakefield is not another man; he has always had dormant within him this virus, this perverse principle. Things unaccountably happen, and if we all had more time, the narrator tells us,

> might I exemplify how an influence, beyond our control, lays its strong hand on every deed which we do, and weaves its consequences into an iron tissue of necessity.

After twenty years away, half of which Hawthorne passes off in a paragraph, Wakefield one evening "is taking his customary walk towards the dwelling which he still calls his own." He is caught in a sudden shower, soaked to the skin, and at last returns home.

> Shall he stand, wet and shivering here, when his own hearth has a good fire to warm him, and his own wife will run to fetch the gray coat and small-clothes, which, doubtless, she has kept carefully in the closet of their bed-chamber?

Well, of course not. We have the option of attaching a happy ending, however unlikely, to this tale—let him go in to his now elderly widow. And so they lived happily ever after. Because it is our story, we can have it that way if we want to, but the narrator has an alternative suggestion. "Stay, Wakefield! Would you go to the sole home that is left you? Then step into your grave!"

Depending on our angle of vision, we are likely to read "Wakefield" in one of two ways. It may be seen as a tediously abstract story featuring two nearly anonymous eighteenth-century Londoners doing nothing much for twenty years. This is perhaps the "dated" and "quaint" Hawthorne to whom the critic took exception. Or it may rather be seen as a participatory narrative, featuring narrator and character and reader, then and now, and reflecting in apparently cheerful but actually chilling fashion on the self-destructive consequences of withdrawal, of watching rather than participating in life.

I cannot report that an infusion of Dr. Hawthorne's early-nineteenth-century narrative techniques resulted in a miraculous and widely admired recovery from late-twentieth-century anonymity for my story. In fact, I have not had a response yet. But "Fred and Kay and Randy and Tish," if I may point a final moral in the Hawthorne manner, is a better, more interesting, more complex, and certainly more distinctive story than it was, particularly, I think, as it offers the reader the opportunity to discover something of him- or herself in the narrative.

Toni Cade Bambara

Toni Cade Bambara was born in 1939 in New York City and ed-ucated at Queens College, the University of Florence, and the City College of the City University of New York. She has worked as a social investigator for the New York State Department of Welfare, as a visiting Professor of African-American Studies at Stephens College, and as a consultant on women's studies at Emory University. Since 1971, she has been writer-in-residence at Spelman College in Atlanta. Among her fiction are the story collections *Gorilla, My Love* (1972), *The Salt Eaters* (1980), and the novel *If Blessing Comes* (1987).

My Man Bovanne

Toni Cade Bambara

Blind people got a hummin jones if you notice. Which is understandable com-pletely once you been around one and notice what no eyes will force you into to see people, and you get past the first time, which seems to come out of nowhere, and it's like you in church again with fat-chest ladies and old gents gruntin a hum low in the throat to whatever the preacher be saying. Shakey Bee bottom lip all swole up with Sweet Peach and me explainin how come the sweet-potato bread was a dollar-quarter this time stead of dollar regular and he say uh hunh he understand, then he break into this *thizzin* kind of hum which is quiet, but fiercesome just the same, if you ain't ready for it. Which I wasn't. But I got used to it and the onliest time I had to say somethin bout it was when he was playin checkers on the stoop one time and he commenst to hummin quite churchy seem to me. So I says, "Look here Shakey Bee, I can't beat you and Jesus too." He stop.

So that's how come I asked My Man Bovanne to dance. He ain't my man mind you, just a nice ole gent from the block that we all know cause he fixes things and the kids like him. Or used to fore Black Power got hold their minds and mess em around till they can't be civil to ole folks. So we at this benefit for my niece's cousin who's runnin for somethin with this Black party somethin or other behind her. And I press up close to dance with Bovanne who blind and I'm hummin and he hummin, chest to chest like talkin. Not jammin my breasts into the man. Wasn't bout tits. Was bout vibrations. And he dug it and asked me what color dress I had on and how my hair was fixed and how I was doin without a man, not nosy but nice-like, and who was at this affair and was the canapés dainty-stingy or healthy enough to get hold of proper. Comfy and cheery is what I'm tryin to get across. Touch talkin like the heel of the hand on the tambourine or on a drum.

But right away Joe Lee come up on us and frown for dancin so close to the man. My own son who knows what kind of warm I am about; and don't grown men call me long distance and in the middle of the night for a little Mama comfort? But he frown. Which ain't right since Bovanne can't see and defend himself. Just a nice old man who fixes toasters and busted irons and bicycles and things and changes the lock on my door when my men friends get messy. Nice man. Which is not why they invited him. Grass roots you see. Me and Sister Taylor and the woman who does heads at Mamies and the man from the barber shop, we all there on account of we grass roots. And I ain't never been souther than Brooklyn Battery and no more country than the window box on my fire escape. And just yesterday my kids tellin me to take them countrified rags off my head and be cool. And now can't get Black enough to suit em. So everybody passin sayin My Man Bovanne. Big deal, keep steppin and don't even stop a minute to get the man a drink or one of them cute sandwiches or tell him what's goin in. And him standin there with a smile ready case someone do speak he want to be ready. So that's how come I pull him on the dance floor and we dance squeezin past the tables and chairs and all them coats and people standin round up in each other face talkin bout this and that but got no use for this blind man who mostly fixed skates and scooters for all these folks when they was just kids. So I'm pressed up close and we touch talkin with the hum. And here come my daughter cuttin her eye at me like she do when she tell me about my "apolitical" self like I got hoof and mouf disease and there ain't no hope at all. And I don't pay her no mind and just look up in Bovanne shadow face and tell him his stomach like a drum and he laugh. Laugh real loud. And here come my youngest, Task, with a tap on my elbow like he the third grade monitor and I'm cuttin up on the line to assembly.

"I was just talkin on the drums," I explained when they hauled me into the kitchen. I figured drums was my best defense. They can get ready for drums what with all this heritage business. And Bovanne stomach just like that drum Task give me when he come back from Africa. You just touch it and it hum thizzm, thizzm. So I stuck to the drum story. "Just drummin that's all."

"Mama, what are you talkin about?"

"She had too much to drink," say Elo to Task cause she don't hardly say nuthin to me direct no more since that ugly argument about my wigs.

"Look here Mama," say Task, the gentle one. "We just tryin to pull your coat. You were makin a spectacle of yourself out there dancing like that."

"Dancin like what?"

Task run a hand over his left ear like his father for the world and his father before that.

"Like a bitch in heat," say Elo.

"Well, uhh, I was goin to say like one of them sex-starved ladies gettin on in years and not too discriminating. Know what I mean?"

I don't answer cause I'll cry. Terrible thing when your own children talk to you like that. Pullin me out the party and hustlin me into some stranger's kitchen in the back of a bar just like the damn police. And ain't like I'm old old. I can still wear me some sleeveless dresses without the meat hangin off my arm. And I keep up with some thangs through my kids. Who ain't kids no more. To hear them tell it. So I don't say nuthin.

"Dancin with that tom," say Elo to Joe Lee, who leanin on the folks' freezer. "His feet can smell a cracker a mile away and go into their shuffle number post haste. And them eyes. He could be a little considerate and put on some shades. Who wants to look into them blown-out fuses that—"

"Is this what they call the generation gap?" I say.

"Generation gap," spits Elo, like I suggested castor oil and fricassee possum in the milk-shakes or somethin. "That's a white concept for a white phenomenon. There's no generation gap among Black people. We are a col—"

"Yeh, well never mind," says Joe Lee. "The point is Mama . . . well, it's pride. You embarrass yourself and us too dancin like that."

"I wasn't shame." Then nobody say nuthin. Them standin there in they pretty clothes with drinks in they hands and gangin up on me, and me in the third-degree chair and nary a olive to my name. Felt just like the police got hold to me.

"First of all," Task say, holdin up his hand and tickin off the offenses, "the dress. Now that dress is too short, Mama, and too low-cut for a woman your age. And Tamu's going to make a speech tonight to kick off the campaign and will be introducin you and expecting you to organize the council of elders—"

"Me? Didn nobody ask me nuthin. You mean Nisi? She change her name?"

"Well, Norton was supposed to tell you about it. Nisi wants to introduce you and then encourage the older folks to form a Council of the Elders to act as an advisory—"

"And you going to be standing there with your boobs out and that wig on your head and that hem up to your ass. And people'll say, 'Ain't that the horny bitch that was grindin with the blind dude?'"

"Elo, be cool a minute," say Task, gettin to the next finger. "And then there's the drinkin. Mama, you know you can't drink cause next thing you know you be laughin loud and carryin on," and he grab another finger for the loudness. "And then there's the dancin. You been tattooed on the man for four records straight and slow draggin even on the fast numbers. How you think that look for a woman your age?"

"What's my age?"

"What?"

"I'm axin you all a simple question. You keep talkin bout what's proper for a woman my age. How old am I anyhow?" And Joe Lee slams his eyes shut and squinches up his face to figure. And Task run a hand over his ear and stare into his glass like the ice cubes goin calculate for him. And Elo just starin at the top of my head like she goin rip the wig off any minute now.

"Is your hair braided up under that thing? If so, why don't you take it off? You always did do a neat cornroll."

"Uh huh," cause I'm thinkin how she couldn't undo her hair fast enough talking bout cornroll so countrified. None of which was the subject. "How old, I say?"

"Sixtee-one or—"

"You a damn lie Joe Lee Peoples."

"And that's another thing," say Task on the fingers.

"You know what you all can kiss," I say, gettin up and brushin the wrinkles out my lap.

"Oh, Mama," Elo say, puttin a hand on my shoulder like she hasn't done since she left home and the hand landin light and not sure it supposed to be there. Which hurt me to my heart. Cause this was the child in our happiness fore Mr. Peoples die. And I carried that child strapped to my chest till she was nearly two. We was close is what I'm tryin to tell you. Cause it was more me in the child than the others. And even after Task it was the girlchild I covered in the night and wept over for no reason at all less it was she was a chub-chub like me and not very pretty, but a warm child. And how did things get to this, that she can't put a sure hand on me and say Mama we love you and care about you and you entitled to enjoy yourself cause you a good woman?

"And then there's Reverend Trent," say Task, glancin from left to right like they hatchin a plot and just now lettin me in on it. "You were suppose to be talking with him tonight, Mama, about giving us his basement for campaign headquarters and—"

"Didn nobody tell me nuthin. If grass roots mean you kept in the dark I can't use it. I really can't. And Reven Trent a fool anyway the way he tore into the widow man up there on Edgecomb cause he wouldn't take in three of them foster children and the woman not even comfy in the ground yet and the man's mind messed up and—"

"Look here," say Task. "What we need is a family conference so we can get all this stuff cleared up and laid out on the table. In the meantime I think we better get back into the other room and tend to business. And in the meantime, Mama, see if you can't get to Reverend Trent and—"

"You want me to belly rub with the Reven, that it?"

"Oh damn," Elo say and go through the swingin door.

"We'll talk about all this at dinner. How's tomorrow night, Joe Lee?" While Joe Lee being self-important I'm wonderin who's doin the cookin and how come no body ax me if I'm free and do I get a corsage and things like that. Then Joe nod that it's O.K. and he go through the swingin door and just a little hub-bub come through from the other room. Then Task smile his smile, lookin just like his daddy and he leave. And it just me in this stranger's kitchen, which was a mess I wouldn't never let my kitchen look like. Poison you just to look at the pots. Then the door swing the other way and it's My Man Bovanne standin there saying Miss Hazel but lookin at the deep fry and then at the steam table, and most surprised when I come up on him from the other direction and take him on out of there. Pass the folks pushin up towards the stage where Nisi and some other people settin and ready to talk, and folks gettin to the last of the sandwiches and the booze fore they settle down in one spot and listen serious.

And I'm thinkin bout tellin Bovanne what a lovely long dress Nisi got on and the earrings and her hair piled up in a cone and the people bout to hear how we all gettin screwed and gotta form our own party and everybody there listenin and lookin. But instead I just haul the man on out of there, and Joe Lee and his wife look at me like I'm terrible, but they ain't said boo to the man yet. Cause he blind and old and don't nobody there need him since they grown up and don't need they skates fixed no more.

"Where we goin, Miss Hazel?" Him knowin all the time.

"First we gonna buy you some dark sunglasses. Then you comin with me to the supermarket so I can pick up tomorrow's dinner, which is going to be a grand thing proper and you invited. Then we goin to my house."

"That be fine. I surely would like to rest my feet." Bein cute, but you got to let men play out they little show, blind or not. So he chat on bout how tired he is and how he appreciate me takin him in hand this way. And I'm thinkin I'll have him change the lock on my door first thing. Then I'll give the man a nice warm bath with jasmine leaves in the water and a little Epsom salt on the sponge to do his back. And then a good rubdown with rose water and olive oil. Then a cup of lemon tea with a taste in it. And a little talcum, some of that fancy stuff Nisi mother sent over last Christmas. And then a massage, a good face massage round the forehead which is the worryin part. Cause you gots to take care of the older folks. And let them know they still needed to run the mimeo machine and keep the spark plugs clean and fix the mailboxes for folks who might help us get the breakfast program goin, and the school for the little kids and the campaign and all. Cause old folks is the nation. That what Nisi was sayin and I mean to do my part.

"I imagine you are a very pretty woman, Miss Hazel."

"I surely am," I say just like the hussy my daughter always say I was.

Character, Politics, and Phrasing in Toni Cade Bambara's "My Man Bovanne"

David Huddle

> **Phrase,** *n* [Gr. *phrasis,* from *phrazein,* to speak.] 1. a manner or style of speech, expression; phraseology. 2. a short, colorful, or forceful expression. . . . 5. in music, a short, distinct part or passage, usually of two, four, or eight measures.—*Webster's Unabridged Dictionary.*

O**n** its way to our minds and hearts, a story—even one read in silence—passes through our ears. For the writer of a conventional story, this is a fact of small consequence. However, for an author with a special ap-

preciation of the powers of language, the sound of a story—its sheer music—
can become its most important element. Consider, for example the opening of
Toni Cade Bambara's "My Man Bovanne":

> Blind people got a hummin jones if you notice. Which is understandable com-
> pletely once you been around one and notice what no eyes will force you into
> to see people, and you get past the first time, which seems to come out of
> nowhere, and it's like you in church again with fat-chest ladies and old gents
> gruntin a hum low in the throat to whatever the preacher be saying. Shakey
> Bee bottom lip all swole up with Sweet Peach and me explainin how come the
> sweet-potato bread was a dollar-quarter this time stead of dollar regular and
> he say uh hunh he understand, then he break into this *thizzin* kind of hum
> which is quiet, but fiercesome just the same, if you ain't ready for it. Which I
> wasn't. But I got used to it and the onliest time I had to say somethin bout it
> was when he was playin checkers on the stoop one time and he commenst to
> hummin quite churchy seem to me. So I says, "Look here Shakey Bee, I can't
> beat you and Jesus too." He stop.

Shocked, astonished, amused, charmed, disoriented, irked, intrigued:
These are likely reader responses to such a paragraph. Someone newly entering
the story will probably experience a combination of all these responses. For
some years now, we Americans have been informally hearing the sound of this
language—or something very close to it—but regardless of our ethnic backgrounds, few of us have encountered it on the printed page. Reading these sentences requires conventionally educated readers to reevaluate some of their
most basic assumptions about the nature of literature.*

The voice that begins "My Man Bovanne" is not that of a minor character
speaking, a mere tenant of the story; this story's rightful owner uses a voice that
defies "acceptable" usage and demands that its reader reconsider syntax, diction, and the basic concept of the English sentence: "Shakey Bee bottom lip all
swole up with Sweet Peach and me explainin how come the sweet-potato
bread was a dollar-quarter this time stead of dollar regular and he say uh hunh
he understand, then he break into this *thizzin* kind of hum which is quiet, but
fiercesome just the same, if you ain't ready for it." As Italian departs from
Latin, as jazz departs from the classical tradition, so does this black American
urban dialect depart from the English we customarily find on the printed page.
The music of this dialect, in a reader's mind's ear, conveys its spirit of rebellion
from its stuffy parent, its satirical mockery and criticism of conventional
English, along with the wit and joy of its own refreshing vitality.†

The voice that utters these sentences makes an immediate and distinct impression on us—because of how different it is from what we are accustomed to
reading, of course, but also because of its individual personality: The person
speaking to us this way—the character we begin constructing in our minds as
we read this opening paragraph—is funny ("a hummin jones" might be

---

*These sentences also raise language-related issues similar to those in James Alan McPherson's
"The Story of a Dead Man."
†The lively speech of Billy Renfro in "Dead Man" entertains us in a similar fashion.

roughly translated as "a habit of humming"), sharply observant ("fat-chest ladies"), opinionated ("quite churchy seem to me"), and a maker of poetically original phrases (*"thizzin* kind of hum which is quiet, but fiercesome"). This character is direct and irreverent enough to open a conversation by making a blunt generalization about "blind people." Though not conventionally sensitive, this character is nevertheless someone who has spent enough time in the company of a blind person to get "used to it," someone who has the capacity to empathize ("notice what no eyes will force you into to see people").

The jazz saxophonist Stan Getz admired the playing of his peer Sonny Rollins for "say[ing] only who he is, what he is." Though we do not consciously register a definitive judgment of the personality of this narrator, every phrase of her speech tells us "who [she] is, what [she] is."* This is the voice of a person so nakedly herself that she is the opposite of an unreliable narrator. The phrasing of this voice ("He ain't my man mind you, just a nice ole gent") instructs us readers to accept it as belonging to someone who has nothing to hide. Perfectly aware of what others think of her, she has unshakable confidence in the truth of her own experience: "And I press up close to dance with Bovanne who blind and I'm hummin and he hummin, chest to chest like talkin. Not jammin my breasts into the man. Wasn't bout tits. Was bout vibrations."

What was it "bout"? *Correctness* is the main issue of "My Man Bovanne." To read the story is to be forced to judge whose perception of people and events, relationships, and even the general human circumstance is most accurate, most humane, most valuable. The language that conveys the story to us, however charming and amusing it may be, is that of a disenfranchised voice: Our culture tells us that people who speak to us this way possess neither truth nor authority—or if truth, then certainly not authority.

What does our culture signify as the language of truth and authority? Well, another voice in the story offers a sampling of it: "That's a white concept for a white phenomenon. There's no generation gap among Black people."†

Disadvantaged phrasing is what Miss Hazel must use to tell us her story. ("And how did things get to this, that she can't put a sure hand on me and say Mama we love you and care about you and you entitled to enjoy yourself cause you a good woman?") She must use these words because they are what her economic, racial, and geographic circumstances have given her to use, but we also understand that she is choosing to use them because they are who and what she is. Unlike Nisi, who has changed her name to Tamu, Miss Hazel is sticking with what she has ("'I wasn't shame'").

As is the case with most first-person narrators, Miss Hazel is characterized primarily by her voice: The way she tells us her story determines the way we

---

*Billy Renfro's voice in "Dead Man" invites us to make similar judgments about the reliability of his "character." In Billy Renfro's case, though his language suggests that he is a "reliable" narrator and that he, like Miss Hazel, is "nakedly himself," his voice also contains, instead of wisdom and compassion, a belligerence calculated to make a reader just as uneasy about him as his cousin William is.

†William, the narrator of "Dead Man," uses such a "voice of authority" in his relentless efforts to gain social and economic advantage.

readers perceive her. Her phrasing, after we get used to it, has the effect of charming us, amusing us, endearing her to us; it also aligns our sympathies with her in her role of the underdog of her situation.* Miss Hazel's black English signifies her minority status; we can also discern with our ears how Miss Hazel's voice contrasts with her children's more up-to-date, hip, and politically aware black English ("His feet can smell a cracker a mile away and go into their shuffle number post haste. And them eyes. He could be a little considerate and put on some shades. Who wants to look into them blown-out fuses . . .").

The way she talks informs us readers, at an almost subconscious level of apprehension, that within this minority gathering Miss Hazel is a minority of one. The way she talks builds our understanding of, and sympathy for, her the more we learn of the forces against which she struggles—her children's disapproval, her friend Bovanne's displaced status in the group, and the gathering's fashionable ideology that would antiquate Miss Hazel's basic values.

The "message" of "My Man Bovanne" (and it is an overtly polemical story)[†] is delivered through the nuance of Miss Hazel's voice. Neither she nor anyone else in the story needs directly to inform us that this woman—marginalized by race, sex, economic circumstance, education, age, and her own helpless honesty—possesses a superior political consciousness in her discerning appreciation of Bovanne, her heartfelt compassion for him, and her truly responsible action toward him. We readers come to know this about Miss Hazel's character through her phrasing:

> Then I'll give the man a nice warm bath with jasmine leaves in the water and a little Epsom salt on the sponge to do his back. And then a good rubdown with rose water and olive oil. Then a cup of lemon tea with a taste in it. And a little talcum, some of that fancy stuff Nisi mother sent over last Christmas. And then a massage, a good face massage round the forehead which is the worryin part. Cause you gots to take care of the older folks. And let them know they still needed to run the mimeo machine and keep the spark plugs clean and fix the mailboxes for folks who might help us get the breakfast program goin, and the school for the little kids and the campaign and all. Cause old folks is the nation.

Language is such an immediate and obvious element of a narrative that both writer and readers often ignore its power and significance. Just as our captivation by the image in a work of visual art might cause us to overlook the actual paint and canvas of the object, a story[‡] can engage us so thoroughly that we might not notice how much is accomplished by the language of its telling. Because we might not adequately take note of its "surface"—the words on the page—we might see character and politics as the most significant elements of

---

*In spite of its belligerence, Billy Renfro's phrasing eventually wins our sympathy for him in a similar fashion.

†McPherson's "Dead Man," by contrast, is a *subtly* polemical story.

‡Katherine Mansfield's "The Garden Party" is a conventional example of such a story.

"My Man Bovanne." The story offers its readers the thrill of intimately witnessing the hard-earned personal triumph of a true underdog. Through her own resourcefulness of spirit, heart, and mind, Miss Hazel wins out and has "her way," so that at the end we feel the pleasure of an admired friend's having overcome adversity to receive a well-deserved reward. However, it is the phrasing of the story that teaches us readers to appreciate both Miss Hazel and her higher consciousness ("Cause old folks is the nation"). Miss Hazel's voice enables a reader to become her confidant ("'I surely am,' I say just like the hussy my daughter always say I was"). The personality of Miss Hazel and the political enlightenment she offers us are the compositions of Toni Cade Bambara's virtuoso phrasing.

Raymond Carver

Raymond Carver, born in 1939 in Clatskanie, Oregon, studied writing in California and at the University of Iowa Writers' Workshop; he spent a number of years holding a variety of odd jobs to support himself and his family while he wrote. Carver published ten volumes of poetry and short fiction in the last twenty years of his life; *Where I'm Calling From* (1988) is a collection of what he considered his best stories. In his later years, Carver taught creative writing and was the recipient of a prestigious MacArthur Fellowship before his death in 1988.

So Much Water So Close to Home

[SHORT VERSION]

Raymond Carver

My husband eats with a good appetite. But I don't think he's really hungry. He chews, arms on the table, and stares at something across the room. He looks at me and looks away. He wipes his mouth on the napkin. He shrugs, and goes on eating.

"What are you staring at me for?" he says. "What is it?" he says and lays down his fork.

"Was I staring?" I say, and shake my head.

The telephone rings.

"Don't answer it," he says.

"It might be your mother," I say.

"Watch and see," he says.

I pick up the receiver and listen. My husband stops eating.

"What did I tell you?" he says when I hang up. He starts to eat again. Then throws his napkin on his plate. He says, "Goddamn it, why can't people mind their own business? Tell me what I did wrong and I'll listen! I wasn't the only man there. We talked it over and we all decided. We couldn't just turn around. We were five miles from the car. I won't have you passing judgment. Do you hear?"

"You know," I say.

He says, "What do I know, Claire? Tell me what I'm supposed to know. I don't know anything except one thing." He gives me what he thinks is a meaningful look. "She was dead," he says. "And I'm as sorry as anyone else. But she was dead."

"That's the point," I say.

He raises his hands. He pushes his chair away from the table. He takes out his cigarettes and goes out to the back with a can of beer. I see him sit in the lawn chair and pick up the newspaper again.

His name is in there on the first page. Along with the names of his friends.

I close my eyes and hold on to the sink. Then I rake my arm across the drainboard and send the dishes to the floor.

He doesn't move. I know he's heard. He lifts his head as if still listening. But he doesn't move otherwise. He doesn't turn around.

He and Gordon Johnson and Mel Dorn and Vern Williams, they play poker and bowl and fish. They fish every spring and early summer before visiting relatives can get in the way. They are decent men, family men, men who take care of their jobs. They have sons and daughters who go to school with our son, Dean.

Last Friday these family men left for the Naches River. They parked the car in the mountains and hiked to where they wanted to fish. They carried their bedrolls, their food, their playing cards, their whiskey.

They saw the girl before they set up camp. Mel Dorn found her. No clothes on her at all. She was wedged into some branches that stuck out over the water.

He called the others and they came to look. They talked about what to do. One of the men—my Stuart didn't say which—said they should start back at once. The others stirred the sand with their shoes, said they didn't feel inclined that way. They pleaded fatigue, the late hour, the fact that the girl wasn't going anywhere.

In the end they went ahead and set up the camp. They built a fire and drank their whiskey. When the moon came up, they talked about the girl. Someone said they should keep the body from drifting away. The took their flashlights and went back to the river. One of the men—it might have been Stuart—waded in and got her. He took her by the fingers and pulled her into shore. He got some nylon cord and tied it to her wrist and then looped the rest around a tree.

The next morning they cooked breakfast, drank coffee, and drank whiskey, and then split up to fish. That night they cooked fish, cooked potatoes, drank coffee, drank whiskey, then took their cooking things and eating things back down to the river and washed them where the girl was.

They played some cards later on. Maybe they played until they couldn't see them anymore. Vern Williams went to sleep. But the others told stories. Gordon Johnson said the trout they'd caught were hard because of the terrible coldness of the water.

The next morning they got up late, drank whiskey, fished a little, took down their tents, rolled their sleeping bags, gathered their stuff, and hiked out. They drove until they got to a telephone. It was Stuart who made the call while the others stood around in the sun and listened. He gave the sheriff their names. They had nothing to hide. They weren't ashamed. They said they'd wait until someone could come for better directions and take down their statements.

I was asleep when he got home. But I woke up when I heard him in the kitchen. I found him leaning against the refrigerator with a can of beer. He put his heavy arms around me and rubbed his big hands on my back. In bed he put his hands on me again and then waited as if thinking of something else. I turned and opened my legs. Afterwards, I think he stayed awake.

He was up that morning before I could get out of bed. To see if there was something in the paper, I suppose.

The telephone began ringing right after eight.

"Go to hell!" I heard him shout.

The telephone rang right again.

"I have nothing to add to what I already said to the sheriff!"

He slammed the receiver down.

"What is going on?" I said.

It was then that he told me what I just told you.

I sweep up the broken dishes and go outside. He is lying on his back on the grass now, the newspaper and can of beer within reach.

"Stuart, could we go for a drive?" I say.

He rolls over and looks at me. "We'll pick up some beer," he says. He gets to his feet and touches me on the hip as he goes past. "Give me a minute," he says.

We drive through town without speaking. He stops at a roadside market for beer. I notice a great stack of papers just inside the door. On the top step a fat woman in a print dress holds out a licorice stick to a little girl. Later on, we cross Everson Creek and turn into the picnic grounds. The creek runs under the bridge and into a large pond a few hundred yards away. I can see the men out there. I can see them out there fishing.

So much water so close to home.

I say, "Why did you have to go miles away?"

"Don't rile me," he says.

We sit on a bench in the sun. He opens us cans of beer. He says, "Relax, Claire."

"They said they were innocent. They said they were crazy."

He says, "Who?" He says, "What are you talking about?"

"The Maddox brothers. They killed a girl named Arlene Hubly where I grew up. They cut off her head and threw her into the Cle Elum River. It happened when I was a girl."

"You're going to get me riled," he says.

I look at the creek. I'm right in it, eyes open, face down, staring at the moss on the bottom, dead.

"I don't know what's wrong with you," he says on the way home. "You're getting me more riled by the minute."

There is nothing I can say to him.

He tries to concentrate on the road. But he keeps looking into the rear-view mirror.

He knows.

Stuart believes he is letting me sleep this morning. But I was awake long before the alarm went off. I was thinking, lying on the far side of the bed away from his hairy legs.

He gets Dean off for school, and then he shaves, dresses, and leaves for work. Twice he looks in and clears his throat. But I keep my eyes closed.

In the kitchen I find a note from him. It's signed "Love."

I sit in the breakfast nook and drink coffee and leave a ring on the note. I look at the newspaper and turn it this way and that on the table. Then I skid it close and read what it says. The body has been identified, claimed. But it took some examining it, some putting things into it, some cutting, some weighing, some measuring, some putting things back again and sewing them in.

I sit for a long time holding the newspaper and thinking. Then I call up to get a chair at the hairdresser's.

I sit under the dryer with a magazine on my lap and let Marnie do my nails.

"I am going to a funeral tomorrow," I say.

"I'm sorry to hear that," Marnie says.

"It was a murder," I say.

"That's the worst kind," Marnie says.

"We weren't all that close," I say. "But you know."

"We'll get you fixed up for it," Marnie says.

That night I make my bed on the sofa, and in the morning I get up first. I put on coffee and fix breakfast while he shaves.

He appears in the kitchen doorway, towel over his bare shoulder, appraising.

"Here's coffee," I say. "Eggs'll be ready in a minute."

I wake Dean, and the three of us eat. Whenever Stuart looks at me, I ask Dean if he wants more milk, more toast, etc.

"I'll call you today," Stuart says as he opens the door.

I say, "I don't think I'll be home today."

"All right," he says. "Sure."

I dress carefully. I try on a hat and look at myself in the mirror. I write out a note for Dean.

Honey, Mommy has things to do this afternoon, but will be back later. You stay in or be in the backyard until one of us comes home.

Love, Mommy

I look at the word *Love* and then I underline it. Then I see the word *backyard*. Is it one word or two?

I drive through farm country, through fields of oats and sugar beets and past apple orchards, cattle grazing in pastures. Then everything changes, more like shacks than farmhouses and stands of timber instead of orchards. Then mountains, and on the right, far below, I sometimes see the Naches River.

A green pickup comes up behind me and stays behind me for miles. I keep slowing at the wrong times, hoping he will pass. Then I speed up. But this is at the wrong times, too. I grip the wheel until my fingers hurt.

On a long clear stretch he goes past. But he drives along beside for a bit, a crewcut man in a blue workshirt. We look each other over. Then he waves, toots his horn, and pulls on up ahead.

I slow down and find a place. I pull over and shut off the motor. I can hear the river down below the trees. Then I hear the pickup coming back.

I lock the doors and roll up the windows.

"You all right?" the man says. He raps on the glass. "You okay?" He leans his arms on the door and brings his face to the window.

I stare at him. I can't think what else to do.

"Is everything all right in there? How come you're all locked up?"

I shake my head.

"Roll down your window." He shakes his head and looks at the highway and then back at me. "Roll it down now."

"Please," I say, "I have to go."

"Open the door," he says as if he isn't listening. "You're going to choke in there."

He looks at my breasts, my legs. I can tell that's what he's doing.

"Hey, sugar," he says. "I'm just here to help is all."

The casket is closed and covered with floral sprays. The organ starts up the minute I take a seat. People are coming in and finding chairs. There's a boy in flared pants and a yellow short-sleeved shirt. A door opens and the family comes in in a group and moves over to a curtained place off to one side. Chairs creak as everybody gets settled. Directly, a nice blond man in a nice dark suit stands and asks us to bow our heads. He says a prayer for us, the living, and when he finishes, he says a prayer for the soul of the departed.

Along with the others I go past the casket. Then I move out onto the front steps and into the afternoon light. There's a woman who limps as she goes down the stairs ahead of me. On the sidewalk she looks around. "Well, they got him," she says. "If that's any consolation. They arrested him this morning. I heard it on the radio before I come. A boy right here in town."

We move a few steps down the hot sidewalk. People are starting cars. I put out my hand and hold on to a parking meter. Polished hoods and polished fenders. My head swims.

I say, "They have friends, these killers. You can't tell."

"I have known that child since she was a little girl," the woman says. "She used to come over and I'd bake cookies for her and let her eat them in front of the TV."

Back home, Stuart sits at the table with a drink of whiskey in front of him. For a crazy instant I think something's happened to Dean.

"Where is he?" I say. "Where is Dean?"

"Outside," my husband says.

He drains his glass and stands up. He says, "I think I know what you need."

He reaches an arm around my waist and with his other hand he begins to unbutton my jacket and then he goes on to the buttons of my blouse.

"First things first," he says.

He says something else. But I don't need to listen. I can't hear a thing with so much water going.

"That's right," I say, finishing the buttons myself. "Before Dean comes. Hurry."

Inference and Information in Raymond Carver's "So Much Water So Close to Home"

Ghita Orth

Some makers of fiction believe in the writing equivalent of Method acting. In this view, you create entire lives for your characters, from the number of their siblings to the brand of their toothpaste, so that, even if these factors don't enter into a story, you will understand the characters so totally that you will know how they would respond to any situation you place them in, and why. Even if writers don't invent a complete biography for a character, if asked they could probably explain if, even where, a protagonist went to college, or to what political party he or she belongs. As creators of fictional worlds, writers must know a great deal about those worlds and the characters who inhabit them. But how much of this to tell a *reader* in the context of a story? Not much, if we are to judge by this version of Raymond Carver's "So Much Water So Close to Home." Reading it, we must rely largely on inference rather than information.

Whatever Carver may know about Claire and Stuart and Dean, he isn't letting us in on it very fully; it's easy to understand from "So Much Water So Close to Home" why much of Carver's fiction is called "minimalist." Even if we aren't familiar with that style, we can deduce from the story its identifying characteristics.

One of the most affecting of these is Carver's casting the story in the present tense, as though its events were being recorded as they occur. We feel as though we are watching unprocessed data unreel before our eyes, rather than seeing events that have been considered by a narrator who has weighed their significance and chosen to focus only on those details that count. Here, because it seems as though a camera is running, impartially recording all details no matter what their relative importance, the reader must assume the responsibility of determining if, in fact, they *are* important.

In "So Much Water So Close to Home," the recording "camera" is Claire, its first-person narrator. We may expect a character narrator to function as a knowing guide through his or her own territory, but due to the style in which she relates its events and the kind of person she seems to be, Claire isn't much help in our attempt to get oriented in the story.

Claire's sentences are short and structurally simplistic: "He looks at me and looks away. He wipes his mouth on the napkin. He shrugs, and goes on eating." The effect of this repetitive, uninflected syntax is, like the present tense, to flatten and neutralize the particulars it narrates; all seem of equal weight. Again, readers are called upon to make judgments on their own. Similarly, Claire's bland and basic diction, employing only the simplest vocabulary, provides no evocative uses of language to point our attention or heighten our responses.

The manner of Claire's storytelling also affects our reactions to her as a character, just as Hazel's does in "My Man Bovanne." If we are to judge from the way she speaks, Claire is, like her narration, without imaginative "style" or intellectual acuity. Because we can't readily gauge her level of awareness or sensitivity, we are left pretty much to our own devices in attempting to understand the import of the events she relates. Furthermore, our feeling that Claire is somehow limited is intensified by the fact that, unlike most first-person narrators, she doesn't *think* very much. Not having access to any of her mental processes, we find it hard to "read" her and her behavior. Claire's motivations remain opaque.

So, too, she never tells us directly what she is *feeling* at any given moment. Her emotions are as sparsely delineated as her thoughts. The only way we know, for example, that Claire feels anger is when she recounts her actions: "I rake my arm across the drainboard and send the dishes to the floor." Although Claire is telling us her own story, we can only watch its events from the outside; we see her do things, but are left to infer why.

Often our sense of why characters behave as they do is clarified by what we know of their peripheral lives—their past experiences, their jobs, the environments they inhabit. Here, however, Claire and Stuart come to us essentially without any lives beyond the present moments of the story. Although Claire refers to the murder of Arlene Hubly in her childhood, her prior relationship with her husband, which might help us understand their current one, is never touched on. Nor do we have much sense of Claire and Stuart as parents; Dean is barely present here. And is Stuart a soccer coach? A doctor? A professional guitarist? Do they live in an old farmhouse? A trailer? A suburban split-level? "So Much Water So Close to Home" provides no answers to such questions that could help us know Claire and Stuart; what the camera records, with no surrounding context, is all that is available to us.

For the reader of "So Much Water So Close to Home," the ultimate effect of these characteristically minimalist devices—present tense, simple syntax and diction, limited presentation of thoughts and feelings, and lack of peripheral context—is that of a direct confrontation with immediate experience, without interference by the writer. Although there is no sense of Carver's presence in the story's style, however, nor of his intervention in the arrangement of its material, "So Much Water So Close to Home" only *seems* artless. Even a choice to deny readers access to characters' pasts, or to use the present tense, is a conscious artistic decision on the writer's part. Carver has as carefully chosen what to withhold here as another writer might choose what to include. His craft, although nearly invisible, is craft nonetheless.

In his essay "On Writing," Carver explains something of what that craft entails:

> All we have, finally, [are] the words, and they had better be the right ones. . . . If the words are heavy with the writer's own unbridled emotions, or if they are imprecise and inaccurate for some other reason—if the words are in any way blurred—the reader's eyes will slide right over them and nothing will be achieved.

The simplicity of Claire's narration, then, is purposeful for Carver—but *what,* exactly, does the minimalist writer hope to achieve with this pared-down style and withholding of elaboration?

More so than other kinds of fiction, minimalist stories like "So Much Water So Close to Home" attempt to engage their readers directly, actually to involve them in the process of making the story by forcing them to read below and through a minimal surface to assumptions of meaning. We are led to participate in the narrative process, as is also the case in Hawthorne's "Wakefield." As we try to understand Claire's behavior, we find ourselves as puzzled as Stuart; like him, we are confused about how to interpret the situation. Similarly, finding ourselves unable to explain what Stuart's behavior means to Claire, we, like her, are reduced to inarticulate response.

We are drawn into participating in the story, then, as we assume the interpretive roles its characters seem unable to fill, and when we feel unsuccessful in our attempts we stand squarely, if uneasily, at the characters' sides. Reading this version of "So Much Water So Close to Home" is a frustrating experience—like Stuart speaking to Claire, we are led to demand of the story, "Tell me what I'm supposed to know."

But the story doesn't really answer. The tension thus created is part of the effect Carver aims for. In his essay he explains:

> There has to be tension, a sense that something is imminent. . . . What creates tension in a piece of fiction is partly the way the concrete words are linked together to make up the visible action of the story. But it's also the things that are left out, that are implied, the landscape just under the smooth (but sometimes broken and unsettled) surface of things.

Readers of "So Much Water So Close to Home," though, can't help but wonder just how available that landscape is to them. It may not matter that we don't know Stuart's occupation or what Claire's kitchen looks like, but what if we

also don't know the nature of the conflict on which the story turns or understand its seeming resolution in the final paragraphs? A writer who chooses to
rely on his readers' powers of inference as much as Carver does here is taking
the chance of being misunderstood.

In this story, for example, the one thing we are certain of is that Claire is
distressed by what Stuart and his friends have done on their fishing trip. We
know this by her breaking the dishes and by the fact that although she passively acquiesced to Stuart's sexual advances before hearing his story, afterward she lies "on the far side of the bed away from his hairy legs" and then
moves even farther, to the sofa. The ways she interacts with Stuart—her judgmental silences, her mysterious assertions that he "knows" something—also
suggest the degree to which the events of the trip have disturbed her. But why?

It is tempting to imagine that Claire thinks Stuart himself has played a part
in the girl's death. She mentions convicted murderers who, like Stuart, "said
they were innocent"; she is not relieved by the arrest of the girl's assailant, saying, "They have friends, these killers"; she sees the man in the green pickup as
himself a potential attacker, perhaps one of those "friends"; she even seems
afraid for Dean while he is in Stuart's care.

And if we assume Claire sees her husband as a murderer, are we to see him
this way too? He does sound guiltily defensive in talking about the incident at
the Naches River and is clearly angered and made nervous by Claire's ac-
cusatory attitude. But although we don't really know Stuart and can't be *sure*
he is innocent of the crime, one would think that if he or his friends had been
involved in the girl's death they would simply have let her body drift down-
river rather than calling the sheriff. As Stuart explains, they reported the body
because "they had nothing to hide," and it appears we are meant to believe
him.

Perhaps, then, Claire is just blindly ignoring the illogic of assuming Stuart
had a hand in the girl's death, but how to explain the story's ending? If she
thought he were a killer, would she allow him again to approach her sexually
and even help and encourage him, "finishing the buttons [her]self?" Claire
does not indicate any real fear of Stuart; there appears to be more to this situation than a wife's thinking her husband is a dangerous killer. In fact, in the
story Claire seems to accept that the girl was already dead when the men found
her. When Stuart says, "She was dead," Claire replies, "That's the point."
Murder is not, then, the crime of which she finds him guilty.

But she does act as though a crime has been committed. What Claire is appalled by may be her husband's callous disregard for the dead, entirely helpless girl. These men have fished, played cards, and drunk whiskey, ignoring
her naked corpse; they have even washed their dishes in the water near where
her body is tied. Stuart's defensiveness about the incident focuses on justifying
the men's blatantly cold and selfish behavior: "We couldn't turn around. We
were five miles from the car. I won't have you passing judgment."

But Claire does pass judgment, and although much of the situation is
murky, it is clear that whatever equilibrium there might have been in their relationship has, when the story begins, been shaken. Something has gone very

wrong between Stuart and Claire as a result of his treatment of the murdered girl. The next thing a reader might ask, then, would have to do with *why* Claire has been made so distraught by these events. It is true that her husband has behaved crudely, but why should she care so much about the dead girl that Stuart didn't care about at all?

Carver has given us so little direct information in "So Much Water So Close to Home" that again we must draw inferences from the smallest details. In this case, when, at the picnic grounds, Claire says, "I look at the creek. I'm right in it, eyes open, face down, staring at the moss on the bottom, dead," we understand that she is somehow identifying with the murder victim. Although this would explain why she is so personally offended by Stuart's treatment of the girl, here, as has happened throughout our reading of the story, the possible answer to a question only raises another question.

We now wonder *why* she makes this identification—what leads her to see herself in the dead girl's place, in a watery grave? And what are we to make of her previous reference to water when she mused, "So much water so close to home"? Was she just referring to the local creek? Because this is the phrase Carver has chosen as the story's title, we sense that it must be thematically central in some way, but *what* way eludes us.

That water appears again in the story's final lines thus also seems important. This is, after all, the most puzzling scene of many. As far as we have been able to tell until now, the fishing incident has caused a significant breach between Claire and Stuart, yet at the story's conclusion she is hurriedly urging on his renewed sexual advances. Because this is a complete reversal of the direction in which the story appeared to have been heading, we look for some causative factor that will help us understand it.

Perhaps Claire's going to the funeral (for reasons that are hard to fathom) has somehow led her to "forgive" Stuart. But from her physical reaction afterward, dizzy while her "head swims," she seems not to have found any ease of mind or balanced perspective there. Only when Claire tells us that, as Stuart begins to undress her, she "can't hear a thing with so much water going" do we find a possible way of understanding her behavior.

She seems, when Stuart comes on to her, again to see herself in the place of the victimized girl. Is Claire going under here, helplessly giving in to the "terrible coldness of the water" like that in which the girl, demeaned by Stuart and his friends, had lain? We begin to sense what she may have meant in asserting there was "so much water so close to home"; the dead girl's situation feels terribly familiar.

Throughout the story, however, Carver has withheld the kinds of information that could have more surely structured our responses to it; we have been forced to help make the story's meanings ourselves, and each of us may have made a slightly different one. As a result, we are left, at story's end, as disconcerted and uneasy as Stuart and Claire have been. So how much do readers need to know about fictional characters and their worlds to come away from a story fully satisfied by it? More, perhaps, than Carver has chosen to offer us here.

There is, however, another, longer "So Much Water So Close to Home"—
the original version, first published in 1977. Later, for his collection *What We
Talk About When We Talk about Love* in 1981, Carver rewrote that story, paring it
down to the minimalist narrative we've just looked at. After two years, though,
given the opportunity to include it in *Fires*, a volume of essays, stories, and
poems, Carver returned to the longer version he had first written and reprinted
it with only slight revisions. That is the story which follows here, the one
Carver included in his final fiction collection, *Where I'm Calling From*, and thus,
at the last, chose as *the* "So Much Water So Close to Home."

So Much Water So Close to Home

[LONG VERSION]

Raymond Carver

My husband eats with good appetite but he seems tired, edgy. He chews
slowly, arms on the table, and stares at something across the room. He looks at
me and looks away again. He wipes his mouth on the napkin. He shrugs and
goes on eating. Something has come between us though he would like me to
believe otherwise.

"What are you staring at me for?" he asks. "What is it?" he says and puts
his fork down.

"Was I staring?" I say and shake my head stupidly, stupidly.

The telephone rings. "Don't answer it," he says.

"It might be your mother," I say. "Dean—it might be something about
Dean."

"Watch and see," he says.

I pick up the receiver and listen for a minute. He stops eating. I bite my lip
and hang up.

"What did I tell you?" he says. He starts to eat again, then throws the napkin onto his plate. "Goddamn it, why can't people mind their own business?
Tell me what I did wrong and I'll listen! It's not fair. She was dead, wasn't she?
There were other men there besides me. We talked it over and we all decided.
We'd only just got there. We'd walked for hours. We couldn't just turn around,
we were five miles from the car. It was opening day. What the hell, I don't see
anything wrong. No, I don't. And don't look at me that way, do you hear? I
won't have you passing judgment on me. Not you."

"You know," I say and shake my head.

"What do I know, Claire? Tell me. Tell me what I know. I don't know anything except one thing: you hadn't better get worked up over this." He gives me what he thinks is a *meaningful* look. "She was dead, dead, dead, do you hear?" he says after a minute. "It's a damn shame, I agree. She was a young girl and it's a shame, and I'm sorry, as sorry as anyone else, but she was dead, Claire, dead. Now let's leave it alone. Please, Claire. Let's leave it alone now."

"That's the point," I say. "She was dead. But don't you see? She needed help."

"I give up," he says and raises his hands. He pushes his chair away from the table, takes his cigarettes and goes out to the patio with a can of beer. He walks back and forth for a minute and then sits in a lawn chair and picks up the paper once more. His name is there on the first page along with the names of his friends, the other men who made the "grisly find."

I close my eyes for a minute and hold onto the drainboard. I must not dwell on this any longer. I must get over it, put it out of sight, out of mind, etc., and "go on." I open my eyes. Despite everything, knowing all that may be in store, I rake my arm across the drainboard and send the dishes and glasses smashing and scattering across the floor.

He doesn't move. I know he has heard, he raises his head as if listening, but he doesn't move otherwise, doesn't turn around to look. I hate him for that, for not moving. He waits a minute, then draws on his cigarette and leans back in the chair. I pity him for listening, detached, and then settling back and drawing on his cigarette. The wind takes the smoke out of his mouth in a thin stream. Why do I notice that? He can never know how much I pity him for that, for sitting still and listening, and letting the smoke stream out of his mouth. . . .

He planned his fishing trip into the mountains last Sunday, a week before the Memorial Day weekend. He and Gordon Johnson, Mel Dorn, Vern Williams. They play poker, bowl, and fish together. They fish together every spring and early summer, the first two or three months of the season, before family vacations, little league baseball, and visiting relatives can intrude. They are decent men, family men, responsible at their jobs. They have sons and daughters who go to school with our son, Dean. On Friday afternoon these four men left for a three-day fishing trip to the Naches River. They parked the car in the mountains and hiked several miles to where they wanted to fish. They carried their bedrolls, food and cooking utensils, their playing cards, their whiskey. The first evening at the river, even before they could set up camp, Mel Dorn found the girl floating face down in the river, nude, lodged near the shore in some branches. He called the other men and they all came to look at her. They talked about what to do. One of the men—Stuart didn't say which—perhaps it was Vern Williams, he is a heavy-set, easy man who laughs often—one of them thought they should start back to the car at once. The others stirred the sand with their shoes and said they felt inclined to stay. They pleaded fatigue, the late hour, the fact that the girl "wasn't going anywhere." In the end they all decided to stay. They went ahead and set up the camp and built a fire and drank their whiskey. They drank a lot of whiskey and when the moon came up they talked about the girl. Someone thought they should do something to prevent the body from floating away. Somehow they thought that this might create a problem for them if it floated away during the night. They took flashlights and stumbled down to the river. The wind was up, a cold wind, and waves from the river lapped the sandy bank. One of the men, I don't know who, it might have been Stuart, he could have done it, waded into the water and took the girl by the fingers and pulled her, still face down, closer to shore, into shallow water, and then took a piece of nylon cord and tied it around her wrist and then secured the cord to tree roots, all the while the flashlights of the other men played over the girl's body. Afterward, they went back to camp and drank more whiskey. Then they went to sleep. The next morning, Saturday, they cooked breakfast, drank lots of coffee, more whiskey, and then split up to fish, two men upriver, two men down.

That night, after they had cooked their fish and potatoes and had more coffee and whiskey, they took their dishes down to the river and rinsed them off a few yards from where the body lay in the water. They drank again and then they took out their cards and played and drank until they couldn't see the cards any longer. Vern Williams went to sleep, but the others told coarse stories and spoke of vulgar or dishonest escapades out of their past, and no one mentioned the girl until Gordon Johnson, who'd forgotten for a minute, commented on the firmness of the trout they'd caught, and the terrible coldness of the river water. They stopped talking then but continued to drink until one of them tripped and fell cursing against the lantern, and then they climbed into their sleeping bags.

The next morning they got up late, drank more whiskey, fished a little as they kept drinking whiskey. Then, at one o'clock in the afternoon, Sunday, a day earlier than they'd planned, they decided to leave. They took down their tents, rolled their sleeping bags, gathered their pans, pots, fish, and fishing gear, and hiked out. They didn't look at the girl again before they left. When they reached the car they drove the highway in silence until they came to a telephone. Stuart made the call to the sheriff's office while the others stood around in the hot sun and listened. He gave the man on the other end of the line all of their names—they had nothing to hide, they weren't ashamed of anything—and agreed to wait at the service station until someone could come for more detailed directions and individual statements.

He came home at eleven o'clock that night. I was asleep but woke when I heard him in the kitchen. I found him leaning against the refrigerator drinking a can of beer. He put his heavy arms around me and rubbed his hands up and down my back, the same hands he'd left with two days before, I thought.

In bed he put his hands on me again and then waited, as if thinking of something else. I turned slightly and then moved my legs. Afterward, I know he stayed awake for a long time, for he was awake when I fell asleep; and later, when I stirred for a minute, opening my eyes at a slight noise, a rustle of sheets, it was almost daylight outside, birds were singing, and he was on his back smoking and looking at the curtained window. Half-asleep I said his name, but he didn't answer. I fell asleep again.

He was up this morning before I could get out of bed—to see if there was anything about it in the paper, I suppose. The telephone began to ring shortly after eight o'clock.

"Go to hell," I heard him shout into the receiver. The telephone rang again a minute later, and I hurried into the kitchen. "I have nothing else to add to what I've already said to the sheriff. That's right!" He slammed down the receiver.

"What is going on?" I said, alarmed.

"Sit down," he said slowly. His fingers scraped, scraped against his stubble of whiskers. "I have to tell you something. Something happened while we were fishing." We sat across from each other at the table, and then he told me.

I drank coffee and stared at him as he spoke. Then I read the account in the newspaper that he shoved across the table: " . . . unidentified girl eighteen to twenty-four years of age . . . body three to five days in the water . . . rape a possible motive . . . preliminary results show death by strangulation . . . cuts and bruises on her breasts and pelvic area . . . autopsy . . . rape, pending further investigation."

"You've got to understand," he said. "Don't look at me like that. Be careful now, I mean it. Take it easy, Claire."

"Why didn't you tell me last night?" I asked.

"I just . . . didn't. What do you mean?" he said.

"You know what I mean," I said. I looked at his hands, the broad fingers, knuckles covered with hair, moving, lighting a cigarette now, fingers that had moved over me, into me last night.

He shrugged. "What difference does it make, last night, this morning? It was late. You were sleepy, I thought I'd wait until this morning to tell you." He looked out to the patio: a robin flew from the lawn to the picnic table and preened its feathers.

"It isn't true," I said. "You didn't leave her there like that?"

He turned quickly and said, "What'd I do? Listen to me carefully now, once and for all. Nothing happened. I have nothing to be sorry for or feel guilty about. Do you hear me?"

I got up from the table and went to Dean's room. He was awake and in his pajamas, putting together a puzzle. I helped him find his clothes and then went back to the kitchen and put his breakfast on the table. The telephone rang two or three more times and each time Stuart was abrupt while he talked and angry when he hung up. He called Mel Dorn and Gordon Johnson and spoke with them, slowly, seriously, and then he opened a beer and smoked a cigarette while Dean ate, asked him about school, his friends, etc., exactly as if nothing had happened.

Dean wanted to know what he'd done while he was gone, and Stuart took some fish out of the freezer to show him.

"I'm taking him to your mother's for the day," I said.

"Sure," Stuart said and looked at Dean who was holding one of the frozen trout. "If you want to and he wants to, that is. You don't have to, you know. There's nothing wrong."

"I'd like to anyway," I said.

"Can I go swimming there?" Dean asked and wiped his fingers on his pants.

"I believe so," I said. "It's a warm day so take your suit, and I'm sure your grandmother will say it's okay."

Stuart lighted a cigarette and looked at us.

Dean and I drove across town to Stuart's mother's. She lives in an apartment building with a pool and a sauna bath. Her name is Catherine Kane. Her name, Kane, is the same as mine, which seems impossible. Years ago, Stuart has told me, she used to be called Candy by her friends. She is a tall, cold woman with white-blonde hair. She gives me the feeling that she is always judging, judging. I explain briefly in a low voice what has happened (she hasn't yet read the newspaper) and promise to pick Dean up that evening. "He brought his swimming suit," I say. "Stuart and I have to talk about some things," I add vaguely. She looks at me steadily from over her glasses. Then she nods and turns to Dean, saying "How are you, my little man?" She stoops and puts her arms around him. She looks at me again as I open the door to leave. She has a way of looking at me without saying anything.

When I return home Stuart is eating something at the table and drinking beer. . . .

After a time I sweep up the broken dishes and glassware and go outside. Stuart is lying on his back on the grass now, the newspaper and can of beer within reach, staring at the sky. It's breezy but warm out and birds call.

"Stuart, could we go for a drive?" I say. "Anywhere."

He rolls over and looks at me and nods. "We'll pick up some beer," he says. "I hope you're feeling better about this. Try to understand, that's all I ask." He gets to his feet and touches me on the hip as he goes past. "Give me a minute and I'll be ready."

We drive through town without speaking. Before we reach the country he stops at a roadside market for beer. I notice a great stack of papers just inside the door. On the top step a fat woman in a print dress holds out a licorice stick to a little girl. In a few minutes we cross Everson Creek and turn into a picnic area a few feet from the water. The creek flows under the bridge and into a large pond a few hundred yards away. There are a dozen or so men and boys scattered around the banks of the pond under the willows, fishing.

So much water so close to home, why did he have to go miles away to fish?

"Why did you have to go there of all places?" I say.

"The Naches? We always go there. Every year, at least once." We sit on a bench in the sun and he opens two cans of beer and gives one to me. "How the hell was I to know anything like that would happen?" He shakes his head and shrugs, as if it had all happened years ago, or to someone else. "Enjoy the afternoon, Claire. Look at this weather."

"They said they were innocent."

"Who? What are you talking about?"

"The Maddox brothers. They killed a girl named Arlene Hubly near the town where I grew up, and then cut off her head and threw her into the Cle Elum River. She and I went to the same high school. It happened when I was a girl."

"What a hell of a thing to be thinking about," he says. "Come on, get off it.

You're going to get me riled in a minute. How about it now? Claire?"

I look at the creek. I float toward the pond, eyes open, face down, staring at the rocks and moss on the creek bottom until I am carried into the lake where I am pushed by the breeze. Nothing will be any different. We will go on and on and on and on. We will go on even now, as if nothing had happened. I look at him across the picnic table with such intensity that his face drains.

"I don't know what's wrong with you," he says. "I don't—"

I slap him before I realize. I raise my hand, wait a fraction of a second, and then slap his cheek hard. This is crazy, I think as I slap him. We need to lock our fingers together. We need to help one another. This is crazy.

He catches my wrist before I can strike again and raises his own hand. I crouch, waiting, and see something come into his eyes and then dart away. He drops his hand. I drift even faster around and around in the pond.

"Come on, get in the car," he says. "I'm taking you home."

"No, no," I say, pulling back from him.

"Come on," he says. "Goddamn it."

"You're not being fair to me," he says later in the car. Fields and trees and farmhouses fly by outside the window. "You're not being fair. To either one of us. Or to Dean, I might add. Think about Dean for a minute. Think about me. Think about someone else besides your goddamn self for a change."

There is nothing I can say to him now. He tries to concentrate on the road, but he keeps looking into the rearview mirror. Out of the corner of his eye, he looks across the seat to where I sit with my knees drawn up under my chin. The sun blazes against my arm and the side of my face. He opens another beer while he drives, drinks from it, then shoves the can between his legs and lets out breath. He knows. I could laugh in his face. I could weep.

II

Stuart believes he is letting me sleep this morning. But I was awake long before the alarm sounded, thinking, lying on the far side of the bed, away from his hairy legs and his thick, sleeping fingers. He gets Dean off for school, and then he shaves, dresses, and leaves for work. Twice he looks into the bedroom and clears his throat, but I keep my eyes closed.

In the kitchen I find a note from him signed "Love." I sit in the breakfast nook in the sunlight and drink coffee and make a coffee ring on the note. The telephone has stopped ringing, that's something. No more calls since last night. I look at the paper and turn it this way and that on the table. Then I pull it close and read what it says. The body is still unidentified, unclaimed, apparently unmissed. But for the last twenty-four hours men have been examining it, putting things into it, cutting, weighing, measuring, putting back again, sewing up, looking for the exact cause and moment of death. Looking for evidence of rape. I'm sure they hope for rape. Rape would make it easier to understand. The paper says the body will be taken to Keith & Keith Funeral Home pending arrangements. People are asked to come forward with information, etc.

He stays in the kitchen a long while, but comes back with his drink just when the news begins.

First the announcer repeats the story of the four local fishermen finding the body. Then the station shows a high school graduation photograph of the girl, a dark-haired girl with a round face and full, smiling lips. There's a film of the girl's parents entering the funeral home to make the identification. Bewildered, sad, they shuffle slowly up the sidewalk to the front steps to where a man in a dark suit stands waiting, holding the door. Then, it seems as if only seconds have passed, as if they have merely gone inside the door and turned around and come out again, the same couple is shown leaving the building, the woman in tears, covering her face with a handkerchief, the man stopping long enough to say to a reporter, "It's her, it's Susan. I can't say anything right now. I hope they get the person or persons who did it before it happens again. This violence. . . ." He motions feebly at the television camera. Then the man and woman get into an old car and drive away into the late afternoon traffic.

The announcer goes on to say that the girl, Susan Miller, had gotten off work as a cashier in a movie theater in Summit, a town 120 miles north of our town. A green, late-model car pulled up in front of the theater and the girl, who according to witnesses looked as if she'd been waiting, went over to the car and got in, leading the authorities to suspect that the driver of the car was a friend, or at least an acquaintance. The authorities would like to talk to the driver of the green car.

Stuart clears his throat, then leans back in the chair and sips his drink.

The third thing that happens is that after the news Stuart stretches, yawns, and looks at me. I get up and begin making a bed for myself on the sofa.

"What are you doing?" he says, puzzled.

"I'm not sleepy," I say, avoiding his eyes. "I think I'll stay up a while longer and then read something until I fall asleep."

He stares as I spread a sheet over the sofa. When I start to go for a pillow, he stands at the bedroom door, blocking the way.

"I'm going to ask you once more," he says. "What the hell do you think you're going to accomplish by this?"

"I need to be by myself tonight," I say. "I need to have time to think."

He lets out breath. "I'm thinking you're making a big mistake by doing this. I'm thinking you'd better think again about what you're doing. Claire?"

I can't answer. I don't know what I want to say. I turn and begin to tuck in the edges of the blanket. He stares at me a minute longer and then I see him raise his shoulders. "Suit yourself then. I could give a fuck less what you do," he says. He turns and walks down the hall scratching his neck.

This morning I read in the paper that services for Susan Miller are to be held in Chapel of the Pines, Summit, at two o'clock the next afternoon. Also, that police have taken statements from three people who saw her get into the green Chevrolet. But they still have no license number for the car. They are getting warmer, though, and the investigation is continuing. I sit for a long while holding the paper, thinking, then I call to make an appointment at the hairdresser's.

I sit under the dryer with a magazine on my lap and let Millie do my nails.

"I'm going to a funeral tomorrow," I say after we have talked a bit about a girl who no longer works there.

Millie looks up at me and then back at my fingers. "I'm sorry to hear that, Mrs. Kane. I'm real sorry."

"It's a young girl's funeral," I say.

"That's the worst kind. My sister died when I was a girl, and I'm still not over it to this day. Who died?" she says after a minute.

"A girl. We weren't all that close, you know, but still."

"Too bad. I'm real sorry. But we'll get you fixed up for it, don't worry. How's that look?"

"That looks . . . fine. Millie, did you ever wish you were somebody else, or else just nobody, nothing, nothing at all?"

She looks at me. "I can't say I ever felt that, no. No, if I was somebody else I'd be afraid I might not like who I was." She holds my fingers and seems to think about something for a minute. "I don't know, I just don't know. . . . Let me have your other hand now, Mrs. Kane."

At eleven o'clock that night I make another bed on the sofa and this time Stuart only looks at me, rolls his tongue behind his lips, and goes down the hall to the bedroom. In the night I wake and listen to the wind slamming the gate against the fence. I don't want to be awake, and I lie for a long while with my eyes closed. Finally I get up and go down the hall with my pillow. The light is burning in our bedroom and Stuart is on his back with his mouth open, breathing heavily. I go into Dean's room and get into bed with him. In his sleep he moves over to give me space. I lie there for a minute and then hold him, my face against his hair.

"What is it, mama?" he says.

"Nothing, honey. Go back to sleep. It's nothing, it's all right."

I get up when I hear Stuart's alarm, put on coffee and prepare breakfast while he shaves.

He appears in the kitchen doorway, towel over his bare shoulder, appraising.

"Here's coffee," I say. "Eggs will be ready in a minute."

He nods.

I wake Dean and the three of us have breakfast. Once or twice Stuart looks at me as if he wants to say something, but each time I ask Dean if he wants more milk, more toast, etc.

"I'll call you today," Stuart says as he opens the door.

"I don't think I'll be home today," I say quickly. "I have a lot of things to do today. In fact, I may be late for dinner."

"All right. Sure." He moves his briefcase from one hand to the other. "Maybe we'll go out for dinner tonight? How would you like that?" He keeps looking at me. He's forgotten about the girl already. "Are you all right?"

I move to straighten his tie, then drop my hand. He wants to kiss me goodbye. I move back a step. "Have a nice day then," he says finally. He turns and goes down the walk to his car.

I dress carefully. I try on a hat that I haven't worn in several years and look at myself in the mirror. Then I remove the hat, apply a light makeup, and write a note for Dean.

Honey, Mommy has things to do this afternoon, but will be home later. You are to stay in the house or in the back/yard until one of us comes home.

Love

I look at the word "Love" and then I underline it. As I am writing the note I realize I don't know whether *back yard* is one word or two. I have never considered it before. I think about it and then I draw a line and make two words of it.

I stop for gas and ask directions to Summit. Barry, a forty-year-old mechanic with a moustache, comes out from the restroom and leans against the front fender while the other man, Lewis, puts the hose into the tank and begins to slowly wash the windshield.

"Summit," Barry says, looking at me and smoothing a finger down each side of his moustache. "There's no best way to get to Summit, Mrs. Kane. It's about a two-, two-and-a-half-hour drive each way. Across the mountains. It's quite a drive for a woman. Summit? What's in Summit, Mrs. Kane?"

"I have business," I say, vaguely uneasy. Lewis has gone to wait on another customer.

"Ah. Well, if I wasn't tied up there"—he gestures with his thumb toward the bay—"I'd offer to drive you to Summit and back again. Road's not all that good. I mean it's good enough, there's just a lot of curves and so on."

"I'll be all right. But thank you." He leans against the fender. I can feel his eyes as I open my purse.

Barry takes the credit card. "Don't drive it at night," he says. "It's not all that good a road, like I said. And while I'd be willing to bet you wouldn't have car trouble with this, I know this car, you can never be sure about blowouts and things like that. Just to be on the safe side I'd better check these tires." He taps one of the front tires with his shoe. "We'll run it onto the hoist. Won't take long."

"No, no, it's all right. Really, I can't take any more time. The tires look fine to me."

"Only takes a minute," he says. "Be on the safe side."

"I said no. No! They look fine to me. I have to go now. Barry. . . . "

"Mrs. Kane?"

"I have to go now."

I sign something. He gives me the receipt, the card, some stamps. I put everything into my purse. "You take it easy," he says. "Be seeing you."

As I wait to pull into the traffic, I look back and see him watching. I close my eyes, then open them. He waves.

I turn at the first light, then turn again and drive until I come to the highway and read the sign: SUMMIT 117 Miles. It is ten-thirty and warm.

The highway skirts the edge of town, then passes through farm country, through fields of oats and sugar beets and apple orchards, with here and there a small herd of cattle grazing in open pastures. Then everything changes, the farms become fewer and fewer, more like shacks now than houses, and stands of timber replace the orchards. All at once I'm in the mountains and on the right, far below, I catch glimpses of the Naches River.

In a little while I see a green pickup truck behind me, and it stays behind me for miles. I keep slowing at the wrong times, hoping it will pass, and then increasing my speed, again at the wrong times. I grip the wheel until my fingers hurt. Then on a clear stretch he does pass, but he drives along beside for a minute, a crew-cut man in a blue workshirt in his early thirties, and we look at each other. Then he waves, toots the horn twice, and pulls ahead of me.

I slow down and find a place, a dirt road off of the shoulder. I pull over and turn off the ignition. I can hear the river somewhere down below the trees. Ahead of me the dirt road goes into the trees. Then I hear the pickup returning.

I start the engine just as the truck pulls up behind me. I lock the doors and roll up the windows. Perspiration breaks on my face and arms as I put the car in gear, but there is no place to drive.

"You all right?" the man says as he comes up to the car. "Hello. Hello in there." He raps the glass. "You okay?" He leans his arms on the door and brings his face close to the window.

I stare at him and can't find any words.

"After I passed I slowed up some," he says. "But when I didn't see you in the mirror I pulled off and waited a couple of minutes. When you still didn't show I thought I'd better drive back and check. Is everything all right? How come you're locked up in there?"

I shake my head.

"Come on, roll down your window. Hey, are you sure you're okay? You know it's not good for a woman to be batting around the country by herself." He shakes his head and looks at the highway, then back at me. "Now come on, roll down the window, how about it? We can't talk this way."

"Please, I have to go."

"Open the door, all right?" he says, as if he isn't listening. "At least roll the window down. You're going to smother in there." He looks at my breasts and legs. The skirt has pulled up over my knees. His eyes linger on my legs, but I sit still, afraid to move.

"I want to smother," I say. "I am smothering, can't you see?"

"What in the hell?" he says and moves back from the door. He turns and walks back to his truck. Then, in the side mirror, I watch him returning, and I close my eyes.

"You don't want me to follow you toward Summit or anything? I don't mind. I got some extra time this morning," he says.

I shake my head.

He hesitates and then shrugs. "Okay, lady, have it your way then," he says. "Okay."

I wait until he has reached the highway, and then I back out. He shifts gears and pulls away slowly, looking back at me in his rearview mirror. I stop the car on the shoulder and put my head on the wheel.

The casket is closed and covered with floral sprays. The organ begins soon after I take a seat near the back of the chapel. People begin to file in and find chairs, some middle-aged and older people, but most of them in their early twenties or even younger. They are people who look uncomfortable in their suits and ties, sport coats and slacks, their dark dresses and leather gloves. One boy in flared pants and a yellow short-sleeved shirt takes the chair next to mine and begins to bite his lips. A door opens at one side of the chapel and I look up and for a minute the parking lot reminds me of a meadow. But then the sun flashes on car windows. The family enters in a group and moves into a curtained area off to the side. Chairs creak as they settle themselves. In a few minutes a slim, blond man in a dark suit stands and asks us to bow our heads. He speaks a brief prayer for us, the living, and when he finishes he asks us to pray in silence for the soul of Susan Miller, departed. I close my eyes and remember her picture in the newspaper and on television. I see her leaving the theater and getting into the green Chevrolet. Then I imagine her journey down the river, the nude body hitting rocks, caught at by branches, the body floating and turning, her hair streaming in the water. Then the hands and hair catching in the overhanging branches, holding, until four men come along to stare at her. I can see a man who is drunk (Stuart?) take her by the wrist. Does anyone here know about that? What if these people knew that? I look around at the other faces. There is a connection to be made of these things, these events, these faces, if I can find it. My head aches with the effort to find it.

He talks about Susan Miller's gifts: cheerfulness and beauty, grace and enthusiasm. From behind the closed curtain someone clears his throat, someone else sobs. The organ music begins. The service is over.

Along with the others I file slowly past the casket. Then I move out onto the front steps and into the bright, hot afternoon light. A middle-aged woman who limps as she goes down the stairs ahead of me reaches the sidewalk and looks around, her eyes falling on me. "Well, they got him," she says. "If that's any consolation. They arrested him this morning. I heard it on the radio before I came. A guy right here in town. A longhair, you might have guessed." We move a few steps down the hot sidewalk. People are starting cars. I put out my hand and hold on to a parking meter. Sunlight glances off polished hoods and fenders. My head swims. "He's admitted having relations with her that night, but he says he didn't kill her." She snorts. "They'll put him on probation and then turn him loose."

"He might not have acted alone," I say. "They'll have to be sure. He might be covering up for someone, a brother, or some friends."

"I have known that child since she was a little girl," the woman goes on, and her lips tremble. "She used to come over and I'd bake cookies for her and let her eat them in front of the TV." She looks off and begins shaking her head as the tears roll down her cheeks.

III

Stuart sits at the table with a drink in front of him. His eyes are red and for a minute I think he has been crying. He looks at me and doesn't say anything. For a wild instant I feel something has happened to Dean, and my heart turns.

"Where is he?" I say. "Where is Dean?"

"Outside," he says.

"Stuart, I'm so afraid, so afraid," I say, leaning against the door.

"What are you afraid of, Claire? Tell me, honey, and maybe I can help. I'd like to help, just try me. That's what husbands are for."

"I can't explain," I say. "I'm just afraid. I feel like, I feel like, I feel like. . . ."

He drains his glass and stands up, not taking his eyes from me. "I think I know what you need, honey. Let me play doctor, okay? Just take it easy now." He reaches an arm around my waist and with his other hand begins to unbutton my jacket, then my blouse. "First things first," he says, trying to joke.

"Not now, please," I say.

"Not now, please," he says, teasing. "Please nothing." Then he steps behind me and locks an arm around my waist. One of his hands slips under my brassiere.

"Stop, stop, stop," I say. I stamp on his toes.

And then I am lifted up and then falling. I sit on the floor looking up at him and my neck hurts and my skirt is over my knees. He leans down and says, "You go to hell then, do you hear, bitch? I hope your cunt drops off before I touch it again." He sobs once and I realize he can't help it, he can't help himself either. I feel a rush of pity for him as he heads for the living room.

He didn't sleep at home last night.

This morning, flowers, red and yellow chrysanthemums. I am drinking coffee when the doorbell rings.

"Mrs. Kane?" the young man says, holding his box of flowers.

I nod and pull the robe tighter at my throat.

"The man who called, he said you'd know." The boy looks at my robe, open at the throat, and touches his cap. He stands with his legs apart, feet firmly planted on the top step. "Have a nice day," he says.

A little later the telephone rings and Stuart says, "Honey, how are you? I'll be home early, I love you. Did you hear me? I love you, I'm sorry, I'll make it up to you. Goodbye, I have to run now."

I put the flowers in a vase in the center of the dining room table and then I move my things into the extra bedroom.

Last night, around midnight, Stuart breaks the lock on my door. He does it just to show me that he can, I suppose, for he doesn't do anything when the door springs open except stand there in his underwear looking surprised and foolish while the anger slips from his face. He shuts the door slowly, and a few minutes later I hear him in the kitchen prying open a tray of ice cubes.

I'm in bed when he calls today to tell me that he's asked his mother to come stay with us for a few days. I wait a minute, thinking about this, and then hang up while he is still talking. But in a little while I dial his number at work. When he finally comes on the line I say, "It doesn't matter, Stuart. Really, I tell you it doesn't matter one way or the other."

"I love you," he says.

He says something else and I listen and nod slowly. I feel sleepy. Then I wake up and say, "For God's sake, Stuart, she was only a child."

More Information in Raymond Carver's "So Much Water So Close to Home"

Ghita Orth

This version of "So Much Water So Close to Home" demonstrates an instructive paradox: The more complex a story, the easier it may be to understand. Here Carver has extended the time frame from two days to five, incorporated additional scenes and dialogue, introduced new characters, and provided characters with past and present contexts. More happens here, to more people, over a longer period of time, but these additions, rather than moving us away from the story's central issues, allow us to see and understand them more fully. By providing the reader with more information, Carver thus provides us with more opportunities for informed response.

But Carver does more here than expand and enrich the material found in the shorter version; he also, surprisingly, changes the concluding events in its plot. The passive, acquiescent Claire of the earlier story now rejects Stuart's advances, physically resists him, and then locks herself away from him in the extra bedroom. This reversal of Claire's behavior reflects the fact that we seem, here, to be dealing with a different Claire.

The changed Claire appears more comfortable with language than did the narrator of the minimalist "So Much Water So Close to Home"; her syntax and diction are less limited and limiting. Compare, for example, the effects of these two passages:

> He raises his hands. He pushes his chair away from the table. He takes out his cigarettes and goes out to the back with a can of beer. I see him sit in the lawn chair and pick up the newspaper again.
>
> [SHORT VERSION]

> "I give up," he says and raises his hands. He pushes his chair away from the table, takes his cigarettes and goes out to the patio with a can of beer. He walks back and forth for a minute and then sits in a lawn chair and picks up the paper once more.
>
> [LONG VERSION]

In addition to the new line of dialogue which helps us to interpret Stuart's gesture, the long version combines basic sentences to create a smoother, less simplistic style. Even substituting "once more" for "again" evidences a more sophisticated voice than the one we heard earlier. Claire seems more articulate and intelligent here, and our response to her as a character is subtly altered.

Not only does Claire speak more gracefully here, she is also more aware of the details of her environment and, to our benefit, includes these in her narration. When "the back" becomes "the patio," that simple change provides the kind of information that helps us to see Claire's house—not an old farmhouse or a trailer after all. And since Stuart now sits in "*a* lawn chair," one of a number, rather than "*the* lawn chair," it seems a comfortably furnished space. We can thus now locate Claire and Stuart in a specific environment with all it implies, just as we know from this version that Stuart carries a briefcase and is an engineer. Such concrete details help to make the characters more real to us by providing a sense of the ongoing circumstances of the lives that surround their immediate interaction.

Although that interaction is still cast in the present tense, Claire's new attention to her world helps to focus our own attention on particulars within it; her narration seems more pointed. Describing Stuart's reaction to hearing her break the dishes, for example, Claire says,

> The wind takes the smoke out of his mouth in a thin stream. Why do I notice that? He can never know how much I pity him for that, for sitting still and listening, and letting the smoke stream out of his mouth. . . .

The reader is thus directed to notice the smoke too, as a detail that matters.

In this version of "So Much Water So Close to Home" we also have some indications of why it matters. Claire's thoughts and emotions are available to us directly; we need not infer them solely from her behavior. Here her "pity" for Stuart's pretense that nothing has occurred is accessible to the reader, and, though we may not yet fully understand the *reason* she feels this way, we are no longer excluded from her interior life. With access to what she thinks and feels, we are on surer ground in our process of understanding her and her story.

A question central to that process in the minimalist "So Much Water So Close to Home," however, remains a question—why does Claire identify with the dead girl and respond to Stuart's treatment of her with such anger, outrage, and disapproval? Here, though, we have surer ways of answering; Claire, an increasingly developed, three-dimensional character, shares her memories, as well as her thoughts and feelings, with us. Carver has given Claire a past, and because we now can know something of the circumstances that have led to and shaped her present responses, we can hope to understand those responses more clearly. The events here are seen as part of a continuum, rather than as isolated present moments.

People, in life, don't act in a vacuum; our behavior reflects the sum of our past experiences. So too in fiction—what characters are is in some measure a reflection of what they have been. It's important then to look at what Claire and Stuart have been, separately and together, in our approach to the crucial questions around which the story turns.

Claire's memories of her childhood are hazy; "there is a film over those early years" as though seen through mist, and Claire's dissociation from her earlier self is emphasized when she refers to that self in the third person as "a girl." Just as the language here reminds the reader of the girl in the river, so too does Claire's passivity in her early relationship with Stuart. She, if we can borrow the term, goes with the flow when, "seeing that's his aim, she lets him seduce her." With this information, the words that Carver has added to the passage in which Claire imagines herself in the dead girl's situation take on significance; Claire now sees herself "float toward the pond," being passively "carried into the lake where [she is] pushed by the breeze." Claire's identification with the dead girl floating powerless at the mercy of wind and currents now seems more clearly connected to a shared inertia.

Too, as Claire now explains to Stuart, the "point" of her disgust at his behavior is that, being dead, the girl "needed help." Totally without defenses, unable to act for herself, the dead girl in the water is much like Claire, who until now seems to have helplessly drifted in her marriage. The image of this girl, who can only acquiesce to any indignities foisted upon her by the men on the fishing trip, who is merely a body, beneath their concern, seems emblematic of Claire's own relation to Stuart.

In recounting that relationship, Claire reveals even closer connections between herself and Susan Miller—and indeed, the fact that the murder victim is here given a name and a family allows us, like Claire, to see her as more than the depersonalized object the men saw. In this version of "So Much Water So Close to Home," Susan Miller is subjected not only to murder but also to sexual violence at the hands of someone she knew, who has "admitted having relations with her that night." That violence also lurks under the surface of Claire's marriage, as she makes clear in her memories.

"Once, during a particularly bad argument," Stuart had said, "someday this affair (his words: 'this affair') [would] end in violence." Claire and Stuart thus have had *many* bad arguments, and his reference to their connection as somehow less than a marriage is as revealing as his prediction. It is no wonder Claire "remembers this"; in fact, her anxiety in response to it resulted in a nervous breakdown. Her daily headaches at the time Stuart is about to get home from work, her secret pleasure "at the doctor's solicitous attention," her feeling that she "spoils everything" by returning home from the hospital speak volumes about her relationship with her husband long before his trip to the Naches River.

The violence that has been done to Susan Miller, then, is not unfamiliar to Claire, and we find evidence of it in the story's new or expanded scenes. When, for example, she sweeps the dishes to the floor, she now does it "knowing all that may be in store" from Stuart as a result. She starts at his touch and his thinly veiled threats: "Be that way if you want. But just remember." And violence unchecked, with a strongly sexual component, appears here when Stuart "steps behind [her] and locks an arm around [her] waist" while fondling her against her will, then throws her to the floor when she tries to stop him.

Although Stuart's violence does stop short of actual rape or murder—he angrily breaks the lock on Claire's door but then "doesn't do anything"—Claire is still victimized by it. The atmosphere of barely repressed hostility and aggression that surrounds her even seems to be contagious; in this version of the story, Claire herself furiously slaps Stuart. When he lifts his hand in return, her identification with Susan Miller intensifies; she drifts "even faster around and around in the pond." In the light of this new information about Claire's marriage, past and present, we can, in this version of "So Much Water So Close to

Home," finally understand the intensity of her empathy with this victim of abusiveness and sexual violence.

Here, too, we have sufficient information to recognize why Claire finds Stuart's response to this victim so appalling. It is not only the girl's helpless passivity or the manner of her death that creates Claire's empathy. Stuart's way of dealing with that death also seems to replicate an ongoing pattern established early in their marriage.

When Claire returned from the hospital, Stuart had promised, "everything [would be] different and better for them." He seems here to be taking note of the necessity to make changes in their relationship in response to Claire's illness, but the passage then makes clear that nothing in Stuart's life was really affected by what had happened to his wife. "In the dark, he goes on stroking her arm. . . . He continues to bowl and play cards regularly. He goes fishing with three friends of his." The elision signals that material has been left out, but because we have come to know Claire and Stuart we can pretty confidently fill in the blanks as we could not when information was withheld in the shorter story. Here, Stuart's response to Claire primarily as a female body who has no real import in the stereotypically masculine pursuits of his life mirrors his response to the dead Susan Miller, whose helpless need he disregarded (even more callously in this version) in the interests of his fishing vacation.

Stuart's capacity to brush almost anything under the rug, to go on with his life despite any untoward occurrence, is also demonstrated in the story's expanded present action. In this version of "So Much Water So Close to Home," Carver's craft is more apparent than it was—the additional actions and dialogue purposefully point us toward the story's central issues. Thus the new scenes with Claire, Stuart, and Dean do more than create the sense of an actual family that had been missing before.

With his son, Stuart is able to behave "exactly as if nothing had happened" on the fishing trip, as he has not been able to with Claire, and when Dean finds out what did happen and begins asking questions, Stuart answers, "It was just a body, and that's all there is to it." It's precisely this denial of Susan Miller's legitimacy as a human being, dead *or* alive, that is so disturbing to Claire, and Stuart's refusal to accept the legitimacy of her horror at what he has done reflects his habitual patterns of behavior.

"What difference does it make?" Stuart asks, that he had not told his wife about the incident before they had sex the night before. But it does make a difference to Claire; when she hears what has happened, she moves her bed to the sofa in what we now see is an uncharacteristic gesture of independent will. Even this rejection, however, doesn't matter to Stuart for very long. His attempt to go on as though nothing has happened, to placate Claire by taking her out to dinner, just confirms her sad recognition that he has "forgotten about the girl already." Although Claire does not want to be touched by Stuart after what he has done, she also faces the terrible probability that, as in the past, she and Stuart will "go on and on and on and on . . . even now, as if nothing had happened."

Carver's expanded text has thus helped us formulate answers to our previous questions about Claire's motivation. It is easy to see why, after her years of living with Stuart culminate in the events at the Naches River, Claire should posit two conclusions: "1) people no longer care what happens to other people; and 2) nothing makes any real difference any longer." It is also easy to see why these generalizations are so distressing to her. Although she accedes to the notion that their lives together are not entirely within their control but have "been set in motion, and . . . will go on and on until they stop," she is troubled that things happen in those lives that "should change something" but then do not. That the presence of the dead Susan Miller, killed violently, does not make a significant difference to the men on the fishing trip is analogous to the way the presence of violence and conflict in Stuart and Claire's marriage does not alter its continuing dailiness. Claire feels something *should* have changed on the trip due to the discovery of the corpse, just as a marriage should reflect whatever horrors it may have confronted. To her, the fact that "nothing makes any real difference" to Stuart is the corollary of his not caring "what happens to other people."

Because Claire does care, the "crisis" she undergoes in the story, one minimized by Stuart, leaves her with a heart that "feels damaged." The issue of her reliability as a narrator thus comes into question, as it does in all instances of first-person narration. When Claire was only recording external events, the reader could assume objectivity in the storytelling. Here, however, Claire is a fleshed-out character rather than a neutral camera, and the reader begins to wonder if she has been made so distraught by the situation that she cannot present it accurately. Since all the information in the story comes to us colored by Claire's attitudes, we need to ask if the perceptions that have led *us* to perception can be trusted.

We can test the reliability of Claire's narration in relation to whatever objective information the story may provide. Stuart, for example, doesn't come across very positively in the minimalist "So Much Water So Close to Home"; here he seems even worse, entirely crude and unfeeling. Is this a reflection of subjective bias on Claire's part? There is, for example, a small but telling addition to her description of what happened at the river; Claire now says: "One of the men, I don't know who, it might have been Stuart, *he could have done it* [my emphasis], waded into the water and took the girl by the fingers and pulled her" to shore, then tied the naked corpse to a tree. The clause italicized here characterizes Stuart as the kind of man who could dispassionately manage this shocking maneuver and not be disturbed by it.

But is this a fair assessment of him? Our sense of what Stuart is like is not dependent only on Claire's comments; we see and hear him. Noting his ability to continue his life while ignoring anything—whether his wife's emotional state or his discovery of a corpse—that might disturb its surface equanimity, we accept the accuracy of Claire's view.

In testing out her trustworthiness as a narrator, we also come to understand the function of the two additional characters Carver has included in this "So Much Water So Close to Home." No matter how minor their roles, fictional characters need *some* purpose to justify their appearance in a story. Here Mrs.

Kane and Barry, the gas station man, may serve to corroborate Claire's reliability.

Initially, Claire's attitude to Stuart's mother seems almost paranoid; she is suspicious and wary of Mrs. Kane, believing "she is always judging, judging." But Carver makes clear to us that Claire is probably right in her assessment of her mother-in-law's judgmental attitude. Stuart's mother had, after all, been called in to take care of Dean during Claire's hospitalization, and it is not unreasonable to think she would be watching for signs of recurring mental instability. Claire's view that Mrs. Kane is perched across town "waiting" is likely to be accurate—when Stuart can no longer cope with Claire's new gestures of independence, he tells her "he's asked his mother to come stay with [them] for a few days." Although Mrs. Kane may be justified in expecting Claire to break down totally again, her role in the story provides evidence that, at least for now, Claire's views of the people around her are not essentially distorted.

Another instance in which Claire might seem more obsessive than objective is her confrontation with the man in the green pickup truck. Whereas in the short version of the story her conviction that he is a potential attacker seemed questionable, here Carver has introduced Barry, a mechanic at Claire's gas station, to suggest that her sense of peril on the road to Summit may be well founded. Barry warns Claire about the dangers of the drive "across the mountains. It's quite a drive for a woman." Although Barry's solicitousness for her safety could suggest a similar motive for the truck driver's stopping, it makes Claire suspicions at least understandable. She seems, if anything, more desperate here than in the shorter version of the scene, but if she is misreading the truck driver's motives, she appears aware that her fear may be due to her own instability rather than his malevolence. "I want to smother," Claire tells him. "I am smothering." Unable to breathe, as though herself drowning, at the side of the Naches River where Susan Miller was degraded, Claire acknowledges her analogous vulnerability.

Claire's willingness to implicate herself in the problematic occurrences she tells us about seems further proof that we can trust the veracity of her perceptions; she does not attempt to present herself as without fault. After slapping Stuart, for example, Claire recognizes their *mutual* failure of communication: "This is crazy, I think . . . We need to lock our fingers together. We need to help one another." She accepts the irrationality of her own actions as well as Stuart's and validates his need as well as her own.

Later, after Stuart's most violent verbal and physical abuse, Claire again demonstrates a level of self-awareness that reinforces our sense of the reliability of her narration. When Stuart sobs after his obscene diatribe, Claire says, "I realize he can't help it, he can't help himself either. I feel a rush of pity for him . . ." By including the word "either" here, Claire makes clear she understands that Stuart's habitual behaviors are as beyond conscious control as are her own. He too is moved by forces he cannot govern, and although this does not excuse his conduct, it at least allows Claire to feel something more complicated than hatred for him. Unadulterated hatred would have distorted her, and thus our, view of him; "pity" suggests that Stuart's faults are human rather than simply monstrous, as may Claire's "pity" for his earlier imperturbability when she smashed the dishes.

As we have seen, then, Carver's expanded "So Much Water So Close to Home" has provided ways of understanding the narration that allow us to be more confident in our reading of it. Writer has admitted reader into the world of the story. At Susan Miller's funeral, Claire realizes why she may have gone to Summit: "There is a connection to be made of these things, these events, these faces, if I can find it." Because of the various kinds of information Carver has imbedded in the longer text, the reader, at least, can make such connections. The dead girl, the passive wife, the husband who denies them both, all finally come together.

Since we now understand Claire and her situation so much more fully, her acquiescing to Stuart's advances, were she to do so here, would be incomprehensible rather than merely puzzling. Instead, when Stuart answers her cry for help by evading it, by wanting to "play doctor," Claire, refusing to be passive, forcibly rejects him. Even so, the basic pattern of their relationship continues— in the morning, as if the ugly scene could be erased, Stuart sends flowers, apologizes, says he loves her. Claire has been proven right in her prediction that their marriage is likely just to go on and on, no matter what.

Claire's moving to the extra room and locking the door behind her thus seems a desperate attempt to call attention to her needs, to *matter* in some way, to force this event, if none other, to make a difference. But though Stuart breaks the lock, he cannot break his characteristic pattern of response; the next day, even after Claire hangs up on him, he is again saying "I love you" as though nothing has seriously changed between them.

And, at this point, he may be right to think so. "It doesn't matter," Claire has told him. "I tell you it doesn't matter one way or the other." Whether "it" refers to Mrs. Kane's coming to stay with them or Stuart's breaking into her room or the events at the Naches River, Claire seems wearily to be giving up and giving in. She sounds just like Stuart.

Had "So Much Water So Close to Home" ended here, we would, despite Claire's prior rejection of Stuart, have been left much as we were in its short version—with the image of a woman, virtually insensate, whose will, like Eveline's in Joyce's story, has been nullified. Here too Claire can barely hear what Stuart is saying and seems "smothering" in emotional lassitude. But with the last line of the story, she reasserts herself: "Then I wake up and say, 'For God's sake, Stuart, she was only a child.'"

In her refusal, even now, to let go of what Stuart has done, Claire might seem just stubbornly unreasonable. However, although her words may be only a minimal protest, they reflect Claire's ultimate unwillingness to accept that people don't care what happens to others and that nothing makes any real difference. In reminding Stuart once again of the callousness of what he has done, Claire, like Carver, speaks up for Susan Miller and also for herself—the other "girl" who had not mattered to Stuart as much more than a body.

The import of the story's title now seems apparent. The situation at the Naches River was essentially present right in Stuart and Claire's own backyard, or rather, their patio. There too we saw a man's inattention to a woman's need for help, his perception of her as a body rather than a person, his ability to ignore the occurrence of violence and continue his life without regard to its effects. As Claire implies, Stuart did not need to go all the way to the Naches River—he could have enacted the trip's events much closer to home, as he had done before, without all the attendant problems and publicity.

In this version of the story, Claire's recognition that, metaphorically, there was "so much water so close to home" makes sense to the reader who has seen the analogies between her situation and Susan Miller's. We can also see why Carver chose this phrase as the title of his narrative; as is often the case, the title points readers toward a work's pivotal issues.

Most of us would have been hard put to know what these *were* in the minimalist version, which left us wondering what the story was "about." Here, however, because we have so many more ways of knowing its characters through Carver's inclusion of descriptive details, thoughts, feelings, and past histories in Claire's seemingly reliable narration, we also have ways of knowing the story's thematic focus.

Fiction writers' ideas often evolve in the process of storytelling, as they move characters through events. Having first written this longer version of "So Much Water So Close to Home," Carver discovered what his story was about and could then pare it down; similarly, if you were now to reread the minimalist version, bringing to it what you know from the longer one, it would make more sense. In later restoring what he had cut, however, Carver no doubt recognized that readers meeting Claire and Stuart *only* in the shorter story, with no way of really comprehending them, would be left to infer what his ideas might be. As Carver acknowledged in a 1987 interview, in writing fiction "you have to presuppose some kind of knowledge on the part of the readers, that they're going to fill in some of the gaps. But you can't leave them drifting around without enough information to make them care about these people."

With the kinds of information Carver provides us with here, we can clearly ascertain some of his thematic concerns: the lack of communication that can keep a husband and wife essentially strangers; the male bonding that allows for the reduction of women to bodies outside the real concerns of men's lives; the underlying habits of violence and/or apathy that may erode a relationship; the destructive ways in which people are often locked into behavioral patterns; and, perhaps most important, the necessity of caring for others and acknowledging those things in our lives that should make a difference in how we lead them.

Although this is a long list, it is certainly not an exhaustive one. No doubt you will be able to add to it from your own sense of the story's meanings as they resonate from increased knowledge of, and informed response to, its characters and events. Here, Raymond Carver has brought so much of the story so much closer to home.

ABOUT _____ Julia Alvarez

Born in the Dominican Republic in 1950, Julia Alvarez moved
with her family to the United States when she was ten years old.
After completing her graduate education at Syracuse University,
she spent twelve years teaching poetry in schools in Kentucky,
California, Vermont, Washington, D.C., and Illinois. In 1986 she
published her first book of poetry, *Homecoming,* and in 1991 her
collection of related stories *How the García Girls Lost Their
Accents.* She lives near Middlebury, Vermont, and teaches writing and literature at Middlebury College.

The Kiss

Julia Alvarez

Even after they'd been married and had their own families and often couldn't
make it for other occasions, the four daughters always came home for their father's birthday. They would gather together, without husbands, would-be husbands, or bring-home work. For this too was part of the tradition: the daughters came home alone. The apartment was too small for everyone, the father
argued. Surely their husbands could spare them for one overnight?

The husbands would just as soon have not gone to their in-laws, but they
felt annoyed at the father's strutting. "When's he going to realize you've grown
up? You sleep with us!"

"He's almost seventy, for God's sake!" the daughters said, defending the
father. They were passionate women, but their devotions were like roots; they
were sunk into the past towards the old man.

So for one night every November the daughters turned back into their father's girls. In the cramped living room, surrounded by the dark oversized furniture from the old house they grew up in, they were children again in a
smaller, simpler version of the world. There was the prodigal scene at the door.
The father opened his arms wide and welcomed them in his broken English:
"This is your home, and never you should forget it." Inside, the mother fussed
at them—their sloppy clothes; their long, loose hair; their looking tired, too
skinny, too made up, and so on.

After a few glasses of wine, the father started in on what should be done if
he did not live to see his next birthday. "Come on, Papi," his daughters coaxed
him, as if it were a modesty of his, to perish, and they had to talk him into staying alive. After his cake and candles, the father distributed bulky envelopes

130

that felt as if they were padded, and they were, no less than several hundreds in bills, tens and twenties and fives, all arranged to face the same way, the top one signed with the father's name, branding them his. Why not checks? the daughters would wonder later, gossiping together in the bedroom, counting their money to make sure the father wasn't playing favorites. Was there some illegality that the father stashed such sums away? Was he—none of the daughters really believed this, but to contemplate it was a wonderful little explosion in their heads—was he maybe dealing drugs or doing abortions in his office?

At the table there was always the pretense of trying to give the envelopes back. "No, no, Papi, it's *your* birthday, after all."

The father told them there was plenty more where that had come from. The revolution in the old country had failed. Most of his comrades had been killed or bought off. He had escaped to this country. And now it was every man for himself, so what he made was for his girls. The father never gave his daughters money when their husbands were around. "They might receive the wrong idea," the father once said, and although none of the daughters knew specifically what the father meant, they all understood what he was saying to them: Don't bring the men home for my birthday.

But this year, for his seventieth birthday, the youngest daughter, Sofía, wanted the celebration at her house. Her son had been born that summer, and she did not want to be traveling in November with a four-month-old and her little girl. And yet, she, of all the daughters, did not want to be the absent one because for the first time since she'd run off with her husband six years ago, she and her father were on speaking terms. In fact, the old man had been out to see her—or really to see his grandson—twice. It was a big deal that Sofía had had a son. He was the first male born into the family in two generations. In fact, the baby was to be named for the grandfather—Carlos—and his middle name was to be Sofía's maiden name, and so, what the old man had never hoped for with his "harem of four girls," as he liked to joke, his own name was to be kept going in this new country!

During his two visits, the grandfather had stood guard by the crib all day, speaking to little Carlos. "Charles the Fifth; Charles Dickens; Prince Charles." He enumerated the names of famous Charleses in order to stir up genetic ambition in the boy. "Charlemagne," he cooed at him also, for the baby was large and big-boned with blond fuzz on his pale pink skin, and blue eyes just like his German father's. All the grandfather's Caribbean fondness for a male heir and for fair Nordic looks had surfaced. There was now good blood in the family against a future bad choice by one of its women.

"You can be president, you were born here," the grandfather crooned. "You can go to the moon, maybe even to Mars by the time you are of my age."

His macho babytalk brought back Sofía's old antagonism towards her father. How obnoxious for him to go on and on like that while beside him stood his little granddaughter, wide-eyed and sad at all the things her baby brother, no bigger than one of her dolls, was going to be able to do just because he was a boy. "Make him stop, please," Sofía asked her husband. Otto was considered the jolly, good-natured one among the brothers-in-law. "The camp counselor," his sisters-in-law teased. Otto approached the grandfather. Both men looked fondly down at the new Viking.

"You can be as great a man as your father," the grandfather said. This was the first compliment the father-in-law had ever paid any son-in-law in the family. There was no way Otto was going to mess with the old man now. "He is a good boy, is he not, Papi?" Otto's German accent thickened with affection. He clapped his hand on his father-in-law's shoulders. They were friends now.

But though the father had made up with his son-in-law, there was still a strain with his own daughter. When he had come to visit, she embraced him at the door, but he stiffened and politely shrugged her off. "Let me put down these heavy bags, Sofía." He had never called her by her family pet name, Fifi, even when she lived at home. He had always had problems with his maverick youngest, and her running off hadn't helped. "I don't want loose women in my family," he had cautioned all his daughters. Warnings were delivered communally, for even though there was usually the offending daughter of the moment, every woman's character could use extra scolding.

His daughters had had to put up with this kind of attitude in an unsympathetic era. They grew up in the late sixties. Those were the days when wearing jeans and hoop earrings, smoking a little dope, and sleeping with their classmates were considered political acts against the military-industrial complex. But standing up to their father was a different matter altogether. Even as grown women, they lowered their voices in their father's earshot when alluding to their bodies' pleasure. Professional women, too, all three of them, with degrees on the wall!

Sofía was the one without the degrees. She had always gone her own way, though she downplayed her choices, calling them accidents. Among the four sisters, she was considered the plain one, with her tall, big-boned body and large-featured face. And yet, she was the one with "non-stop boyfriends," her sisters joked, not without wonder and a little envy. They admired her and were always asking her advice about men. The third daughter had shared a room with Sofía growing up. She liked to watch her sister move about their room, getting ready for bed, brushing and arranging her hair in a clip before easing herself under the sheets as if someone were waiting for her there. In the dark, Fifi gave off a fresh, wholesome smell of clean flesh. It gave solace to the third daughter, who was always so tentative and terrified and had such troubles with men. Her sister's breathing in the dark room was like having a powerful, tamed animal at the foot of her bed ready to protect her.

The youngest daughter had been the first to leave home. She had dropped out of college, in love. She had taken a job as a secretary and was living at home because her father had threatened to disown her if she moved out on her own. On her vacation she went to Colombia because her current boyfriend was going, and since she couldn't spend an overnight with him in New York, she had to travel thousands of miles to sleep with him. In Bogotá, they discovered that once they could enjoy the forbidden fruit, they lost their appetite. They broke up. She met a tourist on the street, some guy from Germany, just like that. The woman had not been without a boyfriend for more than a few days of her adult life. They fell in love.

On her way home, she tossed her diaphragm in the first bin at Kennedy Airport. She was taking no chances. But the father could tell. For months, he kept an eye out. First chance he got, he went through her drawers "looking for my nail clippers," and there he found her packet of love letters. The German man's small, correct handwriting mentioned unmentionable things—bed conversations were recreated on the thin blue sheets of aerogramme letters.

"What is the meaning of this?" The father shook the letters in her face. They had been sitting around the table, the four sisters, gabbing, and the father had come in, beating the packet against his leg like a whip, the satin hair ribbon unraveling where he had untied it, and then wrapped it round and round in a mad effort to contain his youngest daughter's misbehavior.

"Give me those!" she cried, lunging at him.

The father raised his hand with the letters above both their heads like the Statue of Liberty with her freedom torch, but he had forgotten this was the daughter who was as tall as he was. She clawed his arm down and clutched the letters to herself as if they were her babe he'd plucked from her breast. It seemed a biological rather than a romantic fury.

After his initial shock, the father regained his own fury. "Has he deflowered you? That's what I want to know. Have you gone behind the palm trees? Are you dragging my good name through the dirt, that is what I would like to know!" The father was screaming crazily in the youngest daughter's face, question after question, not giving the daughter a chance to answer. His face grew red with fury, but hers was more terrible in its impassivity, a pale ivory moon, pulling and pulling at the tide of his anger, until it seemed he might drown in his own outpouring of fury.

Her worried sisters stood up, one at each arm, coaxing him like nurses, another touching the small of his back as if he were a feverish boy. "Come on, Papi, simmer down now. Take it easy. Let's talk. We're a family, after all."

"Are you a whore?" the father interrogated his daughter. There was spit on the daughter's cheeks from the closeness of his mouth to her face.

"It's none of your fucking business!" she said in a low, ugly-sounding voice like the snarl of an animal who could hurt him. "You have no right, no right at all, to go through my stuff or read my mail!" Tears spurted out of her eyes, her nostrils flared.

The father's mouth opened in a little zero of shock. Quietly, Sofía drew herself up and left the room. Usually, in her growing-up tantrums, this daughter would storm out of the house and come back hours later, placated, the sweetness in her nature reasserted, bearing silly gifts for everyone in the family, refrigerator magnets, little stuffed hairballs with roll-around eyeballs.

But this time they could hear her upstairs, opening and closing her drawers, moving back and forth from the bed to the closet. Downstairs, the father prowled up and down the length of the rooms, his three daughters caging him while the other great power in the house, tidily—as if she had all the time in the world—buttoned and folded all her clothes, packed all her bags, and left the house forever. She got herself to Germany somehow and got the man to marry her. To throw in the face of the father who was so ambitious for presidents and geniuses in the family, the German nobody turned out to be a world-class chemist. But the daughter's was not a petty nature. What did she care what Otto did for a living when she had shown up at his door and offered herself to him.

"I can love you as much as anybody else," she said. "If you can do the same for me, let's get married."

"Come on in and let's talk," Otto had said, or so the story went.

"Yes or no," Sofía answered. Just like that on a snowy night someone at his door and a cold draft coming in. "I couldn't let her freeze," Otto boasted later.

"Like hell you couldn't!" Sofía planted a large hand on his shoulder, and anyone could see how it must be between them in the darkness of their love-making. On their honeymoon, they traveled to Greece, and Sofía sent her mother and father and sisters postcards like any newlywed. "We're having a great time. Wish you were here."

But the father kept to his revenge. For months no one could mention the daughter's name in his presence, though he kept calling them all "Sofía" and quickly correcting himself. When the daughter's baby girl was born, his wife put her foot down. Let him carry his grudge to the grave, *she* was going out to Michigan (where Otto had relocated) to see her first grandchild!

Last minute, the father relented and went along, but he might as well have stayed away. He was grim and silent the whole visit, no matter how hard Sofía and her sisters tried to engage him in conversation. Banishment was better than this cold shoulder. But Sofía tried again. On the old man's next birthday, she appeared at the apartment with her little girl. "Surprise!" There was a reconciliation of sorts. The father first tried to shake hands with her. Thwarted, he then embraced her stiffly before taking the baby in his arms under the watchful eye of his wife. Every year after that, the daughter came for her father's birthday, and in the way of women, soothed and stitched and patched over the hurt feelings. But there it was under the social fabric, the raw wound. The father refused to set foot in his daughter's house. They rarely spoke; the father said public things to her in the same tone of voice he used with his sons-in-law.

But now his seventieth birthday was coming up, and he had agreed to have the celebration at Sofía's house. The christening for little Carlos was scheduled for the morning, so the big event would be Papi Carlos's party that night. It was a coup for the youngest daughter to have gathered the scattered family in the Midwest for a weekend. But the real coup was how Sofía had managed to have the husbands included this year. The husbands are coming, the husbands are coming, the sisters joked. Sofía passed the compliment off on little Carlos. The boy had opened the door for the other men in the family.

But the coup the youngest daughter most wanted was to reconcile with her father in a big way. She would throw the old man a party he wouldn't forget. For weeks she planned what they would eat, where they would all sleep, the entertainment. She kept calling up her sisters with every little thing to see what they thought. Mostly, they agreed with her: a band, paper hats, balloons, buttons that broadcast THE WORLD'S GREATEST DAD. Everything overdone and silly and devoted the way they knew the father would like it. Sofía briefly considered a belly dancer or a girl who'd pop out of a cake. But the third daughter, who had become a feminist in the wake of her divorce, said she considered such locker-room entertainments offensive. A band with music was what she'd pitch in on; her married sisters could split it three ways if they wanted to be sexists. With great patience, Sofía created a weekend that would offend no one. They were going to have a good time in her house for the old man's seventieth, if it killed her!

The night of the party, the family ate an early dinner before the band and the guests arrived. Each daughter toasted both Carloses. The sons-in-law called big Carlos, "Papi." Little Carlos, looking very much like a little girl in his long, white christening gown, bawled the whole time, and his poor mother had not a moment's peace between serving the dinner she'd prepared for the family and giving him his. The phone kept ringing, relatives from the old country calling with congratulations for the old man. The toasts the daughters had prepared kept getting interrupted. Even so, their father's eyes glazed with tears more than once as the four girls went through their paces.

He looked old tonight, every single one of his seventy years was showing. Perhaps it was that too much wine had darkened his complexion, and his white hair and brows and mustache stood out unnaturally white. He perked up a little for his gifts, though, gadgets and books and desk trophies from his daughters, and cards with long notes penned inside "to the best, dearest Papi in the world," each one of which the old man wanted to read out loud. "No you don't, Papi, they're private!" his daughters chimed in, crowding around him, wanting to spare each other the embarrassment of having their gushing made public. His wife gave him a gold watch. The third daughter teased that that's how companies retired their employees, but when her mother made angry eyes at her, she stopped. Then there were the men gifts—belts and credit card wallets from the sons-in-law.

"Things I really need." The father was gracious. He stacked up the gift cards and put them away in his pocket to pore over later. The sons-in-law all knew that the father was watching them, jealously, for signs of indifference or self-interest. As for his girls, even after their toasts were given, the gifts opened, and the father had borne them out of the way with the help of his little granddaughter, even then, the daughters felt that there was something else he had been waiting for which they had not yet given him.

But there was still plenty of party left to make sure he got whatever it was he needed for the long, lonely year ahead. The band arrived, three middle-aged men, each with a silver wave slicked back with too much hair cream. DANNY AND HIS BOYS set up a placard with their name against the fireplace. There was one on an accordion, another on a fiddle, and a third was miscellaneous on maracas and triangle and drums when needed. They played movie themes, polkas, anything familiar you could hum along to; the corny songs were all dedicated to "Poppy" or "his lovely lady." The father liked the band. "Nice choice," he congratulated Otto. The youngest daughter's temper flared easily with all she'd had to drink and eat. She narrowed her eyes at her smiling husband and put a hand on her hip. As if Otto had lifted a finger during her long months of planning!

The guests began to arrive, many with tales of how they'd gotten lost on the way; the suburbs were dark and intricate like mazes with their courts and cul-de-sacs. Otto's unmarried colleagues looked around the room, trying to single out the recently divorced sister they'd heard so much about. But there was no one as beautiful and funny and talented as Sofía had boasted the third oldest would be. Most of these friends were half in love with Sofía anyway, and it was she they sought out in the crowded room.

There was a big chocolate cake in the shape of a heart set out on the long buffet with seventy-one candles—one for good luck. The granddaughter and her aunts had counted them and planted them diagonally across the heart, joke candles that wouldn't blow out. Later, they burned a flaming arrow that would not quit. The bar was next to the heart and by midnight when the band broke out again with "Happy Birthday, Poppy," everyone had had too much to eat and drink.

They'd been playing party games on and off all night. The band obliged with musical chairs, but after two of the dining room chairs were broken, they left off playing. The third daughter, especially, had gotten out of hand, making musical chairs of every man's lap. The father sat without speaking. He gazed upon the scene disapprovingly.

In fact, the older the evening got, the more withdrawn the father had become. Surrounded by his daughters and their husbands and fancy, intelligent, high-talking friends, he seemed to be realizing that he was just an old man sitting in their houses, eating up their roast lamb, impinging upon their lives. The daughters could almost hear his thoughts inside their own heads. He, who had paid to straighten their teeth and smooth the accent out of their English in expensive schools, he was nothing to them now. Everyone in this room would survive him, even the silly men in the band who seemed like boys—imagine making a living out of playing birthday songs! How could they ever earn enough money to give their daughters pretty clothes and send them to Europe during the summers so they wouldn't get bored? Where were the world's men anymore? Every last one of his sons-in-law was a kid; he could see that clearly. Even Otto, the famous scientist, was a schoolboy with a pencil, doing his long division. The new son-in-law he even felt sorry for—he could see this husband would give out on his strong-willed second daughter. Already she had him giving her backrubs and going for cigarettes in the middle of the night. But he needn't worry about his girls. Or his wife, for that matter. There she sat, pretty and slim as a girl, smiling coyly at everyone when a song was dedicated to her. Eight, maybe nine, months he gave her of widowhood, and then she'd find someone to grow old with on his life insurance.

The third daughter thought of a party game to draw her father out. She took one of the baby's soft receiving blankets, blindfolded her father, and led him to a chair at the center of the room. The women clapped. The men sat down. The father pretended he didn't understand what all his daughters were up to. "How does one play this game, Mami?"

"You're on your own, Dad," the mother said, laughing. She was the only one in the family who called him by his American name.

"Are you ready, Papi?" the oldest asked.

"I am perfect ready," he replied in his heavy accent.

"Okay, now, guess who this is," the oldest said. She always took charge. This is how they worked things among the daughters.

The father nodded, his eyebrows shot up. He held on to his chair, excited, a little scared, like a boy about to be asked a hard question he knows the answer to.

The oldest daughter motioned to the third daughter, who tiptoed into the circle the women had made around the old man. She gave him a daughterly peck on the cheek.

"Who was that, Papi?" the oldest asked.

He was giggling with pleasure and could not get the words out at first. He had had too much to drink. "That was Mami," he said in a coy little voice.

"No! Wrong!" all the women cried out.

"Carla?" he guessed the oldest. He was going down the line. "Wrong!" More shouts.

"Sandi? Yoyo?"

"You guessed it," his third oldest said.

The women clapped; some bent over in hilarious laughter. Everyone had had too much to drink. And the old man was having his good time too.

"Okay, here's another coming at you." The eldest took up the game again. She put her index finger to her lips, gave everyone a meaningful glance, quietly circled the old man, and kissed him from behind on top of his head. Then she tiptoed back to where she had been standing when she had first spoken. "Who was that, Papi?" she asked, extra innocent.

"Mami?" His voice rode up, exposed and vulnerable. Then it sank back into its certainties. "That was Mami."

"Count me out," his wife said from the couch where she'd finally given in to exhaustion.

The father never guessed any of the other women in the room. That would have been disrespectful. Besides, their strange-sounding American names were hard to remember and difficult to pronounce. Still he got the benefit of their kisses under cover of his daughters. Down the line, the father went each time: "Carla?" "Sandi?" "Yoyo?" Sometimes, he altered the order, put the third daughter first or the oldest one second.

Sofía had been in the bedroom, tending to her son, who was wild with all the noise in the house tonight. She came back into the living room, buttoning her dress front, and happened upon the game. "Ooh." She rolled her eyes. "It's getting raunchy in here, ha!" She worked her hips in a mock rotation, and the men all laughed. She thrust her girlfriends into the circle and whispered to her little girl to plant the next kiss on her grandfather's nose. The women all pecked and puckered at the old man's face. The second daughter sat briefly on his lap and chucked him under the chin. Every time the father took a wrong guess, the youngest daughter laughed loudly. But soon, she noticed that he never guessed her name. After all her hard work, she was not to be included in his daughter count. Damn him! She'd take her turn and make him know it was her!

Quickly, she swooped into the circle and gave the old man a wet, open-mouthed kiss in his ear. She ran her tongue in the whorls of his ear and nibbled the tip. Then she moved back.

"Oh la la," the oldest said, laughing. "Who was that, Papi?"

The old man did not answer. The smile that had played on his lips through-out the game was gone. He sat up, alert. There was a long pause; everyone leaned forward, waiting for the father to begin with his usual, "Mami?"

But the father did not guess his wife's name. He tore at his blindfold as if it were a contagious body whose disease he might catch. The receiving blanket fell in a soft heap beside his chair. His face had darkened with shame at having his pleasure aroused in public by one of his daughters. He looked from one to the other. His gaze faltered. On the face of his youngest was the brilliant, im-passive look he remembered from when she had snatched her love letters out of his hands.

"That's enough of that," he commanded in a low, furious voice. And sure enough, his party was over.

Ordering the Family Confusion in Julia Alvarez's "The Kiss"

David Huddle

Sandi, Yoyo, Sofía, Carla, Papi, Mami, Otto, little Carlos, an unnamed granddaughter, and a couple of unnamed husbands, not to men-tion assorted "fancy, intelligent, high-talking friends": All these characters come to the party given by the García* girls to celebrate their father's seventi-eth birthday. The sheer logistics† of writing about such a well-attended party might intimidate any but the craftiest of writers. Julia Alvarez manages the task with grace and economy in "The Kiss." Her García family party takes up only 3 pages in her 9-page story. There's plenty of confusion in the room and in the thoughts and feelings of the characters, but a reader is privileged to see—quite clearly—everything that most matters, dramatically and emotionally.

---

*Although the family name García is not mentioned in "The Kiss," the story is one of the related pieces of Julia Alvarez's 1991 collection, *How the García Girls Lost Their Accents*. For the sake of con-venience, the family name is used throughout this essay.

†*Webster's* defines "logistics" as "the branch of military science having to do with moving, supply-ing, and quartering troops."

The method Alvarez uses to grant this "reader's privilege" and to cut through all the confusion is a subtle manipulation of point of view, the most basic technical device of fiction writing. "The Kiss" is, of course, a third-person story, the classic version of which (e.g., Katherine Mansfield's "The Garden Party" and Allen Shepherd's "Lightning") uses the limited-omniscient point of view, which restricts a reader's access to the thoughts and feelings of only one (main) character. Focus is maintained by sticking with the protagonist.

But because it is more concerned with a whole family than it is with any one individual, there is not a traditional "main character" in "The Kiss," and it is not a classic third-person story. This narrative requires a complex mechanism for maintaining focus at the same time it keeps track of the many elements that are important in the sequence of events that occur at Papi's party. The point of view must be sufficiently flexible to grant a reader access to more than one character's thoughts and feelings, but it must not be disorienting through arbitrarily switching from one consciousness to another.*

The opening sentence of "The Kiss," with its third-person plural pronouns, establishes a group consciousness: "Even after they'd been married and had their own families and often couldn't make it home for other occasions, the four daughters always came home for their father's birthday." The same sentence establishes the story's fundamental dramatic circumstance: The daughters are pitted against their father—or they are allied with their father—or they are both pitted against and allied with their father. That push-pull dynamic of the parent-child relationship is what Alvarez means to explore and to explicate here. The parent is spotlighted: "The father opened his arms wide and welcomed them in his broken English: 'This is your home, and never you should forget it.'"

"The Kiss" doesn't even name one of these four daughters until its second page, in this key sentence: "But this year, for his seventieth birthday, the youngest daughter, Sofía, wanted the celebration at her house." For the first time in the story, with the word *wanted*, we readers have access to the interior life of an individual. Such access automatically designates a character as having importance in a story. Ordinarily it's how we readers instinctively recognize a "protagonist": It's the character to whom we're linked, by way of consciousness. But Sofía is not exactly a protagonist in "The Kiss," because too little of her interior life is made available to us and because the story points to another character as equally important.

Papi actually gets more individual attention than any other character in the story. He has more to say, he's described more elaborately, and his important birthday party is the central occasion of the story. But we don't have direct access to his consciousness; for the most part, we readers are linked to the group consciousness of the daughters. The story positions us *with* the daughters; we see and understand Papi as they see and understand him.

---

*Here, as in Louise Erdrich's "Fleur," the technical point-of-view problem has invited the author to generate an imaginative solution.

He looked old tonight, every single one of his seventy years was showing. Perhaps it was that too much wine had darkened his complexion, and his white hair and brows and mustache stood out unnaturally white.

Just prior to the crucial scene of the story, Alvarez executes an exceptional point-of-view maneuver: She lets us into Papi's consciousness. Without disrupting her story's focus, she can't switch directly to Papi's thinking—because we readers have spent the entire story, up to this point, in the company of the daughters. Now she needs to bring the reader much closer to Papi so that the reader will understand and sympathize with him through the scene that follows. How can she have it both ways, remaining in the company of the daughters but moving into the consciousness of the father? Look carefully at the sentence I have italicized below:

> The father sat without speaking. He gazed upon the scene disapprovingly.
>
> In fact, the older the evening got, the more withdrawn the father had become. Surrounded by his daughters and their husbands and fancy, intelligent, high-talking friends, he seemed to be realizing that he was just an old man sitting in their houses, eating up their roast lamb, impinging upon their lives. *The daughters could almost hear his thoughts inside their own heads.* He, who had paid to straighten their teeth and smooth the accent out of their English in expensive schools, he was nothing to them now. . . . But he needn't worry about his girls. Or his wife, for that matter. There she sat, pretty and slim as a girl, smiling coyly at everyone when a song was dedicated to her. Eight, maybe nine, months he gave her of widowhood, and then she'd find someone to grow old with on his life insurance.

By the end of this long paragraph of Papi's pondering the state of his family and his life, Papi's inner frailty has been completely revealed to the reader. With some deft technical maneuvering, Alvarez has made us readers move closer to him and feel for him. Now watch how she backs us away from him and returns us to the group consciousness of the daughters:

> The third daughter thought of a party game to draw her father out. She took one of the baby's soft receiving blankets, blindfolded her father, and led him to a chair at the center of the room. The women clapped. The men sat down. The father pretended he didn't understand what all his daughters were up to.

With these two paragraphs Alvarez has transported us into and back out of Papi García's secret soul, so that now we readers are again viewing him from a distance.* However objectively we see him during what follows, we can't forget what we learned in those intimate moments when we had access to his thoughts and feelings.

With the beginning of the blindfolding game, we readers can almost intuit what the symmetrical pattern of the story calls for: the other important character, Sofía, the youngest daughter, must somehow balance the weight of the story that Papi took on with his long paragraph. Some access to Sofía's interior life is essential to whatever is to happen:

*The word *pretended* conveys a link with Papi's inner life, even though the (literal) point of view has moved to the perceptions of those who are viewing him from some distance.

Sofía had been in the bedroom, tending to her son, who was wild with all the noise in the house tonight. She came back into the living room, buttoning her dress front, and happened upon the game. "Ooh." She rolled her eyes. "It's getting raunchy in here, ha!" She worked her hips in a mock rotation, and the men all laughed. She thrust her girlfriends into the circle and whispered to her little girl to plant the next kiss on her grandfather's nose. The women all pecked and puckered at the old man's face. The second daughter sat briefly on his lap and clucked him under the chin. Every time the father took a wrong guess, the youngest daughter laughed loudly. But soon, she noticed that he never guessed her name. After all her hard work, she was not to be included in his daughter count. Damn him! She'd take her turn and make him know it was her!

Preparation for the crucial moment of "The Kiss" has now been completed. The situation, the characters, and the reader have all been set up.* In another half page the story, like Papi's party, is over. One may be reminded of Katherine Mansfield's "The Garden Party," wherein some eight pages were devoted to the Sheridan family's preparing for their party, which began and ended within the space of half a page. But here in "The Kiss," there is no aftermath. When this party is over, it is all over, and a reader perfectly understands the rich ambiguity and ambivalence of this tiny event in the overall sweep of an extremely complex family history.

A delicate, precise positioning—as in a family portrait—is what gives "The Kiss" its meaning, its resonance in the mind of a reader. Obviously Sofía and Papi stand in the foreground. Behind them are the other three daughters and Mami. In the third row are Otto and the other two husbands, and behind them are the other guests at the birthday party and perhaps even the one divorced husband. In the fourth row are the culture, the history, and the politics of the Dominican Republic from which the García family originated. And in the fifth row is the culture of the United States in the 1960s, the value system that so informs (and conflicts) the consciousness of the family—especially the daughters and most especially Sofía.

In retrospect, with the García family portrait so charmingly before us, the story seems inevitable: Of course everyone had to be positioned and posed just this way, how could it have been otherwise? But when the story first began brewing in the mind of the author, its point-of-view difficulties must have seemed formidable: How could a short story be constructed to convey the way the terrible fight between Papi and Sofía (which came out of their different placements in culture and history) affected the entire family? None of the conventional options of point of view could capture that delicate mix of the two individual consciousnesses, as well as the general family consciousness, that was required by "The Kiss."

Most likely Alvarez, in the earliest stages of her composing, did not even envision the subtle point-of-view requirement of the finished story. Rarely is it

---

*Though the term *set up* has some negative implications (e.g., a con man might "set up" a potential victim), it is ordinarily used among fiction writers to mean "to carry out the necessary preparation to produce a desired effect."

the case that a writer can say, *Ah ha! I see exactly how I'm going to write this story!* Rather more likely, Alvarez proceeded intuitively, as most fiction writers do as they work through the early drafts of a story. Probably in doing so, she discovered what was necessary. Because she came to a point where the story needed "double vision," she found (or discovered or invented) the remarkable sentence that gave her access to Papi's thoughts at the same time it kept the point-of-view focus within the group consciousness ("The daughters could almost hear his thoughts inside their own heads"). Probably by trying one arrangement and then another, Alvarez arrived at the pattern of assembled "parts" of delicately and differently shaded consciousness that became the finished version of "The Kiss."

We can only speculate about the composing process* that brought "The Kiss" onto these pages where we have read it. But we can be certain that the author had to adjust conventional storytelling technique; she had to "customize" the limited-omniscient point of view to suit the individual needs of her story. Certain stories require their creators to extend their innovative powers even to the tools with which they must work.

*The basis of such speculation is, of course, our own individual composing processes, which in the case of the editors are at least partially described in their comments about their own stories.

Yukio Mishima

Yukio Mishima, fiction writer and dramatist, was born Kimitake Hiraoka in 1925. Under his pen name he became a major figure in modern Japanese literature; he was also an actor and director, as well as a public promoter of traditional Japanese values. His works include short fiction collections, novels including *Confessions of a Mask* (1949), *The Sailor Who Fell from Grace with the Sea* (1963), and the tetralogy *The Sea of Fertility,* the last volume of which was published in 1970. In that year Mishima publicly committed ritual suicide, apparently as a political statement.

Swaddling Clothes

Yukio Mishima
Translated by Ivan Morris

He was always busy, Toshiko's husband. Even tonight he had to dash off to an appointment, leaving her to go home alone by taxi. But what else could a woman expect when she married an actor—an attractive one? No doubt she had been foolish to hope that he would spend the evening with her. And yet he must have known how she dreaded going back to their house, unhomely with its Western-style furniture and with the bloodstains still showing on the floor.

Toshiko had been oversensitive since girlhood: that was her nature. As the result of constant worrying she never put on weight, and now, an adult woman, she looked more like a transparent picture than a creature of flesh and blood. Her delicacy of spirit was evident to her most casual acquaintance.

Earlier that evening, when she had joined her husband at a night club, she had been shocked to find him entertaining friends with an account of "the incident." Sitting there in his American-style suit, puffing at a cigarette, he had seemed to her almost a stranger.

"It's a fantastic story," he was saying, gesturing flamboyantly as if in an attempt to outweigh the attractions of the dance band. "Here this new nurse for our baby arrives from the employment agency, and the very first thing I notice about her is her stomach. It's enormous—as if she had a pillow stuck under her kimono! No wonder, I thought, for I soon saw that she could eat more than the rest of us put together. She polished off the contents of our rice bin like that. . . ." He snapped his fingers. "'Gastric dilation'—that's how she explained her girth and her appetite. Well, the day before yesterday we heard groans and moans coming from the nursery. We rushed in and found her squatting on the floor, holding her stomach in her two hands, and moaning like a cow. Next to

143

her our baby lay in his cot, scared out of his wits and crying at the top of his lungs. A pretty scene, I can tell you!"

"So the cat was out of the bag?" suggested one of their friends, a film actor like Toshiko's husband.

"Indeed it was! And it gave me the shock of my life. You see, I'd completely swallowed that story about 'gastric dilation.' Well, I didn't waste any time. I rescued our good rug from the floor and spread a blanket for her to lie on. The whole time the girl was yelling like a stuck pig. By the time the doctor from the maternity clinic arrived, the baby had already been born. But our sitting room was a pretty shambles!"

"Oh, that I'm sure of!" said another of their friends, and the whole company burst into laughter.

Toshiko was dumbfounded to hear her husband discussing the horrifying happening as though it were no more than an amusing incident which they chanced to have witnessed. She shut her eyes for a moment and all at once she saw the newborn baby lying before her: on the parquet floor the infant lay, and his frail body was wrapped in bloodstained newspapers.

Toshiko was sure that the doctor had done the whole thing out of spite. As if to emphasize his scorn for this mother who had given birth to a bastard under such sordid conditions, he had told his assistant to wrap the baby in some loose newspapers, rather than proper swaddling. This callous treatment of the newborn child had offended Toshiko. Overcoming her disgust at the entire scene, she had fetched a brand-new piece of flannel from her cupboard and, having swaddled the baby in it, had lain him carefully in an armchair.

This all had taken place in the evening after her husband had left the house. Toshiko had told him nothing of it, fearing that he would think her oversoft, oversentimental; yet the scene had engraved itself deeply in her mind. Tonight she sat silently thinking back on it, while the jazz orchestra brayed and her husband chatted cheerfully with his friends. She knew that she would never forget the sight of the baby, wrapped in stained newspapers and lying on the floor— it was a scene fit for a butchershop. Toshiko, whose own life had been spent in solid comfort, poignantly felt the wretchedness of the illegitimate baby.

I am the only person to have witnessed its shame, the thought occurred to her. The mother never saw the child lying there in its newspaper wrappings, and the baby itself of course didn't know. I alone shall have to preserve that terrible scene in my memory. When the baby grows up and wants to find out about his birth, there will be no one to tell him, so long as I preserve silence. How strange that I should have this feeling of guilt! After all, it was I who took him up from the floor, swathed him properly in flannel, and laid him down to sleep in the armchair.

They left the night club and Toshiko stepped into the taxi that her husband had called for her. "Take this lady to Ushigom" he told the driver and shut the door from the outside. Toshiko gazed through the window at her husband's smiling face and noticed his strong, white teeth. Then she leaned back in the seat, oppressed by the knowledge that their life together was in some way too easy, too painless. It would have been difficult for her to put her thoughts into words. Through the rear window of the taxi she took a last look at her husband. He was striding along the street toward his Nash car, and soon the back of his rather garish tweed coat had blended with the figures of the passers-by.

The taxi drove off, passed down a street dotted with bars and then by a theatre, in front of which the throngs of people jostled each other on the pavement. Although the performance had only just ended, the lights had already been turned out and in the half dark outside it was depressingly obvious that the cherry blossoms decorating the front of the theatre were merely scraps of white paper.

Even if that baby should grow up in ignorance of the secret of his birth, he can never become a respectable citizen, reflected Toshiko, pursuing the same train of thought. Those soiled newspaper swaddling clothes will be the symbol of his entire life. But why should I keep worrying about him so much? Is it because I feel uneasy about the future of my own child? Say twenty years from now, when our boy will have grown up into a fine, carefully educated young man, one day by a quirk of fate he meets that other boy, who then will also have turned twenty. And say that the other boy, who has been sinned against, savagely stabs him with a knife. . . .

It was a warm, overcast April night, but thoughts of the future made Toshiko feel cold and miserable. She shivered on the back seat of the car.

No, when the time comes I shall take my son's place, she told herself suddenly. Twenty years from now I shall be forty-three. I shall go to that young man and tell him straight out about everything—about his newspaper swaddling clothes, and about how I went and wrapped him in flannel.

The taxi ran along the dark wide road that was bordered by the park and by the Imperial Palace moat. In the distance, Toshiko noticed the pinpricks of light which came from the blocks of tall office buildings.

Twenty years from now that wretched child will be in utter misery. He will be living a desolate, hopeless, poverty-stricken existence—a lonely rat. What else could happen to a baby who has had such a birth? He'll be wandering through the streets by himself, cursing his father, loathing his mother.

No doubt Toshiko derived a certain satisfaction from her somber thoughts: she tortured herself with them without cease. The taxi approached Hanzomon and drove past the compound of the British Embassy. At that point the famous rows of cherry trees were spread out before Toshiko in all their purity. On the spur of the moment she decided to go and view the blossoms by herself in the dark night. It was a strange decision for a timid and unadventurous young woman, but then she was in a strange state of mind and she dreaded the return home. That evening all sorts of unsettling fancies had burst open in her mind.

She crossed the wide street—a slim, solitary figure in the darkness. As a rule when she walked in the traffic Toshiko used to cling fearfully to her companion, but tonight she darted alone between the cars and a moment later had reached the long narrow park that borders the Palace moat. Chidorigafuchi, it is called—the Abyss of the Thousand Birds.

Tonight the whole park had become a grove of blossoming cherry trees. Under the calm cloudy sky the blossoms formed a mass of solid whiteness. The paper lanterns that hung from wires between the trees had been put out; in their place electric light bulbs, red, yellow, and green, shone dully beneath the blossoms. It was well past ten o'clock and most of the flower-viewers had gone home. As the occasional passers-by strolled through the park, they would automatically kick aside the empty bottles or crush the waste paper beneath their feet.

Newspapers, thought Toshiko, her mind going back once again to those happenings. Bloodstained newspapers. If a man were ever to hear of that piteous birth and know that it was he who had lain there, it would ruin his entire life. To think that I, a perfect stranger, should from now on have to keep such a secret—the secret of a man's whole existence. . . .

Lost in these thoughts, Toshiko walked on through the park. Most of the people still remaining there were quiet couples; no one paid her any attention. She noticed two people sitting on a stone bench beside the moat, not looking at the blossoms, but gazing silently at the water. Pitch black it was, and swathed in heavy shadows. Beyond the moat the somber forest of the Imperial Palace blocked her view. The trees reached up, to form a solid dark mass against the night sky. Toshiko walked slowly along the path beneath the blossoms hanging heavily overhead.

On a stone bench, slightly apart from the others, she noticed a pale object— not, as she had at first imagined, a pile of cherry blossoms, nor a garment forgotten by one of the visitors to the park. Only when she came closer did she see that it was a human form lying on the bench. Was it, she wondered, one of those miserable drunks often to be seen sleeping in public places? Obviously not, for the body had been systematically covered with newspapers, and it was the whiteness of those papers that had attracted Toshiko's attention. Standing by the bench, she gazed down at the sleeping figure.

It was a man in a brown jersey who lay there, curled up on layers of newspapers, other newspapers covering him. No doubt this had become his normal night residence now that spring had arrived. Toshiko gazed down at the man's dirty, unkempt hair, which in places had become hopelessly matted. As she observed the sleeping figure wrapped in its newspapers, she was inevitably reminded of the baby who had lain on the floor in its wretched swaddling clothes. The shoulder of the man's jersey rose and fell in the darkness in time with his heavy breathing.

It seemed to Toshiko that all her fears and premonitions had suddenly taken concrete form. In the darkness the man's pale forehead stood out, and it was a young forehead, though carved with the wrinkles of long poverty and hardship. His khaki trousers had been slightly pulled up; on his sockless feet he wore a pair of battered gym shoes. She could not see his face and suddenly had an overmastering desire to get one glimpse of it.

She walked to the head of the bench and looked down. The man's head was half buried in his arms, but Toshiko could see that he was surprisingly young. She noticed the thick eyebrows and the fine bridge of his nose. His slightly open mouth was alive with youth.

But Toshiko had approached too close. In the silent night the newspaper bedding rustled, and abruptly the man opened his eyes. Seeing the young woman standing directly beside him, he raised himself with a jerk, and his eyes lit up. A second later a powerful hand reached out and seized Toshiko by her slender wrist.

She did not feel in the least afraid and made no effort to free herself. In a flash the thought had struck her. Ah, so the twenty years have already gone by! The forest of the Imperial Palace was pitch dark and utterly silent.

The Importance of Where in Yukio Mishima's "Swaddling Clothes"

Ghita Orth

"Barefoot, her hair wringing wet, the girl hurried along, then quickly pushed through the door; she was very hungry." Reading these sentences, we might at first glance think we have a clear sense of the situation being presented; we know *who* is doing *what* and *why*. But do we really understand what's going on here? It's one thing if the girl is rushing along the beach in Galveston, Texas, to a waterside snack bar but quite another if she is on her way down New York's Fifth Avenue to lunch at the Plaza Hotel! And is it June or November? 1892 or 1992? Clearly, *where* things happen—in place and in time—significantly affects how we perceive those happenings.

Because everything that happens to people happens somewhere, we expect the same to be true in fiction; like the girl here, a story needs to be specifically located if the reader is to be drawn into its world and understand the import of what takes place there. Only science fiction occurs in thin air, and even then, galaxies can be as concretely delineated as any earthbound setting and thus be as convincingly believable. Perhaps Shakespeare says it best through Theseus in *A Midsummer Night's Dream*:

> And as imagination bodies forth
> The forms of things unknown, the poet's pen
> Turns them to shapes, and gives to aery nothing
> A local habitation and a name.

If we understand "poet" here to mean any maker of fictions, we also understand that only when a storyteller provides a concrete "local habitation" for the creatures of his or her imagination do these characters, and the ideas they embody, become real for the reader.

Yukio Mishima provides such a habitation in "Swaddling Clothes," a story which demonstrates both the importance of "where" in fiction and the ways in which details of place can be incorporated seamlessly into a work as part of its totality of meaning. Unlike the girl in our example, when Toshiko hurries along she is doing so in a specific location: "the long narrow park that borders the Palace moat. Chidorigafuchi, it is called—the Abyss of the Thousand Birds." And by the time she enters this "abyss," we have come to understand the thematic implications that resonate from it. In "Swaddling Clothes," the general setting and particular places within it play roles as central as any character's.

This doesn't mean, however, that Mishima, like a playwright, must formally "set the stage" for his story. Because a reader is usually less interested in setting for its own sake than in the ways it illuminates action and character, the locations of a story can often best be presented through details and images. If, for example, characters look out windows at specific scenes or walk down streets with specific names and attributes, the writer can provide a story's events with concrete, particular surroundings almost incidentally. Fiction writers thus don't necessarily furnish introductory paragraphs describing setting but usually reveal where a narrative is occurring more naturally, as it unfolds. And "where," here, doesn't just refer to physical place. The setting of a story is its locus in time as well as space, in culture as well as geography.

Even if we did not know that the author of "Swaddling Clothes" was one of modern Japan's most prominent writers, we could, from internal evidence, recognize in what country, and in which decade, its events occur. It is not only the central character's name that tells us the site of the story; references to kimonos and cherry blossoms also make clear its Japanese locale. Clearly, too, Toshiko lives in a large urban center, complete with taxis and streets "dotted with bars," and her visit to the Imperial Palace gardens identifies this city as Tokyo. Yet Tokyo in 1929 was much different from Tokyo in the 1990s; really to understand Toshiko's environment, we need some sense of when her story takes place.

Numerous details here say "twentieth century," from the nightclub Toshiko visits to the maternity clinic where the doctor works to the decorative "electric light bulbs" in the palace garden. But the twentieth century was, for Japan, marked crucially by the military defeat in 1945 that forever separated its imperial past from its democratic future. Since Allied firebombings in that year reduced virtually all of Tokyo to rubble, the "blocks of tall office buildings" that Toshiko notices tells the reader that this is Japan rebuilt after World War II, as does the fact that England, once an enemy, here has an established embassy. Yet this is not Japan in 1992—the Nash car Toshiko's husband drives dates the story considerably earlier. In fact, Mishima published "Swaddling Clothes" in 1966; in this case at least, we can safely assume the story to be set in a time close to its time of composition.

But how is all this important? Why does it matter? By the 1990s Japan's new global identity was well established. In the 1960s, however, still recovering from the destruction of its old identity in the war, the country hovered between two worlds. This pull of opposing cultural forces is one of Mishima's central concerns in "Swaddling Clothes," and indeed in much of his fiction. For Mishima, postwar Japan, influenced by Western ideologies and enamored of the American artifacts introduced by occupying forces, was falling prey to a vulgar materialism that threatened to betray its cultural heritage and traditional character.

This conflict between two ways of living in the world of postwar Tokyo is at the heart of "Swaddling Clothes"; the issues around which the story revolves are rooted in its spatial and temporal setting, in its "where." But this is not a political/sociological treatise—instead, Mishima's concerns about this place at this time are acted out in the narrative that is set there. Its images of Toshiko's American-car-driving film actor husband and the house he has furnished, with its "sitting room" and "parquet floor," suggest his rejection of the Japanese cultural heritage, just as Toshiko's negative responses to the occidental style he affects link her with a more traditional value system.

The focus of narration in "Swaddling Clothes" aligns us with Toshiko by allowing us to know her thoughts and attitudes. To her, their westernized furniture is "unhomely," her husband's tweed coat "garish," and, in his "American-style" suit, he seems almost a stranger to her. These descriptive details imply not only the husband's adoption of an "American-style" materialism, but also his distance from the Asian "delicacy of spirit" that Toshiko embodies and of which he doesn't approve.

Even the unnamed husband's profession as a movie actor (one which Mishima himself had experienced) suggests an artificial life of "flamboyant" posturing. Although the present action of "Swaddling Clothes" takes place only in the taxi carrying Toshiko through Tokyo and in the park bordering the Imperial Palace, other locations are introduced through her memories. Thus her husband's shockingly superficial treatment of the baby's birth as a performance piece occurs, suitably, in a nightclub, where he tells the story "as if in an attempt to outweigh the attractions of the dance band." He is comfortable in this loud showplace, "chat[ting] cheerfully with his friends," while to Toshiko's ears, the American music played by the "jazz orchestra bray[s]" unpleasantly. In this setting, Toshiko is again associated with a traditional Japanese world that contrasts with her husband's hard-edged, westernized modernity.

The callousness of Toshiko's husband, reflected in his recounting "the horrifying happening as though it were no more than an amusing incident," is also clear in his handling of the "happening" itself. In his finely furnished home, the nursemaid's labor is a tawdry intrusion, her giving birth merely a noisy housekeeping disaster that leaves his "sitting room . . . a pretty shambles." When he spreads a blanket on the floor for the woman, who, significantly, dresses in the traditional Japanese kimono, it is not to make her more comfortable but to save his expensive rug (no tatami mats here!) from being sullied.

For Toshiko, however, wrapping the newborn child in flannel is a complex gesture; the "bloodstains . . . showing on the floor" mean nothing to her compared to the ignominious bloodstains on the newspapers in which the baby has been swaddled. Although the squalid scene, reeking of the butcher shop and the trash heap, disgusts her, Toshiko's concern is with its human, rather than material, effects. The soiled, disposable swaddling clothes provided by the scornful modern doctor seem to her indicative of the baby's future—a throwaway life in which the man to come must suffer and be discarded because of his shameful origins. These "bloodstained newspapers" thus become a powerful and unforgettable image to Toshiko even after she has replaced them, and as the story progresses we come to understand why.

Toshiko's fear that her husband would attribute her re-covering the baby merely to an "oversoft, oversentimental" conscience acknowledges not only his inherent coldness but also her own sense that she has been moved by more than an excess of tender feeling. Toshiko's taxi ride provides the necessary setting for her reflections on all that has occurred; essentially alone in the enclosed space of the car, she does what we all would do—looks out the window and thinks.

Doing so, Toshiko, like the reader, puzzles over the "feeling of guilt" that surrounds the incident in her mind despite her having taken the baby "up from the floor [and] swathed him properly in flannel." Her thoughts suggest this guilt may grow from her recognition of the "solid comfort" that has always been her due and her knowledge that even her married life is "in some way too easy, too painless." Toshiko's sharing the pain of the bastard child and re-dressing the wrong done to him may be a way of assuaging this guilt, of feeling something difficult and thus, in its way, satisfying.

This guilt of privilege, expressing itself as a desire to share and alleviate the burdens of the disadvantaged, is often apparent in the workings of our own society. As we understand some of Toshiko's motivations here, we cross the national boundaries between us and recognize a shared humanity. But we cannot turn Toshiko into an American living in the pluralistic 1990s—she is too clearly rooted in the story's "where," in a unique cultural identity. To try to erase the differences between us would be to deny, as Toshiko's husband does, the validity of her Japanese heritage. Instead, in coming to understand Toshiko's specific beliefs about the baby's future and her own, we come to understand something of Japanese custom and tradition.

To those of us raised with a faith in the American Dream that anyone can rise from rags to riches, overcoming adverse conditions by dint of determination and hard work, Toshiko's conviction that the baby's entire future has been compromised by his inauspicious beginnings is hard to accept. Her belief in a society of rigid class/caste stratification, however, seems a reflection of the old Japanese feudal system in which one's place, determined by birth, was inescapable. As Ruth Benedict points out in *The Chrysanthemum and the Sword*, "the extreme explicitness of the Japanese hierarchical system in feudal times, from outcast to Emperor, has left its strong impression on modern Japan."

Toshiko's certainty that the outcast bastard child "can never become a respectable citizen" is less puzzling, then, when we recognize that Japan's traditional hereditary caste system has colored her ways of looking at the world, even in the 1960s; it is part of the culture in which "Swaddling Clothes" is set, one she inhabits psychologically as well as physically. If the "solid comfort" Toshiko has been given in life is somehow unearned, if at birth the pattern of life is cast and her enviable position is accidental, how wretched the equally accidental position of an illegitimate child born in squalor and shame. Such a deterministic view may seem alien to many Western readers, but in the story's Japanese milieu Toshiko's belief that "a baby who has had such a birth" must eventually live a "desolate, hopeless, poverty-stricken existence" is at home.

The "soiled newspaper swaddling clothes" thus become for her not only a potent image of the inescapable disgrace of the baby's birth but also "the symbol of his entire life." This symbol, the bloody newspapers, reverberates through the story much like the "unsettling fancies" they have generated in Toshiko's mind. Here, too, seeing the story as reflecting a specific cultural heritage can help us to understand her obsessive imaginings.

The way in which the baby's shame is made tangible to Toshiko in the symbol of the newspaper swaddling clothes allows us to share the traditional Japanese view of shame as a tangible entity. Failures and rejections weigh heavily, and any shame incurred must somehow be vindicated, as we see in Toshiko's thoughts. According to Ruth Benedict, the Japanese say "'the world tips' . . . so long as any insult or slur or defeat is not requited or eliminated. A good man must try to get the world back into balance again."

And so must a good woman. Because only Toshiko has borne witness to the child's ignominious beginnings, she feels she has incurred the obligation of bearing the secret of his shame and thus, it seems, of requiting it. Somehow Toshiko must right the imbalance between her privilege and the insult done to the child and future man. Convinced that the baby has been "sinned against" by the power of social circumstance that has materially blessed her and will bless her child, Toshiko imagines the retribution that could "by a quirk of fate" be wreaked on her own son by this son of poverty and degradation. She commits herself to suffering in her son's place "when the time comes" in recompense for the shame she has witnessed.

Again the reader may well find Toshiko's attitude troubling, especially since she seemingly has little regard for the terrible effects her martyrdom could have on her son. The puzzling aspects of her motivation here, though, can perhaps be clarified if we understand that even her willingness to sacrifice herself grows from her Japanese habits of mind. Toshiko here demonstrates the Japanese concept of *giri*—a term that might translate as duty, obligation, or honor. As Toshiko's determination makes clear, to honor an obligation is to perform the noblest duty possible, for, as Benedict explains, "the strong, according to Japanese verdict, are those who disregard personal happiness and fulfill their obligations." As the narrator of "Swaddling Clothes" points out, "No doubt Toshiko derived a certain satisfaction from her somber thoughts: she tortured herself with them without cease." In being willing to follow what Toshiko takes to be her *giri*, she is honoring a commitment to the illegitimate, degraded baby that, in the Japanese view, honors her as well, especially because of its personal cost.

This commitment is tested sooner than Toshiko had expected as "Swaddling Clothes" moves to its inexorable resolution. The location of this final scene, and the descriptive details of setting that Mishima provides, serve to reinforce and unify much of what has gone before. In an uncharacteristic "decision for a timid and unadventurous young woman," Toshiko steps alone, as though driven, into the dark night to meet the incarnation of her obsession in a park whose very name, "The Abyss of the Thousand Birds," conjures images of both the terrible and the traditionally beautiful.

That this park where Toshiko is tested borders the ancient moat surrounding the Imperial Palace seems significant. These are the grounds of shoguns and emperors, the seat of traditional Japanese authority; in what little remained of prewar Tokyo after the bombings of World War II, the Imperial Palace environs were a reminder of past nobility and glory. And Mishima's description of the site is entirely accurate—like most writers, he calls upon his familiarity with the location of his fiction to render it as concretely as any guidebook might. In one such guide, the park Toshiko visits is described as "a pleasant green strip of promenade, high on the edge of the moat, lined with cherry trees." But even though fiction writers may set their stories in actual places, unlike guidebook writers they are not committed to presenting them objectively. Thus Mishima here weights his description of this real park to suggest its particular import in the story.

In "Swaddling Clothes," the promenade is not so pleasantly picturesque, despite the fact that its cherry trees are in bloom. The traditional "paper lanterns . . . had been put out"; in their place, modern "electric light bulbs . . . shone dully beneath the blossoms." The atmosphere of this final scene reflects the ambiguity of what occurs in it. Just as the April warmth has not kept Toshiko from "thoughts of the future [that] made [her] feel cold and miserable," the cherry blossoms "in all their purity" do not warm her spirit. In contrast to the sham world of Toshiko's husband, imaged in the "cherry blossoms decorating the front of the theatre" Toshiko had passed earlier that "were merely scraps of white paper," the Abyss of the Thousand Birds is inescapably real.

In the park, strollers are careless of the rubbish surrounding them; "they would automatically kick aside the empty bottles or crush the waste paper beneath their feet," reinforcing Toshiko's certainty of what the newspaper swaddling clothes presage for the bastard child. Here on a bench, an unkempt man, "surprisingly young," lies "systematically covered with newspapers." This insistently symbolic image can leave no doubt in Toshiko's, or the reader's, mind as to what their confrontation portends. The concrete embodiment of all Toshiko's "fears and premonitions," the man seems certain to exact violently from her the price of her terrible knowledge—and she is entirely willing that he do so, thinking only, "Ah, so the twenty years have already gone by!"

What a Western reader might see here as incomprehensible passivity seems, for Toshiko, to be a choice. To the Japanese, Benedict explains, "'voluntary' death in payment of . . . giri . . . achieves an object you yourself desire." As in the ancient samurai code, to choose death is to die honorably and not in vain. Thus Toshiko does not here "feel in the least afraid, and [makes] no effort to free herself."

We cannot, of course, know what will happen to Toshiko in the moments after the story ends—whether or not the man will loosen his grip on her wrist. What we do know is that the psychological imperatives that have brought her alone to the palace grounds have not loosened their grip on her soul. In the "where" of "Swaddling Clothes," the story's final horrifying scene seems both inevitable and conclusive.

But although we, like Toshiko, accede to the cumulative weight of the story's symbols and images, we are left with a sense of ambiguity about their ultimate meaning. In Japanese poetry, for example, cherry blossoms traditionally signify spring, which in turn signifies renewal. Are we then to see what seems likely to be Toshiko's martyrdom in the cherry blossom grove as a symbolic rebirth into earned peace? Toshiko herself first imagines the shape on the bench to be a "pile of cherry blossoms," but clearly it is not. Nor, contrary to her assumption, is it a "garment" carelessly cast aside like the "empty bottles" or "waste paper" that Toshiko has associated with the baby's future life. Is Mishima, then, implying that Toshiko's nemesis is neither an instrument of renewal nor the embodiment of a lost life? Is he merely a disreputable, ordinary "man in a brown jersey," reaching out for Toshiko from the "heavy shadows" to which her beliefs have made her entirely vulnerable?

It is fitting that the last sentence of this story in which general and particular settings are so central to meaning should be a reference to place: "The forest of the Imperial Palace was pitch dark and utterly silent." Perhaps Mishima is suggesting that the traditional value system which seems to have governed Toshiko's behavior has, in postwar Japan, been essentially silenced. There is nothing left to honor Toshiko's martyrdom but mute darkness.

In life, *where* we are—the time, place, and culture we inhabit—influences *who* we are, just as it does fictional characters like Toshiko, or Bambara's Hazel, or Mansfield's Laura. Everything we write, from personal letters to essays to short stories, is indigenous to that particular vantage point from which we see the world. The imagined worlds a writer locates in his or her pages, then, are home not only of the characters who live in them, but also, as with Mishima here, of the writer's unique experience of place. When we, as storytellers, provide "a local habitation" for our fictions, we commit to paper, directly or indirectly, discoveries about the "where" in which we ourselves live; when we, as readers, enter such fictional provinces, our understanding of the times, places, and cultures embodied there is immeasurably expanded.

ABOUT _____

Lynne Sharon Schwartz

Lynne Sharon Schwartz was born in 1939 in New York City, where she lives and where much of her work is set. She was educated at Barnard College, Bryn Mawr College, and New York University and has taught in various writing programs, including the Middlebury, Vermont, Bread Loaf Writers Conference. *Rough Strife* (1980), her first novel, was nominated for an American Book Award; since then she has published two short story collections and two novels, of which *Leaving Brooklyn* was a 1990 nominee for the PEN Faulkner Award for fiction. A selection of her fiction and nonfiction has been collected in *The Lynne Sharon Schwartz Reader*.

What I Did for Love

Lynne Sharon Schwartz

Together with Carl I used to dream of changing the power structure and making the world a better place. Never that I could end up watching the ten o'clock news with a small rodent on my lap.

He was the fourth. Percy, the first, was a bullet-shaped, dark brown guinea pig, short-haired as distinct from the long-haired kind, and from the moment he arrived he tried to hide, making tunnels out of the newspapers in his cage until Martine, who was just eight then, cut the narrow ends off a shoebox and made him a real tunnel, where he stayed except when food appeared. I guess she would have preferred a more sociable pet, but Carl and I couldn't walk a dog four times a day, and the cat we tried chewed at the plants and watched us in bed, which made us self-conscious, and finally got locked in the refrigerator as the magnetic door was closing, so after we found it chilled and traumatized we gave it to a friend who appreciated cats.

Percy had been living his hermit life for about a year when Martine noticed he was hardly eating and being unusually quiet, no rustling of paper in the tunnel. I made an appointment with a vet someone recommended. On the morning of the appointment, after I got Martine on the school bus, I saw Percy lying very still outside the tunnel. I called the vet before I left for work to say I thought his patient might be dead.

"Might be?"

"Well . . . how can I tell for sure?"

He clears his throat and with this patronizing air doctors have, even vets, says, "Why not go and flick your finger near the animal's neck and see if he responds?"

Since I work for a doctor I'm not intimidated by this attitude, it just rolls off me. "Okay, hold on a minute. . . ." I went and flicked. "He doesn't seem to respond, but still . . . I just don't feel sure."

"Raise one of his legs," he says slowly, as if he's talking to a severely retarded person, "wiggle it around and see if it feels stiff." He never heard of denial, this guy. What am I going to tell Martine?

"Hang on. . . ." I wiggled the leg. "It feels stiff," I had to admit.

"I think it's safe to assume," he says, "that the animal is dead."

"I guess we won't be keeping the appointment, then?" I'm not retarded. I said it on purpose, to kind of rile him and see what he'd say.

"That will hardly be necessary."

To get ready for the burial, I put Percy in a shoebox (a new one, not the tunnel one), wrapped the tissue paper from the shoes around him, and added some flowers I bought on the way home from work, then sealed it up with masking tape. Carl and I kept the coffin in our room that night so Martine wouldn't have to be alone in the dark with it. She didn't cry much, at least in front of us. She keeps her feelings to herself, more like me in that way than Carl. But I knew she was very attached to Percy, hermit that he was. The next morning, a Saturday, the three of us set out carrying the box and a spade and shovel we borrowed from the super of the building. Carl's plan was to bury him in the park, but it was the dead of winter, February, and the ground was so frozen the spade could barely break it.

"This isn't going to work," he said.

Martine looked tragic. She's always been a very beautiful child, with a creamy-skinned face and an expression of serene tragic beauty that, depending on the situation, can make you want to laugh or cry. At that moment I could have done either. We were huddled together, our eyes and noses running from the cold, Martine clutching the shoebox in her blue down mittens.

"I know what," Carl said. "We'll bury him at sea."

Martine's face got even more tragic, and I gave him a funny look too. What sea? It was more than an hour's drive to Coney Island and I had a million things to do that day.

"The river. It's a very old and dignified tradition," he told her. "For people who die on ships, when it would take too long to reach land. In a way it's nicer than an earth burial—in the course of time Percy's body will drift to the depths and mingle with coral and anemone instead of being confined in—"

"Okay," she said.

So we walked up to the 125th Street pier on the Hudson River. This is a desolate place just off an exit of the West Side Highway, where the only buildings are meat-processing plants and where in the daytime a few lone people come to wash their cars, hauling water up in buckets, and even to fish, believe it or not, and at night people come to buy and sell drugs. I looked at Martine. She handed me the box like she couldn't bear to do it herself, so I knelt down and placed it in the river as gently as I could. I was hoping it would float for a while, at least till we could get her away, but my romantic Carl was saying something poetic and sentimental about death and it began to sink, about four feet from where we stood. It was headed south, though, towards the Statue of Liberty and the open sea, I pointed out to her. Free at last.

We got her another guinea pig, a chubby buff-colored one who did not hide and was intelligent and interested in its surroundings, as much as a guinea pig can be. We must have had it—Mooney, it was called—for around a year and a half when Carl began talking about changing his life, finding a new direction. He was one of those people—we both were—who had dropped out of school because it seemed there was so much we should be doing in the world. I was afraid he would be drafted, and we had long searching talks, the way you do when you're twenty, about whether he should be a conscientious objector, but at the last minute the army didn't want him because he had flat feet and was partially deaf in one ear. Those same flat feet led all those marches and demonstrations. Anyhow, he never managed to drop back in later on when things changed. Not that there was any less to do, but somehow no way of doing it anymore and hardly anyone left to do it with, not to mention money. You have to take care of your own life, we discovered. And if you have a kid . . . You find yourself doing things you never planned on.

He started driving a cab when Martine was born and had been ever since. It's exhausting, driving a cab. He spent less and less time organizing demonstrations and drawing maps of the locations of nuclear stockpiles. Now he spent his spare time playing ball with the guys he used to go to meetings with, or reading, or puttering with his plants, which after me, he used to say, were his great passion. It was not a terrible life, he was not harming anyone, and as I often told him, driving a cab where you come in contact with people who are going places was more varied than what I do all day as an X-ray technician, which you could hardly call upbeat. Most of the time, you find the patients either have cancer or not, and while you naturally hope for the best each time, you can't help getting to feel less and less, because a certain percentage are always doomed regardless of your feelings. Well, Carl was not satisfied, he was bored, so I said, "Okay, what would you do if you had a totally free choice?"

"I would like to practice the art of topiary."

"What's that?"

"Topiary is the shaping of shrubberies and trees into certain forms. You know, when you drive past rich towns in Westchester, you sometimes see bushes on the lawns trimmed to spell a word or the initials of a corporation? You can make all sorts of shapes—animals, statues. Have you ever seen it?"

"Yes." I was a little surprised by this. You think you know all about a person and then, topiary. "Well, maybe there's someplace you can learn. Take a course in, what is it, landscape gardening?"

"It's not very practical. You said totally free choice. I don't think there could be much of a demand for it in Manhattan."

"We could move."

"Where, Chris?" He smiled, sad and sweet and sexy. That was his kind of appeal. "Beverly Hills?"

"Well, maybe there's something related that you can do. You know those men who drive around in green trucks and get hoisted into the trees in little metal seats? I think they trim branches off the ones with Dutch elm disease. Or a tree surgeon?"

This didn't grab him. We talked about plants and trees, and ambition, and doing something you cared about that also provided a living. Finally he said it was a little embarrassing, but what he really might like, in practical terms, was to have a plant store, a big one, like the ones he browsed in down in the Twenties.

"Why should that be embarrassing?"

"When you first met me I was going to alter the power structure of society and now I'm telling you I want to have a plant store. Are you laughing at me, Chris? Tell the truth."

"I haven't heard you say anything laughable yet. I didn't really expect you to change the world, Carl."

"No?"

"I mean, I believed you meant it, and I believed in you, but that's not why I married you." Lord no. I married him for his touch, it struck me, and the sound of his voice, and a thousand other of those things I thought I couldn't exist without. It also struck me that I had never truly expected to change the power structure but that I had liked hanging out with people who thought they could. It was, I would have to say, inspiring.

"Do you think I'm having a mid-life crisis?"

"No. You're only thirty-three. I think you want to change jobs."

So we decided he should try it. He could start by getting a job in a plant store to learn about it, and drive the cab at night. That way we could save some money for a small store to begin with. He would have less time with me and Martine, but it would be worth it in the long run. Except he didn't do it right away. He liked to sit on things for a while, like a hen.

That summer we scraped together the money to send Martine to a camp run by some people we used to hang out with in the old days, and since it was a camp with animals, sort of a farm camp, she took Mooney along. Her third night away she called collect from Vermont and said she had something very sad to tell us. From her tragic voice, for an instant I thought they might have discovered she had a terminal disease like leukemia, and how could they be so stupid as to tell her—they were progressive types, maybe they thought it was therapeutic to confront your own mortality—but the news was that Mooney was dead. Someone had left the door of the guinea pig's cage open the night before and he got out and was discovered in the morning in a nearby field, most likely mauled by a larger animal. I sounded relieved and not tragic enough, but fortunately Carl had the right tone throughout. At the age of eleven she understood a little about the brutalities of nature and the survival of the fittest and so on, but it was still hard for her to accept.

Martine is a peacefully inclined, intuitive type. She would have felt at home in our day, when peace and love were respectable attitudes. We named her after Martin Luther King, which nowadays seems a far-out thing to have done. Not that my estimation of him has changed or that I don't like the name, only it isn't the sort of thing people do anymore. Just as once we stayed up nights thinking of how to transform the world and now I'm glad I have a job, no matter how boring, and can send her to camp for a few weeks.

Anyway, the people running the camp being the way they were, they immediately bought her a new guinea pig. Aside from her tragedy she had a terrific time, and she came home with a female pig named Elf, who strangely enough looked exactly like Mooney, in fact if I hadn't known Mooney was dead I would have taken Elf for Mooney. I remember remarking to Carl that if things were reversed, if Mooney had been left at home with us and died and we had managed to find an identical bullet-shaped replacement, I might have tried to pass it off as Mooney, in the way mothers instinctively try to protect their children from the harsher facts of life. But Carl said he wouldn't have, he would have told her the truth, not to make her confront harsh reality but because Martine would be able to tell the difference, as mothers can with twins, and he wouldn't want her catching him in a lie. "You know she has such high standards," he said.

In the dead of winter, even colder than in Percy's era, Martine told us Elf wasn't eating. Oh no, I thought. *Déjà vu.* The stillness, then the stiffness, wrapping it in a shoebox, burial at sea . . . Nevertheless, what can you do, so I made an appointment with the vet, the same old arrogant vet—I didn't have the energy to look for a new one. I was feeling sick when the day arrived, so Carl took off from work and went with Martine and Elf.

"There's good news and bad news," he said when they got home. "The good news is that she doesn't have a dread disease. What's wrong with her is her teeth."

I was lying in bed, trying to sleep. "Her teeth?"

"You've got it. Her top and bottom teeth are growing together so she can't eat. She can't separate them to chew." He gave me a demonstration of Elf's problem, stretching his lips and straining his molars.

"Please, this is no time to make me laugh. My stomach is killing me."

"What is it? Your period?"

"No. I don't know what."

"Well, listen—the bad news is that she needs surgery. Oral surgery. It's a hundred twenty-five including the anesthetic."

"This is not the least bit funny. What are we going to do?" Martine was putting Elf back in her cage, otherwise we would have discussed this with more sensitivity.

"Is there a choice? You know how Martine feels—Albert Schweitzer Junior. I made an appointment for tomorrow. She'll have to stay overnight."

"I presume you mean Elf, not Martine."

"Of course I mean Elf. Maybe I should call a doctor for you too."

"No, I'll be okay. What's a stomachache compared to oral surgery?"

"I don't want you getting all worked up over this, Chris." He joined me on the bed and started fooling around. "Thousands of people each year have successful oral surgery. It's nothing to be alarmed about."

"I'll try to deal with it. Ow, you're leaning right where it hurts." Martine came into the room and Carl sat up quickly.

"She's looking very wan," she said.

"Two days from now she'll be a new person," Carl said.

"She's never been a person before. How could she be one in two days?"

"Medical science is amazing."

"I have no luck with guinea pigs." She plopped into a chair, stretched out her legs, and sat gazing at her sneakers. I noticed how tall she was growing. She was nearly twelve and beginning to get breasts. But she wasn't awkward like most girls at that stage; she was stunning, willowy and auburn-haired, with green eyes. There was sometimes a faint emerald light in the whites of her eyes that would take me by surprise, and I would stare and think, What a lucky accident.

"Maybe none of them live long," I said. "I doubt if yours are being singled out."

"They have a four-to-six-year life span. I looked it up in the encyclopedia. But in four years I've gone through almost three."

That night I had such terrible pains in my stomach that Carl took me to the emergency room, where after a lot of fussing around—they tried to send me home, they tried to get me to sleep—they found it was my appendix and it had to come out right away. It was quite a few days before I felt like anything resembling normal, and I forgot completely about Elf's oral surgery.

"Chris, before we go inside, I'd better tell you something." Carl switched off the engine and reached into the back seat for my overnight bag. He was avoiding my eyes.

"What happened? I spoke to her on the phone just last night!" I was about to leap out of the car, but he grabbed my arm.

"Hold it a minute, will you? You're supposed to take it easy."

"Well what's wrong, for Chrissake?"

He looked at me. "Not Martine. Jesus! Elf."

"Elf." I thought I would pass out. I was still pretty drugged.

"She got through the surgery all right. We brought her home the next day. But . . . I don't know whether she was too weak from not eating or what, but she never started eating again. And so . . ."

"I never liked that doctor. How did Martine take it this time?"

"Sad but philosophical. I think she's used to it by now. Besides, she was more concerned about you."

"I'm glad to hear that. So where is the corpse? At sea again?"

"Well, no, actually. That's why I wanted to tell you before you went in the apartment. The temperature has been near zero. The river is frozen."

"Just give it to me straight, Carl."

"She's wrapped in some plastic bags on the bathroom windowsill. Outside. The iron grating is holding her in place. I was going to put her in the freezer with the meat, but I thought you might not care for that."

"Couldn't you find a shoebox?"

"No. I guess nobody's gotten new shoes lately."

"And how long is she going to stay there?"

"They're predicting a thaw. It's supposed to get warm, unseasonably warm, so in a few days we'll take her out to the park. Anyway, welcome home. Oh, there's another thing."

"I hope this is good."

It was. He had found a job working in the greenhouse at the Botanical Garden.

Since Martine never brought the subject up again after the thaw and the park burial, I assumed the guinea pig phase of her life was over. Two weeks after she returned from camp that summer, the super who had loaned us the spade and shovel for Percy came up to say there was a family in the next building with a new guinea pig, but their baby was allergic to it and couldn't stop sneezing. Maybe we wanted to do them a favor and take it off their hands?

Martine and I turned to each other. "What do you think?" I said.

"I'm not sure. They're a lot of expense, aren't they?"

"Not so bad. I mean, what's a little lettuce, carrots . . . "

"The medical expenses. And you don't like them too much, do you, Mom?"

I tried to shrug it off with a blank smile. I looked at Mr. Coates—what I expected I'll never know, since he stood there as if he had seen and heard everything in his lifetime and was content to wait for this discussion to be over. I wondered how much of a tip he would get for the deal. Nothing from us, I vowed.

"I've noticed," Martine said. "You don't like to handle them. You don't like small rodents."

"Not a whole lot, frankly." They looked to me like rats, fat tailless rats. For Martine's sake I had wished them good health and long life, but I tried not to get too close. When she was out with her friends and I had to feed them, I used to toss the lettuce in and step back as they lunged for it. I didn't like the eager squeaks they let out when they smelled the food coming, or the crunching sounds they made eating it. And when I held them—at the beginning, when she would offer them to me to stroke, before she noticed how I felt about small rodents—I didn't like the nervous fluttery softness of them, their darting squirmy little movements, the sniffing and nipping and the beat of the fragile heart so close to the surface I could feel it in my palms. "But they don't bother me so long as they're in the cage in your room." Which was true.

"You could go over and take a look," said Mr. Coates finally. "I'll take you over there if you want."

"Maybe I'll do that, Mom. Do you want to come too?"

"No. I know what guinea pigs look like by now."

"What color is it?" Martine was asking him on the way out.

"I don't know the color. I ain't seen it myself yet."

I didn't pay any more attention to Rusty, named for his color, than I had to the others. I made sure to be in another room while Martine and Carl cut his nails, one holding him down, the other clipping—they took turns. Martine started junior high and got even more beautiful, breasts, hips, the works, with a kind of slow way of turning her head and moving her eyes. She also started expressing intelligent opinions on every subject in the news, test tube babies, airplane hijackings, chemicals in packaged foods, while Carl and I listened and marveled, with this peculiar guilty relief that she was turning out so well—I guess because we were not living out our former ideals, not changing the world or on the other hand being particularly upwardly mobile either. Carl was happier working in the greenhouse, but we still hadn't managed to save enough to rent a store or qualify for a bank loan.

At Martine's thirteenth birthday party in May, we got to talking in the kitchen with one of the mothers who came to pick up her kid. I liked her. She was about our age, small and blonde, and she had dropped out of school too but had gone back to finish and was even doing graduate work.

"What field?" I asked. I was scraping pizza crusts into the garbage while Carl washed out soda cans—he was very big on recycling. In the living room the kids were dancing to a reggae song called "Free Nelson Mandela," and the three of us had been remarking, first of all, that Nelson Mandela had been in prison since we were about their age and in the meantime we had grown up and were raising children and feeling vaguely disappointed with ourselves, and secondly, that dancing to a record like that wouldn't have been our style even if there had been one back then, which was unlikely. Singing was more our style. And the fact that teen-agers today were dancing to this "Free Nelson Mandela" record at parties made their generation seem less serious, yet at this point who were we to judge styles of being serious? The man was still in prison, after all.

"Romance languages," she said. She was playing with the plastic magnetic letters on the refrigerator. They had been there since Martine was two. Sometimes we would use them to write things like Merry Xmas or, as tonight, Happy Birthday, and sometimes to leave real messages, like Skating Back at 7 M. The messages would stay up for the longest time, eroding little by little because we knocked the letters off accidentally and stuck them back any old place, or because we needed a letter for a new message, so that Happy Birthday could come to read Hapy Birda, and at some point they would lose their meaning altogether, like Hay irda, which amused Martine no end. This woman wrote, "Nel mezzo del cammin di nostra vita."

"What does that mean?" Carl asked her.

"'In the middle of the journey of our life.' It's the opening of *The Divine Comedy*. What it means is, here I am thirty-five years old and I'm a graduate student."

"There's nothing wrong with that," said Carl. "I admire your determination. I'm driving a cab, but one day before I die I'm going to learn to do topiary, for the simple reason that I want to."

She said what I knew she would. "What's topiary?"

He stopped rinsing cans to tell her.

I never read *The Divine Comedy*, but I do know Dante goes through Hell and Purgatory and eventually gets to Paradise. All the parts you ever hear about, though, seem to take place in Hell, and so a small shiver ran up my spine, seeing that message on the refrigerator above Happy Birthday. Then I forgot about it.

In bed that night I asked Carl if he was serious about learning topiary. He said he had been thinking it over again. Since he had gotten a raise at the green-house, maybe he might give up the cab altogether, he was so sick of it, and use the money we'd saved for the store to study landscape gardening.

"Well, okay. That sounds good. I can work a half day Saturdays, maybe."

"No, I don't want you to lose the little free time you have. We'll manage. Maybe there's something you want to go back and study too."

"I'm not ambitious. Why, would I be more attractive, like, if I went to grad-uate school?"

"Ha! Did I hear you right?" He let out a comic whoop. "I don't even re-member her name, Chris. Listen, you want me to prove my love?"

That was the last time. The next day he came down with the flu, then Martine and I got it, and just when we were beginning to come back to life he had a heart attack driving the cab. He might have made it, the doctor said, ex-cept he was alone and lost control of the wheel. They told me more details about it, just like a news report, more than I could bear to listen to, in fact. I tried to forget the words the minute I heard them, but no amount of trying could make me stop seeing the scene in my mind. They offered me pills, all through those next insane days, but I wasn't interested in feeling better. Anyhow, what kind of goddamn pill could cure this? I asked them. I also kept seeing in my mind a scene on the Long Island Expressway when Martine was a baby and we were going to Jones Beach. About three cars ahead of us over in the right lane, a car started to veer, and as we got closer we could see the driver slumping down in his seat. Before we could even think what to do, a state trooper appeared out of nowhere and jumped in on the driver's side to grab the wheel. Sirens started up, I guess they took him to the hospital, and a huge pile-up was averted. Watching it, I felt bad about how we used to call cops pigs. That sounds a little simpleminded, I know, but so was calling them pigs. And now I wondered how come a miracle in the form of a cop happened for that person and not for Carl, which is a question a retarded person might ask—I mean, an out-of-the-way street in Queens at eleven at night . . . It happened the way it happened, that's all. A loss to all those who might have enjoyed his topi-ary. I do think he would have done it in his own good time. If only we had had a little more time, I could have taken care of him. I wouldn't have been a mira-cle, but I would have done a good job. The way he vanished, though, I couldn't do a thing, not even say goodbye or hold his hand in the hospital or whatever it is old couples do—maybe the wife whispers that she'll be joining him soon, but I have no illusions that I'll ever be joining him, soon or late. I just got a lot less of him than I expected. Another thing is that the last time we made love I was slightly distracted because of the graduate student he admired for her de-termination, not that anything transpired between them except some ordinary conversation, but it started me wondering in general. Stupid, because I know very well how he felt, he told me every night. Those words I don't forget. I let them put me to sleep. I lie there remembering how it felt with his arms and legs flung over me and can't believe I'm expected to get through decades without ever feeling that again.

So I did end up working half days on Saturdays. In July Martine was supposed to go back to the camp run by the progressives and pacifists, where she had always had such a great time except for her tragedy with Mooney, and I didn't want to begin my life alone by asking for help.

"I don't have to go," she said. "If we don't have the money it's all right. I don't think I even feel like going anymore." My beautiful child with the tragic face. Now she had something worthy of that face.

"You should go, however you feel. When you get there you'll be glad."

"Except there's a slight problem," she said.

"What's that?"

"Rusty. I'm not taking him. Not after what happened to Mooney."

"No," I agreed.

"Which means . . ."

"Oh God! All right, I can do it. How bad can it be? A little lettuce, cabbage, right? A few handfuls of pellets . . ."

"There's the cage to clean too."

"The cage. Okay."

It was hard, her going off on the bus, with the typical scene of cheery mothers and fathers crowding around waving brown lunch bags, but I forced myself through it and so did she. I would force myself through the rest of my life if I had to.

First thing every morning and before I went to bed I put a handful of pellets in Rusty's bowl and fresh water in his bottle, and when I left for work and came home I dropped a few leaves of something green into the cage. Since I never really looked at him I was shocked, the fourth night after Martine left, when Mr. Coates, who had come up to fix the window lock in her room, said in his usual unexcited way, "Your pig's eye's popping out."

The right eye was protruding half an inch out of the socket and the cylindrical part behind it was yellow with gummy pus, a disgusting sight. "Jesus F. Christ," I said.

"He won't be no help to you. You need a vet."

The thought of going back to that arrogant vet who I always suspected had screwed up with Elf was more than I could take, so I searched the yellow pages till I found a woman vet in the neighborhood. When I walked in the next day carrying Rusty in a carton, I knew I had lucked out. She had curly hair like a mop, she wore jeans and a white sweatshirt, and she seemed young, maybe twenty-nine or thirty. Her name was Doctor Dunn. Very good, Doctor Dunn, so there won't be all that other shit to cope with.

To get him on the examining table I had to lift him up by his middle and feel all the squirminess and the beat of the scared delicate heart between my palms.

"It looks like either a growth of some kind pushing it forward, or maybe an abscess. But in either case I'm afraid the eye will have to go. It's badly infected and unless it's removed it'll dry up and the infection will spread and . . . uh . . ."

"He'll die?"

"Right."

Seventy-five dollars, she said, including his overnight stay, plus twenty-five for the biopsy. Terrific, I thought, just what I need. It was lower than the other vet's rates, though.

"I want to explain something about the surgery. He's a very small animal, two pounds or so, and any prolonged anesthesia is going to be risky. What this means is, I can't make any guarantees. I'd say his chances are . . . seventy-thirty, depending on his general condition. Of course, we'll do everything we can. . . ."

"And if I don't do it he'll die anyhow?"

"Right."

Squirming there on the table was this orange rat whose fate I was deciding. I felt very out of sync with reality, as if I was in a science fiction movie and how did I ever arrive at this place. "Okay. I guess we'd better do it."

The receptionist I left him with told me to call around four the next day to see how he came through the surgery. *If* was what she meant. That evening out of habit I almost went in to toss him some celery, then I remembered the cage was empty. There was no reason to go into Martine's room. But I decided to take the opportunity to clean the cage and the room both. I had found that the more I moved around the more numb I felt, which was what I wanted.

On the dot of four, I called from work. Doctor Dunn answered herself.

"He's fine! What a trouper, that Rusty! We had him hooked up to the EKG the whole time and monitored him, and he was terrific. I'm really pleased."

"Thank you," I managed to say. "Thank you very much." In one day she had established a closer relationship with him than I had in a year. That was an interesting thought. I mean, it didn't make me feel emotionally inadequate; I simply realized that's why she went through years of veterinary school, because she really cared, the way Carl could have about topiary, I guess.

"Can you come in and pick him up before seven? Then I can tell you about the post-op care."

Post-op care? I had never thought of that. I had never even thought of how the eye would look. Would it be a hole, or just a blank patch of fur? Would there be a bandage on it, or maybe she could fix him up with a special little eye patch?

I found Rusty in his carton on the front desk, with the receptionist petting him and calling him a good boy. "We're all crazy about him," she said. "He's quite a fella, aren't you, Rusty-baby?"

Where his right eye used to be, there was a row of five black stitches, and the area around it was shaved. Below the bottom stitch, a plastic tube the diameter of a straw and about an inch long stuck out. That was a drain for the wound, Doctor Dunn explained. He had a black plastic collar around his neck that looked like a ruff, the kind you see in old portraits of royalty. To keep him from poking himself, she said.

"Was he in good condition otherwise?" I thought I should sound concerned, in this world of animal-lovers.

"Oh, fine. Now . . . The post-operative care is a little complicated, so I wrote it down." She handed me a list of instructions:

1. Cold compresses tonight, 5–10 minutes.
2. Oral antibiotics, 3× a day for at least 7 days.
3. Keep collar on at all times.
4. Feed as usual.
5. Call if any excessive redness, swelling, or discharge develops.
6. Come in 3–4 days from now to have drain pulled.
7. Call early next week for biopsy results.
8. Make appointment for suture removal, 10–14 days.
9. Starting tomorrow, apply warm compresses 5–10 minutes, 2× a day for 10 days.

"Here's a sample bottle of antibiotics. Maybe I'd better do the first dose to show you how." She held him to her chest with one hand, while with the other she nudged his mouth open using the medicine dropper and squeezed the drops in, murmuring, "Come on now, that's a good boy, there you go." As she wiped the drips off his face and her sweatshirt with a tissue, I thought, Never. This is not happening to me. But I knew it was, and that I would have to go through with it.

When I went to get some ice water for the cold compress that night, I saw the message the graduate student mother had left on the refrigerator near Happy Birthday, which was now Happ Brhday. "Ne mezz I camn di nstr vita," it read. I knew some letters were missing though not which ones, and those that were left were crooked, but I remembered well enough what it meant. I sat down to watch the ten o'clock news with Rusty on my lap and put the compress on his eye, or the place where his eye used to be, but he squirmed around wildly, clawing at my pants. Ice water oozed onto my legs. I told him to cut it out, he had no choice. Finally I tried patting him and talking to him like a baby, to quiet him. Don't worry, kiddo, you're going to be all right—stuff like that, the way Carl would have done without feeling idiotic. It worked. Only hearing those words loosened me a little out of my numbness and I had this terrible sensation of walking a tightrope in pitch darkness, though in fact I was whispering sweet nothings to a guinea pig. I even thought of telling him what I'd been through with my appendix, a fellow sufferer, and God knows what next, but I controlled myself. If I freaked out, who would take care of Martine?

I figured seven and a half minutes for the compress was fair enough—Doctor Dunn had written down 5–10. Then I changed my mind and held it there for another minute so if anything happened I would have a clear conscience when I told Martine. I held him to my chest with a towel over my shirt, feeling the heart pulsing against me, and squirted in the antibiotic. I lost a good bit, but I'd have plenty of chances to improve.

In the morning I found the collar lying in the mess of shit and cedar chips in his cage. I washed it and tried to get it back on him, but he fought back with his whole body—each time I fitted it around his neck he managed to squirm and jerk his way out, till beyond being repelled I was practically weeping with frustration. Two people could have done it easily. Carl, I thought, if ever I needed you . . . Finally after a great struggle I got it fastened in back with masking tape so he wouldn't undo it. But when I came home from work it was off again and we wrestled again. The next morning I rebelled. The drops, the compresses, okay, but there was no way I was going to literally collar a rodent morning and night for ten days. There are limits to everything, especially on a tightrope in the dark. I called Doctor Dunn from work.

"Is he poking himself around the eye?" she asked. "Any bleeding or discharge? Good. Then forget it. You can throw the collar away."

I was so relieved.

"How is he otherwise? Is he eating?"

"Yes. He seems okay. Except he's shedding." I told her how when I lifted him up, orange hairs fluttered down into his cage like leaves from a tree. When leaves fell off Carl's plants, which I was also trying to keep alive though that project wasn't as dramatic, it usually meant they were on their way out. I had already lost three—I didn't have his green thumb. It seemed my life had become one huge effort to keep things alive, with death hot on my trail. I even had nightmares about what could be happening to Martine at camp. When I wrote to her, though, I tried to sound casual, as if I was fine, and I wrote that Rusty was fine too. Maybe Carl would have given her all the gory details, but I didn't mind lying. He was going to be fine. I was determined that pig would live even if it was over my dead body. Luckily I wasn't so far gone as to say all this to Doctor Dunn. "Is that a bad sign?"

"Shedding doesn't mean anything," she said. "He doesn't feel well, so he's not grooming himself as usual. It'll stop as he gets better."

I also noticed, those first few days, he would do this weird dance when I put the food in his cage. It dawned on me that he could smell it but not see it. While he scurried around in circles, I kept trying to shove it towards his good side—kind of a Bugs Bunny routine. Then after a while he developed a funny motion, turning his head to spot it, and soon he was finding it pretty well with his one eye. I told Doctor Dunn when I brought him in to have the drain removed. She said yes, they adapt quickly. They compensate. She talked about evolution and why eyes were located where they were. Predators, she said, have close-set eyes in the front of their heads to see the prey, and the prey have eyes at the sides, to watch out for the predators. How clever, I thought, the way nature matched up the teams. You couldn't change your destiny, but you had certain traits that kept the game going and gave you the illusion of having a fighting chance. We talked about it for a good while. She was interesting, that Doctor Dunn.

A few days later she plucked out the stitches with tweezers while I held him down.

"I have to tell you," she said, "not many people would take such pains with a guinea pig. Some people don't even bother with dogs and cats, you'd be amazed. They'd rather have them put away. You did a terrific job. You must really love animals."

I didn't have the heart to tell her that although it didn't turn my stomach anymore to hold him on my lap and stroke him for the compresses, he was still just a fat rat as far as I was concerned, but a fat rat which fate had arranged I had to keep alive. So I did.

"Well, you could say I did it for love."

She laughed. "Keep applying the warm compresses for another day or two, to be on the safe side. Then that's it. Case closed."

"What about the biopsy?"

"Oh yes, the lab report. It's not in yet, but I have a feeling it wasn't malignant. He doesn't look sick to me. Call me on it next week."

In eleven days Martine will be back. Beautiful Martine, with her suntan making her almost the color of Rusty. I'll warn her about the eye before she sees him. It doesn't look too gruesome now, with the stitches out and the hair growing back—soon it'll be a smooth blank space. In fact, if not for the missing eye she would never have to know what he went through. The house will feel strange to her all over again without Carl, because whenever you're away for a while you expect to come home to some pure and perfect condition. She'll be daydreaming on the bus that maybe it was all a nightmare and the both of us are here waiting for her. But it'll be an altogether different life, and the worst thing is—knowing us, sensible, adaptable types—that one remote day we'll wake up and it'll seem normal this way, and in years to come Carl will turn into the man I had in my youth instead of what he is now, my life. I even envy her— he'll always be her one father.

So I'm applying the warm compresses for the last time, sitting here with a one-eyed guinea pig who is going to live out his four-to-six-year life span no matter what it takes, in the middle of the journey of my life, stroking him as if I really loved animals.

The Uses of Time in Lynne Sharon Schwartz's "What I Did for Love"

Ghita Orth

As unlikely as it might first appear, all the stories in this book have one character in common—time, an often unacknowledged though seldom invisible presence in any fiction. Like the other characters in a story, time is a significant participant in the action, whether events occur over a period of hours, as in "My Man Bovanne"; days, as in "So Much Water So Close to Home"; or years, as in "The Third Bank of the River." And just as writers concern themselves with the development and presentation of the *people* who move through their stories, they consider the uses of time and the ways it can be made to move.

In life, of course, events always follow one another in neat chronological sequence—the alarm rings, you get up, dress, eat breakfast, and begin the first activity of your day. Even if you eat breakfast before you get dressed, you are following a clearly ongoing series of actions. Fiction writers can move stories forward in the same way, by recounting events in their chronological progression.

In fiction as in life, however, time is usually not so neatly contained in a direct forward march. Even though we move ahead in present time, that isn't the *only* time that affects our behavior. As you get dressed, you may remember what you wore yesterday and decide on a different sweater today; as you eat breakfast you may look forward to a pepperoni pizza at lunch and decide to go easy on the pancakes.

So too, even when a fiction writer chooses to present plot events in strict chronological order, characters' memories of the past and projections into the future often complicate and enrich the ongoing forward motion of events. In Mishima's "Swaddling Clothes," for example, Toshiko's thoughts of past and future during her taxi ride and visit to the Imperial Gardens resonate through the story's present time and affect her actions in it.

And present time usually passes more quickly in fiction than in life. We don't need to follow characters through every moment of their day in order to move with them through a story's consequential events, and choosing to depict only those events which are *of* consequence, the ones that "count" in developing character or delineating plot, can leave writers with time on their hands. Thus, the various devices that signal the passage of unnarrated, because irrelevant, time in a story.

You might choose a time-marking phrase to get a character past potentially insignificant actions like pouring milk on the Rice Krispies, or to move her past dead time to the story's next important event—"after breakfast," or "a week later." You can even indicate the passage of time with *visual* markers—a row of asterisks, or a blank line.

Joyce makes use of this last device in "Eveline," where the extra space near the end makes clear that time has elapsed and the story has moved on to its next scene. "Eveline" also demonstrates the importance of deciding *when* to begin a chronological narration. Instead of beginning his depiction of Eveline's conflict at its actual beginning—perhaps with scenes of her first meeting with Frank or, even earlier, of her mother's illness and death—Joyce opens the narrative *in medias res.*

That Latin phrase, meaning "in the middle of things," describes a use of time that can help to intensify a story's focus. By beginning "Eveline" at a moment close to its critical climax, Joyce captures the reader's attention immediately. As we've said, information about relevant prior events can be brought into a story through a character's thoughts, and starting the chronological presentation of events in the thick of things, close to the narration's crucial fulcrum, can heighten its dramatic tension.

Fictional time, then, unlike real time, can be manipulated. In fact, a story's sequence of events need not be presented chronologically at all. The action of Huddle's "Little Sawtooth," for example, opens in the present, reverts to past scenes in a lengthy flashback which in itself doesn't proceed chronologically, and then returns to the narrator's present life. This time frame is further complicated by the fact that "Little Sawtooth" is a story within a story—time passes in the life of the narrator rather differently than it does in the life of the character whose story he is presenting. As fictional characters are rich and various, then, so are the fictional uses of time.

In Lynne Sharon Schwartz's "What I Did for Love," time—the passage of years—is almost literally a central character, and Schwartz's manipulation of chronology in the storytelling serves to enrich and emphasize her thematic concerns. The events in the plot are presented in a series of flashbacks—not memories but actual scenes of prior occurrences—that cover the six years before the time at which the story begins and ends. The most crucial event of those years is clearly Carl's death—shouldn't the story have begun *in medias res* near this climactic moment to emphasize its centrality? Or is it possibly *not* central—of little more significance than the deaths of Percy, Mooney, or Elf, with which it forms a chain of losses? And if that were the case, why not just tell the story chronologically, beginning with guinea pig No. 1 and moving on from there?

That Schwartz has chosen a retrospective approach in which all of the story's "action" occurs in the narrator's past, however, suggests that the focus of her attention is on time itself and the incremental effects of its passage; as Chris says later, "If only we had had a little more time." But she and Carl did not, and the way his sudden death is immersed without prior reference into the narration shockingly reminds us that time sweeps all before it as it all too quickly turns present into past.

The opening paragraph of "What I Did for Love" sets up its framing situation; Chris is tending Rusty when the story begins just as when it ends. Yet in this present moment she refers immediately to the shrinking of earlier dreams, and the ten o'clock news turns the day's events into history. Time past has made its appearance even before Chris's re-creation of it begins.

The intruding presence of "then" in the story's "now," however, may paradoxically be the means by which Chris can move her life and Martine's, as well as Rusty's, onward. As T. S. Eliot suggests in "Burnt Norton," "Time present and time past / Are both perhaps present in time future / And time future contained in time past." It is the nature of this containment that Schwartz investigates in "What I Did for Love."

Eliot also wrote that his J. Alfred Prufrock "measured out [his] life in coffee spoons." Here, Chris seems to measure out her life in guinea pigs; for her their presences are markers of the passing of time, and their accelerated, untimely dyings are as unnerving as they are comic. The story is thus organized into structural units relating to her daughter's sequence of pets, beginning with Percy, the furthest in the past.

Chris's wry evocation of Percy's life and death introduces a number of themes that will play themselves out through the tenures of succeeding guinea pigs. Martine, the eight-year-old child with "an expression of serene tragic beauty," will become an adolescent who finally, in her father's death, has "something worthy of that face." Chris, whose protection of Martine leads her to keep dead Percy's "coffin" in her bedroom and then consign it to the river because Martine "couldn't bear to do it herself," will be committed to the even more bizarre task of performing complex medical procedures to keep a "fat rat" alive for her daughter's sake. And in the process, the woman who here admits that she, unlike Carl, keeps her feelings to herself will in his terrible absence be "whispering sweet nothings to a guinea pig" and find that "hearing those words loosened [her] a little out of [her] numbness."

Time thus changes this family while the guinea pigs come and go, just as times themselves change. Chris's "Free at last" as Percy's shoebox heads to the open sea ironically invokes an outdated liberal oratory—"teen-agers today were dancing to this 'Free Nelson Mandela' record at parties," and practicing a new "[style] of being serious." Because the past they grew up in no longer exists, Chris and Carl are trying to find some way to move beyond it—to move *with* time. This process is anticipated here by Carl's homage to mutability as he promises Martine that "in the course of time Percy's body will drift to the depths and mingle with coral and anemone."

Percy's sea change prefigures the alterations that time exacts on Schwartz's characters as their story progresses toward the present. For example, a year and a half into the "era" of Mooney, guinea pig No. 2, Carl "began talking about changing his life, finding a new direction." The story's retrospective time frame now reaches back into the even more distant past as Chris explains who she and Carl were, or thought they were, thirteen years earlier. Acknowledging how the attrition of the years has turned sixties philosophical dropouts into a cab driver and an X-ray technician, Chris recognizes that it was "[n]ot that there was any less to do, but somehow no way of doing it anymore."

Carl's aborted dreams of changing the world thus now find belated expression in his ambition to own a plant store and "practice the art of topiary." His old impetus to "alter the power structure of society" is transmuted into a desire to shape "shrubberies and trees into certain forms." Like Carl, Chris finds herself having to modify an earlier idealism; in her job she "can't help getting to feel less and less," for she has come to learn that feelings can't save the lives of her patients, much less the world. Unlike Carl, however, she has not yet found any substitute for her lost idealistic commitments. In Mooney's section of the story, then, we see Chris and Carl coping with time's reductive effects; their present is not the future they had envisioned, the past has not been prologue.

In Martine, however, their earlier selves live on—even her name is anachronistic, since calling children after political idols "isn't the sort of thing people do anymore." As Chris points out, Martine "would have felt at home in our day, when peace and love were respectable attitudes." Instead, all three of them need to find ways of feeling at home in a new era. When Mooney dies and is immediately replaced by the seemingly identical Elf, that process continues.

In the time period defined for Chris by Elf's arrival and departure, Carl finds work in a greenhouse and Martine continues to grow toward womanhood. "[N]early twelve and beginning to get breasts," she is also growing beyond her mother's ability to "protect [her] from the harsher facts of life," as embodied by the lengthening chain of dead pets. Having gone through "almost three" guinea pigs in four years despite their documented life spans, Martine must confront the cost of time's accelerating passage.

The guinea pigs go too quickly, like time itself; Chris's sense of *"déjà vu"* when Elf sickens may be predicated as much on her own previous experience of time's headlong rush and her inability to control it as on her prior dealings with dying "rodents." That Schwartz has constructed this brief segment of the story with a beginning (Elf's summer arrival) and end (her death in "the dead of winter"), while skipping over the intervening months of her presence with the family, further emphasizes her, and time's, speedy progress through their lives.

The longest section of "What I Did for Love" encompasses the reign of Rusty, Martine's fourth pet, who survives into the story's present. Here Schwartz confronts most fully the story's central concerns and clarifies Rusty's emblematic role in them. "The guinea pig phase" of Martine's life, and of Chris's, is not yet over after all.

Rusty is in residence at the time of Martine's thirteenth birthday. Marking as it does the traditional advent of adulthood, the occasion is also a marker for Chris; even as the passing years are making her daughter "more beautiful" and more able to express "intelligent opinions" about her world, she and Carl are still "not living out [their] former ideals . . . or . . . being particularly upwardly mobile either." Martine's evolution into a caring young woman affords them a "peculiar guilty relief" in relation to their own inability to move substantially forward in their lives as time advances.

Chris is pointedly reminded that she is, in fact, already "[i]n the middle of the journey of [her] life" when the mother of one of Martine's friends uses magnetic letters to spell out Dante's phrase on the refrigerator. It is not only what the message says that points to Chris's stasis and makes her uneasy, it is also who put it there—a woman of about her age who "had dropped out of school too but had gone back to finish and was even doing graduate work," to Carl's admiration. Perhaps one need not be passively victimized by time as the phrase itself will be—like Chris's earlier ambitions, the words will "erod[e] little by little" as letters are knocked off or reused until "at some point they [will] lose their meaning altogether." The phrase on Chris's refrigerator is thus the concrete embodiment of the concern with time and change that has informed the story thus far.

Carl's unexpected sudden death comes upon the reader with the same shock it came to Chris: "That was the last time," Chris says, referring to their lovemaking the night of Martine's party.

We always know when we are experiencing something for the first time, but we usually cannot know until after a last experience that it will never come again. Like Chris, then, the reader does not pay significant attention to the lovemaking while it is happening; its import is clear only after the fact, when the poignant recognition of its finality shakes us as it does her. Schwartz thus emphasizes the capriciousness of life and death; Carl's dying "happened the way it happened, that's all," and his sudden vanishing serves as a reminder that we have little time to spare or leave unconsidered. Carl might have done his topiary and many other things "in his own good time," but is time ever really our own, to manage at will?

For Chris, then, Carl's death initiates a reconsideration of how to live *in* time. The past has deserted her, and the future does not promise any spiritual reunion. Instead, Chris says, "I lie there remembering how it felt with his arms and legs flung over me and can't believe I'm expected to get through decades without ever feeling that again." Once more, rather than allowing her to move forward, her memories of the past seem to negate her future.

At first, Chris's temporary adoption of Rusty appears only an attempt to preserve some kind of familiar continuity in Martine's life. Her responsibilities to her daughter, however, lead to a responsibility for Rusty that in turn requires her to be vulnerable in ways she had renounced. Whereas Chris had previously "tried not to get too close" to the guinea pigs, fearing "the beat of the fragile heart so close to the surface," in Rusty's illness she must touch him, actually feel "the beat of the scared delicate heart between [her] palms."

Directly confronting the ongoing pulse of life in the guinea pig, Chris acknowledges her own prior detachment from it. When she notes how quickly and easily the woman vet has "established a . . . relationship" with Rusty, she does not feel "emotionally inadequate" but "simply realize[s] . . . [the vet] really cared, the way Carl could have about topiary, I guess." In Carl's absence, then, Chris' ability to "really care" is tested—single-handedly she will tend his plants and prevent Rusty from dying; as she explains, "It seemed my life had become one huge effort to keep things alive, with death hot on my trail."

All the specific duties that effort will require for Rusty, as listed by the vet, entail a heightened attention to time—in minutes, hours, days, or weeks. Whether calculating the length of compress applications, remembering feeding and medication schedules, or noting phone calls and appointments to be made at future dates, Chris is caught up in an ongoing temporal process.

The symbolic weight of this process is also emphasized by the amount of "story time" Schwartz allocates to it. Whereas Carl's death was recounted in only one long paragraph, Chris's efforts to keep death *from* Rusty take up more than six pages of the narrative. By devoting this much time/space to Rusty's illness, Schwartz points our serious attention to what might otherwise seem a minor matter. Chris's taking care of Rusty is thus clearly the story's focal activity. "The way [Carl] vanished . . . [she] couldn't do a thing." Here is something that, over time, she *can* do.

In her active commitment to keep Rusty alive, Chris is, in effect, finally fighting the entropic effect of time that has claimed Carl and her past, as well as the previous guinea pigs. Though the Dante phrase on the refrigerator has become altered and garbled over the months, Chris "remembered well enough what it meant." Taking responsibility for Rusty's life, Chris seems to be taking control of her own, fighting the pull toward stasis, and investing in a future for Martine and herself.

The two concluding paragraphs of "What I Did for Love" return the narration to the immediate present, and Chris can now concede the possibilities of that future. The place where Rusty's eye had been will soon "be a smooth blank space," much like the different life she and Martine will move into. Schwartz does not here suggest this future will necessarily be a happy one but emphasizes Chris's acceptance of the interrelationship of past, present, and future and the necessity of moving with time from one to the other. As Chris acknowledges, "in years to come Carl will turn into the man I had in my youth instead of what he is now, my life." Rather than thinking of her future as a black hole, Chris can now see it as containing, in Eliot's words, "time present and time past."

Although Chris is actually stroking Rusty in the final scene of "What I Did for Love" and may look "as if [she] really loved animals," her language makes clear that "what [she] did" was not "for love" of the guinea pig. Clearly love of Martine is a motivating factor in her heroic efforts to ensure Rusty's full life span, as is love of Carl, but also, perhaps, Chris has done it for herself—to garner meaning for "the middle of the journey of [her] life" with a determination Carl would have admired. As she once had in the past, in the story's present Chris has again found the value of "doing something you cared about" as she safely delivers Rusty into Martine's future and her own.

The issues that "What I Did for Love" encompasses are thus large, and largely serious, yet the story's tone is wryly comic. As writers, we need not feel that a natural, colloquial voice can't speak to "big" concerns; in fact, the lively style of "What I Did for Love" goes a long way toward keeping it from seeming lugubrious or sentimental. Too, rather than undermining Schwartz's seriousness of purpose, the narrative's comic tone further emphasizes its central focus—as Chris explains, "You couldn't change your destiny, but you had certain traits that kept the game going and gave you the illusion of having a fighting chance." Chris's observant eye and ironic wit seem to be the traits that help ensure her survival; the "illusion of having a fighting chance" in our dealings with time may be all we can hope for.

Just as Chris learns something about the uses of real time through the events in her life, our attention to Schwartz's uses of fictional time in this story can suggest possibilities for our own work. The word "time" itself, in all its various guises, echoes and resonates through the story, emphasizing its importance here. So too, the passing parade of guinea pigs. While most of us don't keep track of time by counting up "small rodents," we do tend to have personal markers for passing years—another birthday, another ski season, another batch of new textbooks; we see here how evocations of such recurrent milestones in a character's personal calendar can become guideposts to a story's progression in time.

Although Chris's guinea pigs are an idiosyncratic reference point, they acquire a wider significance in the story through Schwartz's use of detailed and accurate particulars about them. This writer *knows* guinea pigs, through research or experience; the authority we hear in Chris's description of them lends weight to their emblematic presence in the story. The reader comes to take the animals, and their import, as seriously as Chris does—their dying begins to mean something to us.

In addition to accruing symbolic weight through their specificity, the guinea pigs are allotted significant space in the storytelling itself. So much narrating time, as well as attention, is given over to Rusty's illness that we feel its thematic importance even before we closely consider what that importance might be. Using the elasticity of time possible in fiction, Schwartz thus structures her readers' responses to characters and events. As we participate in the carefully wrought retrospective chronology of "What I Did for Love," we can find suggestions for our own fictions and, like Chris about to take on Rusty, say, "All right, I can do it. How bad can it be?"

Katherine Mansfield

Katherine Mansfield was born in New Zealand in 1888, later settled in England, and died in France in 1923. Many of her short stories are set in New Zealand and reflect her childhood experiences and social concerns. Her best-known collections are *Bliss* (1920), *The Garden Party* (1922), and *The Dove's Nest* (1923). Mansfield's *Collected Stories* appeared in 1945, and volumes of her letters and her journal have also been published in the years since her death.

The Garden Party

Katherine Mansfield

And after all the weather was ideal. They could not have had a more perfect day for a garden-party if they had ordered it. Windless, warm, the sky without a cloud. Only the blue was veiled with a haze of light gold, as it is sometimes in early summer. The gardener had been up since dawn, mowing the lawns and sweeping them, until the grass and the dark flat rosettes where the daisy plants had been seemed to shine. As for the roses, you could not help feeling they understood that roses are the only flowers that impress people at garden-parties; the only flowers that everybody is certain of knowing. Hundreds, yes, literally hundreds, had come out in a single night; the green bushes bowed down as though they had been visited by archangels.

Breakfast was not yet over before the men came to put up the marquee.

"Where do you want the marquee put, mother?"

"My dear child, it's no use asking me. I'm determined to leave everything to you children this year. Forget I am your mother. Treat me as an honored guest."

But Meg could not possibly go and supervise the men. She had washed her hair before breakfast, and she sat drinking her coffee in a green turban, with a dark wet curl stamped on each cheek. Jose, the butterfly, always came down in a silk petticoat and kimono jacket.

"You'll have to go, Laura; you're the artistic one."

Away Laura flew, still holding her piece of bread-and-butter. It's so delicious to have an excuse for eating out of doors, and besides, she loved having to arrange things; she always felt she could do it so much better than anybody else.

Four men in their shirt-sleeves stood grouped together on the garden path.

175

They carried staves covered with rolls of canvas, and they had big tool-bags slung on their backs. They looked impressive. Laura wished now that she had not got the bread-and-butter, but there was nowhere to put it, and she couldn't possibly throw it away. She blushed and tried to look severe and even a little bit short-sighted as she came up to them.

"Good morning," she said, copying her mother's voice. But that sounded so fearfully affected that she was ashamed, and stammered like a little girl, "Oh —er—have you come—is it about the marquee?"

"That's right, miss," said the tallest of the men, a lanky, freckled fellow, and he shifted his tool-bag, knocked back his straw hat and smiled down at her. "That's about it."

His smile was so easy, so friendly that Laura recovered. What nice eyes he had, small, but such a dark blue! And now she looked at the others, they were smiling too. "Cheer up, we won't bite," their smile seemed to say. How very nice workmen were! And what a beautiful morning! She mustn't mention the morning; she must be businesslike. The marquee.

"Well, what about the lily-lawn? Would that do?"

And she pointed to the lily-lawn with the hand that didn't hold the bread-and-butter. They turned, they stared in the direction. A little fat chap thrust out his under-lip, and the tall fellow frowned.

"I don't fancy it," said he. "Not conspicuous enough. You see, with a thing like a marquee," and he turned to Laura in his easy way, "you want to put it somewhere where it'll give you a bang slap in the eye, if you follow me."

Laura's upbringing made her wonder for a moment whether it was quite respectful of a workman to talk to her of bangs slap in the eye. But she did quite follow him.

"A corner of the tennis-court," she suggested. "But the band's going to be in one corner."

"H'm, going to have a band, are you?" said another of the workmen. He was pale. He had a haggard look as his dark eyes scanned the tennis-court. What was he thinking?

"Only a very small band," said Laura gently. Perhaps he wouldn't mind so much if the band was quite small. But the tall fellow interrupted.

"Look here, miss, that's the place. Against those trees. Over there. That'll do fine."

Against the karakas. Then the karaka-trees would be hidden. And they were so lovely, with their broad, gleaming leaves, and their clusters of yellow fruit. They were like trees you imagined growing on a desert island, proud, solitary, lifting their leaves and fruits to the sun in a kind of silent splendor. Must they be hidden by a marquee?

They must. Already the men had shouldered their staves and were making for the place. Only the tall fellow was left. He bent down, pinched a sprig of lavender, put his thumb and forefinger to his nose and snuffed up the smell. When Laura saw that gesture she forgot all about the karakas in her wonder at him caring for things like that—caring for the smell of lavender. How many men that she knew would have done such a thing? Oh, how extraordinarily nice workmen were, she thought. Why couldn't she have workmen for friends rather than the silly boys she danced with and who came to Sunday night supper? She would get on much better with men like these.

It's all the fault, she decided, as the tall fellow drew something on the back of an envelope, something that was to be looped up or left to hang, of these absurd class distinctions. Well, for her part, she didn't feel them. Not a bit, not an atom. . . . And now there came the chock-chock of wooden hammers. Some one whistled, some one sang out, "Are you right there, matey?" "Matey!" The friendliness of it, the—the— Just to prove how happy she was, just to show the tall fellow how at home she felt, and how she despised stupid conventions, Laura took a big bite of her bread-and-butter as she stared at the little drawing. She felt just like a work-girl.

"Laura, Laura, where are you? Telephone, Laura!" a voice cried from the house.

"Coming!" Away she skimmed, over the lawn, up the path, up the steps, across the veranda, and into the porch. In the hall her father and Laurie were brushing their hats ready to go to the office.

"I say, Laura," said Laurie very fast, "you might just give a squiz at my coat before this afternoon. See if it wants pressing."

"I will," said she. Suddenly she couldn't stop herself. She ran at Laurie and gave him a small, quick squeeze. "Oh, I do love parties, don't you?" gasped Laura.

"Ra-ther," said Laurie's warm, boyish voice, and he squeezed his sister too, and gave her a gentle push. "Dash off to the telephone, old girl."

The telephone. "Yes, yes; oh yes. Kitty? Good morning, dear. Come to lunch? Do, dear. Delighted of course. It will only be a very scratch meal—just the sandwich crusts and broken meringue-shells and what's left over. Yes, isn't it a perfect morning? Your white? Oh, I certainly should. One moment—hold the line. Mother's calling." And Laura sat back. "What, mother? Can't hear."

Mrs. Sheridan's voice floated down the stairs. "Tell her to wear that sweet hat she had on last Sunday."

"Mother says you're to wear that *sweet* hat you had on last Sunday. Good. One o'clock. Bye-bye."

Laura put back the receiver, flung her arms over her head, took a deep breath, stretched and let them fall. "Huh," she sighed, and the moment after the sigh she sat up quickly. She was still, listening. All the doors in the house seemed to be open. The house was alive with soft, quick steps and running voices. The green baize door that led to the kitchen regions swung open and shut with a muffled thud. And now there came a long, chuckling absurd sound. It was the heavy piano being moved on its stiff castors. But the air! If you stopped to notice, was the air always like this? Little faint winds were playing chase, in at the tops of the windows, out at the doors. And there were two tiny spots of sun, one on the inkpot, one on a silver photograph frame, playing too. Darling little spots. Especially the one on the inkpot lid. It was quite warm. A warm little silver star. She could have kissed it.

The front door bell pealed, and there sounded the rustle of Sadie's print skirt on the stairs. A man's voice murmured; Sadie answered, careless, "I'm sure I don't know. Wait. I'll ask Mrs. Sheridan."

"What is it, Sadie?" Laura came into the hall.

"It's the florist, Miss Laura."

It was, indeed. There, just inside the door, stood a wide, shallow tray full of pots of pink lilies. No other kind. Nothing but lilies—canna lilies, big pink flowers, wide open, radiant, almost frighteningly alive on bright crimson stems.

"O-oh, Sadie!" said Laura, and the sound was like a little moan. She crouched down as if to warm herself at that blaze of lilies; she felt they were in her fingers, on her lips, growing in her breast.

"It's some mistake," she said faintly. "Nobody ever ordered so many. Sadie, go and find mother."

But at that moment Mrs. Sheridan joined them.

"It's quite right," she said calmly. "Yes, I ordered them. Aren't they lovely?" She pressed Laura's arm. "I was passing the shop yesterday, and I saw them in the window. And I suddenly thought for once in my life I shall have enough canna lilies. The garden-party will be a good excuse."

"But I thought you said you didn't mean to interfere," said Laura. Sadie had gone. The florist's man was still outside at his van. She put her arm round her mother's neck and gently, very gently, she bit her mother's ear.

"My darling child, you wouldn't like a logical mother, would you? Don't do that. Here's the man."

He carried more lilies still, another whole tray.

"Bank them up, just inside the door, on both sides of the porch, please," said Mrs. Sheridan. "Don't you agree, Laura?"

"Oh, I *do*, mother."

In the drawing-room Meg, Jose and good little Hans had at last succeeded in moving the piano.

"Now, if we put this chesterfield against the wall and move everything out of the room except the chairs, don't you think?"

"Quite."

"Hans, move these tables into the smoking-room, and bring a sweeper to take these marks off the carpet and—one moment, Hans—" Jose loved giving orders to the servants, and they loved obeying her. She always made them feel they were taking part in some drama. "Tell mother and Miss Laura to come here at once."

"Very good, Miss Jose."

She turned to Meg. "I want to hear what the piano sounds like, just in case I'm asked to sing this afternoon. Let's try over 'This Life is Weary.'"

Pom! Ta-ta-ta *Tee*-ta! The piano burst out so passionately that Jose's face changed. She clasped her hands. She looked mournfully and enigmatically at her mother and Laura as they came in.

This Life is *Wee*-ary,
A Tear—a Sigh.

A Love that *Chan*-ges,
  This Life is *Wee*-ary,
A Tear—a Sigh.
A Love that *Chan*-ges,
And then . . . Goodbye!

But at the word "Goodbye," and although the piano sounded more desperate than ever, her face broke into a brilliant, dreadfully unsympathetic smile.

"Aren't I in good voice, mummy?" she beamed.

This Life is *Wee*-ary,
Hope comes to Die.
A Dream—a *Wa*-kening.

But now Sadie interrupted them. "What is it, Sadie?"

"If you please, m'm, cook says have you got the flags for the sandwiches?"

"The flags for the sandwiches, Sadie?" echoed Mrs. Sheridan dreamily. And the children knew by her face that she hadn't got them. "Let me see." And she said to Sadie firmly, "Tell cook I'll let her have them in ten minutes."

Sadie went.

"Now, Laura," said her mother quickly. "Come with me into the smoking-room. I've got the names somewhere on the back of an envelope. You'll have to write them out for me. Meg, go upstairs this minute and take that wet thing off your head. Jose, run and finish dressing this instant. Do you hear me, children, or shall I have to tell your father when he comes home to-night? And—and, Jose, pacify cook if you do go into the kitchen, will you? I'm terrified of her this morning."

The envelope was found at last behind the dining-room clock, though how it had got there Mrs. Sheridan could not imagine.

"One of you children must have stolen it out of my bag, because I remember vividly—cream cheese and lemon-curd. Have you done that?"

"Yes."

"Egg and—" Mrs. Sheridan held the envelope away from her. "It looks like mice. It can't be mice, can it?"

"Olive, pet," said Laura, looking over her shoulder.

"Yes, of course, olive. What a horrible combination it sounds. Egg and olive."

They were finished at last, and Laura took them off to the kitchen. She found Jose there pacifying the cook, who did not look at all terrifying.

"I have never seen such exquisite sandwiches," said Jose's rapturous voice. "How many kinds did you say there were, cook? Fifteen?"

"Fifteen, Miss Jose."

"Well, cook, I congratulate you."

Cook swept up crusts with the long sandwich knife, and smiled broadly.

"Godber's has come," announced Sadie, issuing out of the pantry. She had seen the man pass the window.

That meant the cream puffs had come. Godber's were famous for their cream puffs. Nobody ever thought of making them at home.

"Bring them in and put them on the table, my girl," ordered cook.

Sadie brought them in and went back to the door. Of course Laura and Jose were far too grown-up to really care about such things. All the same, they couldn't help agreeing that the puffs looked very attractive. Very. Cook began arranging them, shaking off the extra icing sugar.

"Don't they carry one back to all one's parties?" said Laura.

"I suppose they do," said practical Jose, who never liked to be carried back. "They look beautifully light and feathery, I must say."

"Have one each, my dears," said cook in her comfortable voice. "Yer ma won't know."

Oh, impossible. Fancy cream puffs so soon after breakfast. The very idea made one shudder. All the same, two minutes later Jose and Laura were licking their fingers with that absorbed inward look that only comes from whipped cream.

"Let's go into the garden, out by the back way," suggested Laura. "I want to see how the men are getting on with the marquee. They're such awfully nice men."

But the back door was blocked by cook, Sadie, Godber's man and Hans.

Something had happened.

"Tuk-tuk-tuk," clucked cook like an agitated hen. Sadie had her hand clapped to her cheek as though she had toothache. Hans's face was screwed up in the effort to understand. Only Godber's man seemed to be enjoying himself; it was his story.

"What's the matter? What's happened?"

"There's been a horrible accident," said cook. "A man killed."

"A man killed! Where? How? When?"

But Godber's man wasn't going to have his story snatched from under his very nose.

"Know those little cottages just below here, miss?" Know them? Of course, she knew them. "Well, there's a young chap living there, name of Scott, a carter. His horse shied at a traction-engine, corner of Hawke Street this morning, and he was thrown out on the back of his head. Killed."

"Dead!" Laura stared at Godber's man.

"Dead when they picked him up," said Godber's man with relish. "They were taking the body home as I come up here." And he said to the cook, "He's left a wife and five little ones."

"Jose, come here." Laura caught hold of her sister's sleeve and dragged her through the kitchen to the other side of the green baize door. There she paused and leaned against it. "Jose!" she said, horrified, "however are we going to stop everything?"

"Stop everything, Laura!" cried Jose in astonishment. "What do you mean?"

"Stop the garden-party, of course." Why did Jose pretend?

But Jose was still more amazed. "Stop the garden-party? My dear Laura, don't be so absurd. Of course we can't do anything of the kind. Nobody expects us to. Don't be so extravagant."

"But we can't possibly have a garden-party with a man dead just outside the front gate."

That really was extravagant, for the little cottages were in a lane to themselves at the very bottom of a steep rise that led up to the house. A broad road ran between. True, they were far too near. They were the greatest possible eyesore, and they had no right to be in that neighborhood at all. They were little mean dwellings painted a chocolate brown. In the garden patches there was nothing but cabbage stalks, sick hens and tomato cans. The very smoke coming out of their chimneys was poverty-stricken. Little rags and shreds of smoke, so unlike the great silvery plumes that uncurled from the Sheridans' chimneys. Washerwomen lived in the lane and sweeps and a cobbler, and a man whose house-front was studded all over with minute bird-cages. Children swarmed. When the Sheridans were little they were forbidden to set foot there because of the revolting language and of what they might catch. But since they were grown up, Laura and Laurie on their prowls sometimes walked through. It was disgusting and sordid. They came out with a shudder. But still one must go everywhere; one must see everything. So through they went.

"And just think of what the band would sound like to that poor woman," said Laura.

"Oh, Laura!" Jose began to be seriously annoyed. "If you're going to stop a band playing every time some one has an accident, you'll lead a very strenuous life. I'm every bit as sorry about it as you. I feel just as sympathetic." Her eyes hardened. She looked at her sister just as she used to when they were little and fighting together. "You won't bring a drunken workman back to life by being sentimental," she said softly.

"Drunk! Who said he was drunk?" Laura turned furiously on Jose. She said, just as they had used to say on those occasions, "I'm going straight up to tell mother."

"Do, dear," cooed Jose.

"Mother, can I come into your room?" Laura turned the big glass door-knob.

"Of course, child. Why, what's the matter? What's given you such a color?" And Mrs. Sheridan turned round from her dressing-table. She was trying on a new hat.

"Mother, a man's been killed," began Laura.

"*Not* in the garden?" interrupted her mother.

"No, no!"

"Oh, what a fright you gave me!" Mrs. Sheridan sighed with relief, and took off the big hat and held it on her knees.

"But listen, mother," said Laura. Breathless, half-choking, she told the dreadful story. "Of course, we can't have our party, can we?" she pleaded. "The band and everybody arriving. They'd hear us, mother; they're nearly neighbors!"

To Laura's astonishment her mother behaved just like Jose; it was harder to bear because she seemed amused. She refused to take Laura seriously.

"But, my dear child, use your common sense. It's only by accident we've heard of it. If some one had died there normally—and I can't understand how they keep alive in those poky little holes—we should still be having our party, shouldn't we?"

Laura had to say "yes" to that, but she felt it was all wrong. She sat down on her mother's sofa and pinched the cushion frill.

"Mother, isn't it really terribly heartless of us?" she asked.

"Darling!" Mrs. Sheridan got up and came over to her, carrying the hat. Before Laura could stop her she had popped it on. "My child!" said her mother, "the hat is yours. It's made for you. It's much too young for me. I have never seen you look such a picture. Look at yourself!" And she held up her hand-mirror.

"But, mother," Laura began again. She couldn't look at herself; she turned aside.

This time Mrs. Sheridan lost patience just as Jose had done.

"You are being very absurd, Laura," she said coldly. "People like that don't expect sacrifices from us. And it's not very sympathetic to spoil everybody's enjoyment as you're doing now."

"I don't understand," said Laura, and she walked quickly out of the room into her own bedroom. There, quite by chance, the first thing she saw was this charming girl in the mirror, in her black hat trimmed with gold daisies, and a long black velvet ribbon. Never had she imagined she could look like that. Is mother right? she thought. And now she hoped her mother was right. Am I being extravagant? Perhaps it was extravagant. Just for a moment she had another glimpse of that poor woman and those little children, and the body being carried into the house. But it all seemed blurred, unreal, like a picture in the newspaper. I'll remember it again after the party's over, she decided. And somehow that seemed quite the best plan. . . .

Lunch was over by half-past one. By half-past two they were all ready for the fray. The green-coated band had arrived and was established in a corner of the tennis-court.

"My dear!" trilled Kitty Maitland, "aren't they too like frogs for words? You ought to have arranged them round the pond with the conductor in the middle on a leaf."

Laurie arrived and hailed them on his way to dress. At the sight of him Laura remembered the accident again. She wanted to tell him. If Laurie agreed with the others, then it was bound to be all right. And she followed him into the hall.

"Laurie!"

"Hallo!" He was half-way upstairs, but when he turned round and saw Laura he suddenly puffed out his cheeks and goggled his eyes at her. "My word, Laura! You do look stunning," said Laurie. "What an absolutely topping hat!"

Laura said faintly, "Is it?" and smiled up at Laurie, and didn't tell him after all.

Soon after that people began coming in streams. The band struck up; the hired waiters ran from the house to the marquee. Wherever you looked there were couples strolling, bending to the flowers, greeting, moving on over the lawn. They were like bright birds that had alighted in the Sheridans' garden for this one afternoon, on their way to—where? Ah, what happiness it is to be with people who all are happy, to press hands, press cheeks, smile into eyes.

"Darling Laura, how well you look!"

"What a becoming hat, child!"

"Laura, you look quite Spanish. I've never seen you look so striking."

And Laura, glowing, answered softly, "Have you had tea? Won't you have an ice? The passion-fruit ices really are rather special." She ran to her father and begged him. "Daddy darling, can't the band have something to drink?"

And the perfect afternoon slowly ripened, slowly faded, slowly its petals closed.

"Never a more delightful garden-party . . ." "The greatest success . . ." "Quite the most . . ."

Laura helped her mother with the good-byes. They stood side by side in the porch till it was all over.

"All over, all over, thank heaven," said Mr. Sheridan. "Round up the others, Laura. Let's go and have some fresh coffee. I'm exhausted. Yes, it's been very successful. But oh, these parties, these parties! Why will you children insist on giving parties!" And they all of them sat down in the deserted marquee.

"Have a sandwich, daddy dear. I wrote the flag."

"Thanks." Mr. Sheridan took a bite and the sandwich was gone. He took another. "I suppose you didn't hear of a beastly accident that happened today?" he said.

"My dear," said Mrs. Sheridan, holding up her hand, "we did. It nearly ruined the party. Laura insisted we should put it off."

"Oh, mother!" Laura didn't want to be teased about it.

"It was a horrible affair all the same," said Mr. Sheridan. "The chap was married too. Lived just below in the lane, and leaves a wife and half a dozen kiddies, so they say."

An awkward little silence fell. Mrs. Sheridan fidgeted with her cup. Really, it was very tactless of father . . .

Suddenly she looked up. There on the table were all those sandwiches, cakes, puffs, all uneaten, all going to be wasted. She had one of her brilliant ideas.

"I know," she said. "Let's make up a basket. Let's send that poor creature some of this perfectly good food. At any rate, it will be the greatest treat for the children. Don't you agree? And she's sure to have neighbors calling in and so on. What a point to have it all ready prepared. Laura!" She jumped up. "Get me the big basket out of the stairs cupboard."

"But, mother, do you really think it's a good idea?" said Laura.

Again, how curious, she seemed to be different from them all. To take scraps from their party. Would the poor woman really like that?

"Of course! What's the matter with you today? An hour or two ago you were insisting on us being sympathetic, and now—"

Oh, well! Laura ran for the basket. It was filled, it was heaped by her mother.

"Take it yourself, darling," said she. "Run down just as you are. No, wait, take the arum lilies too. People of that class are so impressed by arum lilies."

"The stems will ruin her lace frock," said practical Jose.

So they would. Just in time. "Only the basket, then. And, Laura!"—her mother followed her out of the marquee—"don't on any account—"

"What, mother?"

No, better not put such ideas into the child's head! "Nothing! Run along."

It was just growing dusky as Laura shut their garden gates. A big dog ran by like a shadow. The road gleamed white, and down below in the hollow the little cottages were in deep shade. How quiet it seemed after the afternoon. Here she was going down the hill to somewhere where a man lay dead, and she couldn't realize it. Why couldn't she? She stopped a minute. And it seemed to her that kisses, voices, tinkling spoons, laughter, the smell of crushed grass were somehow inside her. She had no room for anything else. How strange! She looked up at the pale sky, and all she thought was, "Yes, it was the most successful party."

Now the broad road was crossed. The lane began, smoky and dark. Women in shawls and men's tweed caps hurried by. Men hung over the palings; the children played in the doorways. A low hum came from the mean little cottages. In some of them there was a flicker of light, and a shadow, crab-like, moved across the window. Laura bent her head and hurried on. She wished now she had put on a coat. How her frock shone! And the big hat with the velvet streamer—if only it was another hat! Were the people looking at her? They must be. It was a mistake to have come; she knew all along it was a mistake. Should she go back even now?

No, too late. This was the house. It must be. A dark knot of people stood outside. Beside the gate an old, old woman with a crutch sat in a chair, watching. She had her feet on a newspaper. The voices stopped as Laura drew near. The group parted. It was as though she was expected, as though they had known she was coming here.

Laura was terribly nervous. Tossing the velvet ribbon over her shoulder, she said to a woman standing by, "Is this Mrs. Scott's house?" and the woman, smiling queerly, said, "It is, my lass."

Oh, to be away from this! She actually said, "Help me, God," as she walked up the tiny path and knocked. To be away from those staring eyes, or to be covered up in anything, one of those women's shawls even. I'll just leave the basket and go, she decided. I shan't even wait for it to be emptied.

Then the door opened. A little woman in black showed in the gloom.

Laura said, "Are you Mrs. Scott?" But to her horror the woman answered, "Walk in please, miss," and she was shut in the passage.

"No," said Laura, "I don't want to come in. I only want to leave this basket. Mother sent—"

The little woman in the gloomy passage seemed not to have heard her. "Step this way, please, miss," she said in an oily voice, and Laura followed her.

She found herself in a wretched little low kitchen, lighted by a smoky lamp. There was a woman sitting before the fire.

"Em," said the little creature who had let her in. "Em! It's a young lady." She turned to Laura. She said meaningly, "I'm 'er sister, miss. You'll excuse 'er, won't you?"

"Oh, but of course!" said Laura. "Please, please don't disturb her. I—I only want to leave—"

But at that moment the woman at the fire turned round. Her face, puffed up, red, with swollen eyes and swollen lips, looked terrible. She seemed as though she couldn't understand why Laura was there. What did it mean? Why was this stranger standing in the kitchen with a basket? What was it all about? And the poor face puckered up again.

"All right, my dear," said the other. "I'll thenk the young lady."

And again she began, "You'll excuse her, miss, I'm sure," and her face, swollen too, tried an oily smile.

Laura only wanted to get out, to get away. She was back in the passage. The door opened. She walked straight through into the bedroom, where the dead man was lying.

"You'd like a look at 'im, wouldn't you?" said Em's sister, and she brushed past Laura over to the bed. "Don't be afraid, my lass—" and now her voice sounded fond and sly, and fondly she drew down the sheet—"'e looks a picture. There's nothing to show. Come along, my dear."

Laura came.

There lay a young man, fast asleep—sleeping so soundly, so deeply, that he was far, far away from them both. Oh, so remote, so peaceful. He was dreaming. Never wake him up again. His head was sunk in the pillow, his eyes were closed; they were blind under the closed eyelids. He was given up to his dream. What did garden-parties and baskets and lace frocks matter to him? He was far from all those things. He was wonderful, beautiful. While they were laughing and while the band was playing, this marvel had come to the lane. Happy . . . happy. . . . All is well, said that sleeping face. This is just as it should be. I am content.

But all the same you had to cry, and she couldn't go out of the room without saying something to him. Laura gave a loud childish sob.

"Forgive my hat," she said.

And this time she didn't wait for Em's sister. She found her way out of the door, down the path, past all those dark people. At the corner of the lane she met Laurie.

He stepped out of the shadow. "Is that you, Laura?"

"Yes."

"Mother was getting anxious. Was it all right?"

"Yes, quite. Oh, Laurie!" She took his arm, she pressed up against him.

"I say, you're not crying, are you?" asked her brother.

Laura shook her head. She was.

Laurie put his arm round her shoulder. "Don't cry," he said in his warm, loving voice. "Was it awful?"

"No," sobbed Laura. "It was simply marvelous. But, Laurie—" She stopped, she looked at her brother. "Isn't life," she stammered, "isn't life—" But what life was she couldn't explain. No matter. He quite understood.

"*Isn't* it, darling?" said Laurie.

The Finely Shaded Prose of Katherine Mansfield's "The Garden Party"

David Huddle

Style is the means by which a story makes its reader perceive and feel many things all at once. As most of the stories in this book demonstrate, even more than what happens in it, the way in which a narrative is recounted determines its effect on a reader. The beginning and ending sections of Katherine Mansfield's "The Garden Party" demonstrate how significantly the nuances of each sentence contribute to a rich and complex story.

From the opening, "And after all the weather was ideal," giddy anticipation is the mood of "The Garden Party." The Sheridan family's preparations for the party require approximately eight pages of description, whereas the party itself begins and ends in less than half a page. The story's opening sets forth the weather, the sky, the season. In the middle of the first paragraph, an image is delivered in one deft sentence, the writerly equivalent of one of those Corot paintings so small and so finely detailed that a viewer must stand no more than a foot or two away to see it properly:

> The gardener had been up since dawn, mowing the lawns and sweeping them, until the grass and the dark flat rosettes where the daisy plants had been seemed to shine.

A reader sees this gardener, and the results of his labor, from a distance, as if looking down on him from an upstairs window. One of Mansfield's primary resources is her visual artistry; not only does she make the world of her story intensely visible, she does it with maximum efficiency. Speed is important to this story, and so in one sentence she paints what another writer might accomplish in three or four.

The gardener at work in the distance is the right image for the reader to hold in mind while entering the story. One of its major thematic concerns is class differences, the tension between workers and masters. Throughout the "preparation" phase of the story, masters scurry about, concerning themselves with frivolous matters, while workers carry out the labor necessary for their masters' ritual of pleasure. Mansfield explicates the tension with the lightest of hands and with a delicate irony. The servant-master relationship here, in turn-of-the-century New Zealand, is an old-fashioned colonial one, almost as ideal for the masters as the day's weather.

From the initial "And after all," we readers are in the company of the Sheridans, seeing things from their point of view, experiencing the story through the chatty language of Sheridan sensibility: "As for the roses, you could not help feeling they understood that roses are the only flowers that impress people at garden-parties . . ." This sensibility is so privileged that its standards for being impressed by flowers are very high, and "you" are being addressed as if "you" shared the same values. The "tilt" of the language (the sensibility) is sufficient to affect us readers, to amuse and charm us with the Sheridans' innocence, and to invite us to imagine how the workers might view the Sheridans. But finally we attend this garden party as the Sheridans' guests, and we can't help humoring them, even collaborating with them, by seeing just exactly what they mean, understanding exactly how they feel. The language won't allow us any other role; we're insiders whether we like it or not.

For instance, if the story's one-sentence second paragraph read, "The men arrived, ready to put up the marquee, while the Sheridans were still eating breakfast," we would have an entirely different perception of the circumstance than the one we actually receive from the sentence of the text: "Breakfast was not yet over before the men came to put up the marquee." In the former case, we would be standing impatiently outside with the men, irked at the decadence of people who'd still be dawdling over breakfast at this hour. In the latter case, we're at the table with the Sheridans, rushing to swallow our last bites and irked at having to deal with workmen at such an inconvenient hour. Mansfield's sentence gives the impression of being an objective report, but its point-of-view shading is her trick. With the hundreds of other more or less shaded sentences, she maneuvers readers into kinship with the Sheridans.

For its reader, as well as for its protagonist, Laura, the story is an education in Sheridanism, the primary source of which is the mother. Though a minor character, the mother is crucial in her role of defining what it means to be a Sheridan. When asked where she wants the marquee put, Mrs. Sheridan replies,

> "My dear child, it's no use asking me. I'm determined to leave everything to you children this year. Forget I am your mother. Treat me as an honored guest."

This four-sentence speech establishes both a character and a set of values. Mrs. S. is affectionately ironic toward her children. She aspires to be irresponsible and pampered. She's nervy and witty enough to present herself this way, as insufferably spoiled and wanting to be even more so. She's cunningly providing her children with on-the-job training in the giving of garden parties. As readers, we may be mildly horrified by this *grande dame*, but we're also amused by her. We withhold judgment of her because she has let her guard down. The gardener may toil in the distance, but Mrs. S. sits right beside us at the breakfast table, treating us to an intimate view of her.

If we've cooperated with Mrs. Sheridan in her desire to be treated as an "honored guest," we can hardly refuse the private, familial logic that prevents two of the sisters from telling the men where to put up the marquee:

> But Meg could not possibly go and supervise the men. She had washed her hair before breakfast, and she sat drinking her coffee in a green turban, with a dark wet curl stamped on each cheek. Jose [whose name, incidentally, is probably pronounced as if it were spelled "Josie"], the butterfly, always came down in a silk petticoat and a kimono jacket.

At this point in the story, we've been drawn into a deep absurdity: The issue here is merely to decide where to put this thing and to convey that decision to the men who will do the work of putting it up. Mrs. Sheridan could have said, "Tell them to put it there by the karakas," and a daughter could have shouted her order back through the kitchen. But, as the story goes on instructing us, the Sheridans are who they are—people of a certain class—and such simple matters as decision making and communicating take on the consequence of enormous labor.

The image that embodies that absurdity is the "piece of bread-and-butter" Laura ("the artistic one") carries with her when, having been dispatched by her mother and sisters, she goes out to deal with the workmen. Mansfield establishes Laura as the story's protagonist with the sentence "It's so delicious to have an excuse for eating out of doors, and besides, she loved having to arrange things; she always felt she could do it so much better than anyone else." With one exception, Laura Sheridan is the only character in the story to whose inner life we readers have access. Ultimately it is Laura's story, and this "so delicious" sentence is the moment of her taking possession of it. Henceforth we experience the story in the close company of Laura. We never know exactly how old she is, but we see her as being somewhere in the vicinity of fourteen to sixteen. Already we know enough about her mother and her sisters not to be surprised that Laura feels she can arrange things "so much better than anyone else."

Awaiting Laura's direction are four workmen, sketched in sufficient detail for us to understand how Laura might be taken aback by them: "They carried staves covered with rolls of canvas, and they had big tool-bags slung on their backs." Although the main source of tension in the story is class difference, a subtle secondary source is gender difference. Both sources inform this tableau—of a young girl facing four grown workmen, the girl at least in theory, by virtue of her class, holding authority over the men:

> Laura wished now that she had not got the bread-and-butter, but there was nowhere to put it, and she couldn't possibly throw it away. She blushed and tried to look severe and even a little bit short-sighted as she came up to them.

If we've been quickly and efficiently drawn into the social fabric of the world of "The Garden Party," we've also been drawn closer to Laura. We appreciate her youthful exuberance and naiveté ("How very nice workmen were! And what a beautiful morning! She mustn't mention the morning; she must be businesslike"). And we appreciate her bemused monitoring of her place in this world, her ongoing attempts to figure out exactly how things work, or how they ought to work ("Laura's upbringing made her wonder for a moment whether it was quite respectful of a workman to talk to her of bangs slap in the eye. But she did quite follow him").

We understand that in this encounter with the workmen, Laura is in a little over her head, but she's equipped with wits and poise, she's sensitive to every nuance of their exchange, and she's *learning* immensely from it. She's carrying out an apprenticeship, and we have become involved in the process of her learning. Since we witnessed her mother's witty high-handedness, we are now aware of how Laura is shadowed by her mother in this exchange with the workmen, and we like Laura all the more for her clumsy apologies for her privileged life. ("'Only a very small band,' said Laura gently. Perhaps he wouldn't mind so much if the band was quite small.")

We are also touched by Laura's intense response to the world around her:

> And [the karaka trees] were so lovely, with their broad, gleaming leaves, and their clusters of yellow fruit. They were like trees you imagined growing on a desert island, proud, solitary, lifting their leaves and fruits to the sun in a kind of silent splendour.

The beauty of the natural world stimulates Laura's imagination. Such description makes us see this "garden" in the moment of Laura's seeing it, thereby making us unusually aware of her youthful vitality.

The last sentence of the paragraph describing the karaka trees asks the question, "Must they be hidden by a marquee?" and the beginning of the next paragraph answers the question: "They must. Already the men had shouldered their staves and were making for the place." There's a cheerful wit at work here; obviously this question and the answer register Laura's thinking of the moment, but they also seem to come from a more disinterested "witness." We readers are both inside and outside Laura's consciousness in these moments. "The Garden Party" depends on a reader's apprehension of Laura's experience both from within and from without, a simultaneous identification with its protagonist and an objective witnessing and judging of her from some distance.

So by the end of the second page a reader has been made aware of Laura's family values and her apprenticeship in those values, her youth, sensitivity, and imagination, her almost unconscious wit, her status as a representative from the world of women to the world of men, and her exact place in this society of unequal but ironically benign division of power between the classes:

> Only the tall fellow was left. He bent down, pinched a sprig of lavender, put his thumb and forefinger to his nose and snuffed up the smell. When Laura saw that gesture she forgot all about the karakas in her wonder at him caring for things like that—caring for the smell of lavender. How many men that she

knew would have done such a thing? Oh, how extraordinarily nice workmen were, she thought. Why couldn't she have workmen for friends rather than the silly boys she danced with and who came to Sunday night supper? She would get on much better with men like these.

The reader's response to Laura has become increasingly complex. Here we see her being condescending, as befits her class, but also romantic and idealistic, as befits her age. We suddenly understand how limited her world is; even though she's privileged enough to attend dances, she's known only a few "boys" of her own class. Of course she makes too much of the workman's "caring for the smell of lavender"; nevertheless, we judge Laura's ignorance not to be of the stupid, dangerous variety but instead sweet and admirably humane.

Then we encounter of one of Mansfield's overtly stylish sentences: "It's all the fault, she decided, as the tall fellow drew something on the back of an envelope, something that was to be looped up or left to hang, of these absurd class distinctions." With Laura's thought left suspended through that long dependent clause, we are pinned to the moment, watching the tall fellow's artwork right along with Laura. And since we have to wait for it, the phrase "these absurd class distinctions" gains some emphasis. At the same time, the lengthy interruption undercuts Laura's conviction; it conveys the impression that her condemnation of class distinctions is such a casual matter that her mind can stray even while it makes the observation. That undercutting carries over into her observations that follow: "Well, for her part, she didn't feel them. Not a bit, not an atom. . . ." Well, for our part, since we've seen that she has class distinctions very much on her mind, we understand her not to be stating a fact but to be coaching herself toward a more democratic sensibility. Laura is impelled toward both truth and illusion. She's both noble and silly:

> Some one whistled, some one sang out, "Are you right there, matey?" "Matey!" The friendliness of it, the—the— Just to prove how happy she was, just to show the tall fellow how at home she felt, and how she despised stupid conventions, Laura took a big bite of her bread-and-butter as she stared at the little drawing. She felt just like a work-girl.

When Laura is called to the phone, Mansfield transports her with a gorgeous sentence, using exactly the right verb for Laura's state of mind as well as for her physical movement and using a syntax that makes a reader see her moving through the elements of her world: "Away she skimmed, over the lawn, up the path, up the steps, across the veranda, and into the porch." These stacked-up prepositional phrases make us register her exertion almost physiologically.

This opening section engages a reader more and more intensely with Laura and her giddy experience on the morning's preparations for her family's garden party. These scenes also lightly demonstrate Laura's struggle to be and not to be a Sheridan. The darker passages that conclude the story deepen the physical/mental/spiritual connection between the reader and the young protagonist; they also provide us readers with an awareness of the hard decisions Laura must face in her quickly approaching adult life.

The beginning of Laura's journey toward a confrontation with mortality is rendered in painterly terms with a deftly shaded transition into Laura's introspection:

> It was just growing dusky as Laura shut their garden gates. A big dog ran by like a shadow. The road gleamed white, and down below in the hollow the little cottages were in deep shade. How quiet it seemed after the afternoon. Here she was going down the hill to somewhere where a man lay dead, and she couldn't realize it. Why couldn't she? She stopped a minute. And it seemed to her that kisses, voices, tinkling spoons, laughter, the smell of crushed grass were somehow inside her. She had no room for anything else. How strange! She looked up at the pale sky, and all she thought was, "Yes, it was the most successful party."

It is significant that she's journeying "down the hill" toward "where the man lay dead." "Down" and "darkness" (or shadow) are associated with death; "up" and "light" are associated with the party. Entirely to Laura's credit, she's able to articulate for herself the terms of her dilemma: "realizing" (an oddly precise word choice: "making real for herself") the death of the man or remembering the party—and this opposition, death versus party, provides the basic tension of the entire story. But after she looks "up at the pale sky," her vacuously social phrasing, "Yes, it was the most successful . . . ," invites us to see Laura in this moment as lost to Sheridanism at least temporarily.

The next paragraph parallels the previous one in moving through description to Laura's thinking, but it demonstrates both a more intensely affecting external world and a more vulnerable Laura:

> Now the broad road was crossed. The lane began, smoky and dark. Women in shawls and men's tweed caps hurried by. Men hung over the palings; the children played in the doorways. A low hum came from the mean little cottages. In some of them there was a flicker of light, and a shadow, crab-like, moved across the window. Laura bent her head and hurried on. She wished now she had put on a coat. How her frock shone! And the big hat with the velvet streamer—if only it was another hat! Were the people looking at her? They must be. It was a mistake to have come; she knew all along it was a mistake. Should she go back even now?

The pattern of light and darkness is elaborated here, and the crablike shadow is an ominous "realization" of the previous paragraph's "dog [that] ran by like a shadow." Laura's frock shines with a light that we must associate with the garden party. But the imagery is not simplemindedly symmetrical; Laura's hat, the ultimate symbol of the party, is a black one. Even so, it makes her stand out distinctly in comparison with these working women wearing "men's tweed caps." Laura's anxiety here over her appearance and being looked at is augmented for us by our memory of Laura's self-consciousness around the marquee installers and of the basic Sheridan obsession with matters of appearance. Although silly from an objective point of view, her doubts about her journey and her wondering if she should turn back seem reasonable enough to us. Instead of judging her from some distance, we are sympathetically *with* Laura on her journey, sharing her state of heightened self-consciousness when she reaches "the house":

> A dark knot of people stood outside. Beside the gate an old, old woman with a crutch sat in a chair, watching. She had her feet on a newspaper. The voices stopped as Laura drew near. The group parted. It was as though she was expected, as though they had known she was coming here.

The word *knot* conveys an ugly constriction—something Laura is feeling as well as something she is seeing. The image of a *knot* of people drastically contrasts her earlier description of the garden party, where "there were couples strolling, bending to the flowers, greeting, moving on over the lawn."

As her innocent happiness of the morning transformed the Sheridan home into paradise, now Laura's fear has transformed her errand into a journey into the underworld. She departed through a gate; now she must arrive through another gate, this one guarded by a figure who must appear ominous to Laura, though the actual description of her ("old, old . . . with a crutch . . . watching . . . her feet on a newspaper") implies neither threatening nor benign qualities. The voices stopping and the group parting must also appear ominous to Laura, though again, to Mansfield's readers, they are neutral phenomena. That these people appear to have "expected" Laura, to have "known she was coming," is ambiguous in a way that enhances the scene: The clairvoyance is eerie, but in social terms, to be "expected" is to be welcomed. It's likely that the group's expectation is for visitors in general and that it is mostly imagined by Laura to be directed at her. In their silence and standing aside, the people are probably just responding politely and naturally to Laura in her party clothes. But in light of what we've seen of the social fabric of the culture—and especially of the working people's solicitous attitude toward the Sheridans—we can imagine that if one of them were dead, the working people would have made gestures of condolence to the Sheridan family. So it really isn't all that surprising. The ambiguity of Laura's reception marks a transition from her fearful journey down into the dark neighborhood into the oddly hospitable territory of the dead man's house—a hospitality felt more strongly by the reader than by Laura:

> Laura was terribly nervous. Tossing the velvet ribbon over her shoulder, she said to a woman standing by, "Is this Mrs. Scott's house?" and the woman, smiling queerly, said, "It is, my lass."

"Tossing the velvet ribbon over her shoulder" is Laura's attempt to play down both the garden party and the fact of her being a Sheridan. The woman's words, "It is, my lass," have that tone of kind deference that we first encountered in the lanky marquee installer's "That's right, miss," but the queerness of the woman's smile serves to maintain the dark mood of the scene. Laura's level of anxiety remains very high:

> Oh, to be away from this! She actually said, "Help me, God," as she walked up the tiny path and knocked. To be away from those staring eyes, or to be covered up in anything, one of those women's shawls even. I'll just leave the basket and go, she decided. I shan't even wait for it to be emptied.

Does this circumstance call for prayer—especially when we've seen no evidence of even the slightest spiritual concern in the Sheridans' house? Well, no, it doesn't, and Mansfield's undercutting "actually" makes that clear to us. But since a scene soon to come holds spiritual content, this little prayer is an unobtrusive introduction of a spiritual *motif.* And even if her anxiety is merely an acute case of self-consciousness, Laura's prayer conveys to us the gravity she sees in her circumstance as she stands on the threshold of the dead man's house.

> Then the door opened. A little woman in black showed in the gloom.
> Laura said, "Are you Mrs. Scott?" But to her horror the woman answered, "Walk in please, miss," and she was shut in the passage.
> "No," said Laura, "I don't want to come in. I only want to leave this basket. Mother sent—"
> The little woman in the gloomy passage seemed not to have heard her. "Step this way, please, miss," she said in an oily voice, and Laura followed her.

Both "gloom" (or "gloomy") and "passage" are repeated here, and "passage" (a word with a neatly apt figurative application to the scene) will reappear a few paragraphs later. Mansfield is moving Laura through the scene at a crisp pace; she's not about to linger here in the hallway, but she is taking care to establish the intensely claustrophobic qualities of the setting.

This is the third cronelike woman Laura has encountered at the dead man's house (the other two being the "old, old [one] with a crutch" and the one who smiled "queerly"). This third one will be Laura's escort in death's inner sanctum. Women are presiding over the ritual of death as earlier they presided over the garden party. And this woman, though she is kind and deferential in her manner, directs Laura, against Laura's wishes, to carry out what the woman deems to be the appropriate behavior for the occasion. Laura's encounter with the marquee installers at the beginning of the story has prepared us for her encounter with this woman. Since Laura let the men put up the marquee in front of the karaka trees, we certainly don't expect her to disobey this woman. Mansfield has established malleability as essential to Laura's character, and it is against her will that Laura carries out this last stage of her journey. It would be against any Sheridan's will to go farther than the front door of the dead man's house. The difference between Laura and all the other Sheridans is that she has it in her character to defer to this lower-class woman. On the one hand, we see her acting out of her democratic impulse, out of basic human decency; on the other hand, we wish she had a little more backbone. Although we understand that she is the only Sheridan who's capable of carrying this journey to its conclusion, her weakness is what prevents us from seeing her as excessively good, her actions as overly noble. The odd combination of weakness and courage in her actions is now a fresh dimension of Laura's character for this late section of the story. But Mansfield is taking care to show Laura to be "better" than the other Sheridans only to the extent that she is more wholly human.

> She found herself in a wretched little low kitchen, lighted by a smoky lamp. There was a woman sitting before the fire.

"Em," said the little creature who had let her in. "Em! It's a young lady."
She turned to Laura. She said meaningly, "I'm 'er sister, miss. You'll excuse 'er,
won't you?"

"Oh, but of course!" said Laura. "Please, please don't disturb her. I—I only
want to leave—"

But at that moment the woman at the fire turned round. Her face, puffed
up, red, with swollen eyes and swollen lips, looked terrible. She seemed as
though she couldn't understand why Laura was there. What did it mean? Why
was this stranger standing in the kitchen with a basket? What was it all about?
And the poor face puckered up again.

"All right, my dear," said the other. "I'll thenk the young lady."

By reverting to her mother's phrasing with "wretched little low kitchen" and
"the little creature," Laura is staving off her fear. And Mansfield isn't romanticizing her portrait of the lives of working people: The lamp is "smoky," and the
widow's name (or as much of it as we're able to hear) is one crude syllable. Nor
is Mansfield romanticizing Laura's response to the situation; the girl is blurting
the absolute truth when she says, "I only want to leave." The personality of the
widow's sister, the "little creature," emerges unobtrusively in her speech: She
appears to be savoring this death. The power of the widow's grief is made evident by her silence—in stark contrast to her sister's obsequious utterances—
and by Mansfield's explicit description of her face. The effect of that description
is intensified by Mansfield's having described no one's face until this moment.
We're seeing the widow's face through Laura's eyes, and the effect of it on
Laura is to inspire a leap of empathy: Laura imagines the widow's impression
of her, so that in this moment, visually and emotionally, both characters
sharply register in a reader's consciousness. Laura and the widow can't bring
themselves to speak to each other, but the widow's sister is intent on performing the manners called for by the occasion:

> "All right, my dear," said the other. "I'll thenk the young lady."
> And again she began, "You'll excuse her, miss, I'm sure," and her face,
> swollen too, tried an oily smile.

If Laura's reading of the widow's face is at all accurate, then with "All right, my
dear," the widow's sister is merely pretending to be in communication with
her; in spite of her own grieving (her face is "swollen too"), she is doing her
best to carry out what she sees as suitable behavior. Em's sister is the only character in the story we hear using such dialect as "thenk," "'er," and "'e," though
we heard a "yer" from cook and a "matey" sung out by one of the marquee installers; even though the story is so much about class differences, Mansfield
uses lower-class dialect with a very light hand. But in this scene, this is the third
time "swollen" and the second time "oily" have been used, their effect being to
deepen our sense of Laura's revulsion at her circumstance:

> Laura only wanted to get out, to get away. She was back in the passage. The
> door opened. She walked straight through into the bedroom, where the dead
> man was lying.

Although inconspicuous, this is an artful paragraph. We're aware of Laura's emotional condition, and so we understand how, when she's "back in the passage" (that word again), she'd assume that an opening door would take her back outside. That this door opens without visible human agency must be attributed to Laura's nightmarish state of mind. And either "the passage" is a different one or the door that opens is not the door that Laura came in through earlier—Mansfield deliberately does not clarify which is the case, but it doesn't matter because we understand that Laura is disoriented anyway. So intensely do we feel her desire to escape that we understand how she can take several steps into the bedroom before she realizes she's "where the dead man was lying"; Mansfield's syntax saves the dead man for last, and so we come upon him with a surprise similar to Laura's. A considerable complexity is conveyed by this thirty-one-word paragraph.

Mansfield has established and developed this minor character of Laura's escort for a number of reasons, not the least of which is that she serves as a kind of ambassador for the community outside the Sheridans' gate; Laura has more interaction with this woman than with any other working-class character in the story. The widow's sister is also here for purposes of tone and pacing and for the dramatic highlighting of this moment. She is also the one character in the story who can credibly make this presentation of the dead young man. After "the little creature" accomplishes the task, she disappears from the story.

> "You'd like a look at 'im, wouldn't you?" said Em's sister, and she brushed past Laura over to the bed. "Don't be afraid, my lass—" and now her voice sounded fond and sly, and fondly she drew down the sheet—" 'e looks a picture. There's nothing to show. Come along, my dear."

This woman's comforting "There's nothing to show" is her delicate way of telling Laura that the man's body has not been visibly damaged by the accident that killed him. Her final words, "Come along, my dear," have the ominous, seductive ring of the wolf's voice in "Little Red Riding-Hood."

The ritual that's being performed here is remarkable; "the little creature" may be a minor character, but in this moment, she's a high priestess. She is initiating Laura in the mystery of death; she's also showing Laura a man, as an object or specimen; she's allowing the girl "a look" of greater thoroughness and intensity than she has likely ever been able to have of any living man—because she doesn't have to feel self-conscious while she's looking. Death, of course, is the primary thematic element here, but the scene is also charged by romantic and erotic undercurrents. In the same way that Mansfield's not having previously described anyone's face gives special emphasis to her description of the widow's face, her not having previously given men any more than passing attention now adds dramatic force to Laura's encounter with this man.

Of more interest than the last two-word paragraph we encountered ("Sadie went") is "Laura came." It conveys Laura's following an order, just as Sadie followed one. Throughout the story we've seen Laura carrying out the will of others, doing almost nothing of her own accord. A reader imagines that she feels torn by the invitation; probably she both wants and doesn't want "a look," but Mansfield is telling us nothing of her thinking and feeling. Another writer might have seen Laura's decision—to look or not to look—as the very crux of the story, but Mansfield doesn't linger an instant because she sees the next moment as the crucial one:

> There lay a young man, fast asleep—sleeping so soundly, so deeply, that he was far, far away from them both. Oh, so remote, so peaceful. He was dreaming. Never wake him up again. His head was sunk in the pillow, his eyes were closed; they were blind under the closed eyelids. He was given up to his dream. What did garden-parties and baskets and lace frocks matter to him? He was far from all those things. He was wonderful, beautiful. While they were laughing and while the band was playing, this marvel had come to the lane. Happy . . . happy. . . . All is well, said that sleeping face. This is just as it should be. I am content.

Instead of being the horrifying sight a reader expects, the dead man is, through Laura's view of him, "wonderful, beautiful," a sleeping fairy-tale prince. But the source of the young man's beauty is not his physical appearance; it is his being dead. Laura is seeing through the young man to his death, which she interprets as a dream; death is a "marvel" to her because it is so remote from the worldly "fray" of "garden-parties and baskets and lace frocks." Laura's romantic vision is at work in constructing both these worldly and spiritual versions of happiness, but the story presents the latter as a "truer happiness." To Laura, the dead man's body is a revelation of his spirit, which is "given up to his dream." Through Mansfield's excessively positive language, we understand Laura's response to the dead man to be romantically exaggerated, but we don't feel that response to be completely invalid—just as we don't feel that her democratic impulses are invalid. A relevant ambiguity is at work in this "extravagant" diction ("wonderful, beautiful . . . marvel . . . Happy"); it is at one and the same time garden-party chitchat and the language of awe. While Laura is probably the only Sheridan capable of experiencing awe, she's nevertheless stuck with the Sheridan vocabulary for articulating it even to herself. Almost as a way of protecting the truth she has received from the dead man, Laura remembers her manners and agrees with herself to put on an act for him:

> But all the same you had to cry, and she couldn't go out of the room without saying something to him. Laura gave a loud childish sob.
>   "Forgive my hat," she said.

The hat here reverberates back through the story, so that, silly as it sounds for Laura to ask forgiveness for her hat, we understand her actually to be asking forgiveness for her entire life. Her hat is her identity as a Sheridan, as a vain creature, as a person devoted only to worldly matters. The truth of the spirit is what she has witnessed in the dead man, a truth that stands in direct opposition to the worldly values with which she has been raised. A reader's response to Laura's plea for forgiveness is to laugh—what an absurd thing for her to say!—but we have been so instructed by the story that another part of what makes us laugh is our shock in apprehending the profundity of the moment. On the backlash of understanding, we know that nothing Laura could say would be as meaningful and correct as "Forgive my hat."

These words have a cathartic effect: They release the pressure the entire story has directed toward Laura's encounter with the dead man. Now Mansfield quickens the pace for Laura's escape:

> And this time she didn't wait for Em's sister. She found her way out of the door, down the path, past all those dark people. At the corner of the lane she met Laurie.
>> He stepped out of the shadow. "Is that you, Laura?"
>> "Yes."
>> "Mother was getting anxious. Was it all right?"
>> "Yes, quite. Oh, Laurie!" She took his arm, she pressed up against him.
>> "I say, you're not crying, are you?" asked her brother.
>> Laura shook her head. She was.

However profound her encounter with the dead man has been, the Sheridanesque phrasing of her perception of "all those dark people" demonstrates that Laura has not been transformed by it into a completely new person. In fact, her escort back to her own world is that Sheridan most like herself, her soul-mate brother. Having just carried out a spiritual exchange with the dead man, she responds to the living Laurie by "press[ing] up against him," a phrase that echoes the garden party's happiness in the form of "press[ing] hands, press[ing] cheeks." Laurie's phrasing of his question suggests the official Sheridan surprise at—and perhaps disapproval of—crying over a dead workman; Laura, in shaking her head to deny her crying, accepts that view, though the amusingly contradictory next sentence ("She was") reflects the complex truth of her tears: They are not out of sorrow over the workman's death; they are the tears she brought forth as a performance for the dead man, but she has nevertheless gone on crying. So we know that even though Laura is going back to her house and her worldly life as a Sheridan, she has been deeply affected by her spiritual experience in the dead workman's house. What remains for the story to tell us?

> Laurie put his arm round her shoulder. "Don't cry," he said in his warm, loving voice. "Was it awful?"
>> "No," sobbed Laura. "It was simply marvelous. But, Laurie—" She stopped, she looked at her brother. "Isn't life," she stammered, "isn't life—"
>> But what life was she couldn't explain. No matter. He quite understood.
>> "*Isn't* it, darling?" said Laurie.

On the surface of it, this is certainly a happy ending, a moment of affection and rare understanding between brother and sister. But it is also an ending that invites us to scratch that surface and to reconsider the whole story in light of its final vision. Laura's "It was simply marvelous" is a trifaceted pronouncement: (1) It has that Sheridanesque ring of garden-party chitchat, (2) it's an odd thing to say about an encounter with the dead, and (3) it lightly touches the reader's memory of the bedside scene ("while the band was playing, this marvel had come to the lane"). Under scrutiny, the happiness of the final vision considerably diminishes: The understanding between Laura and Laurie, as they phrase it here, is resounding testimony to their need—an essential of Sheridanism—to stay entirely on the surface of "life." In beginning to phrase her question, Laura essays bravely toward some kind of truth, but she lets herself be too easily stopped by Laurie's response. All of their training—as we have seen it demonstrated throughout the first three-quarters of the story—prevents Laura and Laurie from having a real exchange about anything of consequence, let alone matters of mortality. Indeed, one of the echoes of Laura's stopped observation in this passage is her mother's warning ("And, Laura! . . . don't on any account—"), a warning that might specifically have been against entering the dead man's house, or perhaps even against looking at the dead man's body, but that in general terms might have been something like "don't on any account penetrate the surface of experience."

Closer examination of this passage darkens the ending's vision still further: There is a hollowness to this brotherly understanding suggested by the two previous brief scenes in which we have seen Laurie. Just before the party, Laura wanted to tell him about the accident that killed the workman, but he prevented her from even starting to tell him. The sentence "He quite understood" is Laura's thinking, but we readers have been taught to see very little capacity to understand in Laurie's character. And after all, even if he were a brother of unusual sensitivity and depth of character, how could he understand the remarkable moments Laura experienced at the dead man's bedside? So what the ending demonstrates beneath its cheerful warmth is Laura's essential isolation. Earlier in the story we witnessed her wrongly thinking that Jose would understand her and then that her mother would understand her; the argument of the story is clearly that the Sheridans can't comprehend Laura's non-Sheridan qualities. The complex shading of Mansfield's prose has insinuated a disturbing perception into the deeper levels of a reader's consciousness: A sensitive, spiritually inclined young woman is so trapped within her delusions that she can't "realize" how isolated she is within her family.

Laura Sheridan participates in the preparation for and giving of a party, then journeys into a slum where she briefly encounters a dead man before she starts to walk back home. By themselves, the events of "The Garden Party" are of only mild interest and small consequence. However, when invested with the subtle power of Mansfield's style, the account of these events takes on force, complexity, and substance: A life we come to understand as remarkable is shown at a crucial point of development. Style does all the work; the way this story is told *is* the story. "The Garden Party" would be no story at all without the fine shading of Katherine Mansfield's prose.

ABOUT ## Barry Hannah

A native Mississippian, Barry Hannah was born in 1942 and is presently writer-in-residence at the University of Mississippi at Oxford. He has published novels, among them *Geronimo Rex* (1972), *Ray* (1980), and *Never Die* (1991), short story collections, among them *Airships* (1978) and *Bats Out of Hell* (1993), and screenplays.

Love Too Long

Barry Hannah

My head's burning off and I got a heart about to bust out of my ribs. All I can do is move from chair to chair with my cigarette. I wear shades. I can't read a magazine. Some days I take my binoculars and look out in the air. They laid me off. I can't find work. My wife's got a job and she takes flying lessons. When she comes over the house in her airplane, I'm afraid she'll screw up and crash.

I got to get back to work and get dulled out again. I got to be a man again. You can't walk around the house drinking coffee and beer all day, thinking about her taking her brassiere off. We been married and divorced twice. Sometimes I wish I had a sport. I bought a croquet set on credit at Penney's. First day I got so tired of it I knocked the balls off in the weeds and they're out there rotting, mildew all over them, I bet, but I don't want to see.

Some afternoons she'll come right over the roof of the house and turn the plane upside down. Or maybe it's her teacher. I don't know how far she's got along. I'm afraid to ask, on the every third night or so she comes in the house. I want to rip her arm off. I want to sleep in her uterus with my foot hanging out. Some nights she lets me lick her ears and knees. I can't talk about it. It's driving me into a sorry person. Maybe Hobe Lewis would let me pump gas and sell bait at his service station. My mind's around to where I'd do nigger work now.

I'd do Jew work, Swiss, Spanish. Anything.

She never took anything. She just left. She can be a lot of things—she got a college degree. She always had her own bank account. She wanted a better house than this house, but she was patient. She'd eat any food with a sweet smile. She moved through the house with a happy pace, like it meant something.

I think women are closer to God than we are. They walk right out there like they know what they're doing. She moved around the house, reading a book. I never saw her sitting down much, unless she's drinking. She can drink you under the table. Then she'll get up on the spot of eight and fix you an omelet with sardines and peppers. She taught me to like this, a little hot ketchup on the edge of the plate.

199

When she walks through the house, she has a roll from side to side. I've looked at her face too many times when she falls asleep. The omelet tastes like her. I go crazy.

There're things to be done in this world, she said. This love affair went on too long. It's going to make us both worthless, she said. Our love is not such a love as to swell the heart. So she said. She was never unfaithful to me that I know. And if I knew it, I wouldn't care because I know she's sworn to me.

I am her always and she is my always and that's the whole trouble.

For two years I tried to make her pregnant. It didn't work. The doctor said she was too nervous to hold a baby, first time she ever had an examination. She was a nurse at the hospital and brought home all the papers that she forged whenever I needed a report. For example, when I first got on as a fly in elevated construction. A fly can crawl and balance where nobody else can. I was always working at the thing I feared the most. I tell you true. But it was high pay out there at the beam joints. Here's the laugh. I was light and nimble, but the sun always made me sick up there under its nose. I got a permanent suntan. Some people think I'm Arab. I was good.

When I was in the Navy, I finished two years at Bakersfield Junior College in California. Which is to say, I can read and feel fine things and count. Those women who cash your check don't cause any distress to me, all their steel, accents and computers. I'll tell you what I liked that we studied at Bakersfield. It was old James Joyce and his book *The Canterbury Tales.* You wouldn't have thought anybody would write "A fart that well nigh blinded Absalom" in ancient days. All those people hopping and humping at night, framming around, just like last year at Ollie's party that she and I left when they got into threesomes and Polaroids. Because we loved each other too much. She said it was something you'd be sorry about the next morning.

Her name is Jane.

Once I cheated on her. I was drunk in Pittsburgh. They bragged on me for being a fly in the South. This girl and I were left together in a fancy apartment of the Oakland section. The girl did everything. I was homesick during the whole time for Jane. When you get down to it, there isn't much to do. It's just arms and legs. It's not worth a damn.

The first thing Jane did was go out on that houseboat trip with that movie star who was using this town we were in in South Carolina to make his comeback film. I can't tell his name, but he's short and his face is old and piglike now instead of the way it was in the days he was piling up the money. He used to be a star and now he was trying to return as a main partner in a movie about hatred and backstabbing in Dixie. Everybody on board made crude passes at her. I wasn't invited. She'd been chosen as an extra for the movie. The guy who chose her made animalistic comments to her. This was during our first divorce. She jumped off the boat and swam home. But that's how good-looking she is. There was a cameraman on the houseboat who saw her swimming and filmed her. It was in the movie. I sat there and watched her when they showed it local.

The next thing she did was take up with an architect who had a mustache. He was designing her dream house for free and she was putting money in the bank waiting on it. She claimed he never touched her. He just wore his mustache and a gold medallion around his neck and ate yogurt and drew houses all day. She worked for him as a secretary and landscape consultant. Jane was always good about trees, bushes, flowers and so on. She's led many a Spare That Tree campaign almost on her own. She'll write a letter to the editor in a minute.

Only two buildings I ever worked on pleased her. She said the rest looked like death standing up.

The architect made her wear his ring on her finger. I saw her wearing it on the street in Biloxi, Mississippi, one afternoon, coming out of a store. There she was with a new hairdo and a narrow halter and by God I was glad I saw. I was in a bus on the way to the Palms House hotel we were putting up after the hurricane. I almost puked out my kidneys with the grief.

Maybe I need to go to church, I said to myself. I can't stand this alone. I wished I was Jesus. Somebody who never drank or wanted nooky. Or knew Jane.

She and the architect were having some fancy drinks together at a beach lounge when his ex-wife from New Hampshire showed up naked with a single-shotgun gun that was used in the Franco-Prussian War—it was a quaint piece hanging on the wall in their house when he was at Dartmouth—and screaming. The whole bar cleared out, including Jane. The ex-wife tried to get the architect with the bayonet. She took off the whole wall mural behind him and he was rolling around under the tables. Then she tried to cock the gun. The policeman who'd come in got scared and left. The architect got out and threw himself into the arms of Jane, who was out on the patio thinking she was safe. He wanted to die holding his love. Jane didn't want to die in any fashion. Here comes the nude woman, screaming with the cocked gun.

"Hey, hey," says Jane. "Honey, you don't need a gun. You got a hell of a body. I don't see how Lawrence could've left that."

The woman lowered the gun. She was dripping with sweat and pale as an egg out there in the bright sun over the sea. Her hair was nearabout down to her ass and her face was crazy.

"Look at her, Lawrence," said Jane.

The guy turned around and looked at his ex-wife. He whispered: "She was lovely. But her personality was a disease. She was killing me. It was slow murder."

When I got there, the naked woman was on Lawrence's lap. Jane and a lot of people were standing around looking at them. They'd fallen back in love. Lawrence was sucking her breast. She wasn't a bad-looking sight. The long gun lay off in the sand. No law was needed. I was just humiliated. I tried to get away before Jane saw me, but I'd been drinking and smoking a lot the night before and I gave out this ninety-nine-year-old cough. Everybody on the patio except Lawrence and his woman looked around.

But in Mobile we got it going together again. She taught art in a private school where they admitted high-type Negroes only. And I was a fly on the city's first high-rise parking garage. We had so much money we ate out even for breakfast. She thought she was pregnant for a while and I was happy as hell. I wanted a heavenly blessing—as the pastors say—with Jane. I thought it would form the living chain between us that would never be broken. It would be beyond biology and into magic. But it was only eighteen months in Mobile and we left on a rainy day in the winter without her pregnant. She was just lean and her eyes were brown diamonds like always, and she had begun having headaches.

Let me tell you about Jane drinking punch at one of the parties at the University of Florida where she had a job. Some hippie had put LSD in it and there was nothing but teacher types in the house, leaning around, commenting on the azaleas and the evil of the administration. I never took any punch because I brought my own dynamite in the car. Here I was, complimenting myself on holding my own with these profs. One of the profs looked at Jane in her long gown, not knowing she was with me. He said to another: "She's pleasant to look at, as far as *that* goes." I said to him that I'd heard she was smart too, and had taken the all-Missouri swimming meet when she was just a junior in high school. Another guy spoke up. The LSD had hit. I didn't know.

"I'd like to stick her brain. I'll bet her brain would be better than her crack. I'd like to have her hair falling around my honker. I'd love to pull on those ears with silver loops hanging around, at, on, above—what is it?—*them*."

This guy was the chairman of the whole department.

"If I was an earthquake, I'd take care of her," said a fellow with a goatee and an ivory filter for his cigarette.

"Beauty is fleeting," said his ugly wife. "What stays is your basic endurance of pettiness and ennui. And perhaps, most of all, your ability to hide farts."

"Oh, Sandra!" says her husband. "I thought I'd taught you better. You went to Vassar, you bitch, so you wouldn't say things like that."

"I went to Vassar so I'd meet a dashing man with a fortune and a huge cucumber. Then I came back home, to assholing Florida and you," she said. "Washing socks, underwear, arguing with some idiot at Sears."

I met Jane at the punch bowl. She was socking it down and chatting with the librarian honcho who was her boss. He was a Scotsman with a mountain of book titles for his mind. Jane said he'd never read a book in thirty years, but he knew the hell out of their names. Jane truly liked to talk to fat and old guys best of all. She didn't ever converse much with young men. Her ideal of a conversation was when sex was nowhere near it at all. She hated all her speech with her admirers because every word was shaded with lust implications. One of her strange little dreams was to be sort of a cloud with eyes, ears, mouth. I walked up on them without their seeing and heard her say: "I love you. I'd like to pet you to death." She put her hand on his poochy stomach.

So then I was hitting the librarian in the throat and chest. He was a huge person, looked something like a statue of some notable gentleman in ancient history. I couldn't do anything to bring him down. He took all my blows without batting an eye.

"You great bastard!" I yelled up there. "I believed in You on and off all my life! There better be something up there like Jane or I'll humiliate You! I'll swine myself all over this town. I'll appear in public places and embarrass the shit out of You, screaming that I'm a Christian!"

We divorced the second time right after that.

Now we're in Richmond, Virginia. They laid me off. Inflation or recession or whatever rubbed me out. Oh, it was nobody's fault, says the boss. I got to sell my third car off myself, says he. At my house, we don't eat near the meat we used to, says he.

So I'm in this house with my binoculars, moving from chair to chair with my cigarettes. She flies over my house upside down every afternoon. Is she saying she wants me so much she'd pay for a plane to my yard? Or is she saying: Look at this, I never gave a damn for anything but fun in the air?

Nothing in the world matters but you and your woman. Friendship and politics go to hell. My friend Dan three doors down, who's also unemployed, comes over when he can make the price of a six-pack.

It's not the same.

I'm going to die from love.

Outrage in Barry Hannah's "Love Too Long"

Allen Shepherd

Writing about what you know is all very well so long as following such standard good advice doesn't lead you to set up shop in front of the mirror too long or repeatedly to depict adventures in the lives of your friends. The secret, I think, is not to be too modest or too restrictive concerning what you know well enough to write about. Clearly, a narrative of life aboard a present-day Russian fishing trawler or in the camp of Julius Caesar near the Rubicon is beyond most of us, but one should probably try to get beyond one's immediate environment, to venture away from one's customary mind-set. A price to be paid for such healthy ambition is almost certain to be some (unintentionally) funny work. Thus, many years ago after reading Hemingway's *The Old Man and the Sea*, I was inspired (I use the term very loosely) to produce my own mini-epic, entitled *The Old Dog and the Forest*. I will not burden you with a plot summary; you can imagine it well enough—an old dog, a young dog, and so it went, and went, and went. I was crushed when the teacher fortunate enough to receive it inquired whether it was a satire.

The moral of all this, as it pertains to Barry Hannah's story "Love Too Long," is that, for me, Hannah's fiction offered admission to a world which seemed, at first, very different from, even alien to, my own, or my chosen part of my own world, about which I was accustomed to write most naturally and easily. Maybe a few lines from the *Random House College Dictionary*'s definition of "outrage" would help at this point: "1. An act of wanton violence; any gross violation of law or decency. 2. Anything that outrages the feelings. 3. Passionate or violent behavior or language; fury or insolence." The most common, accessible form of outrage is that cited in No. 2. We all know something about outraged (not just hurt) feelings.

How the outraged person may respond is suggested by No. 3. Reflecting on how Hannah's characters behave has been most instructive for me as a writer because I have seen that potential, hitherto usually unrealized, in my own work. Because my world, personal and fictional, is so different from Hannah's, a little of his sort of outrage will likely go a long way, but some of my characters have it in them and occasionally, of recent years, have gotten it out. To register my Hannah-inspired point, it really isn't necessary in all cases that a character should enact outrage; it is sufficient (and often more appropriate) that he or she merely contemplate the act.

For example, being middle-aged and divorced, I feel I have a handle on middle-aged, divorced male characters. Such a character (Fred) would naturally, if his lady love were away during a snowstorm, shovel a path for her return, perhaps even her driveway, if it weren't too long. But suppose he had reason to be outraged? Suppose she were away with somebody else? All kinds of new possibilities suggest themselves. Instead of shoveling neat paths, might he not completely bury her front steps, so that she couldn't get into the house? And a character who would do or contemplate doing such a thing clearly needs to be rethought, since he is not at all what he seemed to be.

No. 1 of my dictionary definitions I recognize readily enough, but it isn't usually useful to me. There are limits, that is to say, to what I can manage or want to work with. It is "wanton violence" rather than a "gross violation of law or decency" that I have most difficulty with. Violation of decency reflects Hannah's dedication to dismaying and offending just about everyone. In that respect, he's rather like Henry Miller. "Art consists," Miller argued, "in going the full length." When Hannah in an interview says, however, "I just frankly enjoy violence," we part company. His pursuit of outrage results in Hannah's work being notably uneven and vulnerable to all sorts of charges, regularly made: of failures of taste, tact, morals, subject, tone, craft, seriousness, and political correctness.

"Love Too Long" comes from Hannah's first (and thus far best) collection of stories, *Airships* (1978). The narrators of most of the stories are of the walking wounded or disabled variety, literally or metaphorically battered veterans. Almost all of Hannah's work jumps with sex, violence, and sadism; the unsettling combination of comedy and cruelty has predictably led to his being associated with a sizable group of supposed antecedents—everyone from Céline to Faulkner to John Hawkes to Flannery O'Connor. The first sentence of "Love Too Long" puts us on notice that we are in the presence of a desperate man, one who tells us, "My head's burning off and I got a heart about to bust out of my ribs." He has had his epiphany, and it's driving—or has already driven—him crazy. How is his outrage displayed? In the overall busyness of the plot (a great many things going on), and even in the first paragraph, the disjointedness and broken rhythms dramatize a man distraught and intimate some of the reasons for his condition. He is out of work and earthbound while his wife is well employed and flying—right over the house, in fact.

His feelings are outraged, but he hasn't been able to enact any passionate or violent behavior; even his language is that of defeat. The core of his misery is bared in variations on a refrain, "I got to be a man again." Instead, he is or sees himself as a helpless dependent, an overgrown fetus, a mildewed croquet ball lost in the grass, a "sorry person"; he's sick with hopeless, jealous, humiliating, long love. He would do anything, he says, but there's nothing to do. He doesn't believe he deserves his wife and, worse still (for him), strongly suspects that women are generically superior to men anyway. Every which way she has it over him: Of an evening she could drink him under the table and then the next morning, pretty and bright, fix him the best omelette in the world. For two years he tried to impregnate her and could not, and even though she was, according to her doctor, too nervous to hold a baby, she had him beat medically—she was a nurse.

The preceding recitation is to suggest that "Love Too Long" is a funny story about a desperate man, far gone (it seems) in masochism and paranoia. And there's worse to come, because there is absolutely no way this man can win, except of course in the telling of his story. While there are a number of detached, transferable bits of humor (for instance, as the narrator, happily unaware of his mistaken attribution, recollects enjoyment taken in junior college in "old James Joyce and his book *The Canterbury Tales*"), Hannah preserves our pleasure in the narrator's distress by a combination of sheer manic inventiveness and formulaic sequences in which bad plus worse somehow always equals worst. Predictability directs and limits empathy. Probably of equal importance is our awareness that this man sees himself pretty much as we do. For all his embarrassing public self-scrutiny, however, the narrator knows and tells a good story. Of that undertaking he is the master.

Self-abasement, however inspired, will carry such a story only so far; thus there occurs a strategic shift in focus to Jane, the narrator's wife, which certainly proves that she is inimitable. During their first divorce, she is relentlessly pursued by assorted males and effortlessly secures a bit part in a movie with "that movie star who was using this town we were in in South Carolina to make his comeback film." There are a good many supporting characters in such vignettes which help carry forward the story and allow the reader to draw an easy breath. After the movie venture, Jane takes up a platonic relationship with an architect with a mustache, whose homicidally jealous ex-wife shows up at a cozy *tête-à-tête* naked and drunk and armed with an aged shotgun, bayonet attached. Another manifestation of outrage. Jane, who is both agile and articulate, manages to make even this near-fatal encounter into a happy reunion. No one could fail to be impressed, and it is, for Hannah, a hard act to follow.

The climax is reached at a faculty party at the University of Florida, where the punch is spiked with LSD, as a consequence of which all present (with the exception of the narrator, who has brought his own stuff and doesn't know about the punch) actually speak and overtly act just as our poor paranoiac protagonist has imagined people have always thought and spoken of him and have habitually done behind his back. He had thought that for once he'd been holding his own, and then this had to happen. When Jane's sexual potential is crudely appraised by her current boss, the librarian, a "huge person," the narrator attacks, but the enemy—as in a nightmare or in the Uncle Remus stories—absorbs his blows "without batting an eye."

In the last paragraph Jane, who has divorced him a second time, is flying over the house again, upside down, and the narrator doesn't know what, if anything, she's telling him. "Is she saying," he wonders, "she wants me so much she'd pay for a plane to my yard? Or is she saying: Look at this, I never gave a damn for anything but fun in the air?" Or is she about to land the plane *on* the house, with him in it? When in the story's last line the poor man says, "I'm going to die from love," we know how to take it, and would gladly give him an indefinite reprieve, if only he would tell us all about it.

What is there about this anecdote-sprinkled monologue that keeps us reading? It isn't in the usual sense much of a story; there's little dramatic tension or suspense or depth of characterization and not much narrative momentum either. The man rambles, one thing reminding him of another, but we keep listening essentially because he keeps saying more and more outrageous things. We are witnessing a performance, and we wonder how long this man will be able to continue to outdo himself.

What all this suggests is the broad range of possibilities for a reader's relationship to a story. For example, Price, in "A Chain of Love," offers us his favorite heroine, whose company he expects we'll enjoy. Chekhov, in "A Dead Body," renders with detached sympathy a seriocomic sequence in peasant life (and death). Price, that is, invites us to fall in love with Rosacoke, while Chekhov invites us to share his sharp-eyed delight in the ridiculous and mysterious. Hannah, by contrast, aims to dismay, disorient, and offend and to these ends gives us a voice we'll listen to regardless of what it has to say. "Love Too Long" features an iconoclastic, aggressively anything-goes sensibility, whose articulation depends on oral style, distinctive voice, and generally manic perspective. Hannah refuses to go beyond astonishment, refuses to question it or convert it into rational explanation. No lesson is drawn, no wisdom offered. None of this, of course, precludes the reader from trying to make good handy common sense of it all, nor the writer from experimenting with a little down-home outrage in his or her own work.

Reynolds Price

Born in Macon, North Carolina, in 1933, Reynolds Price was educated at Duke and Oxford universities and is presently a professor of English at Duke. He is the author of short stories, novels, poems, plays, essays, and biblical translations. He has written for the screen and for television and has written song lyrics as well. Among his principal works are *A Long and Happy Life* (1962), *The Surface of Earth* (1975), *Kate Vaiden* (1986), winner of the National Book Critics Circle Award, and *The Collected Stories* (1993).

A Chain of Love

Reynolds Price

They had observed Papa's birthday with a freezer of cream even if it was the dead of winter, and they had given him a Morris chair that was not brand-new but was what he had always wanted. The next morning he was sick, and nobody could figure the connection between such nice hand-turned cream that Rato almost froze to death making and a tired heart which was what he had according to Dr. Sledge. Papa said "Tired of what?" and refused to go to any hospital. He said he would die at home if it was his time, but the family saw it different so they took him to Raleigh in Milo's car—pulled out the back seat that hadn't been out since Milo married the Abbott girl and spread a pallet and laid him there on pillows with his head resting on the hand-painted one off the settee, the gray felt pillow from Natural Bridge, Virginia that he brought Pauline his wife six years before she died, off that two-day excursion he took with the County Agent to the model peanut farms around Suffolk.

Much as she wanted to, Mama couldn't stay with Papa then. (Mama was his daughter-in-law.) She made him a half a gallon of boiled custard as he asked her to, to take along, and she rode down to Raleigh with them, but she had to come back with Milo in the evening. It worried her not being able to stay when staying was her duty, but they were having a Children's Day at the church that coming Sunday—mainly because the Christmas pageant had fallen through when John Arthur Bobbitt passed around German measles like a dish of cool figs at the first rehearsal—and since she had organized the Sunbeams single-handed, she couldn't leave them then right on the verge of public performance. So they took Rosacoke and Rato along to sit for the first days till Mama could come back herself. Dr. Sledge said there was no need to take on a full-time nurse with two strong grandchildren dying to sit with him anyhow.

And there wasn't. From the minute Papa had his attack, there was never a question of Rosacoke going if Papa had to go—no question of *wanting* to go—and in fact she almost liked the idea. There was just one thing made her think twice about it, which was missing one Saturday night with Wesley. Wesley Beavers was Rosacoke's boyfriend even if Mama didn't like the idea of her riding in to town with a boy two years older every Saturday night to the show and sitting with him afterwards in his car—Rato there on the porch in the pitch dark looking—and telling him goodbye without a word. That was the best part of any week, telling Wesley goodbye the way she did when he pulled his Pontiac up in the yard under the pecan tree, and if it was fall, nuts would hit the car every now and then like enemy bullets to make them laugh or if it was spring, all those little rain frogs would be singing-out over behind the creek and then for a minute calming as if they had all died together or had just stopped to catch their breath. But Wesley would be there when she got back, and anyhow going to the hospital would give her a chance to lay out of school for a week, and it would give her extra time with Papa that she liked to be with. Rosacoke's Papa was her grandfather. Her own father was dead, run over by a green pick-up truck one Saturday evening late a long time ago, almost before she could remember.

But Rato could remember. Rato had seen a lot of things die. He was named for their father—Horatio Junior Mustian—and he was the next-to-oldest boy, nearly eighteen. He didn't mind staying with Papa either. He didn't go to school, hadn't gone in four years, so he didn't have the pleasure of laying out the way Rosacoke did, but seeing all the people would be enough for Rato. Not that he liked people so much. You could hardly get him to speak to anybody, but if you left him alone he would take what pleasure he needed, just standing there taller than anybody else and thinner and watching them.

Dr. Sledge had called on ahead, and they didn't have any trouble getting Papa in the hospital. He even had the refusal of a big corner room with a private bath, but it cost twelve dollars a day. Papa said there was no use trying the good will of Blue Cross Hospital Insurance so he took a ten-dollar room standing empty across the hall, and they wheeled him in on a rolling table pushed by a Negro who said he was Snowball Mason and turned out to be from Warren County too, up around Sixpound, which made Papa feel at home right away and limber enough to flip easy onto the bed in all the clothes he insisted on riding in. But before he could get his breath good, in came a nurse who slid around the bed on her stumpy legs as smooth and speedy as if she was on roller skates with dyed black hair screwed up and bouncing around her ears. She called Papa "darling" as if she had known him all her life and struggled to get him in one of those little night shirts the hospital furnished free without showing everything he had to the whole group. Everybody laughed except Rosacoke who had undressed Papa before and could do it in the dark. She gritted her teeth and finally the nurse got him fixed and stepped back to look as if she had just made him out of thin air. Milo said, "Papa, if you have somebody that peppy around you all the time, you won't be tired long." The nurse smiled and told Papa she would be seeing lots of him in the daytime and then left. Milo laughed at the "lots" and said, "That's what I'm afraid of, Papa—you getting out of hand down here," but Rosacoke said she could manage fine and wasn't exactly a moper herself and Papa agreed to that.

Soon as the nurse got out—after coming back once to get a hairpin she dropped on the bed—they began inspecting the room. There was a good big sink where Rosacoke could rinse out her underwear that she hadn't brought much of and Rato's socks. (Anywhere Rato went he just took the clothes on his back.) And Mama liked the view out the window right over the ambulance entrance where you could see every soul that came in sick. She called Rato's attention to it, and the two of them looked out awhile, but it was getting on towards four o'clock, and much as she wanted to stay and see what Snowball was serving for supper, she told Milo they would have to go. She couldn't stand to ride at night.

Practically before the others left the building, Rosacoke and Rato and Papa had made their sleeping arrangements and were settled. There was one easy chair Rosacoke could sleep in, and since Rato couldn't see stretching out on the floor with his bones, he shoved in another chair out of the parlor down the hall. That dyed-haired nurse saw him do it. She gave him a look that would have dropped anybody but Rato dead in his tracks and said, "You camping out or something, Big Boy?" Rato said, "No'm. Setting with my Papa." Then he went off roaming and the first thing Rosacoke did was open her grip and spread out her toilet articles all over the glass-top bureau. They were all she had brought except for two dresses and a copy of *Hit Parade Tunes and Lyrics* so she could get in some good singing if there was a radio and there was—over Papa's bed, two stations. And at the last minute Mama had stuck in what was left of the salt-water taffy Aunt Oma sent from Virginia Beach that summer. It seemed like a good idea—nurses hung around a patient who had his own candy like Grant around Richmond, Mama said—so she took a piece and gave one to Papa and began to paint her face, trying it out. Papa gummed his candy and watched in the mirror. Mama would have jerked a knot in her if she could have seen the sight Rosacoke was making of herself but Papa smiled. He had always said Rosacoke looked like an actor, and since the only picture show he ever saw was *Birth of a Nation*—and that was forty years ago in the old Warrenton Opera House with a four-piece band in accompaniment—then it must have been Lillian Gish he thought Rosacoke looked like. And she did a little that winter—not as small but thin all the same though beginning to grow, with a heart-shaped face and long yellow hair and blue eyes. That was what Rosacoke liked the best about her face, the eyes. They were big and it was hard to say where the blues left off and the whites began because everything there was more or less blue, and out the far corner of her left eye came this little vein close under the skin that always seemed to Rosacoke to be emptying off some of all that blue, carrying it down to her pale cheek.

But she couldn't stand there staring at herself all the time—she wasn't that good looking and she knew it already—so after the doctors began to ease up with the visits on the second day, Rosacoke got a little tired. That is, till the Volunteer Worker from the Ladies' Guild came in in a pink smock and asked if maybe they wouldn't want some magazines or a deck of cards maybe? She had a pushcart with her full of razor blades and magazines and things, and all Rosacoke had to do was look at Papa, and he—so happy with a lady visitor—

pointed to his black leather purse on the table. The best thing she bought was a deck of Bicycle Playing Cards, and Mama would have jerked another knot if she could have seen Rosacoke right in Papa's bed, teaching him to play Honeymoon Bridge and Fish which she had learned awhile back from town girls on rainy days at little recess. But she never mentioned Slap Jack, her favorite game. She knew in advance Papa would get excited waiting for a Jack to turn up and maybe have a stroke or something so they stuck to quiet games which Papa took to easily, and you could have knocked Rosacoke off the bed with a feather when *he* started teaching her and Rato to play Setback, playing the extra hand himself.

They could count on the cards keeping them busy till Sunday, but they would have to do something with them then. Mama had said she would come down on Sunday to sit her turn with Papa. Milo would bring her after Children's Day. Milo was her oldest boy and he pretty well ran the farm alone with what help Rato could give him. He would probably have to bring Sissie along for the ride even if Papa couldn't stand her. Sissie was Milo's new wife. Just try leaving Sissie anywhere.

The doctors didn't tell Papa what was wrong with him, and he didn't tell them but one thing either which was that he wanted to die at home. He told them they had been mighty nice to him and he appreciated it, but he couldn't think of anything worse than dying away from home. They said they would take care of that and for him to rest till they told him to stop and they would send Dr. Sledge a full report. And Papa didn't worry. He had left it in their hands, and if a doctor had walked in one morning and said he had come to saw his head off, Papa would have just laid his neck out on the pillow where the doctor could get at it. But the doctors didn't bother him for much of his time, and taking them at their word, he slept the best part of every day. That was when Rato would roam the halls, never saying "p-turkey" to anybody, just looking around. And when Rosacoke could see Papa was asleep good, she would tip over and listen to his chest to make sure his heart was beating regular before she would walk across the hall to the corner room, the one they had offered Papa. It was still empty. The door stayed open all the time, and she didn't see any reason for not going in. There was reason *for* going—the view out the window of that room, a white statue of Jesus standing beside the hospital, holding his head bowed down and spreading his hands by his side. His chest was bare and a cloth was hanging over his right shoulder. Rosacoke couldn't see his face too well, but she knew it, clear, from the day they brought Papa in. It was the kindest face she had ever seen. She was sure of that. And she went to that empty room more than once to look out at him and recollect his face the way she knew it was.

But that didn't go on long because on the third day Rato came in from sitting in the hall all morning and said they had just now put some fellow in that empty room. Rosacoke was sorry to hear it. It meant she wouldn't get to go over there in the afternoon any more but she didn't say that. She would rather have died than tell Rato how much time she spent there, looking out a window. Papa wanted to know who it was that could take a twelve-dollar room, and Rato said it was a big man. Papa was disappointed too. He had got it figured there was something wrong with that room, lying empty three days or more. Rato said the man's wife and boy were with him—"I expect it was his boy. Looked like he was anyhow. The man hisself didn't look a bit sick. Walked in on his own steam, talking and laughing." Rosacoke wanted to know if they were rich, but Rato couldn't say, said he didn't know. You couldn't ever tell about Rato though, how much he knew. He wasn't anybody's fool. He just liked the idea of not telling all he knew. Keeping a few secrets was everything Rato had. So Rosacoke said, "Well, he's getting a beautiful room" and then walked over and buttoned Papa's night shirt. She made him stay buttoned square up to the neck all the time because she couldn't stand to look at his old chest. Papa said he was hot as a mink in Africa and that his chest had been that hairy ever since he shaved it to be Maid of Honor in the womanless wedding Delight Church put on when he was seventeen years old.

The night before, when the lights were out but they were still awake, Papa asked Rato to name the best thing he had seen since arriving, and Rato said, "That old lady with all the cards in the big ward down the hall." Rosacoke said, "What sort of cards?" "Every sort there is—Mother's Day, Valentine, Birthday, Christmas . . ." Papa said, "Get-Well cards?" "She ain't going to get well. She's too old." Rosacoke said, "How old?" and Rato said, "What's the oldest thing you know?" She thought and said "God." "Well, she's something similar to that." Rosacoke and Papa laughed but Rato said, "I'm telling the truth. Go take a look if you get the chance. She sleeps all the time." Then they went to sleep but Rosacoke knew he was telling the truth, and anyhow he spoke of his doings so seldom she thought she would take his advice. So the afternoon the man took the twelve-dollar room, she went down while Papa was nodding, and at first it looked the way Rato promised. There was a lady older than God in the bed by the door (saving her a walk past nine other beds), covered to the chin and flat as a plank with no pillow under her head, just steel-colored hair laid wild on the sheets. Rosacoke stepped close enough to see her eyes were shut, and thinking the lady was asleep, she looked up towards a sunburst of greeting cards fanned on the wall over the bed, but she hadn't looked fifteen seconds when the lady shot bolt-upright and spoke in a voice like a fingernail scraping down a dry blackboard—"Praise my Jesus." Rosacoke said "Yes'm" and the lady smiled and said, "Step here, honey, and take a seat and I'll tell you how I got saved at age eighty-one in the midst of a meeting of two hundred people. Then I'll show you my cards—sent by my Sunday school class and my many friends"—and commenced scratching her hair. But Rosacoke said, "No thank you, ma'm" and walked out quicker than she came. She went a few feet outside the door and stopped and thought, "I ought to be ashamed, getting her hopes up. I ought to go back and let her talk." Then she heard the lady's voice scraping on to the empty air so she said to herself, "If I went for five minutes, I'd be there all afternoon, hearing about her cards. Papa is *my* duty." And anyhow she didn't like the lady. It was fine for your friends to send you cards, but that was no reason to organize a show as if you were the only person in the hospital with that many friends and all of them with nothing in the world to do but sit down and write you cards all day. She thought that out and then headed for Papa.

She was walking down the mile-long hall when she saw him—not right at first. At first she was too busy looking at people laid back with their doors open. She didn't know a one of them, not even their faces the way Rato did. The only thing she knew was Snowball Mason in one room, talking to some old man that looked so small in his little outing pajamas with his legs hanging off the bed no more than an inch from the floor like thin dry tan gourds swinging in a wind on somebody's back porch somewhere. Snowball saw her and remembered her as being from Warren County and bowed. She stopped to talk but she happened to look towards the left, and there he was—Wesley—sitting way down across from Papa's door, dressed to the ears and watching the floor the way he always did, not studying people. Still he had come sixty miles to see her so she whispered to Snowball she had to go and went to meet Wesley, holding back from running and trying not to look as if she had seen a ghost which was close to what she had seen, considering this was the last hope she had. He hadn't seen her yet and she could surprise him. She hadn't really missed him so much till now, but when she got nearer she knew how sorry she would be to miss this Saturday with him, and she speeded her steps but kept them quiet. She was almost on him and he put his hands across his eyes—it would be Wesley all over to go to sleep waiting for her—so she came up to him and smiled and said, "Good afternoon, Mr. Beavers, is there something I can do for you?"

But it wasn't Wesley at all. It was somebody she hadn't ever seen before, somebody who didn't really look very much like Wesley when she thought about it. It took whoever it was a little while to realize she was speaking to him, and when he looked up he looked sad and nearly as young as Rosacoke. He looked a little blank too, the way everybody does when you have called them by the wrong name and they don't want you to know it. In a minute he said, "Oh no ma'm, thank you." "No ma'm"—as if Rosacoke was some kind of nurse.

It just about killed her to have done that like some big hussy. The only thing left to say was "Excuse me," and she almost didn't get that out before shutting Papa's door behind her, the hot blood knocking in her ears. Papa was still asleep but Rato was standing by the window, having some Nabs and a Pepsi for dinner, and when she could speak she said would he please peep out and see who that was sitting in the hall. As if Rato had ever peeped in his life. He had done plenty of looking but no peeping so he just pulled open the door as if he was headed for dinner and gave the boy a look. Before he got the door closed good, he said, "Nobody but that man's boy from across the hall. That man they moved in today." Rosacoke said "Thank you" and later on that afternoon she wondered if since he looked like Wesley, that boy could say goodbye like Wesley could.

If they didn't do anything else, those people across the hall at least gave Papa something to think about. They kept their door shut all the time except when somebody was going or coming, and even then they were usually too quick for Rato to get a good enough look to report anything. Something was bound to be wrong though because of all the nurses and doctors hanging around and the way that boy looked whenever he walked out in the hall for a few minutes. Rato reported he saw the man's wife once. He said she was real pretty and looked like she was toting the burden of the world on her shoulders. Even Rato could tell that. So Papa couldn't help asking Snowball the next time he got a chance what was wrong with that man. Snowball said he didn't know and if he did he wouldn't be allowed to say and that made Papa mad. He knew Snowball spent about two-thirds of his time in the man's room, taking bedpans in and out, and he told Snowball at the top of his voice, "That white coat you got on has gone to your head." Rosacoke could have crawled under the bed, but there was no stopping Papa once he got started. You just pretended hadn't a thing happened and he would quiet down. She could tell it got Snowball's goat though and she was sorry. He walked out of Papa's room with his ice-cream coat hanging off him as if somebody had unstarched it.

But that evening when it was time for him to go home, Snowball came back in. He didn't have his white coat on, and that meant he was off duty. He had on his sheepish grin, trying to show he had come on a little social call to see how Papa was making out, but Rosacoke knew right off he had come to apologize to Papa who was taking a nap so she shook Papa and said Snowball wanted to speak to him. Papa raised up blinking and said "Good evening, Snow," and Rosacoke couldn't help smiling at how Snowball turned into a snake doctor, dipping up and down around Papa. He said he just wondered how Mr. Mustian was coming on this afternoon, and did they have any old newspapers he could take home to start fires with? Papa said he was tolerable and hadn't looked at a newspaper since the jimpson weeds took over the Government. What he meant was the Republicans, and he said, "The bad thing about jimp-son weeds, Snow, is they reseeds theyselves."

Snowball hadn't come in on his own time to hear that though, and it didn't take him long to work his way to Papa's bed and lean over a lot closer than Papa liked for anybody to get to him and say it the same way he would have told a secret. "Mr. Mustian, they fixing to take out that gentleman's lung."

"What you talking about?"

"That Mr. Ledwell yonder in the room across the hall. He got a eating-can-cer. That's what I hear his nurse say. But don't tell nobody. I just thought you might want to know so soons I found out . . ."

"A eating-cancer? That's what it is?"

"They don't seem to be no doubt about it. I done already shaved his chest for surgery. He taking his operation in the morning at eight."

Papa wanted to know, "Is he going to live, Snowball?"

"Can't say, Mr. Mustian. He spit the first blood today, and alls I know is they ain't many lives past that. They ain't many. And if they lives you almost wish they hadn't. That's how bad they gets before it's over."

And Papa remembered that was the way it was with Mr. Jack Rooker who swelled up to twice his natural size and smelled a long time before he died. "I can recollect sitting on the porch in the evening and hearing Jack Rooker screaming clean across two tobacco fields, screaming for his oldest boys to just let him rest because there won't nothing nobody could do for him, not nothing. And I'd say to Pauline, 'Pauline, it don't look like Jack Rooker is ever going to die, does it?'" But that was a long time ago when Papa was a lot younger and a lot farther away from dying himself. That was why he could feel so for Jack Rooker back then. It had just seemed as if Jack Rooker was going through something wouldn't anybody else ever have to go through again.

Snowball was nodding his head up and down, saying, "I know. Yes sir, I know," but Rosacoke could tell he had made his peace with Papa and was ready to leave so she stopped Papa from running on about Jack Rooker and told him it was time for Snowball to go home. Papa thanked Snowball for coming in, as if he had never been mad a minute, and said he would count on him keeping them posted on all that happened to that fellow across the hall.

Rosacoke followed Snowball out. "Snowball, what's that man's name again?"

"Mr. Ledwell."

"Is he really going to die, you think?"

"Yes'm, I believe he is. But Miss Rosacoke, you don't have to worry yourself none about that. You ain't going to see him."

"I know that. I just wondered though. I didn't even remember his name."

Snowball said he would be stepping along and would see her in the morning. But Rosacoke didn't hear from him till way in the next afternoon. Papa was taking his nap and she was almost asleep herself when Snowball peeped in and seeing Papa was asleep, whispered that the gentleman across the hall was back from his operation.

"How did it come out, Snow?"

"They tell me he doing right well, Miss Rosacoke."

"Has he waked up yet?"

"No'm, he lying in yonder under his oxygen tent, running on about all sorts of foolishness like a baby. He be in some pain when he do come to though."

"Are his people doing all right?"

"They holding up right well. That's his two sisters with his wife and his boy. They setting there looking at him and waiting to see."

She thanked Snowball for letting them know and said she would tell Papa when he woke up. After Snowball left she stepped into the hall herself. The door over there was closed, and for the first time it said "No visitors." She wanted to wait until somebody opened it. Then she could at least hear the man breathing, if he was still breathing. But there wasn't a sound coming through that oak door thick as her fist, and she wasn't going to be caught snooping like Rato so she went back in to where Papa was awake, spreading a game of Solitaire which that dyed-haired nurse had taught him to play. That was *all* she had done for him.

Since they were away from home, they went to bed around ten o'clock. That is they cut out the lights, and Rosacoke would step in the closet and undress with the door half shut. The first evening she had shut it all the way, and Papa told her there was no use to be so worried about him seeing her as he had seen her stripstrod naked two or three hundred times before she was old enough to walk, but she kept up the practice, and when she was in her nightgown, she would step out and kiss Papa and tell Rato "Sleep tight" and settle in her easy chair under a blanket. Then they would talk a little about the day and home till the talk ran down of its own accord though Papa was liable to go on another hour in the dark about things he remembered. But it would all be quiet soon enough, and Rato would be the first to sleep. After Rosacoke's eyes had opened full to the dark, she could look over and see her brother stretched sideways in his chair, still dressed, with his long hands caught between his drawn-up knees and his head rolled back on his great thin neck and his mouth fallen open. Most people seemed to be somebody else when they were asleep. But not Rato. Rato went to sleep the way you expected he would, like himself who had stopped looking for a while. Then Papa would fall off, sometimes right in the middle of what he was remembering, and Rosacoke could see him too, but he was different—sweeter and with white hair that seemed in the night to be growing into the white pillow his dark leather head rested on, holding him there forever.

After Papa slept Rosacoke was supposed to but she couldn't this night. She kept thinking about it, the man and his boy. Papa had forgotten all about Mr. Ledwell. She hadn't told him anything about the operation, and she had asked Snowball not to tell him either. She didn't want Papa to start back thinking and talking about that poor man and asking questions and sending Rato out to see what he could. She had it all to herself now. Snowball had told her Mr. Ledwell's boy was staying there with him through the nights. Mr. Ledwell had made the boy promise him that before he would go to the operating room, and the boy would be over there now, awake maybe with his father that was dying and she here on her chair trying to sleep with her Papa and Rato, her Papa turned into something else in the night.

Still she might have gone on to sleep if she hadn't thought of Wesley. If she was at home she could go to sleep knowing she would see Wesley at seven-thirty in the morning. He drove the schoolbus and went nearly four miles out of his way on the state's gas to pick her up first so they could talk alone a few minutes before they looked up and saw all those Gupton children in the road, knocking together in the cold and piling on the bus not saying a word with purple splotches like thick cobwebs down their legs that came from standing by an open fire, Mama said, and in winter afternoons Wesley would put her out last into the cold white yard that would be nearly dark by five, and she would walk on towards the light that was coming already from the kitchen windows, steamed on the inside like panes of ice stretched thin on frames. And huddled there she thought how Wesley had said they would to go Warrenton this coming Saturday for a traveling show sponsored by the Lions Club—an exact copy of the Florida State Electric Chair with some poor dummy strapped in it, waiting for the end. Wesley was interested in anything mechanical, and she would have gone with him (no charge for admission the paper said, just a chance to help the Club's Blind Fund) if that was how he wanted to pass time—striking up friends with the owner of the chair whoever it was and talking till time to head back home. But that would have been all right with Rosacoke. She would have waited and been glad if she had got the chance, but she wouldn't now and like as not Wesley would take Willie Duke Aycock which was what Willie Duke had waited for all her life. That was just Wesley. Let her miss school even two days at hog killing and he practically forgot her.

It was thinking all this that kept Rosacoke from going on to sleep. She tried once or twice to empty her head the way she could sometimes at home by closing her eyes and thinking way out in front of her, but she couldn't manage that tonight so she listened till she heard slow breathing from Rato and Papa. Then she got up in her bare feet and felt for the closet door and took down her robe from a hook and put it on. It was peach-colored chenille. She had made it herself and it had been honorable mention at the 4-H Fall Dress Revue in the Warren County Armory. She took her shoes in her hand and opened the door. The hall was empty and the only light was the one at the nurses' desk, and that was so white, shining into both ends of the long hall and against the white charts hanging in tiers. The two night nurses were gone or she could have talked to them. She hadn't ever talked to them, but they seemed nice enough not to mind if she did want to talk. She guessed they were out giving sleeping pills so she walked towards the big ward to pass time.

It was dark down there and all these sounds came out to meet her a long time before she got to the door like some kind of Hell she was hearing from a long way away—a little moan strained out through old dry lips and the grating of each private snore as it tore its way up the throats of the ones who were already asleep. Rosacoke stopped in the open door. The nurses were not there. Nobody seemed to be walking in the dark anyhow. All she could really see was, close to the door, an old woman set up in bed, bent all over on herself and scratching at her hair real slow. But she knew the others were there, and she knew there ought to be something you could do for such people, something you could say even in the dark that would make them know why you were standing there looking—not because you were well yourself and just trying to walk yourself to sleep but because you felt for them, because you hadn't ever been that sick or that old or that alone before in all your life and because you wished they hadn't been either. You couldn't stand there and say to the whole room out loud, "Could I bring you all some ice water or something?" because they probably wouldn't want that anyhow, and even if they did the first ones would be thirsty again and pitching in their hot sheets before you could make it around the room. You would be there all night, and it would be like trying to fill up No-Bottom Pond if it was ever to get empty. So she turned in the open door and saw one nurse back at the desk and walked in that direction, stopping to look at the flowers waiting outside the room of an old man who said they breathed up too much good air at night.

She was some way off when she saw the man's boy. There was no doubt about it being him this time and she was not surprised. The boy walked fast towards the desk, his shirt open down the front, the white tails sweeping behind him in the light of the one lamp and his chest deep brown almost as if he had worked in the field but you knew he hadn't. When he got to the nurse he shut his eyes and said, "My father's nurse says please call Dr. Davis and tell him to come now. It's serious." His voice was low and fast but Rosacoke heard him. The nurse took her time staring at a list of numbers under the glass on her desk before she called. She told whoever she talked to that Mr. Ledwell had taken a turn for the worse. Then she stood and walked to his room. The boy went close behind her so she stopped at the door and said "Wait out here." When she shut the door it stirred enough breeze to lift his shirttail again. He was that close and without stepping back he stood awhile looking. Then he sat by the door where Rosacoke had seen him that first awful time.

She looked on at it from the dark end of the hall (she was not walking by him in her robe even if it had won honorable mention), but she saw him plain because a table was by his chair and he had switched on a small study lamp that lighted his tired face. His chin hung on his hand like dead weight on delicate scales and his eyes were shut. Rosacoke knew if he looked towards the dark he might see her—at least her face—and she pressed to the blackest wall and watched from there. For a long time he was still. No noise came through his father's door. Then clear as day a woman's voice spoke in the open ward, "I have asked and asked for salt on my dinner"—spoke it twice, not changing a word. Some other voice said "Hush" and the boy faced right and looked. Rosacoke didn't know if he saw her or not (maybe he was just seeing dark) but she saw him—his eyes, far off as she was, and they were the saddest eyes in the world to Rosacoke, that pulled hard at her and called on her or just on the dark to do something soon. But she didn't. She couldn't after the mistake of that first time. She shuddered in the hard waves that flushed over her whole body and locked her there in the shadow. Once she put out her hand and her foot and took one small step towards the boy whose head had dropped onto his folded arms, but the bleached light struck her robe, and she dropped back the way one of those rain snails does that is feeling its path, damp and tender, across the long grass till you touch its gentle horns, and it draws itself back, hurt and afraid, into a tight piece you would never guess could think or move or feel, even.

She couldn't have said how long she stood there, getting so tired she knew how it felt to be dead, before the doctor they called came in. He didn't have a tie on, and sleep was in his eyes. He saw the boy and touched him and said something, and they both walked into the room. Before they shut the door a sound like a mad child catching at his breath after crying ran out behind them to where Rosacoke was. She didn't know what was happening, but the boy's father might be dying. She knew that much. She felt almost sure that if the man died they would make some kind of public announcement. But he didn't die and she had waited so long she was nearly asleep. The hall she had to walk through back to Papa's was as quiet now as a winter night in an attic room when you could look out the window and see a sky, cold and hard as a worn plow point shining with the moon. All those people in the ward were asleep or maybe they had given up trying and waited. It seemed as if when you waited at night for something—maybe you didn't know what—the only thing happened was, time made noise in a clock somewhere way off.

It was the next morning that Rosacoke made up her mind. If Mr. Ledwell had lived through the night, she was going to call on him and his family. It was the only thing to do, the only Christian thing to do—to go over there and introduce yourself and ask if there was anything you could do to help such as setting up at night. The way she felt she might have gone over that morning if the room hadn't been so quiet. She hadn't seen a soul come or go since she woke up. She didn't know how Mr. Ledwell was getting along after everything that happened the night before. She didn't know if he had lived out the night. All she could do was wait for Snowball to tell her. She wasn't going to ask Rato to do any more looking for her after the last time.

Snowball was late coming by that morning, but he got there finally and called her out in the hall to talk. He said Mr. Ledwell had a relapse the night before, and they thought he was passing away, but he pulled through unexpectedly. "He not going to last though, Miss Rosacoke. The day nurse tell me he full of the cancer. It's a matter of days, they say, and he know that hisself so all of us try to keep his spirits up. He ain't a old man. I old enough to be his Daddy. He resting right easy this morning, but he was bad sick last night. In fact he was dead for a few minutes before the doctor come and brought him around. They does that right often now you know."

That made Rosacoke think of the day the Phelps boy fell off the dam at Fleming's Mill backwards into twenty feet of water, and three men who were fishing dived in in all their clothes and found his body face-down on the bottom and dragged it out, the mouth hanging open in one corner as if a finger was pulling it down. He had stayed under water four or five minutes, and his chest and wrists were still. They said he was dead as a hammer for half an hour till one man pumped air in him and he belched black mud and began to moan through his teeth. But what Rosacoke always wondered was, where did they go if they died for a while—Mr. Ledwell and the drowned Phelps boy—and if you were to ask them, could they tell you where they had been and what it was like there or had they just been to sleep? She had heard that somebody asked the Phelps boy when he got well enough to go back to school what dying was like, and he said he couldn't tell because it was a secret between him and his Jesus. Mama had said that was all you could expect out of a Phelps anyhow—that she wouldn't ask him if you paid her cash money and that you couldn't just suppose he had gone to Heaven and if he hadn't, you could be sure he wouldn't admit going elsewhere. (She had smiled but she meant it. She had never had a kind word for that branch of Phelpses since they bootlegged their way to big money some years before.) But not everybody felt the way Mama did. A church of Foot-Washing Baptists up towards South Hill heard about it and invited the boy up to testify but he wouldn't go. And from then on

Rosacoke had watched him as if he was something not quite natural that had maybe seen Hell with his own eyes and had lived to tell the tale—or not tell it— and she had followed after him at little recess, hiding where he couldn't notice her so she could watch his face close up and see if his wonderful experience had made him any different. As it turned out it had. He was the quietest thing you could imagine, and his eyes danced all the time as if he was remembering and you couldn't ever know what, not ever.

By the time Rosacoke thought that, Snowball had to leave, but before he went she asked what he thought about her going over to see Mr. Ledwell and his family.

"It couldn't do no harm I can think of, Miss Rosacoke, if you don't stay but a little while. He can't talk much with his one lung, but he be happy to have a visitor. You wait though till he get a little of his strength back from last night."

She nodded Yes but she hadn't planned to pay her visit that morning any-how. She had made up her mind not to go over there till she could take some-thing with her. She might be from Afton, N.C., but she knew better than to go butting into some man's sickroom, to a man on his deathbed, without an ex-pression of her sympathy. And it had to be flowers. There was that much she could do for Mr. Ledwell because he didn't have friends. He and his family had moved to Raleigh less than six months ago. Snowball had found out the Ledwells were from Baltimore. But of course there wasn't a flower for sale any-where in the hospital, and anyhow it wasn't cut flowers Rosacoke had in mind. She got a dime from Papa by saying it was time she sent Mama word as to how they were getting along. Then she hunted down one of the Volunteers and bought two cards with the Capitol on them. She wrote one to Mama.

Dear Mama,
  We like it here alot. I hope you and Baby Sister, Milo and Sissie are all O.K. Papa and I are getting plenty rest. Rato is the one taking exercise. When you come down here would you bring some of your altheas if they have bloomed yet?
                                                                    Yours truly,
                                                            Rosacoke Mustian

She wrote the other one to Wesley Beavers.

Dear Wesley,
  How are you getting along? I am fine but miss you alot. Do you miss me? When you go to see the Florida Electric Chair think of how much I would like to be there. If you see Willie Duke Aycock tell her I said hello. I hope to see you Monday early.
                                                                  Your friend,
                                                                    Rosacoke

Then she mailed them and waited and hoped the altheas had bloomed. Mama had got an idea out of *Life* magazine that you could force things to flower in winter, and she had dug up an althea bush and set it in a tub and put it in the kitchen by the stove and dared it not to bloom. If it had she would gladly pick a handful of oily purple flowers that bruised if you touched them and hold them in her big lap the whole way to Raleigh on Sunday.

And Sunday came before Rosacoke was ready. She woke up early enough (Rato saw to that—he could wake the dead just tying his shoes), but she took her time getting washed and dressed, straightening the room and hiding things away. She didn't expect the family till after dinner so it was nearly noon before she set Papa up and lathered his face and started to shave him. She had finished one side without a nick, singing as she worked—the radio was on to the final hymn at Tabernacle Baptist Church—when the door burst open, and there was Baby Sister and Mama close behind her with flowers. Baby Sister said "Here I am." Rosacoke got her breath and said, "Blow me down. We sure didn't look for you early as this. Mama, I thought you had Children's Day to get behind you before you could leave."

Mama kissed her and touched Papa's wrist. "I did. I did. But once I pulled the Sunbeams through 'Come and Sing Some Happy Happy Song,' I felt like I could leave so we didn't stay to hear Bracey Overby end it with Taps. I know he did all right though. I hope he did—he practiced till he was pale anyhow. Then after leaving church like Indians in the middle of everything to get here early of course some Negroes drove up at the house just as we was starting— some of those curious Marmaduke Negroes with red hair. Well, they had heard about Baby Sister, and they had this skinny baby and wanted her to blow down his throat." (Negroes were always doing that. A child who had never seen its father could cure sore throat by breathing on it.) "It's a awful thing but Baby Sister enjoys it—don't you?—and I can't deny her any powers she may have, especially on Sunday." (Nobody had denied Baby Sister—six years old and big for the name—anything she wanted since she was born six months to the day after her father died. Even the nurses didn't try. Mama marched her in past a dozen signs that plainly said *No Children Under 12* and Baby Sister in Sweetheart Pink and nobody uttered a sound.) All through her story Mama looked around, and when she was done she said "Where is Rato?"

Rosacoke said, "Patrolling, I guess. He'll show up for dinner," and before she could wonder where were Milo and Sissie, they strolled in from parking the car. Milo kissed Rosacoke and said, "Wesley sent you that." Mama said, "No he didn't. We haven't seen Wesley." Then he laughed and kissed Papa— "Miss Betty Upchurch sent you that, but I don't tickle as good as her." (Miss Betty was a crazy old widow with whiskers that he teased Papa about.) Everybody laughed except Sissie. When they quieted down Sissie said "Good morning" and showed her teeth and settled back to looking as if a Mack truck had hit her head-on so Milo explained it to Papa. "Sissie will be off the air today. She's mad—woke up mad but didn't find reasons till we were leaving home. Then she found two good ones. One was she had to shell butter beans all the way up here because Mama didn't read the directions and froze her damn beans in the shell. The other thing was she had to sit on the back seat to do it be- cause Mama and Baby Sister had spoke to sit up front with me and the heater. Well, she sat back there shelling, and when she finished—it took her a hour and we were on the outskirts of Raleigh—she lowered the glass on her side, in- tending to empty out the hulls, but Baby Sister said, 'Shut that pneumonia hole,' and Sissie got flustered and threw out the beans instead. Mama capped

the climax by laughing, and Sissie ain't spoke a word since except just now."
He turned to Sissie who was already staring out the window—"Say something,
Doll Baby. Turn over a new leaf." She wouldn't even look so Milo laughed and
that did seal her. It was a good thing. Nobody could make Papa madder than
Sissie when she started running her mouth.

Mama frowned at Milo and said, "Everybody calm down. We got half a
day to get through in this matchbox." She meant Papa's room that was ten by
twelve. Then she went to the bureau and while Rosacoke scraped chairs
around, she took off her hat and her white ear bobs and combed her hair and
put on a hair net and slipped off her shoes. She went to the chair where Rato
slept—in her stocking feet—and said, "Rosacoke, get me my bed shoes out of
my grip." Rosacoke got them. Then Mama settled back and blew one time with
relief. She had come to stay and she had brought three things with her—dinner
for seven in a cardboard suit box, her grip, and enough altheas to fill a zinc tub.
She made it plain right away that Rosacoke would go on home with Milo and
Sissie and Baby Sister but Rato would stay on to help her with Papa. Milo said
he planned on leaving between eight and nine o'clock. (What he had in mind
was to pacify Sissie by taking her to supper at the Chinese café she liked so
much and then going on to a Sunday picture. But he didn't tell Mama that.)
And Rosacoke couldn't object to leaving. In some ways she would be glad to
get home, and Milo's plans would give her time to pay her visit to Mr. Ledwell,
time to do all she wanted to do, all she thought she could do—to step over
when she had seen her family and pay her respects and give them the flowers
that would say better than she could how much she felt for Mr. Ledwell, dying
in this strange place away from his friends and his home, and for his people
who were waiting.

So she had that day with her family (Rato appeared long enough for dinner), and the day went fine except for three things. One thing was Sissie but nobody ever looked for Sissie to act decent. Another thing was, after they had
eaten the dinner Mama packed, Papa reached over to his bedside table and
pulled out the playing cards. Rosacoke had taken pains to hide them way back
in the drawer, but Papa pulled them out in full view and set up a game of
Solitaire and looked at Mama and grinned. She made a short remark about it
appeared to her Papa was learning fancy tricks in his old age. Papa said
couldn't he teach her a few games, and she drew up in her chair and said she
had gone nearly fifty years—seven of them as a deaconess in Delight Baptist
Church—without knowing one playing card from the other, and she guessed
she could live on in ignorance the rest of the time. But she didn't stop Papa. He
just stopped offering to teach her and lay there the rest of the afternoon, dealing out hands of Solitaire till he was blue in the face. He played right on
through the nap everybody took after dinner. You couldn't have stopped him
with dynamite. The third thing was after their naps. When they all woke up it
was nearly three-thirty and the natural light was dim. Rosacoke stood up to
switch on the bulb, but Milo said "No don't," and even closed the blinds. Then
he went to Papa and pointed at his necktie and said, "Watch this. Pretty soon
it'll start lighting up." It was something he had got that week by mail, and he

claimed it would say "Kiss Me In The Dark!" when the room got dim enough, but they waited and the only thing the tie did was shine pale green all over. Rosacoke was glad he didn't get it working but Papa was disappointed. He asked Milo to leave the tie with him so he could test it in total darkness and show it around to the nurses, but Milo said he was intending to wear it to some crop-dusting movies at the high school that coming Thursday.

In a few more minutes it was five o'clock, and Milo started his plans by saying he and Sissie were going for a little ride and for Rosacoke to be packed for home by nine. Then he got Sissie up and into her coat and they left. Whenever Milo left a place things always quieted down. Papa went back to his Solitaire, and Mama crocheted on a tablecloth that she said would be Rosacoke's wedding present if the thread didn't rot beforehand. Even Baby Sister, who had pestered all afternoon to make up for Sissie being on strike, was worn out and sat still, sucking her thumb, so in the quiet room Rosacoke took down her grip and packed in almost everything. But she kept out her only clean dress and took it down to the nurses' utility closet and pressed it and put it on. She had washed it in the hall bathtub the night before. When she came back to the room, nobody paid her any mind. They thought she was just getting ready to go home. She washed her hands and face and stood in front of the mirror, combing her hair and working up her nerve. She turned her back to Mama and put on a little lipstick and rouge to keep from looking so pale. Then she took the altheas up out of the water Mama set them in and dried the stems with a clean towel and wrapped tissue paper around them. Mama said, "You are dressing too soon," and Rosacoke said, "I reckon I am," but before anybody had seen her good, she slipped out the door in her yellow dress, holding the flowers. She had tied a white card to them. Snowball had got it for her the day before. It said "From a Friend Across the Hall."

She took three steps and stopped and stood in front of the oak door, taller than she would ever be, that said "Ledwell." Behind it was where Mr. Ledwell was and his people that she didn't know, where he had laid down that first day Rato saw him talking and laughing, where he had gone out from to take his operation, and where it was not his home. Rosacoke was nervous but she told herself she looked as good as she could, and she had the altheas in her hands to hide the shaking. She knocked on the door and she must have knocked too soft because nobody came. She knocked again and put her ear to the wood. There were dim sounds coming from the other side so she pushed the door open a little, but the room was dark and quiet as an open field at night with only the sky, and she was drawing back to leave when the moving light of candles caught her, streaming from a part of the room she couldn't see into, drawing her on. So she went inside and pressed the door silent behind her and stood up against it, waiting till her eyes had opened enough to halfway see. There were five or six people in the room. Mr. Ledwell was a ridge on the bed that the sheets rose and fell over in gullies like after a rain, and his boy was by his head, holding one of the candles. In the yellow light the boy looked a way Wesley Beavers might never look, and the same light fell through a clear tent that covered his father's head and chest. A little of it fell on three ladies off in a corner, kneeling on the hard floor, and on a man standing near the bed by a table with two candles on it. He was all in black and falling from his neck was a narrow band of purple cloth with fine gold crosses at the ends. He was talking in words Rosacoke didn't know, almost singing in a voice that was low and far away because he was old with white hair and was looking down, but finally he looked up at Mr. Ledwell's boy, and the two of them pulled the tent back off him. Rosacoke knew he was alive. She could hear the air sucking into his throat, and his eyes were open on the boy and on the yellow candle.

The old man in black moved his hands in the air three times carefully, wide and long over Mr. Ledwell. Then he took a piece of cotton and waited for Mr. Ledwell to shut his eyes. He wiped the cotton over the lids, and they were shining for a second, wet and slick under the light before Mr. Ledwell opened them again and turned them back to the boy. The boy rolled his father's head to one side and then to the other while the old man touched the cotton to the ears that looked cold, and all the time Mr. Ledwell was trying not to take his eyes off the boy as if that sad face in the soft light that came and went was what kept him from dying. And except for that same soft light, the walls of the room would have disappeared and the ceiling, and Rosacoke could have walked out through where the window had been that she used to stand by. It seemed to be time for her to leave anyhow. She didn't know how long this would go on. She didn't know what it was. She only knew they were getting Mr. Ledwell ready to die in their own way, and she had taken the first step to leave when the boy's face turned and saw her through all that dark. His face changed for a minute, and you might have thought he smiled if you hadn't known that couldn't have happened now, not on his face. That was why Rosacoke didn't leave. He had looked at her as if he knew why she was there, almost as if he would have needed her if there had been time. But the old man touched Mr. Ledwell's lips, and Mr. Ledwell strained his head off the pillow and sucked at the cotton before the old man could pull it back. He thought they were giving him something to drink. And it went on that way over his hands that had to be pulled out from under the cover and his feet that seemed to be tallow you could gouge a line in with your fingernail. When they finished with his head, they put the tent back over him, and Rosacoke couldn't hear his breathing quite so loud. From his feet the old man walked back to his head. He put a black wood cross that had Jesus, white and small, nailed on it into Mr. Ledwell's hand. Then he shook a fine mist of water over him and made the sign again, and Rosacoke heard words she could understand. The old man told Mr. Ledwell to say, "Thy will be done." Mr. Ledwell nodded his head and his eyes opened. He took his hand and tapped on the inside of the clear tent. When his boy looked at him, his voice came up in pieces—but Rosacoke heard him plain—"Don't forget to give Jack Rowan one of those puppies." The boy said he wouldn't forget. Mr. Ledwell looked easier and when the old man reached under the tent to take the cross and Jesus away from him, he nodded his head over and over as he turned the cross loose.

The old man went over to speak to the lady who must have been Mr.

Ledwell's wife. She was still on her knees, and she never took her face out of her hands. That was when Rosacoke left. They might switch on the light, and there she would be looking on at this dying which was the most private thing in the world. She had stayed that long because the boy had looked at her, but he might have forgotten by now. He had never looked again. A chair was by the door. She laid her flowers there. In the light somebody might see them and be glad that whoever it was stepped over to bring them, stepped over without saying a word.

She waited in the hall for the sound of his dying because he had seemed so ready, but it didn't come—nobody came or went but a colored girl, pushing a cart load of supper towards the ward—so she had to walk back into Papa's room, dreading questions. The room was dim though and still with only the light over Papa's bed that shined on his hair and the cards spread out on his knees. But he was just turning them over now, not really playing, and when Rosacoke shut the door, he looked and put one finger to his mouth and pointed towards Baby Sister, asleep at last in Mama's lap, and Mama nodding. Rosacoke thought she was safe and halfway smiled and leaned on the door, waiting for breath. But Papa stared at her and then tried to whisper—"You are leaving me, ain't you?"—and Mama jerked awake. It took her a while to get her bearings, but finally she said, "Where in the world have you been with Papa's flowers?" Rosacoke said, "To see a friend." Papa said, "I didn't want no flowers. Who is your friend?" She said "Mr. Ledwell" but Papa didn't show recollection. Mr. Ledwell hadn't crossed his mind since the operation, but just to say something he asked was the man coming on all right? Rosacoke said, "He ain't doing so good, Papa" and to Mama who had never had a secret, never wanted one, "Mama, please don't ask me who that is because I don't know."

Then she went to her grip and turned her back on the room and began packing in the things she had left till last. She was almost done when Rato walked in. Nobody had seen Rato since dinner. He walked in and said it the way he might walk in the kitchen and drop a load of wood in the box—"That man over yonder is dead. Ain't been five minutes." Mama said she was always sorry to hear of any death, and Rato said if they left the door cracked open they could see the man because a nurse had already called the undertaker to come after the body. But Rosacoke faced him and said "No" and said it so Rato wouldn't dare to crack the door one inch. He just left fast and slammed it behind him. But Baby Sister slept through it all, and Mama didn't speak for fear of disturbing her so the room was still again. To keep her hands busy Rosacoke rearranged the few little things in her grip, but she stood sideways to look at Papa and have him to fill her mind. Papa had his cards that he went back to, but he dealt them slow because he was thinking. He was so old himself you couldn't expect him to be too sad. Lately he always said he knew so many more dead men than live ones that there wasn't a soul left who could call him by his first name. And that was the truth. That was what took the edge off death for Papa—grieving over so many people, so many of his friends, burying so much love with each one of them till he had buried them all (everybody he had nearly) and pretty nearly all his love, and death didn't hold fear for him any more. It wasn't as if he didn't know where he was going or what it would be like when he got there. He just trusted and he hoped for one thing, he tried to see to one last thing—for a minute he stopped his card playing and asked Mama could he die at home, and Mama told him he could.

That was what made Rosacoke think so long about Mr. Ledwell who had died in that dark room. She wouldn't be able to go to his funeral, wouldn't even be asked. But that wasn't so bad. She had done what she could, being away from home, hadn't she, and didn't she know his name at least and hadn't he died not cut up or shot or run over but almost in his sleep with his wife and his boy there, and with all that beautiful dying song, hadn't he surely died sanctified? If he had to die wasn't that as good a way as any, leaving his living picture back here in that boy? But she hadn't ever seen him alive really. She hadn't ever told him or any of his kind—out loud—that she felt for them. She hadn't ever said it so loud she could hear her own voice—that Rosacoke Mustian was sorry to see it happen. That was why she spoke at last. She had been quiet so long, and now her slow lean voice cut through all the dark in the room. "It don't seem right," she said. "It just don't seem right. It seem like I had got to know him real well." And her words hung in the room for a long time— longer than it took Papa to pick the cards up off the bed and lay them without a sound in the drawer, longer even than it would have taken Rosacoke to say goodbye to Wesley if it had been Saturday night and she had been at home.

Doing Goodness: Issues of Sentiment and Sentimentality in Reynolds Price's "A Chain of Love"

Allen Shepherd

As the two terms have customarily been used and defined, there is a clear difference between sentiment and sentimentality in literature. Sentiment, one usually hears, is good; sentimentality is not. Sentiment refers to feeling or emotion; without it, literature would certainly be barren and uninteresting. Definitions of sentimentality are often harshly judgmental, as the following example—taken from C. Hugh Holman's *A Handbook to Literature*—suggests.

> Sentimentality: the effort to induce an emotional response disproportionate to the situation, and thus to substitute heightened and generally unthinking feeling for normal ethical and intellectual judgment. It is a particularly pernicious form of anti-intellectualism.

You surely wouldn't want to be guilty of that if you could possibly help it. To commit sentimentality, it seems, is to be disproportionate, unthinking, abnormal, and pernicious.

It should be observed, however, that present-day feminist literary critics have undertaken to rehabilitate sentimentality in certain contexts, particularly in nineteenth-century women's literature, for instance in Harriet Beecher Stowe's *Uncle Tom's Cabin*. They argue essentially that the denigration of sentimentality can be traced to many influences having to do with the intertwining histories of gender, class, and esthetics. For instance, as regards class, when members of the audience of a high-art theatrical production, *King Lear*, for example, weep, the tears are likely to be ascribed to the tragedy's power and validity. But if a nineteenth-century popular text, *Uncle Tom's Cabin*, for example, makes readers cry, references are commonly made to its manipulative characteristics, to its being an exploitative tearjerker.

About one thing, however, the two critical camps are likely to agree, and that is that intelligent, experienced readers may disagree as to whether a given piece of fiction is sentimental or not. Reynolds Price's "A Chain of Love" is one such story, offering a number of problematic passages. In the following pages we will take a look at the story, consider the evidence, and try to come to some conclusions.

It's commonly observed that sentimentality entails cheating or exaggeration, and the cheating comes when a writer asks us to feel for a character without having given us good reason to do so. That is to say the writer tries to get an effect without providing an adequate cause. It's the writer's responsibility, we can probably agree, to establish that a character is indeed worthy of our sympathy, our admiration, our love; once that's done, by any number of different means, strong sentiment (not sentimentality) is the earned result.

Some of the clearest signs of the sentimentalist at work are a writer's employment of simple melodrama, rhetorical clichés, or appeals to stock responses. The object of the melodramatist is to simplify the world and to keep readers thrilled by evoking strong feelings of joy, pity, or horror. To accomplish this purpose, the writer usually dramatizes the conflict of characters who are extremely virtuous or profoundly vicious, with little attention to convincing motivation, in the end effecting poetic justice, according to which all characters are appropriately rewarded or punished for their deeds. Rhetorical clichés assure us that a good woman's love regularly works miracles or that Father infallibly knows best. When we are called upon for a stock response, we are meant to grow misty-eyed at the mere display of our flag, a small child—better yet, a small child with a large dog—or the prospect of universal peace.

The writer employing such materials depends on their evoking built-in responses from the unsophisticated, hence vulnerable, reader. Now of course Father may in fact know best, just as people uncommonly virtuous and vicious may be dramatically opposed, but the reader wishes (we assume) to be taken seriously by the writer, who ought to provide solid grounds for the desired responses within the story.

How does one provide such solid grounds, how best to convey a character's sentiments in fiction? I have learned that, for me at least, two ways don't work. One is to invest the character with long meditations, uninterrupted blocks of introspection. Another is to describe the emotion itself. What I can usually depend on is showing the effects of emotion on a character in action.

For instance, what will be the behavior of a person who has just received a telephone call or a letter containing very good news? Assume that there are other people around but that the happy recipient isn't going to tell them. Perhaps it's too personal, perhaps she wishes to savor it herself, perhaps she's wondering what happens next. How will she act? How do you do someone who is very happy? She will display, I imagine, uncommon animation; she smiles, her eyes are bright. She is interested, sympathetic, ready to laugh, pleased with the world.

In our reflections on sentiment and sentimentality, we have also to recognize that what is accounted sentimental in one time or place isn't necessarily so in another. For example, it seems to me that readers of my parents' generation are sometimes more accepting of what I regard as sentimentality than I usually am, although I may mistake nostalgia for sentimentality. Or, to be a little less self-congratulatory, I, who discovered and was enthralled by Ernest Hemingway in my early teens, was very slow (perhaps reluctant) to recognize his subtractive simplicity, his core-vocabulary understatement as itself being a kind of covert sentimentality or self-pity: Jake Barnes having a good cry in *The Sun Also Rises* or the older waiter reflecting on sleeplessness in "A Clean, Well Lighted Place."

What is most striking about Rosacoke Mustian, protagonist of Price's "A Chain of Love," is that she is indeed a very likable, virtuous, admirable person, attractive (it seems) in almost every way. "Nice" doesn't do her justice, but she is that, too. She is, reviewers have continued to say, a thoroughly endearing character, abounding with goodness. And the author himself certainly seems to have become attached to her, since she is featured not only in this story but also in three novels, *A Long and Happy Life* (1962), *A Generous Man* (1966), and then, returning at age forty-eight, after twenty-eight years of marriage to Wesley Beavers, in *Good Hearts* (1988).

My own experience, writing and reading, suggests that Rosa, as an uncommonly good person, makes substantial imaginative demands on the reader, not to mention the writer. It is much easier, I find, to imagine someone who is less virtuous than you believe yourself to be, perhaps because you can impute to such a character a number of your own least creditable motives and deeds. Try, on the other hand, to imagine a story as told from the perspective of Mother Teresa. An admirable person, no doubt, some would say a saint, but very difficult to grasp. To do a very good person, one risks being saccharine, abstract, incomprehensible, or boring. So to most nonacademic readers Dante's *Inferno*, with its damned (and frequently eloquent) souls suffering eternal punishment, makes for more engaging reading than the *Paradiso*, in which Dante, in the realm of the blessed, receives answers to questions about the nature of good and evil, original sin and transubstantiation.

Is the characterization of Rosacoke Mustian sentimental? One last contextualizing observation is necessary—that in much twentieth-century southern literature one finds a strong sense of family, of place, and of history, all complemented by the significance attached to religion. The works of William Faulkner, Eudora Welty, and Robert Penn Warren are examples often cited. Thus we ought at least to speculate, in evaluating Price's practice, to what extent Rosa's wholeheartedly compassionate response to the Ledwells' troubles, dramatized in her reflections on family, place, history, and religion, may be common rather than unique. I am inclined to believe that although Rosa has good genes and has benefited from her upbringing, that is, she's like her mother, other characters in the story, particularly her sister-in-law Sissie, a foil, make clear that Rosa's goodness is an individual rather than a generic concern.

It seems equally clear, however, that her goodness expresses itself in ways substantially determined by the culture. To understand, to evaluate the unquestioned assumption that all available members of the family will travel to Raleigh to take their turns (not a few hours, but unbroken days and nights) sitting with Papa in his hospital room, one has to remember that the date of the action is about 1950, when hospital rooms could be had for $12 a day, and that the Mustian clan are very-small-town North Carolinians. Where they are, in time and place, affects who they are.

A phrase which Price coined to describe Rosa's motivation, "the ethic of the freely given gesture," further suggests why she does what she does, since it identifies the moral duty of making other people happy, an act being right to the degree that it does this or is undertaken to this end. That Rosa is not an angel of mercy is evident in her disinclination to include the elderly "Praise my Jesus" patient in the circle of those owed a duty. "And anyhow [Rosa] didn't like the lady." Such statements are reassuring; they tend to humanize Rosa. From the very beginning of "A Chain of Love" Price clearly takes seriously the writer's responsibility to establish why Rosa merits our affection as he displays links in the chain of love through allusions to family, marriages, death, generations, home, church, and food—all of this on the first page.

Familial connections extend even to Snowball Mason, the orderly, who "turned out to be from Warren County too, . . . which made Papa feel at home right away." Contrasted with Mason is an anonymous nurse of whom Rosa strongly disapproves—stumpy legs and dyed black hair and she "called Papa 'darling' as if she had known him all his life." Along with the "Praise my Jesus" patient, the nurse is beyond the pale: no freely given gestures to them. What principally inhibits performance of the ethic, however, is Rosa's own ignorance or innocence, her own mixed motives, and the unhappy fact that other people often don't understand or can't respond.

Rosa is wonderfully wholesome, forthright, loving; there is an almost childlike naiveté about her. The issue is not whether we believe such people exist; it is whether we are prepared to value this character as Price directs us to. How much direction is enough? Too much? I'd suggest that Price's situating "a white statue of Jesus" directly in front of the hospital window for Rosa's observation is too much, particularly as we are told that "Rosacoke couldn't see his face too well, but she knew it, clear, from the day they brought Papa in. It was the kindest face she had ever seen." Rosa does not need this kind of reinforcement. Price insists, tells us again what we already know, planting a great big symbol directly in her path and ours. The kindest face is followed, seven pages later, by "the saddest eyes in the world to Rosacoke," these belonging to Mr. Ledwell's grieving son. Is this response excessive? Is this sentimental? It doesn't seem so to me, but I can imagine other readers disagreeing.

One person who would certainly disagree with my earlier characterization of the white statue of Jesus is the author, who observes in an essay on his own work that Rosa's "whole vision was a religious one." This brings to mind two points. Price developed what he calls "elaborate notes" about the story, a practice which I would like to commend. My own story notebooks are filled with speculations on works in progress, with an occasional answer. A second point has to do with the content of Price's observation: It's clear that he speaks of what he planned to do, of authorial intention, while I speak of a reader's perception. The image/symbol still strikes me as laid on, excessive, sentimental; what I'm claiming here is only the reader's usual interpretive prerogative to say what a story means, as Ghita Orth claims it in her comments about my own story, "Lightning."

Since the whole of the story concerns Rosa's failed effort to do what probably couldn't be done, to ease the Ledwells' pain and grief, her perception of the Ledwells' son is appropriately complex, compounded as it is of embarrassment, sympathy, unease, compassion, and yearning for Wesley Beavers. Such human complexity of response, much like Laura's to the dead man in "The Garden Party," is diametrically opposed to the sort of oversimplification which is the essence of sentimentality. I suppose one might argue that Rosa's effort was in fact successful, in that it was a gesture at least as much for herself as for them, and she derived some benefit from the undertaking.

Wesley is very important to Rosa, hence to the story, even though he's not present. From the little we're told about him—his interest in the Florida electric chair and Willie Duke Aycock, for example—it would seem that Rosa deserves better. If we are led to feel protective of Rosa, are such details sentimental? Not, I think, if the feeling is evoked through detail much of which is comic, as is true, for instance, of Rosa's transparent postcard to Wesley.

The conclusion of the story leaves open what Rosacoke will or can do next, how she will complete the gesture, how she will connect. It is right that the story should end this way, that Rosa (for all her rustic, naive qualities) should show herself to be a large, spacious, generous person. She is, I think, the only character in the story (perhaps Papa is another) who is, in E. M. Forster's sense of the term, "round" rather than "flat," multidimensional rather than seen from a single perspective.

If I were pressed finally to say why I think sentimentality is to be avoided, I suppose I would say because it often doesn't work. The sentimentalist, that is, often aims for one response but gets another, gets not tears but a smile, not acceptance but resistance. Some readers may agree that Rosa's "whole vision was a religious one" and thus find her viewing of the statue of Jesus both appropriate and moving. Other readers, however, may feel that Price's planting the statue is overly insistent, condescending, and distrustful of the reader's perceptiveness.

Whether sentimentality will work also, of course, depends on one's audience. Thus, to cite but one example, contemporary academics (present company excepted) are likely to pride themselves on their intellectual toughness and on their ability to take apart any text and propose explanations for how and to what ends it was put together. For such a group, sentimentality would seem very ill advised. But (to get off this at last) Price is himself an English professor at Duke University.

"A Chain of Love" is, paradoxically enough, an often funny, occasionally poignant story about death and dying. Mr. Ledwell dies, Papa's death is anticipated, his wife's death is recalled, while the old, the sick, and the dying dominate the cast of characters, at least numerically. Rosa is an uncommonly though not beatifically good person, possessed of (not by) a powerful sense of Christian charity, of duty owed not to her family alone but to the "Friend Across the Hall" as well. That her best efforts produce little demonstrable benefit, that she is moved in part by the chance resemblance to Wesley Beavers of Mr. Ledwell's son, that Price (not for the first time) in the story's last paragraph, as if he were still unsure of what he'd earlier accomplished, seems unnecessarily to press the reader for a final commitment to Rosa, doesn't, in my judgment, make "A Chain of Love" sentimental. But I can sense that somebody is getting ready to dispute the point, which is just the way it should be.

ABOUT _____ Benjamin Carlisle

Benjamin Carlisle, born in Lakeville, Connecticut, in 1968, was a
student in a creative writing class at the University of Vermont
when he wrote "In the Woods." Since his graduation he has continued to make his home in Burlington, Vermont.

In the Woods

Benjamin Carlisle

Robbie is in the kitchen trying to teach Omar to sit, when suddenly the dog
freezes and his ears shift forward. Seconds pass before Robbie hears the car.
Outside the kitchen window he sees the snow blaze up briefly as headlights
swing through the turn in the driveway. The car stops in front of the garage,
and the engine is cut. Omar's head tilts to one side. He whines, a long ascend-
ing note, gouging the silence.

"Stay," Robbie whispers, resting his hand on Omar's head. He feels the
muscles at the top of the dog's neck, feels Omar's whole body craning toward
the door. "Good dog."

The car's horn beeps—two quick blasts. Omar jolts as if he's being shot and
springs to his feet, but Robbie has him by the collar.

"Sit, Omar. Omar . . . sit." Gently Robbie eases the dog's bottom to the floor.
Omar glances up at him and relaxes his ears for a moment, wagging his tail,
then is immediately focused back on the door, tense, still. Several seconds of silence pass, and Omar's tail begins to sweep slowly back and forth over the
linoleum.

Footsteps crunch in the snow, then Joyce's face appears in the window of
the door. Robbie looks up and sees her—only her face aglow in the light from
the kitchen, her dark hair soaked into the night that frames her. Their eyes meet
momentarily. Joyce mouths words at Robbie and hoists a bag of groceries up to
the window, but he turns back to the dog. Omar's rear hovers several inches off
the floor, and Robbie tries to talk it down. Sit, Omar. Stay. He doesn't want to
have to force the dog to sit. He wants progress. He does not hear—or does not
register hearing—the sound of Joyce struggling with the doorknob. The door
swings open, and he senses Joyce as she steps inside. Omar jumps to his feet.

"Sit," Robbie commands, but the dog scrambles for the open door. Robbie
barks sharply at Joyce, "Don't let him out," but Omar is already skittering
across the surface of the snow.

"Damn it," Robbie says.

"What do you want me to do, throw the groceries at him?" Joyce says.

Robbie doesn't answer.

She walks over to the counter and dumps the bags roughly. "Didn't you hear me honk?"

"I was testing him."

"Terrific."

"He was doing pretty well."

"Well, I was doing pretty shitty. It's icy out there."

Robbie tips back on the hind legs of his chair. "I didn't know it was you," he lies.

Joyce shakes her head. She crosses the kitchen and steps out the open door.

"Where are you going?" Robbie calls after her, but she doesn't stop.

Robbie lets his chair fall forward with a thud. He looks down at the socks on his feet. Joyce has left the door open, and the darkness mounts up outside, a great void, sucking the warmth and comfort from the room. Robbie stands, thinking to close the door at least part of the way, but considers the symbolism Joyce might divine from such an action and sits back down. He can hear Omar barking from the woods. Not another skunk, Robbie thinks. Please, not a skunk. You'd expect Omar would learn, he thinks, but nothing seems to dampen his spirit, just as nothing sharpens his brain.

Joyce comes in with two more bags of groceries, and Robbie jumps up to shut the door behind her. "Thank you," she says. "What a gentleman."

"Any more?" he asks belatedly.

"No, that's it." Joyce sets the bags on the counter. She takes off her jacket and gloves, drapes the jacket over the back of a chair, and stuffs the gloves into a side pocket. She begins to put away groceries.

Robbie walks over to the kitchen table and stands with his hands thrust deep into his pants pockets, watching Joyce move about. Her cheeks are flushed from the cold, and as she stretches to put a bag of flour in an upper cabinet, a wave of guilt and longing rushes over him. He did not intend for their evening to get off to such a start. He feels inept, idiotic, but it is too late to offer to help. He picks at the wool of his sweater.

"How was work?" he says.

"Fine."

"Just 'fine'?"

"Just fine."

Joyce sets two rolls of toilet paper on the counter, off to one side. Robbie hesitates a moment, then advances, takes these, and heads into the downstairs bathroom. He is stashing them among the soaps and detergents under the sink when he hears Joyce remark, barely audibly (as if unconcerned that he hear): "One upstairs." So he returns with a single roll and leaves it on the table. As he is crossing the room, his right foot strays into a puddle of melting snow from Joyce's boots. He cringes but remains silent.

Joyce puts two yellow tomatoes on the window sill. Taking a six-pack of beer from one of the bags, she lays the bottles individually on their sides in the bottom of the refrigerator. She puts butter in the door, a box of cereal in a cabinet above and to the right of the sink. She takes a quart of milk out of a bag. From the refrigerator she pulls a gallon container less than a quarter full of milk and pours the fresh quart into it.

"Why did you do that?" Robbie says.

Joyce turns and looks at him. "Do what?"

"That."

"To save space," she says. "It wasn't sour."

"Yes, I know."

"Then what's the problem?"

"No problem."

"It's all milk," she says. "It's homogenized. It's safe."

"I just look forward to the fresh stuff."

"Yes, well we all need something to look forward to, don't we?"

"Exactly," Robbie mumbles, then falls quiet. He looks away, but Joyce continues to eye him steadily. Then, with exaggerated care, she places onto the counter the empty milk carton she has been holding, walks by Robbie, and sits down at the kitchen table. She folds her arms across her chest and glares at him.

Robbie wanders over to the counter. His back to Joyce, he rustles randomly through the grocery bags. He grabs a box of tea, opens it. Earl Grey. He turns on the stove. In a cabinet to the left of the sink he finds a small tin pot and fills it with water. He can feel Joyce watching him.

The electric burner lights up like a cattle brand, and as he sets the pot of water on, Robbie pictures the cheap tin melting over the surface of the stove. He pictures water cascading over the sagging lip of the pot and sputtering across the molten puddle, partially dousing it, steaming. And the handle of the pan, black and erect—he sees it droop and sink like a mast into the solder, swallowed, and the last silver bubbles rise, slow with their belch.

"Tea?" he asks, still facing the stove.

"Robbie."

"No? Coffee? Decaf?"

"Come on, Robbie. Look at me."

He turns around. Joyce is leaning across the table at him. He smiles. "What?"

"Nothing."

"You wanted something?"

Joyce shakes her head and laughs sadly. "No," she says.

"Okay," he says. He turns back to the stove. The pot of water has begun to tick and rasp like emphysema—a dry, breathy hiss. Robbie looks on. A minute passes, and a layer of tiny bubbles begins to form on the bottom of the pot. They look like pinheads, silvery and lustrous at once, and Robbie wonders at this: how the bubbles seem more a product of the tin than of the water itself.

Another minute goes by. Soon the pot begins to shake softly. The water inside tumbles upon itself as bubbles the size of marbles are birthed from the seamless tin bottom. Robbie lowers his head over the pot and sniffs, tries to smell the stale air being cooked from the water. Shutting his eyes, he brings his face as close as the heat permits. Steam envelops him, the roar of the pot. His skin becomes slick with condensation, and when finally he backs off and straightens, needing to breathe, beads of moisture roll down his cheeks and accumulate on his chin. He catches the scent of his own shaving cream—as if the steam had opened his pores and released that smell. But it is noticeable only for a moment.

He wipes his face on his sleeve, then flicks off the burner and takes a mug from a hook. He turns to gesture to Joyce with the mug—"Last chance," he is going to say—but she is no longer sitting at the table. He hears footsteps on the stairs, the measured clomp of her boots. Then the bedroom door slams.

Outside there is just enough moonlight to make out the edge of the woods. Omar's barking has grown feeble and seems to be receding farther and farther into the distance. Robbie sets off across the meadow for the trees north of the house. He has put on his boots and Joyce's jacket; his was up in their bedroom. His forearms telescope a foot out of the sleeves and the jacket doesn't quite make it down to his waist, but the parka is thick and otherwise warm. Rather than stretch Joyce's wool gloves, Robbie searched through the hall closet and discovered an old pair of boxing gloves from high school. They are huge, generously stuffed and warm, and the moonlight glistens off the black cracked-leather orbs hanging at Robbie's sides like buoys, like planets.

The snow is deep and covered with a crust of ice that can't quite hold Robbie's weight. He lifts his foot high to set it on the surface, then, just as he jerks his weight up over the foot and is completely off balance, the foot plunges through and his whole body drops drastically. Every step is this way. Robbie is struck by how absurd he must look: like a chicken crossing a barnyard, the gesture of each step so awkwardly huge and reaching, yet so pitiful considering the results.

Finally Robbie reaches the edge of the woods and starts in. Here the snow is less deep. He moves relatively quickly for five minutes, picking his way through the trees, before he stops to listen for Omar. The barking continues, steady, not high-pitched and feverish as it might be if Omar had something cornered. It seems to be coming from off to the east. He moves in this direction for a minute or so, then stops. He doesn't seem any closer. In fact, now the barking appears to be coming from back toward the south, far to the south—perhaps from the woods on the other side of the house. He takes a step in this direction but immediately hears barks behind him. The barks are all the same—the same tone, same texture—but they seem to be careening through the forest, coming from everywhere and nowhere at once. Probably has his head down a hole, Robbie thinks. He calls out to the dog. Several times he repeats Omar's name,

shouting as loud as he can, then abruptly stops, discouraged by the hopeless-
ness of it and unnerved by a tone of desperation he hears in his own voice, as if
he and not Omar were the one lost and in need of help. There is no point getting himself worked up.

He stands among the dark outlines of the trees and for a moment is motionless. He breathes deeply, and the cold air stings his lungs. He likes the sensation. He breathes heavily, sucking in the brittle air with powerful heaves of
his chest. His lungs burn. This is when you know you are alive, he tells himself.
This is when you realize you will be lucky to wake up alive tomorrow. He begins to bounce on his toes. Shaking out his arms, he takes a few tentative
swings with the boxing gloves. The parka is restricting, but soon he is dancing
in the snow, throwing jabs and uppercuts and feinting to the right and left with
his head. Omar's barks whip out at him from the trees. Robbie ducks, lashes
back at them in flurries, then lunges with a roundhouse right. The gloves cut
through the night in short, broken orbits. This is life, he tells himself.

He slows quickly—footwork taxing in the snow—and soon is still, gasping
for breath. Tears from the cold sting his eyes, and he stands for several minutes,
feeling dizzy, light-headed, darkness swimming about him. The snow, up
around the top of his calves, steadies him as he waits for his wind to return.

Gradually Robbie's breathing slows, and as it does the night seems to settle
around him. He listens, but there is nothing, only the vast hush of a breeze
through the treetops, rising and cresting softly, then dropping off into silence.
His own breaths seem now to disturb the night with their coarse, uneasy vitality. He looks around him. On all sides stretch the moonlit plane of snow, sec-
tioned erratically by trees and shadows, punctured by his own dark footholes.
What now? he wonders. He is wide awake, alert, and ready but feels no urge to
move. His boots, snug in the imprints of his last steps, feel to Robbie to have
frozen in place. The dead weight is both comforting and frightening.

Minutes pass. Finally Robbie uproots his feet and starts home. What else is
there to do? And now, once he is moving and can picture in his mind the lamp-
lit house huddled atop the small rise of the meadow, he begins to feel cold.
Under the parka, his sweat begins to chill. And he walks faster, stepping in his
old tracks to make the going easier.

Robbie straddles Joyce's sleeping body. He nuzzles her cheeks and forehead
with his face. The heat emitting from her body is startling, almost oppressive,
like a blast of heat from an open furnace door. He kisses her lips and she rolls
her face away, mumbling groggily.

Robbie kisses her again and again, smothers her with kisses, and slowly she
awakens. She is half conscious. He kisses her eyes, and she moans. He blows
softly into her ear. She seems to smile. Robbie rolls off the bed and undresses.
He slips under the covers and slides over close to Joyce. Touching her side, he
finds to his surprise that she is still wearing her sweater from work. He feels
with his hand down to her waist to her belt and corduroys.

"What are you doing?" she says.

Her voice is distant and dreamy, childlike.

Robbie pushes aside her sweater and manipulates the buttons of her shirt front.

"Oh," she says.

He runs his hand up her stomach to her breast. She squirms, her nipple hardening under his touch.

"You're cold," she says. She pushes at his chest with her forearm. "Stop, Robbie. You're cold and sticky."

"I've been outside," he says. But he removes his hand.

He lies there for a minute, then gets out of bed and goes into the bathroom. His legs itch from the quick change in temperature; he bends and scratches them at length. He moistens a washcloth with warm water and runs it over his chest and face. His body smells good to him; the washcloth smells good. He presses it to his temples—one, then the other—looks at his face in the mirror for several minutes, then urinates. On the way out the door he stops at the mirror for one last look and remembers his teeth. He brushes them. Finally he returns to the bedroom and climbs under the covers.

"Joyce?" he says. He reaches out blindly and touches her covered body.

She jerks violently.

"Joyce?" Slowly Robbie's eyes adjust, and he sees she has the covers pulled up over her head. He tugs them down.

"Don't!" Joyce screams and snatches the covers back.

Robbie recoils in surprise. She is sobbing. "Joyce?" he says. "What's wrong? I thought you were happy." There is more sobbing. "Tell me what's wrong, honey."

Several minutes pass. Robbie sits still, slumped forward on the bed, and watches Joyce shake. He thinks about Omar—if Omar will freeze being out all night. He tries to picture Omar frozen, imagines the dark wet lip at the corners of Omar's mouth, loose nubbined flesh, smooth and faintly rubbery like the whip of meat from the tip of a lobster's claw. What would it look like frozen?

He tries again. "Joyce? What's wrong?"

But there is no answer.

She'll get over it, Robbie thinks. Tomorrow she won't remember a thing. He lies back and pulls the covers up under his chin. These things are always gone the next day.

He closes his eyes. The bedsprings tremble beneath him.

Minutes pass, and Robbie realizes that he isn't going to be able to sleep. He isn't tired. It occurs to him that he hasn't eaten dinner. He is hungry, starving even, and he contemplates getting up to make something. But he is already naked and in bed and can't be bothered. The covers are just starting to warm up. He wonders what time it is. It can't be much past eight, but it's hard to tell. Winter is deceiving that way, he thinks. It's still early, but it has already been dark for hours.

ABOUT _____ ### Maria Hummel

A native Vermonter, Maria Hummel was born in 1972 and began writing seriously in high school. She published her first poem at age eighteen while a student at the University of Vermont, where she majored in English and environmental studies. Hummel spent a semester in Prague and, before her graduation, was a teaching assistant for a course in nature writing, which she designed.

The Music of Detail: Creating a Character's Perception

Maria Hummel

In the film *Amadeus,* Mozart rushes to greet the emperor after the performance of his first opera in Vienna.

"Well, Your Majesty, what do you think?" he questions the emperor eagerly.

His Majesty replies encouragingly that it was a good effort, especially for his first opera. The disappointed composer asks him what exactly was wrong with the piece he thought already perfect, whereupon the emperor consults with his musical Cabinet and concludes that the opera had "too many notes," and Mozart should "just cut a few."

While this advice justifiably enraged the genius Mozart, who heard entire compositions in his head before he ever committed them to paper, not all artists can claim that their work is perfect from the moment they create it. For writers particularly, the problem of "too many notes" arises when not every detail is relevant, not every word necessary to convey the writer's meaning.

Benjamin Carlisle's story "In the Woods" demonstrates a balance of detail and conciseness that many writers struggle to achieve. Carlisle's judicious use of dialogue coupled with extensive sense detail builds a story from events that do not seem notable at first: teaching a dog to sit, unpacking groceries, walking in the woods. Yet, like a composer creating a fugue, he uses each of these moments to explore a theme with variations. This theme is the perception of the main character, Robbie.

Robbie perceives his own inability to communicate with Joyce, the woman he lives with, through details, small things that bother him, like Joyce's pouring the fresh milk into the old container. Through specific moments, Carlisle also conveys Robbie's longing to escape, as the character thrusts his face into

237

the boiling water's steam while Joyce attempts to confront him about their relationship.

When Joyce first comes home, Robbie is immersed in teaching his dog,
Omar, how to sit. Robbie's attention frequently focuses on Omar throughout
the story. That is a relationship he is comfortable with, and he uses it to ignore
Joyce as she carries in the groceries. Robbie's absorption is invariably single-
minded and often purely sensuous. When Joyce beckons at the door, he does
not answer her silent request for assistance but only sees "her face aglow in the
light from the kitchen, her dark hair soaked into the night that frames her."
This moment signifies the breach in their perceptions of the relationship. What
grates on Joyce about Robbie is not what grates on Robbie about Joyce. Later,
Carlisle plays out this disparity when Joyce is irritated by Robbie's lack of sensitivity to her while Robbie is annoyed only that she pours new milk into the
old.

Carlisle also portrays this difference through dialogue. Robbie does not
know what to say to mollify Joyce.

> "How was work?" he says.
> "Fine."
> "Just 'fine'?"
> "Just fine."
> Joyce sets two rolls of toilet paper on the counter, off to one side.

Robbie takes the toilet paper and puts it away. When he returns, he steps
into a pool of melting snow from Joyce's boots and "cringes but remains
silent." While the lack of communication between them seems to hurt Joyce,
the melting snow and the poured milk are among the little things that bother
Robbie. Carlisle uses these details to create his focal character's unique perception of the events.

As Robbie and Joyce continue to sidestep real conversation, he starts to boil
water for tea. His vivid imagination plays with the pot as the water heats:

> Robbie pictures the cheap tin melting over the surface of the stove. He pictures
> water cascading over the sagging lip of the pot and sputtering across the
> molten puddle, partially dousing it, steaming. And the handle of the pan, black
> and erect—he sees it droop and sink like a mast into the solder, swallowed,
> and the last silver bubbles rise, slow with their belch.

This image of impotence and submersion mirrors Robbie's wish to escape
the situation he is in. Joyce tries to bring their conversation beyond the groceries, but he thrusts his face over the pot, enjoying the steam on his skin as it
drowns out Joyce's words. When he turns around, she is stomping off to the
bedroom.

After Joyce's exit, Carlisle abruptly switches the scene to the woods where
Robbie walks, searching for Omar. This change of location echoes Robbie's apparent lack of sympathy for Joyce. The story, like Robbie, is inattentive to her
and her emotions and focuses back on the dog. In the woods Robbie achieves

the dark solitude he was looking for. Away from the accusing light of the kitchen, of Joyce's face, he listens for Omar's barks, which surround him no matter which direction he goes in. Black boxing gloves dangle at the ends of Robbie's arms like "planets" that contrast with the white snow he lurches across, his feet cracking through the thin crust:

> Robbie is struck by how absurd he must look: like a chicken crossing a barn-yard, the gesture of each step so awkwardly huge and reaching, yet so pitiful considering the results.

Carlisle's meticulous description of Robbie's walk illuminates through image Robbie's obsession with the small details of living. Minor irritations like the thinness of the crust do not allow Robbie to progress evenly across the snow. Similarly, in his emotional relations he cannot make any "huge and reaching" gestures before he is distracted by daily events, such as the puddle of snow wetting his sock when he wants to apologize to Joyce.

Robbie, submerged in the woods, feels comfortable and happy. "This is when you know you are alive, he tells himself" as he swings punches at Omar's invisible barking, the dark planets of his gloves volleying about him. Through this portrait of a man boxing the air, Carlisle shows Robbie's desire to fight back at the little things that consume his daily life. In the woods, in the dark-ness, Robbie is expressive, yet when he returns home he must confront Joyce, who does not communicate on the same physical level that he does.

When he climbs into bed with her, Robbie still feels safe, under the cover of darkness. For him the evening dispute is resolved, and he touches her, waking her and renewing her irritation with him. She tells him to go away, and he heads to the bathroom, where he scratches his legs, itchy from the temperature change. When he returns and tries to touch her again, she pushes him from her and huddles under the covers, crying.

After a few fumbling attempts to discover what has upset Joyce, Robbie lies back, still satisfied: "Tomorrow she won't remember a thing," he tells himself. "These things are always gone the next day." Carlisle reinforces his character's self-absorption with this statement, showing that Robbie cares about Joyce but does not see emotional problems as being on a different level than concerns about fresh milk. Robbie idly wonders what Omar's lips would look like if the dog froze to death outside. In another story, descriptions of tea bags, leg scratching, or dog lips might not fit. Yet these sensuous images are part of Robbie's outlook; these details are what he notices.

Carlisle never produces too many notes because his details are part of Robbie's observation. The author weaves these commonplace experiences into a piece, creating a character whose perception of events runs as a theme throughout the story—a character for whom the little things are most impor-tant. Carlisle's choice of detail shows writers where embellishment enhances art and where sparse language heightens a reader's attention.

Unlike operas, short stories are limited to what they can tell in a brief block of time. Carlisle uses one evening to build the scope of Robbie's character, and the resulting story teaches about the use of detail as well as about human perception. As the layers of a fugue weave a theme from variations, the descriptions of "In the Woods" build together to create a character who is easy to recognize but difficult to forget in his blend of perceptiveness and insensitivity. Like a good musical composition, Carlisle's creation of Robbie lingers in the mind even after the last line is read, after the last word sounds across the page.

David Huddle

David Huddle was born in the small town of Ivanhoe, Virginia, in 1942 and grew up there. He graduated from the University of Virginia and the MFA programs of Hollins College and Columbia University and is a veteran of the Vietnam War. Huddle's first collection of stories, *A Dream with No Stump Roots in It,* appeared in 1975. Since then he has published three more story collections, of which *Intimates* (1993) is the most recent, and three volumes of poetry, *Paper Boy* (1979), *Stopping by Home* (1988), and *The Nature of Yearning* (1992). His essays on writing have been collected in *The Writing Habit* (1992), and *A David Huddle Reader* was published in 1994. He teaches at the University of Vermont and the Bread Loaf School of English.

Little Sawtooth

David Huddle

My living room is twelve feet wide and twenty-five feet long; it feels both large and cozy. I work there in the hours just before and after dawn, the hours when my wife and daughters sleep most deeply in the bedrooms upstairs. Since my laptop computer screen is lighted, I don't have to turn on any lamps. I write while sitting on the sofa with the fireplace opposite me and the empty wing chairs facing me as if they held ghosts whose duty is to watch me struggle with my early morning compositions.

More and more, my writing has caused me to examine my past—or maybe more accurately, my past has begun to examine *me.* Surprising things have come back to me for no discernible reason.

Someone I knew at the University of Idaho twenty-two years ago has been paying me some memory calls this past month. She's a woman I knew from what was a particularly harsh period for me, the beginning of my separation from my first wife. I was finding living alone almost unbearable, but I was afflicted with Recent Divorcé's Syndrome, the symptoms of which are simultaneous desire and hostility. It's a good thing I'd enrolled in graduate school, because anything more structured than that would have had me committing crimes of violence.

Michelle Gonyaw was the young woman with whom I fell into acquaintanceship. She, too—though it took me a while to see it—was a case-study in pain that year. I of course thought I was the only human being on the planet who'd ever been so severely singed by love. After our Whitman-and-Crane seminar was over each Tuesday and Thursday afternoon, I'd catch up with Michelle and chat with her while we walked toward town. Actually I was doing most of the talking and most of it about myself, but of course that's not what I thought I was doing. And she wasn't friendly either, which is probably why I persisted.

A few years younger than I was, Michelle dressed in the plainest, darkest, loosest clothes she could find and kept her black hair cut short. She tried to make herself invisible, but people noticed her anyway—I did at the very first meeting of our seminar. She couldn't hide her big violet eyes and her skin that was the lightest I've ever seen on a healthy person. At the time I took pride in not being sexually attracted to her—I just thought she was odd and probably an outcast like me—but my guess now is that her way of presenting herself allowed me to be sexually attracted to her without my realizing it.

"You know you dress like a god-damn nun," I told her one afternoon, walking toward town. That was the tone I used with her most of the time.

She snorted, the first time she'd shown any sign of being amused by me. "Yes," she said. "That exactly what I am, a god-damn—a god-*damned* nun."

I looked at her while we walked, but she didn't say anything else. After a while I said, "That's a mystifying thing to say."

She shrugged, which marked the end of our conversation for that afternoon.

But I persisted, and though she remained detached in her attitude toward me, Michelle did begin to let me accompany her inside her apartment. I had to ask her if I could come in; after she stopped saying no to that, then I had to ask her if I could have a cup of tea. Later on I even got to where I'd ask her if maybe she had a sandwich or something to eat. But the point is that she obliged me— usually with a shrug, as if she didn't care whether or not I came in with her, or whether or not she had to put the water on to boil or had to make a sandwich.

Our acquaintanceship proceeded just this way for months. I did all the talking and most of the tea-drinking and sandwich-eating, while Michelle sat at her kitchen table and stared out the window. I got used to seeing how the fall light—and then the winter light—shone over her hacked-off black hair and her pale face on which there was never a trace of make-up.

One Thursday afternoon in Michelle's apartment kitchen, while she was staring out her window, I asked her if I could borrow a stamp. Not even glancing at me, she told me to go into her living room where I'd find one in her top desk drawer. I took that as a sign of her getting used to me, letting me rummage in her stuff like that, and I'll confess I was more than a little curious about what she'd have in her desk. A minute later she walked into the room where I was absentmindedly holding this pair of glasses in my hands and looking at them.

When I glanced up at her, I couldn't imagine what was wrong. She stood sort of tilted forward and her mouth gaped. Still, it might not have come to anything except that I noticed what her eyes were focused on. "Michelle, whose glasses are these?" I asked her.

She spun back toward the kitchen door, but she didn't walk out of the room. Instead, she put her face in her hands. I set the glasses down on her desk, walked over to her, and almost put my hand on her shoulder. I didn't of course, but I was surprised that she even continued to stand there near me because nothing I'd seen in her up to that point had indicated that she had it in her to cry like that or to let anyone give her comfort.

"What's the deal here, Michelle?" I asked her. She shook her head. But then she said, "Yes, I'll tell you. But not right now. Please." In another moment, she moved away from me—not rudely but just in a this-has-gone-on-long-enough kind of way. She walked over to her desk, picked up the glasses, returned them to the drawer, and turned back to me, by which I understood her to mean that she wanted me to leave her alone.

"So I'll come by for you tonight," I said on my way out. She didn't say anything. "We'll go get a drink," I said with the door open. She didn't say anything. "Around ten," I said from the hallway. She shrugged. I took that to mean that she'd go with me, and I shut the door behind me.

That was the beginning of phase two of our acquaintanceship. We started walking down to the Moscow Hotel for drinks around ten or eleven almost every night. And Michelle started telling me about the glasses. Again, I had to be the one who made it happen. I'd show up at her door and knock—but then it wouldn't take her long to get ready to go. At the hotel bar, when we had our table in the corner and our drinks in front of us, I'd ask her a question, and she'd start talking. If she stopped, I'd ask her another question. Sometimes I wanted her to go on, and sometimes it was fine with me for her to stop and let me think about what she'd told me. It took quite a few nights to get the whole story out of her.

From Spirit Lake, north of Coeur d'Alene, where she'd grown up, Michelle had gone to college down in Boise. She wanted to be a teacher. She had what she thought of as a standard liberal arts education until her senior year when she signed up to take English history from a new instructor, just out of graduate school at the University of North Carolina. He had all these fancy fellowships—and had even studied at Cambridge University in England—but Professor Hammett Wilson had never taught any classes before he showed up for his first one at Boise State.

He spoke about English history the way revivalist preachers talk about Jesus, except that instead of repeating everything three or four times and shouting and carrying on, Hammett Wilson was brilliantly articulate. Michelle said he'd be broken out in a sweat, pacing the floor and gesturing, but he'd be speaking with this incredible lucidity and precision.

According to Michelle, he wasn't anything special to look at, a man of medium height and build, average taste in clothes, brown eyes, brown hair that fell over his forehead, and glasses, which he wore all the time, except when he lectured. Michelle said you could almost hear the whole class exhaling when Hammett Wilson set all his books and notes down on the desk, stood up straight, smiled at them, and took off his glasses.

What happened between Hammett Wilson and Michelle Gonyaw was that one morning when he took his glasses off to begin lecturing, he was looking straight into Michelle's eyes. He seemed to want to look away but to be unable to manage it for a long moment. For the rest of the class Michelle felt paralyzed. Hammett took up the lecture in his normal manner, except that again and again his eyes came back to Michelle's. At the end of class, he walked over to her desk to ask her to stop by his office that afternoon. He hadn't even learned her name, so that he had to ask her that: "Sometime after two o'clock, Miss—?"

Michelle said she knew she shouldn't have gone, but she had no more choice about it than she did about taking her next breath. She knew Hammett was married. He was the kind of man who, even though he'd been in town only a couple of months, had taken his wife and two young boys with him to every-thing on campus that might be of interest to a new teacher. Michelle had been raised a Catholic. She said that in the student union snack bar she sat alone like a hypnotized person until two o'clock. When she stood up to walk over to Hammett's office, she knew her old life was over.

His door was open, but she knocked anyway, standing just inside the threshold. He'd been looking out the window with his back to the door. When he heard her, he stood up and turned. They stayed like that a moment or two, until he finally stepped around behind her to close the door. Michelle wouldn't spell it out for me, but I gather that he let his hand brush across her shoulders when he turned back from the closed door.

"What he mostly did was whisper—because the walls of his office were so thin," she said. "But it was very intense whispering. He liked to have long talks like that, the two of us standing there holding each other, whispering with our mouths almost touching each other's ears." Michelle said she thought it was strange, but she didn't mind it.

She also said, "I was the one of us who was more physically aggressive," meaning me to understand, I think, that she wasn't some innocent country girl who had let herself be seduced.

But I think nothing much more than whispering, kissing, and maybe a lit-tle touching happened in that office. How many times she visited him there is not clear to me, but I doubt if it was very many. No one suspected them of any-thing. It was still early enough in the fall for them to think about taking a drive out Sunset Peak Road toward the National Forest.

Having been a member of the Outing Club since her freshman year, Michelle had come to know that mountainous countryside between Boise and Sun Valley. About fifty miles out of Boise, there was a place called Little Sawtooth Falls that she wanted Hammett to see. Michelle considered it her own private park. She had the idea they could talk there in their normal voices.

That second week of October Hammett's wife had taken their two boys to visit her sister in Portland. When Hammett told Michelle that his family was leaving him at home for a couple of days, both of them were quick to say that it wouldn't do for Michelle to visit his house.

The arrangement they worked out was that after his Thursday afternoon class, Hammett would walk from his office a few blocks over to a shopping center parking lot where Michelle would wait for him. Her aunt and uncle had just given her a second-hand car for her birthday because they'd promised her one if she wouldn't smoke or drink until she was twenty-one.

I was amazed that anybody could get to be twenty-one without smoking or drinking, but Michelle just shook her head at me and muttered, "I never thought about it. It wasn't hard." I raised my glass to her, she raised hers to me, and we toasted the young woman she had been.

Thursday worked out just as they had wanted it; they even got warm, sunny weather for their trip. When he reached the parking lot, Hammett looked all around to make certain no one he knew was there before he stepped into Michelle's car. To keep from being seen while she drove out of Boise, he lay down in the seat with his head in her lap. Michelle said that was the part of it that later hurt her the worst to remember, driving her car with the weight of Hammett's head on her right thigh.

She said that as she drove, they talked, mostly about their families and the way they had been brought up, Hammett an only child in Chevy Chase, Maryland, and Michelle the second of five children in Spirit Lake. His mother worked for the Department of the Interior, his father for the Department of Justice; her father, with two of her uncles, ran the biggest building supplies business in northern Idaho. So much did Michelle like the talking with Hammett that she asked him not to sit up even after they were well out of town. That way, she didn't think he'd notice when she started driving slower to make the trip last longer.

Little Sawtooth Falls was a tiny park tucked away in the side of a fair-sized mountain. The state had put up only a couple of small signs marking the turnoffs to it and had cleared out a ten-space parking area. When they stepped out of the car and stretched in the warm air, it was just as Michelle had thought it would be; they had the park to themselves. Hammett came around to her side, grinning at her. A small sign pointed toward the path to the falls. She touched his arm and turned him in that direction. They walked slowly out of the late afternoon sunlight into the deep aspen shade and the smell of the mountain water.

The path wound along a stream that a rock formation prevented them from seeing, but the stream's noise grew louder as they moved through the trees. They descended a set of stone steps to a small wooden bridge. When they stood in the middle of the bridge and looked back up the way they'd come, the whole of Little Sawtooth Falls opened up to them, this immense, narrow chasm through which water billowed in tiers down to a pool spilling over right at eye level, then plunging to another deep green pool immediately below the bridge. Sunlight shafted through the trees; mist rose from the white water and the pools; high walls of gray rock jutted up to the sky.

For long minutes they stood there, Hammett just smiling and looking around them and she pretending to look down at the water, but mostly sneaking looks at him.

In noticing his glasses, she remembered how alive he was in class without them; so she reached up to take them off him. He seemed very boyish to her then. Hammett smiled at her and said she'd have to help him navigate.

Hammett's depending on her to help him move appealed to Michelle. She put his glasses in her skirt pocket, took his hand, and led him up the path on the other side of the bridge. Over there was a steep set of stone steps leading to a single bench where they could sit, where they could see the bridge and the stream far below them winding down through the trees and rocks away from the falls. The bench was a quirky fixture, something a ranger might have put up on his own because he'd decided that spot would be the ideal place to sit and study Little Sawtooth Falls. In front of Hammett and Michelle, maybe fifteen yards away, a powerful column of water caught the last sunlight of the day in a cloud of rising mist.

That bench was one reason why Michelle claimed a spiritual ownership of the place: every other time she'd come to Little Sawtooth Falls, it had been unoccupied. Sitting there with Hammett was utterly natural to her; in no place in the world would she have felt more at home. She joked with him that this was her office, and now she was holding office hours.

With their talking and stopping to kiss and touch each other, the time passed without their noticing it. Hammett didn't have to be back home, because his family was in Portland. And Michelle's suitemates might have wondered where she was, but even if she did still live in a dorm, she was a senior and could do what she wanted. She figured her suitemates would be delighted if she stayed out late for the first time since they'd known her.

The light very slowly sifted up out of the woods around them, so that when they first noticed it, they were softly encased in a deep blue grayness, but they could look up through the leaves and limbs and still see a lighted sky. They were pleased with themselves for having forgotten about time. The darkness brought them still closer to each other.

She kept thinking that she was embarrassed by what they began to do, but instead of holding her back, the embarrassment fueled her desire to go further, to do more. It wasn't something either one of them would have even thought possible, but somehow they managed to have intercourse on that bench. This wasn't easy for her to tell me about—there was a lot of stopping on her part and a lot of questioning from me, but finally she made it clear to me how things went. It was Michelle's first real sex, and though aroused, she wasn't as satisfied by it as Hammett apparently was. But she was able to give herself over to the deep twilight, the sound of the water, the smell of the woods, the absolute aloneness and intimacy of the two of them.

When they stood up to leave, they realized they might as well have been blind. No light came from the sky, from the water, from the road, no light came from anywhere: it was the darkest kind of dark.

The situation was funny to them, a little trick they'd played on themselves—or rather a trick desire had played on them. When they started inching their way down the hill in the direction of the bridge, they were holding onto each other's hands and even giggling nervously. Their feet hadn't located the stone steps that had brought them up there—those steps had probably been set by hand into the mountainside by the ranger who'd installed the bench in the first place, but that ranger had probably never imagined two people getting themselves stuck up there in the dark.

Hammett was in front, stepping gingerly and teasing Michelle about having stolen his glasses. She was teasing him back, saying that if he had them, he'd just be worse off because it would only mean that he'd have a clearer vision of the dark.

Michelle realized she was shivering; she knew some of it was because of that mountain coolness that rises up out of the ground. She also realized how all of her senses had opened up, so that she was like this night-blooming plant that had become sensitive to even the slightest current of air.

She was a little scared, but mostly she was excited by the adventure, by the sheer craziness of what she and Hammett were doing. Until recently, she could not have dreamed of moving through absolute dark in the company of a man with whom she'd just made love.

The sound of the water was clearly audible; all they had to do was slowly make their way down the slope in that direction; eventually they'd find the little bridge. Then the path up the other side would be easy.

While Michelle was imagining their coming down to the bridge, imagining the way their footsteps would sound on the flat wooden planks, Hammett's hand slipped out of hers.

Hammett hadn't spoken, hadn't made a sound; he was just suddenly gone.

Down the hill from her there was a little noise, a scraping like a foot sliding through loose dirt and rocks. Then from farther down the slope there came a slight brushing sound like a shoulder scraping the bark of a tree. That was it.

Michelle stood still a moment, listening. She called Hammett's name, softly at first, then louder. He wouldn't play a joke on her; if he wasn't answering, she knew he must be hurt. Fear was rising in her so that if she didn't do something to stop it, she was going to start shaking.

Getting down on her hands and knees, she crawled slowly in the direction she thought Hammett had fallen.

Almost immediately she came to a drop-off of about a foot and a half from one shelf of rock to another. Michelle encountered it with a hand reaching out and down into nothing until she was touching the ground with her shoulder. If she'd been walking, she'd have pitched forward off that shelf the same as Hammett had. So finding it that way made her feel both worse and better. She figured Hammett had knocked himself unconscious somewhere farther down the slope. That brought the fear rising back up in her. But she also figured that worming her way down the slope the way she was doing was probably safe, and that going as she was, even if it took hours, finally she was sure to find him.

It did take hours—or it seemed like hours to Michelle. As she made her way downhill, the noise of the water kept getting louder. Finally she reached the top edge of a cliff-face that plummeted all the way to the water. By now she had been crawling through the dark, blind and alone and scared, for too long to be able to feel much of anything new. But when she stretched her arm down over the cliff-face, she said it was like that huge pit of rock opened up inside her. She backed away a couple of feet and lay down in the leaves and dirt, curled up tight.

Too cold to lie there any longer, she crawled back to the edge of the cliff, crawled in the upstream direction for a long way, then back in the downstream direction. When she reached the little wooden bridge, that was when she knew she had been holding onto this shred of a fantasy of finding Hammett sitting there, waiting for her.

By now she didn't know how much time had passed. She was shivering hard, sitting on the bridge, hunched over and hugging her scraped knees until it began raining. Figuring she might be in danger of going into hypothermia, she made herself stand up and start picking her way along the path back toward the parked car.

It was just so easy to get from that bridge to her parked car. She hated how easy it was.

She'd been carrying her car keys in her skirt; taking them out, she remembered what she had in the other pocket. It hurt her whole body to remember Hammett's glasses, which she thought she could feel now, pressing ever so slightly against her upper thigh. She didn't touch them.

She got into her car, started it, turned on the heater, then sat there thinking. The clock said it was close to three. It kept raining. By the time she had warmed up enough to stop shivering, she had decided that whatever she did, it would have to be the right thing for Hammett. She tried to think what that would be. He'd avoided telling her much about his wife and children even though their pictures were on his desk and even though she'd asked him about them quite a few times. She wondered what that evasion meant—probably that he'd wanted to protect them from what he and Michelle were doing in his office. She took a deep breath and made herself think even harder about Hammett. It came to her then that he'd probably been afraid she'd want him to leave his family for her. She had a quick flash of hating him.

She wasn't sleepy, and she hoped she was thinking with a clear head. She had faced up to the likelihood that Hammett was dead, or at the very least, hurt badly. When daylight came, she'd go down there and find him.

Even after the inky blue world outside her windshield started lightening, she made herself wait longer, because she knew she'd need more than just a little bit of light. Still, the rain slowed daylight's coming; when she started down the path again, she couldn't see very far in front of her.

At the bridge there wasn't a lot she could do except stare down at the rock and water below it. The rain was soft and steady.

She made her way up the stone steps to the bench where only hours ago she and Hammett had sat. The rain had smoothed out the mud and leaves around the bench.

By guessing about what angle they would have started moving in, she found what she was pretty certain to be the rock ledge that had caused

Hammett to pitch forward in the dark. She found some marks that looked like they were her knee prints from the crawling she'd done down the hill. When she came down to the side of the cliff, she couldn't see over it all the way to the bottom. Like the soul of a stone, a draft of cold air rose into her face.

Michelle wasn't about to give up. She walked downstream from the bridge until she discovered a path that led her to the water's edge. Moving beside the stream, she worked her way back toward the bridge, stepping on rocks and ledges, sometimes even wading in the foot-numbing water. "Step up here, stupid," she'd say, or, "Over there, over there!" She was aware of how tired her body was while her mind kept driving her.

She was able to maneuver herself under the bridge and all the way up to the edge of the pool where Hammett should have fallen. From that point, she was able to see all around several tiers of the falls and down into the water. Beneath the surface she saw no shape or shadow that could have been Hammett.

So she walked slowly back downstream, then up again to the bridge and from there to the parking lot and the car. She got in and started it. Now she put her hand in her skirt pocket to hold onto Hammett's glasses. There were no other cars in the parking lot; there wasn't another person around. Shivering, she sat for a while with one hand in her pocket and the other on the steering wheel. Finally she put the car into gear and headed back to school.

Around ten that morning she drove into her dormitory's parking lot. The building itself was almost empty; she saw no one who knew her by name. No one seemed to take note of her coming in, even though she was wet and her skirt was muddy. It was an hour in which almost everyone was in class; her suite was empty. When she unlocked her room—she had a single—and went in and closed the door, she stood listening to the silence, staring at the rainy light at her window. In a trance, she removed Hammett's glasses from her skirt pocket and set them in her desk drawer, at the front. Then she undressed and put on her robe. She had the shower to herself. She didn't come out until the water had stopped stinging her scraped knees and palms. Back in her room, she lay down on the bed to wait.

Her mind darted in and out of sleep. She stayed where she was until well after dark. Then she dressed in her regular studying clothes and went out. She was sure her suitemates would ask her questions that would lead her to something, questions that would make her tell them what had happened or lie to them or something.

In the bathroom, a girl said hi to her; two others, chatting in the common room, smiled at her and gave her little finger-waves; Michelle felt almost invisible. She began to understand that they hadn't known she'd been gone. If they'd thought about her at all, they must have figured she was in her room, studying or sleeping or whatever they thought she usually did.

Standing in the common room leafing blindly through a magazine, Michelle had the eerie sensation of having dreamed the night that burned so vividly in her mind. She swayed on her feet. Then she felt her body sharply insist that every bit of it had happened.

She wished that she'd had somebody she'd confided in about Hammett. There ought to have been somebody she had to answer to.

She knew she had to get out of that dormitory. When she put on her jacket, picked up her backpack of books and headed for the door, no one even asked her where she was going. She was already outside before she heard somebody call out to her, "Bye, Michelle."

In a snack-bar booth with her Shakespeare text open on the table in front of her so that she'd be less likely to be bothered, Michelle worked it through in her mind to the point where she saw that it wasn't likely that anybody would connect her with Hammett's disappearance. She sipped her coffee. If anybody was even going to mention her name with his, she would have to be the one.

She tried to read the signs of everything she'd been through since that moment in class she'd found Hammett looking into her eyes. She could feel herself wanting to tell it all to somebody, tell it just so that it wouldn't evaporate. But she couldn't help feeling that telling somebody would be indulging herself. She knew she had to discern the answer to one simple question: should she walk out to the pay phone in the hallway, make a call, and tell someone what had happened? Staring at the back of her hand, she stopped it from shaking. A vision came to her, of Hammett Wilson sitting in his office waiting for her to come visit him and smiling at the pictures of his wife and sons on his desk.

So she decided. And walking back to her dormitory that night Michelle wrapped that secret around herself like some kind of invisible coat. She understood that holding it to herself made her experience with Hammett something that was hers and only hers. She set her mind to what she knew wouldn't be easy, carrying herself in such a way that no one would suspect how her life had been changed.

Something she never did tell me about, though I asked her, was what it was like at school when Hammett didn't show up for his classes or what it was like at his house when his wife and boys showed up and he wasn't there. She shook her head, as if she didn't want to say. "But, Michelle, wasn't there a huge investigation?" I asked her.

"Yes, there was," she said, nodding, but she went no further than that.

The last week of school that spring, Michelle made excuses not to go with me to the Moscow Hotel for our evening drinks. When I stopped by her place, she was polite enough in her refusals—saying she had vast amounts of work to accomplish in order to finish the semester. I was preoccupied with schoolwork, too, and so I didn't press her.

On my last morning in town, I called Michelle to try to persuade her to have breakfast with me over at the Moscow Hotel. She didn't need any persuading. She said she'd been planning to see me before I went back east.

The morning was bright, and we were both a little giddy at having finished up our schoolwork. Over our last cups of coffee, we were chatting very pleasantly, I thought, when Michelle startled me by taking Hammett's glasses out of her purse.

"You remember these," she said, holding them in front of her.

I nodded.

"These have been with me all this time." She curled her fingers around them. "I've kept them in my purse or else in my desk drawer, near the front, where you found them that time. I decided that if anyone ever asked me about them, I'd tell them the story, as best I could. That was how I worked it out: I wouldn't ever volunteer to tell anybody, but I wouldn't try to protect myself either." She spoke very softly, with her eyes almost closed. We were sitting in a dark corner but near a window that cast Michelle in a bright beam of sun, with flecks of dust floating all around her in the light. Her skin was clear and pale as a cup of fresh milk.

She leaned forward and asked in a near whisper, "But you know what?"

I shook my head.

She didn't seem to see me, but she went on anyway, still whispering. "I hated every single word I told you." She paused before she spoke again, this time so softly it was more like a message to herself than to me. "And I won't ever tell it again." She kept her eyes on the glasses in her hand on the table.

While we sat there, I had the oddest sensation of being with her and not with her. I had a sense of her making important decisions, and there was a crazy moment when I thought maybe she was getting ready to ask something of me; though I couldn't imagine what it might be, I felt a vague dread about it. I was pretty sure I would let her down because I wasn't ready that morning to be responsible for anyone but myself. But Michelle kept her silence, and we sat still until the window's shaft of sunlight had moved well past her. When we stood up, she quickly tucked the glasses back into her purse, as if she'd just stolen them. She came around the table toward me, meaning to give me a hug, I guess, but I wasn't ready for that either, because I backed away, facing her with no suitable gesture to make except a stupid handshake.

Michelle and I hadn't pretended we'd write to each other or keep in touch. Watching her walk away from me, I couldn't help thinking about Hammett's glasses riding along with her in her purse; the thought came to me that she was going to drop them in the first trash can she came to. I shook off that notion, but at a distance, I followed her out onto the street and watched her dark figure steadily diminish as she walked away. With my hands in my pockets, I stood out there in the spring sunlight until I couldn't see her any more.

Lately Michelle's story has been coming back to me, not the way it came, through her twangy Idaho voice but with such a visual clarity that it might have been a movie I saw lots of times years ago. The telling of it those nights in the bar of the Moscow Hotel seemed to make her cold, and I guess it made me cold, too. I remember the two of us hunkering over the table, hugging ourselves and shivering.

But when Michelle enters my thinking now, I welcome her almost as if she's a source of warmth. I understand how her telling me her story released me into the world where, every day, people carry out their lives with their stories locked inside themselves.

At the time, I didn't realize how she was affecting me, and I'm ashamed to say that I don't have the slightest idea what happened to Michelle. I can't imagine where she would have gone or what she would have done with her life. In my first years of teaching, I hardly thought of her. But as I gradually settled into my writing life, she began paying me more and more visits; I feel as if I have finally begun to be able to receive whatever signals her story means to send me.

Nowadays, my mornings of solitude are powerfully informed by Michelle Gonyaw and Hammett Wilson. More than once the thought has occurred to me that they may be the shades who inhabit the wing chairs that sit opposite me, while I tap out my sentences on my computer. If Michelle is alive, I know that she must spend some part of every day of her life on her hands and knees, crawling over cold dirt and moss and reaching out into the dark. And I know that thanks to her, I spend some part of almost every day of my life lost only in my writing, while light makes its way into my living room.

Try, Try Again: The Evolution and Construction of "Little Sawtooth"

David Huddle

"Yeah, you, you're 'Mr. Try, Try Again,' if I ever met him," my wife said in one of those throwaway remarks in which a family member casually summarizes one's whole life with one quick sentence. I felt insulted because she was pointing out my incompetence but complimented because she at least recognized my determination to try to get something right— I don't remember what the something was, probably my tennis backhand, which I've been trying to improve for half my life.

My inclination to revise is my primary resource as a writer. It's a natural impulse, one that in its small-change mode just about drives me nuts; printing up a final copy of a manuscript, I'll notice that I can improve a sentence or cut or change or add a word or streamline some punctuation—another manuscript will have to be printed up. Again and again this will happen until my entire morning has been lost to work that seems of no consequence whatsoever.

Big changes are another matter. I'm not so obsessive about them, but I'm always willing to try out a major renovation of a story when I see how it might result in an improvement. I'm blessed with a foolhardy confidence, a certainty that my revision is going to improve the piece of writing. Usually I'm right. "Little Sawtooth" is one of the half dozen of my stories that I'm proudest of, the source of that pride being the many hundreds of changes I made in it—of all sizes and varieties.

"Little Sawtooth" came out of—was begat by—a novel I was writing called *Loving Stupid*. In this novel—which has long since been consigned to the oblivion of a computer disk in a little file box—my two main characters went out to dinner with a couple of minor characters. The female minor character began telling the tale of Michelle Gonyaw. My vague intention with the scene was that she would offer a brief anecdote for after-dinner conversation—five or ten minutes of monologue, a page or two of typing. But she wouldn't stop talking. The tale she recounted became so interesting to me that I stopped worrying about bringing it to an end. I let her talk her way all the way through to an ending. At the time, I figured that with a little tinkering on my part to help transform it from part of a novel into a piece that could stand on its own, her tale would probably make a good short story. I knew it was too big and too distracting to work as a scene in my novel, but I proceeded with writing the novel anyway, knowing I'd come back to edit that runaway narrative, or maybe even just throw it away. As it turned out, I threw the whole novel away, keeping just a few of its parts like "Little Sawtooth."

Certain autobiographical elements are present in this story, which is mostly—say, about 88 percent—made up.

- At the time I wrote the story, I had a student in one of my classes who looked like Michelle Gonyaw. Her name was Jodi Gonyaw; her last name snagged in my mind the way certain names or words sometimes do; *Somebody Gonyaw* seemed especially right for a character in a story. Jodi had pale skin and dark hair. She had a rural background and a lot of gumption. I'm not certain what color her eyes were. I always meant to check them out in class, but I never remembered to do it. While I was teaching, I almost never remembered that my student looked like my character. Only in the first day or so of my writing Michelle's narrative did I think of Jodi and Michelle as resembling each other; they quickly became separate entities.

- Little Sawtooth Falls may or may not exist in Idaho—I don't know, though I did examine a map of Idaho to see if such a place seemed probable; the Sawtooth Mountain range does of course exist to the east of Boise. But the actual place I had in mind in writing my story was Texas Falls, Vermont, near the Bread Loaf School of English, where I teach in the summers. It is such a vivid and intricate landscape that if you're a story writer, you automatically begin to consider it as a potential setting for a story. I'd been familiar with Texas Falls for a number of years before it ever made its way into my writing.*

- In October and November 1987 I taught as a visiting writer at the University of Idaho. I sometimes had drinks with friends at the Moscow Hotel. On several occasions of having breakfast at the Moscow Hotel, I witnessed an unusually intense quality of light that shone through the restau-

---

*Using a *real* setting for a *made-up* story is apparently something I do fairly often without thinking about it. Here is how I recently explained it to an editor: "[My familiarity with the place] is probably what gave me the nerve to risk entering the imagined territory of what happens in the story: I could step into the dark unknown if I tightly clutched the teddy bear of what I knew so well."

rant windows. One weekend during my brief tenure out west, I drove my rented car south to Ketchum, Idaho, to pay my respects at the Hemingway Memorial there; then I drove west and north back to Moscow by way of Boise. The mountainous landscape I passed through on that journey made a strong impression on me. By my eastern standards, those mountains were vast; I felt small, alone, and insignificant. I took some shortcuts on roads that were narrow, with steep drop-offs down into deep wilderness; I suspected that if I had an accident on that journey, it might be months before I was found.

The basic narrative of "Little Sawtooth"—the account of Michelle's emotional collision with Hammett Wilson, their journey to the falls, his disappearance, and her return to her dormitory—remained more or less unchanged from the first draft to the last. That main element seemed so solid to me that I never imagined how difficult it would be to solve the main "problem" of the composition: Who was to convey that narrative to the reader?

The original teller of this tale, the minor character from my failed novel, wasn't anybody I knew or understood well enough to bring into a short story, but it seemed to me essential that the teller be female: I thought the person retelling Michelle's story ought to be someone in whom Michelle would have intimately confided. I tried having a female former roommate of Michelle's convey her story to the reader. Though I worked very hard to make this roommate a substantial character, I couldn't bring her far enough along—couldn't develop her "character" sufficiently—to make her telling the story an event that came to any consequence.*

I also tried having Hammett Wilson's wife tell the story retrospectively, having received, years after the incident, the news of what had happened in a letter from Michelle from across the country. Again the problem was character development: I couldn't empathize sufficiently with Mrs. Wilson to let her tell the story credibly.

I tried having Michelle tell the story directly to the reader. This maneuver had the odd effect of bringing up questions I couldn't quite answer. *Well, why did you do that, Michelle? What in the world were you thinking?* For example, Michelle's decision not to report Hammett's disappearance seems much more believable as reported by someone who can't really explain it in any depth.

---

*Twenty-five years of writing short stories have taught me a few basic principles, one of which is that a "frame" for a short story can never be *merely* a frame if the story is to be successful. That is, the external (or framing) story, even if much shorter than the internal story, must nevertheless *matter*. This principle applies to "Little Sawtooth" in that if there is to be someone who retells Michelle's story, that narrator's "story" must be, in its own way, of equal importance to Michelle's story. In *Writing in General and the Short Story in Particular*, Rust Hills offers useful and illuminating discussion of these matters; particularly valuable is Hill's suggestion that a story's "point-of-view character" must also be its "moved character." His classic example is *The Great Gatsby*, in which, though Gatsby gets most of the ink, Nick Carraway is both the "point-of-view character" and the "moved character." In the case of "Little Sawtooth," the teacher-writer who narrates Michelle's story must at the end convey to the reader how he has been "moved" by his acquaintance with her.

Trying to write "Little Sawtooth" as a first-person story forced me to see that my understanding of Michelle was only partial. I could tell her story second-hand, from the safe distance of someone who had heard it from her many years ago, but I really couldn't move directly into her thoughts, her feelings, her voice. So if I were going to get by with telling it at all, I was stuck with having to *re*tell Michelle's story. And I couldn't seem to find the right person or the right voice to do that *re*telling.

Although I've listed only a few options above, I tried them in many variations. I worked on the story off and on for well over a year before I hit upon a solution to the problem of who should tell the story. The solution arrived more or less by accident as well as by necessity.

Customarily I give a reading of my work each summer at the Bread Loaf School of English. Although there's some turnover in this audience from one year to the next, essentially the same people are kind enough to listen to me read to them every summer. It is an audience I respect a great deal, one made up almost entirely of English teachers. Unless I want to disgrace myself, I have to read something new, but this particular summer I had no new work in which I had any confidence. I knew that in spite of my not yet having found the right narrator for it, "Little Sawtooth" nevertheless contained a powerful basic narrative element that would hold an audience's attention. When I learned the date, I assigned myself the project of revising "Little Sawtooth" into shape for the reading. I had about four weeks. Maybe I wouldn't be able to solve its basic problem, but I knew I could make it a better story if I continued to revise.*

It had been a while since I'd picked up the story to review it. This time, as I read it over, the idea came to me: Why couldn't I—or somebody almost exactly like me—tell this story? It's impossible to reconstruct the circumstances that produced this notion; they would be powerfully informed by what I had been reading and teaching, as well as by the conversations I'd had with friends and family, along with the ongoing, intertwining threads of my thoughts and feelings. Any writer's daily experience is informed by the possibility of writing about it; a small department of a writer's consciousness monitors every waking and sleeping moment in terms of its place in a current writing project or its place in a writing project of the future. What is on a writer's mind—emotionally and intellectually—over periods of days, weeks, months, or years will usually surface in his or her writing.

Comfort and *luck* have been on my mind for quite a long while now, almost for as long as I can remember. My life is comfortable; I've had some luck. I possess good health, a family, friends, a job, a house, a car, food, and music; I have time to read, watch television, play tennis, and write. Though not a profoundly grateful person, I am nevertheless aware of the simple fact of fate's arbitrariness. Having done things no differently, having made exactly the same deci-

---

*Revising a story in order to give a public reading is a common practice of mine. The pressure of the occasion seems to serve as an incentive for me to give an unfinished story the concentrated attention it needs to bring it to a more finalized form. A similar pressure to finish a story can be usefully located in the occasion of submitting it for publication, passing it along to a friend for criticism, or even meeting a due date for a creative writing class.

sions I have made throughout my life, I could as easily be on the street, in a hospital, or in my grave. If I had to name some personal preoccupations, this would certainly be one of the first I'd mention, fate's benign quirks that have granted me my life.

Writing is the ultimate luxury. To have a life that allows one to write is the ultimate good luck. These are perhaps the main discoveries I made in writing "Little Sawtooth." They came to me in the final steps of revision, when I made a character like myself become the narrator of the story. Putting together those two opposite lives, Michelle's and my own, produced a narrative configuration that resonated in my consciousness. Enlightenment wasn't the only result of my bringing Michelle's story closer to myself; I also came to *feel* the story in a way that I hadn't until then.

Conway Twitty said of country-and-western music, "You can't sing it if you don't feel it"; I believe that the most powerful stories an author writes are those he or she *feels* most deeply. Of course, to produce a story that will emotionally affect a reader, the writer's feeling must be embodied in craft, but to my way of thinking, *feeling* is slightly more necessary than *craft*. Neither craft nor feeling alone will produce a strong story. In my efforts to craft "Little Sawtooth," in my trying it in many different versions, I stumbled upon a narrator who enabled me to write with feeling. I found a way to *take possession* of a story that didn't really belong to me.

Alas, Poor Hammett!

Allen Shepherd

In his autobiographical study, *The Education of Henry Adams*, Adams—casting himself as a representative modern man—concludes that chaos is the law of nature, order the dream of mankind. One of the more common aims of fiction writers seems to be to try to synthesize such order in their own or others' lives, to make sense of things, and to this end writing (and reading) may provide, if not answers to their questions, then at least shape and substance to their speculations. The narrator of David Huddle's "Little Sawtooth," who observes that "my writing has caused me to examine my past," appears to be engaged in such a process, his account of it complicated and made more substantial by the fact that he is telling us a story about (or within) a story earlier told to him.

The story-within-the-story offers writers and readers special compositional and interpretive problems and rewards: Perhaps Conrad's *Heart of Darkness* is the best-known example. As we read such stories, we are likely to wonder at some point whether the characters, subject matter, and thematic concerns really require for their articulation the complexity, irony, and ambiguity which this mode of storytelling seems to engender. It's the old question, for writers as well as readers: What's the best way to tell *this* story? We may wonder, more specifically, how and what the narrators know and how accurate their perceptions are. Or what the inner narrative (Michelle Gonyaw's, in "Little Sawtooth") finally means to the outer narrator.

So as to pursue these matters, let me do a little chronological overviewing of the story. About twenty-two years before the opening of the frame story, at the University of Idaho, one graduate student, Michelle Gonyaw, told another graduate student, the narrator, of her own earlier affair with and the accidental death of a young, apparently gifted, and certainly nearsighted history professor, Hammett Wilson. Thus "Little Sawtooth" offers three layered time periods: the freshman year of Michelle Gonyaw, featuring Professor Wilson, living and dead; a graduate school year of Gonyaw and the narrator, during which for his own reasons he extracts from her the Wilson narrative; and, after an interval of another twenty-two years, early mornings in the life of the writer-narrator, whose (second?) wife and two daughters are outside the loop, or will be, until they read the story.

Of the three principal characters, Wilson is surely the simplest, because least developed: We are not privy to such stories as *he* might have told. In Henry Adams's terms, chaos overtook him. In our experience of the story, he simply vanishes; X marks his spot. Gonyaw is a considerably more complex figure; that is to say, the narrator's response to her, early and late, is much more involved. At the time of their friendship he pursued her, questioned her, speculated about her, needed her; now, alone in his living room, he "welcome[s] her almost as if she's a source of warmth." She presides like a muse over his work, and he concludes his narrative with citation of two related lessons learned from her. First, he now understands "how her telling me her story released me into the world where, every day, people carry out their lives with their stories locked inside themselves." She *released* him; that is, she presided over the narrator's coming-of-age as storyteller and, even more, seems to have exemplified the nature of the subject matter of those stories. Second, in an image which epitomizes the human need for hope and order, he knows "she must spend some part of every day of her life on her hands and knees, crawling over cold dirt and moss and reaching out into the dark." I wonder about "every day," after all these years. In his own more comfortable domestic version of her desperate search, the narrator closes by telling us, he continues to "spend some part of almost every day of my life lost only in my writing, while light makes its way into my living room." What I have described, then, abstractly regarded, is a story-within-a-story, about writing stories, about the creative process, about what one needs to know, cast in an increasingly suspenseful narrative and employing conventional but very effective imagery—coldness and warmth, darkness and light, Gonyaw's beautiful violet eyes and Wilson's heavy glasses.

This is probably not the way Huddle imagined or wrote the story, nor is it how, line by line and scene by scene, we read the story. Reflecting on "Little

Sawtooth" afterward, however, we can see that it represents an account of the narrator's education as a writer, or at least a part of it, although as we are actually reading we don't think in such elevated abstractions. We are more likely to wonder about what's going to happen next, how it's all going to come out; why the characters behave as they do, what motivates them; perhaps why some things don't happen or aren't included; and finally, about the adequacy of the ending, whether it satisfies us or not.

I want to consider these issues one at a time. It's accurate to say, I think, that each of the chronological layers in the story has its own distinctive kind of suspense. Thus we want to know how the affair of Michelle and her professor will end; we also want to know how the "acquaintance" (not "relationship") of Michelle and the narrator will evolve; and finally, we want to know how over time the narrator has been affected by or has come to understand the young woman and her remarkable story. With regard to motivation, we may wonder why the narrator so insistently pursues Michelle. And why does she endure his companionship, about which she doesn't seem very enthusiastic? The narrator several times reflects on his motives concerning Michelle. At the time, he says, he "took pride in not being sexually attracted to her," but now he inclines to think that "her way of presenting herself allowed me to be sexually attracted to her without my realizing it." Really? We may add a few garden-variety explanations of their odd pairing. The narrator had recently separated from his first wife and required someone to listen to him recount his woes. And however much Michelle hated "every single word" she told him, she continued to feel, as she had immediately after the accident, that there "ought to have been somebody she had to answer to." They needed and used each other, in familiar fashion.

We may wonder similarly about Michelle and Hammett Wilson—why are they so powerfully attracted to each other, and why is it mutual? Huddle seems not very interested in exploring the motives of the freshman and the professor. Their affair is probably best accepted as a given; it doesn't violate commonplace credibility, and besides, if the two were passionately in love, contemplating marriage, and Hammett were agonizing over leaving his wife and two children, it would be an equally credible but very different story, and Michelle's response to her lover's sudden demise, the center of the whole fictional undertaking, would presumably require alteration.

What's important about the liaison is the way it ends. What we must believe implicitly is the veracity of the account of what happened at the park near Little Sawtooth Falls. We need to grasp the geography of the park and be able to see it as we read; Huddle is careful to give us all the help we require. We also need to believe that the narrator knows all these things, that he assimilated them in successive conversations with Michelle and has remembered them these many years. We need to credit what Michelle did after Hammett Wilson disappeared and also what she didn't do. We need to believe that she would not call to him, that she would not, once she had reached her car, go for help, and that afterward she was intent on doing "the right thing for Hammett." We need to believe that Michelle would keep the story to herself, waiting, as it were, for a deliverer, an uncharming prince, who turns out to be the narrator. We need to accept that all of the details subsequent to Michelle's return to the dorm, interesting though they might be, have no place in this narrative.

Any first-person narrative is inescapably a self-portrait of the narrator, all the more so when the narrator, as in "Little Sawtooth," is both observer and a principal actor. Regarding his younger self, the narrator exercises an indulgent humor, as, for instance, when he recalls the pangs of "Recent Divorcé's Syndrome." He seems now to have reached a snug harbor, from which both the stormy past and the peaceful present may be meditatively observed. Yet as we are told that Professor Wilson is one of the two shades visiting in the wing chairs, I wonder. The narrator was once a successor of sorts to Professor Wilson in Michelle Gonyaw's life, though he insists on the absence of conscious sexual attraction. At the opening of his story he remarks that "My past has begun to examine *me*," an odd locution, and I wonder whether twenty-odd years out of grad school, with a wife and two children (like someone else we remember), he hasn't perhaps undertaken some sort of extramarital liaison of his own, becoming yet again a successor to Hammett Wilson. What do you think? Is the story the narrator's effort to order his own confusion?

On the last page of "Little Sawtooth" I was gratified to read that the narrator, though he's ashamed to admit it, hasn't "the slightest idea what happened to Michelle." I was gratified because it rings absolutely true (that's the not-very-creditable way things often happen); because it makes the narrative manageable (imagine the consequences of several intervening reunions with her, indicative of all the other ways the story might have gone); and because it gives to the story that sense of closure (of a substantial number but not all things considered and made sense of) which prepares me to contemplate nature's law of chaos and man's dream of order.

To do a story-within-a-story well, as Huddle does here, is a difficult undertaking. Among the principal dangers are that the structure will seem an unnecessary, artificial appurtenance, that parallels between inner and outer narratives will seem problematic or forced, or that the narrator will appear not to be laying himself out on the page but practicing escape and evasion. Most successful practitioners, I suspect, probably don't come to such an elaborate structure in a first or second draft—not, in my own experience, until other structures have proved inadequate. The story-within-the-story is particularly effective when the narrator is seeking to discern or impose order on experience, to make connections, and to come to conclusions.

Ghita Orth

Ghita Orth grew up in New York City, where she was born in 1936, and is a graduate of Brandeis University and the University of Vermont. Her volume of poetry, *The Music of What Happens,* was published in 1982 as winner of the Eileen W. Barnes Award, and her poems have appeared in a variety of journals. A teacher of literature and creative writing at the University of Vermont, she wrote, in collaboration with Allen Shepherd, the fiction section of *Angles of Vision* (1992).

Handling Charges

Ghita Orth

She was glad he could not read. She was glad of that every time they pushed, hugged together in one triangular wedge, through the revolving door under the outpatient sign that told any passerby walking his dog or heading for the luncheonette on the corner why they were there—"For Cancer and Allied Diseases." Not that Jeff would have known at barely three what the words meant could he have read them, but surely he would have asked. Tova was prepared for certain complicated questions that were his due; she knew all the right words—not "real mother" but "first mother" for that unknown woman who had borne him, not "adopted" but "chosen" for the mysterious process that had brought him to them, his question-answerers. Now she was glad Jeff could not read, did not ask, did not yet ask. Instead, dutifully she read to herself all the signs as they waited for the elevator. "Up" and "Down" were too vague, too easy. She sought out "Radiation Therapy" and "Chemotherapy" and "Pharmacy," each with a little bright arrow pointing around and among the slick leather barrel chairs in the lobby. With its reception desk and uniformed doorman it could almost have been the lobby of a hotel in some foreign country where "Pharmacy" simply meant "telephone." She hoped it seemed like that to Jeff.

As she watched the red light tick its way down the numbers on the flat panel in front of her, the boy looked instead at the grey metal doors, and finally at the wheelchair that was pushed through them toward the man who stood at their backs. Tova had noticed that before; Jeff liked wheelchairs, often spoke to the people he found in them, was spoken to. For a long time, when their daily visits to the hospital had just begun, she had not understood. Assuming that he would share or learn her natural, courteous aversion to blatant difference, she had, at first, tried to direct his attention to whatever was handy, animal wall

260

posters, a water fountain, the stethoscope hanging out of some doctor's pocket, but wheelchairs brought people into his line of sight. As he walked with her up and down hospital corridors, these people were accessible, had faces that could turn to his.

He had always liked to see his world head-on, directly, without mediators. When he had sat, newly arrived at six weeks, in his infant seat centered on the round dining room table, he had ignored peripheries, reached only for what was before his eyes. Even when, older, he had recognized the lure of things beyond his touching, he had wanted to be as close to them as possible. Once she had held him up to the moon to which he pointed, held him as high as she could in front of the tall glass doors which separated their house from the Vermont winter, the frost-glass moonrays. "The moon's an egg," Jeff had said, as her arms tremored with the strain of his twenty-five pounds. "I will eat it." Then she had laughed, proud of the cold, straight line of his vision. Now, as the wheelchair slid past them, Jeff stopped to smile.

The woman seated in it smiled back. Her lap was piled with evidence of long days and nights in residence on one of the hospital's far, unimaginable upper floors: a few paperback books, a gym bag, a flat white box emblazoned "R. H. Macy," and in her hand a small bunch of pinkish flowers wrapped in paper towels instead of a florist's green tissue. She was going home, she said to the boy, only to the boy. Tova stood irresolutely above them. The doors of the elevator were surely about to close, the man surely about to accept the wheelchair from its attendant, but the woman and Jeff were talking softly about the pretty flowers, how nice it was not to have to stay in the hospital. Finally the man did take the chair, began to wheel it toward the exit. The elevator doors twitched a warning and Tova urged Jeff inside, knowing that as the woman was propelled past the barrel chairs, the desk, the arrows, she would be able to read all the signs for herself.

When the elevator left them on the third floor, Tova and Jeff walked companionably again, almost gaily, his hand in hers, toward what she tried to label "Control Room" in her head. Here a long row of chairs for waiting patients led to a battery of machines, each knobbed and warted with buttons and switches and lighted glass bulbs like the tops of coffee percolators, each with its own video screen, its own crew. She could not begin to understand these machines which manipulated and interpreted the betatrons and scanners leaded behind tall doors at the far end of the room, but she was glad for their metallic glow and hum. Here, at least, fantasy was possible; she imagined Jeff saw the room as something out of *Star Trek*.

They always had to wait here, even though they were always on time. The waiting room had become an expected part of each morning, like her private game of identifying the flowers on the handkerchief that one of the radiation therapists always wore in a pocket high on her chest. It was pinned there, fanned out in an intricate origami-like design exactly like the handkerchiefs worn by the waitresses in Schrafft's when there was still a Schrafft's on Broadway and Eighty-second Street and she had been taken there by her mother on special occasions, as a treat.

There had been many ordinary events masquerading as special when Tova was a child—going to the planetarium, the zoo, even buying school shoes at the Indian Walk store. There she had had to stand on the treads of a black machine and put her feet, socks and all, into two slots that allowed the shoe salesman to peer into an eyepiece right through the cotton knit, the skin, down to the multiple, interlocking bones of her feet. Although they had a different salesman each year, the pattern was always the same; after he had made a notation on his pad and smiled to her mother at the fine condition of her metatarsals, the larger size necessary for her oxfords or saddle shoes, he would say, "Why not have a look and see how well our shoes take care of your feet?" the way store clerks now said "Have a good day" after each anonymous transaction. And she would look down the metal tube that was like an upside-down periscope and find her own grey skeleton. Even that was a special occasion, and Tova and her mother would have banana splits at Schrafft's afterward, not at the counter but at a linened table with a waitress, for reasons she didn't quite understand.

Pieces of New York were missing or dislocated each time Tova came back from Vermont, but she still saw the city in which she had grown up with its ceremonies of childhood intact. This summer, Jeff had his own incomprehensible ceremonies in her city. The three of them had driven down from Vermont with scarcely packed tote bags, hangered clothes straight from the closet, the diagnosis with its Latinate, multisyllabic name echoing unspoken in the tight air of the car. Wearing the diagnosis was easier for Jeff than hearing it had been for Tova and Rob, especially for Rob, who was a pathologist and knew about rampant, malevolent cells irregularly drawing dark stain to their centers, and about prognoses. It was a mistake to think that grief brought people together, as Tova had often read in women's magazines; rather, it did and it didn't. When she and Rob lay together on his weekend nights in New York, each twined arms around the other's body but hugged an inviolate, singular pain. When Tova saw Rob suddenly stop pouring a cup of coffee and stare, empty-eyed, she read her own loss in his shaking hand and touched his fingers for the thinning of Jeff's tousled, unruly curls, for his raw, peeling cheek, for the maimed and altered vision of Son. She did not know why Rob's hand shook; to touch it was only to touch her own prickly, resentful skin, her own tremors of anger.

She knew that she had always taken an unjust pleasure in Jeff's curls, his perfect, gentle features—unjust because they were a gift, as he had been, and evidence of a genetic heritage with which she had had nothing to do, like the embryonic beginnings of his disease. That he had been the kind of baby who elicited clucking comments from checkers in the supermarket as she pushed him, king of the milk cartons and bags of vegetables that surrounded him in the cart, toward their adulation, had always seemed to her sheer luck. She was certain that she and Rob could never have produced a child as beautiful as he, and was secretly and hotly pleased to find that no one seemed to notice the discrepancy between what Jeff was and what she could have made of her own blood, her own plain chromosomes. When strangers commented on Jeff's prettiness, for that was the right word, Tova would often respond, "I think so too," rather than with the modest "thank you" that a real mother, responsible for having produced that prettiness, would have earned. She was innocent of responsibility in his separate beauty; she loved that beauty because it was gratuitous. Sitting beside Jeff on the neatly aligned chairs in the Control Room, Tova wondered if anything was really gratuitous at all, or if, like the Free Gift offer from Sears that Rob had brought down with the mail on Friday, every Memorandum Pad with Attached Address Book and Pencil Holder that was given to you absolutely free in life would cost you $2.98 for handling charges the following month before it was really yours.

Jeff sat quietly in his seat, only getting up now and then to investigate the child-sized water fountain across from where they sat. He was often thirsty, peculiarly so, from some strange side effects of the drugs that thinned his hair or the radiation that blistered his skin, but Tova knew that he particularly liked the fountain for its size. No one had to lift him to press its button, hold him to the warm spurt of water. He could do it all himself, and he did, again and again, as they waited each day. There were only three people waiting with them this Monday—people she knew by sight but not by name or medical history, information which was offered her in chance hospital encounters more often than she liked. She had taken to avoiding people's eyes as she and Jeff moved from floor to floor in their daily progress at Memorial, or rather, avoiding patients' eyes. She did not want to offer up Jeff's diagnosis, his course of treatment, even his name to the common pool of guiltless catastrophe that swirled through the hospital corridors.

One of the women waiting with them was obviously, like Tova, only the mother of a patient; she looked furtive, closed. The woman sat with a girl of ten or eleven who was reading a book, incongruously dressed in a ruffly violet party dress and patent Mary Janes as though coming to Radiation Therapy were an Occasion. Perhaps that was the effect her mother, small, furiously knitting something long and striped, had intended when she buttoned the child into the frilled organdy: "We're not regulars, you see. This is not really our life." Jeff, who was now sliding slowly, with much care, along the padded seats in the direction of the girl, wore the clothes of everyday, shorts, the red shirt with its blatant green alligator that had been a nonbirthday present from an aunt of Tova's who shopped at Bloomingdale's. Jeff was accumulating presents in increasing numbers—it would take two trips to get all his Fisher-Price garages and farms and loading depots back to Vermont. Even people who were on the outskirts of what they were living brought sacrifices to Jeff's illness; the superintendent of her parents' apartment building, their temporary home, had given him a 1927 silver dollar wrapped carefully in tinfoil.

Although Jeff wore his ordinary clothes (Tova wondered if, by having him dress this way, she was striving to be blasé as the other mother was striving not to be) and was now running through his ordinary routine with strange children met by chance—the silent sidle up to the child's seat, the stare, the proffered lure (this time an offer to show the girl the water fountain)—he must have known that his days were somehow different from those of other children, that this girl and this room were different too. Other kids were riding Big Wheels round and round the dead-end street on which they lived at home, making larger and larger circuits from the gravelly roadway over dangerous rain-gutter gullies into the trimmed lawns and daffodil beds of the yards that de-limited their adventures, and here in New York, city kids were roller-skating along the park's bicycle paths, or climbing the riggings of ladder and rope in Adventure Playgrounds, or watching Captain Kangaroo. Instead, by eight-thirty each morning, Tova and Jeff were being bussed from her parents' apart-ment beyond the neighborhoods of ordinary children. The red-brick, square fortress of a city school across from the hospital was closed for the summer the only children Jeff talked with were those who waited, as he did, for the next step in a pattern only their parents saw whole.

Jeff and the organdied girl were taking turns controlling the water foun-tain's spray with their thumbs when Tova heard his name called, called to him, took him to the thick grey door at the back of the room. He was met by the handkerchiefed attendant, and Tova took up her place at one of the buzzing consoles that orchestrated his being there. On the small television screen over the panel of buttons and flashing lights she watched Jeff lifted to the table, po-sitioned, his ragged blanket a grey blotch under his head. She had resisted that—bringing the disreputable blanket here to the hospital each day in a flow-ered plastic bag. It seemed a throwback to a babyhood out of place in this fu-turistic machine whirr and glint. Unlike other mothers she knew, Tova had never let Jeff drag his blanket with him to the store or even to the doctor's of-fice when he went for checkups or shots. It was a comfort for night only, for real darkness. But after the first day she and Rob had brought him to Memorial, left him in the hands of the curiously comforting strangers for tests, for further di-agnoses, she had carried the blanket with them; perhaps as Jeff felt it against his face it would smell of dreams to him, of mother.

Tova felt vaguely self-conscious waiting for the crews around her to begin their maneuvers. On the tiny screen she watched the woman leave Jeff's side, close the thick door; she heard her polite voice, a waitress's voice, say to the technician, "All right, we're ready now," and Tova began the story. Jeff never seemed to object to the blinking red eye of the machine that, as she watched, bent slowly to meet his own. He never cried, but he wriggled a lot. To keep him still, to keep them from having to bind him still with webbed bands of gauze, she told him stories each day over the intercom that led across the distance from where she sat into the closeted silence. It had been the doctor's idea, that first day. "Why don't you talk to him on the mike," he had said. "Just ask him to lie still, tell him it will just take a minute." But she couldn't do that, it seemed too much like a truce. Instead, almost without realizing what she was doing, Tova had begun that day to tell him a story, making it up as she went along, hoping his time under the small florid sun would be over before her story reached a conclusion, before Edgar the Elephant had to decide what to do that day or actually eat his breakfast. It seemed to work. Jeff would lie quietly, and the story would still be moving when the machine pulled back and the waitress-woman helped Jeff hop off the table, collect his blanket, find her, asking, "Then what happened?" and she could make continuity a promise for the day that would follow.

They walked back toward the elevator, Tova stuffing the stringy, splotched blanket into its bag and reaching for Jeff's hand to keep him from the water fountain and the girl, who was carefully putting a felt marker into her book to keep her place in its story. Jeff never seemed to mind their daily visits to the Control Room, for its strange ritual did not hurt, and his mother obviously thought it important. He could not have been concerned with what the betatron was doing to the knotted hive of busy, illicit cells behind his cheekbone; he did not have to be. Each day, though, as they elevatored down, left the shiny, imperturbable lobby, Tova planned a treat for the way home—a taxi, perhaps, so that Jeff could chat with the driver and spin an imaginary wheel as they followed the lines of traffic through the park, or an ice cream pop from the Good Humor man on the corner, or the zoo—as though to reward him for what he did not know he had done, was doing.

When they stepped into the midmorning glare from under the hospital marquee, Tova handed Jeff his hat, a red felt cowboy hat with lariat strap, white embossed horses around its crown. As usual, he grinned when its twined string hung jauntily under his narrow chin and he could proceed to their homeward adventures suitably fitted out. The hat, though, was more necessity than costume for fantasy. Jeff had to wear it to protect his blistered cheek from further prickling and peeling under a real sun that did not turn off with a *ping* at the end of some prescribed dosage. Face shaded under the red cowboy brim, Jeff galloped toward the bus stop, knowing they would be going somewhere on the way home, not knowing why. Tova wanted to avoid the zoo. Mondays, she had discovered, brought out neat lines of day-campers clutching balloons and brown-bagged lunches, herded from cage to cage by zealous counselors and curiously looking at Jeff's hat, his face, blocking his view of Rose the hippopotamus. He was getting nearly too heavy to lift, and Tova tried to keep the zoo for weekends when Rob could hold him up, evading the rows of hatless heads.

The bus pulled to the curb, and Tova gave Jeff their fare money to deposit ceremoniously in the glassed-in box. They sat toward the back, and as the bus, more than half empty, began its lumbering chug toward the park, Jeff got up to swing two-handed round and round the silver pole near the rear door. Tova hoped he was feeling all right—some days, she never knew which or why, the treatments made him sick to his stomach and he would gag uncontrollably, even throw up, no matter where they were or what he had or had not eaten. One morning on the way home he had thrown up on the bus, and an elderly gentleman in the next seat had clucked in commiseration, offering up the paper towels he was unaccountably carrying in his shopping bag along with *The Daily News* and a worn pair of brown shoes. Tova had silently mopped up the mess, mopped up Jeff, tried for the rest of the trip to ignore the dark, irregular stain that spread below the collar of his shirt.

It was odd how the therapy seemed so much worse to Tova than the disease itself. Although Jeff's right eye had teared as the muscles around its orbit burgeoned with unruly cells, he had felt fine until those cells began to struggle against the drugs and beta rays in the hospital's arsenal. He had good days and bad days now, and did not look fine any more. Sometimes Tova wondered if the disease really existed at all; it was not hers, and all she ever saw of it were its peripheries. She knew that something tough and hard lived behind Jeff's eye, yet all she could visualize was a grey blur nestled softly against the fine clean bones of Jeff's skull on the X-ray films that Rob had shown her at the beginning.

Jeff was timing his swings around the pole to the stops and starts of the bus as it nosed through the crosstown traffic, and Tova decided on the carousel. Tomorrow, perhaps, it would make him queasy; today he could obviously handle it. She held the heavy doors open when the bus stopped at the edge of Central Park, and Jeff swung down and through them to walk beside her toward its stone-hedged entrance. He had not asked where they were going, yet he didn't bear left and zooward at the first fork in the path but skipped, slightly ahead of her, toward the tunnel that would bring them to the carousel. Perhaps he thought he had decided the day's ceremony for himself, perhaps he needed to think that.

The tunnel under the roadway was dark; as a child on Sunday outings with her father, Tova had loved to clomp her feet heavily inside it, sometimes even to shout vague, resounding syllables that would bounce and echo off the rounded brick walls curving over her head. Now whenever she walked through the tunnel she hurried against its darkness, conscious of every footfall that was not her own, hurried to the semicircle of daylight at the other end, ignoring the white and red swirls of graffiti on the cement ceiling by not looking up. When Jeff hurried with her, as he did now, she knew he was pulled by the lure of the carousel, not pushed from behind, invisibly.

The carousel too was a place out of Tova's childhood, sheltered in its small, octagonal house, constantly repainted, the same. It was a picture-book merry-go-round, the animals all horses, manes frozen into arabesques by invisible winds just the way they were supposed to be—no zebras or garlanded bears, and certainly no characters from Walt Disney or *Sesame Street*. Interspersed among the horses were stationary sleighs pulled by stationary ponies for those children who had to be held in arms, too young even to be strapped onto the glossy stallions that moved up and down their greased brass poles in time to the music that could be for nothing else.

The music led Jeff running to the ticket booth guarding the painted entrance. He never wanted Tova to go on the carousel with him; he did not want her standing carefully by the side of his glorious steed as her father had always done, and they both knew she did not want to ride awkwardly on its companion, clutching her handbag, legs hanging graceless below the silver stirrups. Tova bought Jeff's ticket, stood with him until the music slowed and the spinning platform ground toward stillness, children spewing from its edges. She watched while he walked, solemn with the responsibility of choice, round the circuit of horses and sleighs until he stopped at a black Arabian, carapaced in scarlet, white maned. Only then did Tova step onto the slatted carousel floor to hoist Jeff up to the bright back of his tall horse, to buckle its leather strap tight around his waist while he held the cracked brown reins, ignoring her as best he could, his cowboy hat suitable, right.

In the silence before the new round of music that would begin the horses' stately progress, Tova found a space on the park bench in front of an umbrel-laed hot dog stand whose vendor sold brown paper bags of peanuts in their shells, though this was far from the zoo. The wooden bench slabs were rough with peeling paint and gouged initials, and she felt their splinters against her legs, white and vulnerable after the long winter of snows in thick woolen slacks. The mechanical pipe organ began revving up to tinny fullness, and the platform began to turn, slowly at first, then, as if assured of its route, more and more quickly. It was easy for Tova to find Jeff among the many colors of lac-quer and overalls and pinafores; she sat on the bench waving at the red hat that swooped in and out of her line of vision above a horse that rose and fell like breath. Tova and Jeff smiled as their worlds revolved—eyes meeting, then blurring until they caught each other again, then another blur.

Insulated already in these weeks, accustomed to Jeff's difference, to her own, Tova was startled when the woman in the rose-printed dress sitting and waving next to her turned to speak, as though Tova were really the mother of a child simply having a turn on the carousel. "Which is your child?" the woman said, smiling, used to such conversations on the benches surrounding cement-walled sandpiles and skating rinks. Tova was not used to them; the words came to her thin and mechanical, voiced through lead. Vaguely, Tova began to point in the direction of the carousel, hoping the woman would focus on some real child, when the music began to falter, like a record turning still after its source of power has been cut off. A man who had been holding a small, fat-cheeked boy on the back of the horse next to Jeff's unbuckled the child, then turned to Jeff and lifted them both down and off the wooden platform.

Rushing to Tova, eager for more, asking please, please could he have an-other ride, Jeff had separated himself from the undistinguishable others. "My," the woman said, still smiling. "Is this your son? That's a terrible burn on his face, it must be very painful. How did it happen?" Tova gave Jeff the dollar, watched him hurry for a place in the newly forming ticket line, and knew she could not stand back and spill the chanceness of her disaster into the woman's flower-strewn lap, could not dirty another life with it, could not watch the smile curl into mere blameless pity on the woman's bare face. This she knew, but she did not know, not till the words were circling hot and red in the air be-tween them, that she would answer, "It was boiling water. A pot on the stove. I knocked it over."

The woman was satisfied. Redeemed from innocence, flushed with sudden having, Tova got up and ran to bear, finally, her son high to the back of the black horse that rode up and down and never away.

The Poem That Got Away

Ghita Orth

"Handling Charges" is the first story I've written, and I wrote it only because its material didn't want to be a poem.

Poetry is the genre that's always been most congenial to me as a writer, for a number of reasons—it allows me to look closely at a small moment of experience and find out as much as I can about it as I try to embody it in language; to handle words one at a time, testing their heft and possibilities; to get nearly instant gratification when I complete a piece of writing in a matter of days rather than weeks or months. I was comfortable with poetry, and then along came material that was pressuring me to write about it and to try out a new, unfamiliar way of doing that.

I work best when I feel compelled to give voice to some idea or issue that's inched into my consciousness, that's pestering me by hanging around the edges of my daily life and asking to be acknowledged. Until "Handling Charges" and since, the concerns that did that for me were poem-sized, rooted in a single cluster of images or a single, pivotal moment. But the material of "Handling Charges" didn't want to be a poem. I had a problem.

Any content, of course, is legitimate in poetry or fiction. What troubled me about the issues in "Handling Charges" was not that they turned on such "unpoetic" circumstances as cancer and radiation therapy. A poem can be flexible enough to contain any world; in fact, I had already published a poem dealing with some of that material:

ELEPHANTS—A MYTHOLOGY

Your quick childhood
was trumpeted by elephants—
a tuskless one, calicoed
red and white, hugged into bursting,
leaking its plastic cells
like seeds into your hair;
small grey models ranked staunchly
on your shelf, Indian, African,
their fat knees wrinkled by the carver's hand
over unbending joints; and the elephant
of seamless words I made for you
when you were made to lie, unmoving,
on the steel table in the steel room
under a red-flowering machine eye.

Microphoned through deaf, lead walls,
Edgar the Elephant, galumphing loose
in Central Park, smiled shyly

under his trunk and stroked the backs
of small boys just like you,
saying *lie still, lie still.*
Then, after the room unclenched
we rode the crosstown bus
to Zoo elephants, slit-eyed and real,
who pointed soft hairy mouths
at the peanuts slipping from your lax hand.

When you begged elephant drawings
from the doctor charting your disappearance
with his blunt pen,
when you marched elephants
heavy-footed through your imaginings,
was it so you might see
calves holding tight
to their parents' rope-tough tails,
trunks twined fast to such bulking safety
that you could dream of never letting go
or getting lost?

Because the poem is written in the first person, whatever assumptions one might make about its autobiographical origins seem justified, but I wrote it enough years after the events that engendered it to be able to see those events with some perspective, to consider them and their implications. It's only when we can step back from a situation that we gain the distance necessary to write *about* it, not *in* it. In writing this poem, then, I tried, as fiction writers (like the narrator in "Little Sawtooth") often do, to discover some coherent shape in what had been essentially disordered, inexplicable. Like telling the story of Edgar the Elephant, writing the poem gave me, or rather my language, some way, after the fact, of ordering a world that had gone out of control.

So it was neither the grim content of the situation nor its emotional load that kept me from trying to put the whole day covered in "Handling Charges" into a poem. It wasn't even the fact that I had a "story" to tell; poems can bear the weight of narrative as readily as fiction. The reason I thought the "story" wouldn't work as a poem, or rather that I didn't know how to *get* it to work as a poem, had something to do with the nature of the issues I wanted to confront.

In the poem, the speaker muses about her son's feelings; her own aren't really dealt with except by implication. What I wanted to think about more closely, and make discoveries about, were the mother's complex attitudes and responses as she stood at the edges of her son's illness.

Like most writers, I can't say there was "a message I tried to get across" (a phrase I'd like to see self-destruct along with any student paper in which it appears), but I did want to deal with some concerns that seemed to grow out of the situation's complexities. I wondered especially about the burden of being guiltless, and what one could do about it, issues similar to those troubling Toshiko in "Swaddling Clothes."

Usually, we think of guilt as only a negative emotion, best gotten rid of, but to be guilty is also to bear responsibility for something, to own it. Just as the mother (not yet "Tova" in my mind) wasn't genetically responsible for her adopted son's good looks, she wasn't responsible for his illness; guiltless, she was separated from it and thus, to a degree, from him, when she least wanted to be. Her son was a gift she felt she hadn't earned, the disease a curse she felt she hadn't deserved. Can something be *really* ours if we haven't paid for it in one way or another?

As I began to wonder how a woman in such a circumstance might free herself from this weight of innocence in relation to her son, I realized that she would have to take responsibility for his illness. Since she couldn't literally do that, she would have to *make* herself guilty through the power of words, just as her words had made her son quiet in the treatment room. She would, then, have to tell someone she had a causative role in what had happened, and that meant dialogue, of characters with names, interacting in a scene. And *that*, to me, meant a story rather than a poem.

That also meant I now had the uncomfortable task of attempting to *make* characters, dialogue, and scenes. I chose a third-person narration to remind myself that Tova was a fictional character, but as the story shows, essentially I tried to get around these challenges by avoiding them. Reading "Handling Charges" now, a number of years after it was written, however, I am no longer embarrassed by its lack of a cast of fleshed-out characters or real interactive dialogue or scenes of ongoing action. I don't think the story's gotten any better, I just think I understand more fully now that a story need not be cast in the kind of traditional narrative mold that had been my model and that I hadn't come close to filling.

Looking at the story now, I see it more as a poem that got away. Unlike David Huddle and Allen Shepherd, who polish and hone their stories with many structural revisions, I wrote "Handling Charges" very quickly, and only tinkered with it afterward. I could not have recast it because I didn't know any other way to manage a piece of fiction; I knew theoretically how a story operated but not how to create the seemingly requisite dialogue or character interactions. So I revised the story as I revise my poems—reseeing individual words and phrases, getting back into the work at the level of its language.

The actual composition of the story essentially operated on that level as well. I tried to attend to the rhythms of phrases and sentences, to the sounds of words. I found that the processes familiar to me from poem making were what propelled my story writing. Focusing on some concrete detail—say, the flowered handkerchief of the radiation attendant—I would find myself moving on to a whole string of related images—Schrafft's, the visit to the shoe store, and then the store's X-ray-like machine, which later seemed to me so right an image in the context of the narrative that I could not have purposely hunted down a much better one. In effect, I was led through the writing by such connections and associations of images, just as I am when a poem seems to be going well.

In other ways, too, the story reflects my approach, not necessarily the best one, to making a poem. "Elephants—A Mythology" is a pretty fair example of how my poems tend to move toward a strong sense of closure. Although I don't really know *where* they will end when I begin them, I find myself waiting for the detail that will somehow provide a kind of "click" at the end and focus what has gone before. So too in "Handling Charges"—the ending signals itself, I hope not too heavy-handedly, as climax and conclusion all at once. And the story closes with an image. In poetry I try to trust a picture to do the work of the proverbial thousand words, especially as the last thing a reader meets on the page, and that's what happens here. In writing the story, then, I discovered that poetry and fiction are not as entirely different species as I had thought.

This is the first time "Handling Charges" has been published. Shortly after I wrote it I sent it off to *The New Yorker* in a spirit of bravado; I didn't expect an acceptance as much as I hoped for some response that would help me better to understand fiction writing and my initial unease with it. When the rejection came, a scrawled note from an editor pleased me greatly. Although he found Jeff's character too sketchily presented and worried that the situation could be seen as potentially sentimental, he talked about "Handling Charges" as though it were a real story. Amazingly, I had made a piece of fiction, however flawed, and I owned it now, for better or worse.

Handling the Bad News in Ghita Orth's "Handling Charges"

David Huddle

Imagine "Handling Charges" as a Hollywood movie made for a popular audience. In its penultimate scene, Tova, the heroine, decides to confide her troubles to a polite stranger and to speak openly about her son's illness. The two women have a good talk out there by the carousel. The stranger, it turns out, has just read an article in an obscure medical journal about a new surgical procedure being experimented with by doctors in Switzerland. The movie ends with Tova's carrying Jeff onto a plane bound for Zurich. At the last moment she turns to wave at the woman in the rose-printed dress, who brushes tears from her eyes while watching the departure of her brave new friend and her friend's terribly-ill-but-perhaps-soon-to-be-miraculously-saved son.

In Ghita Orth's short story "Handling Charges," the main character decides to lie to the polite stranger rather than share the disaster she is facing. In the final sentence, Tova "bear[s] . . . her son high to the back of the black horse," a horse we readers cannot avoid seeing as symbolic of imminent death.

The producers of the Hollywood movie intend to make their audience feel good walking out of the theater; the film reminds its viewers of human mortality and the arbitrariness of fate—which reminders set them up to appreciate what a relief it is to share one's burdens, what a comfort friendship can be, and how one should never give up hope.

Is it Ghita Orth's intention to make her readers feel bad when they finish the last paragraph of "Handling Charges"? Not only does her main character lie and refuse a stranger's offer of friendship and a chance to share her troubles, she also chooses to "bear . . . her son high to the back of the black horse." If the black horse is a figure of death, this mother must be figuratively *delivering* her son to the death that awaits him.

Bad news in several varieties is delivered by this short story. Children suffer and die. Parents sometimes must act as "bearers"—they have to collaborate with the painful medical procedures as well as simply having to accompany their children through their final days, hours, and minutes. People who might be better off sharing their troubles sometimes choose not to share them. People lie. The story makes no attempt to soften these blows. In fact the story intends to deliver its bad news clearly and directly to the reader. "Let there be no mistake," this story tells us. "Bad news exists, dear reader, and here is some of it."

A work of art presents a view of the universe and the human circumstance; it articulates hope or despair or some combination of hope&despair. Though it may be subtle, ambiguous, or enigmatic, a work of art, even one of very low quality, can't help saying *something*.

Hollywood movies (such as the one we've imagined here) often present a "warm, fuzzy" view of the universe and the human circumstance. Makers of such films have learned that more money is to be made from movies that tell us life is sweet and death far away than from movies that tell us life is difficult and death hovers nearby.

Here in Western civilization in the final decade of the twentieth century, there is very little money to be made from writing short stories, regardless of what they tell us. Even for "name writers," better hourly wages would be available waiting tables in a good restaurant or painting houses. So, since money isn't really an issue, today's short story writers are free to write as they choose, free to use the occasion of writing a story to discover their own truths, their own views of the universe and the human circumstance.

An intelligent, sensitive boy is beaten—not terribly but badly enough, and frequently—by his stepfather from the age of three or four until he is almost fourteen; the beatings then stop because suddenly the boy has grown to be taller and stronger than his stepfather. With this bad news in his past, at the age of eighteen the young man enters college; at the age of twenty he takes a creative writing class. He is assigned to write a short story about a topic of his choice. For reasons that anyone could sympathize with, the young man may choose not to write about anything having to do with that bad news in his personal history. But let's assume that he wants to write *something* about that painful experience of his boyhood; what are his options?

A. A story that presents the negative experience, then transforms it into a positive experience for the reader: Just as he is about to be beaten beside a highway, the boy saves the stepfather from being hit by a truck; the stepfather stops drinking; they become pals and go fishing together.

B. A story that exaggerates the negative experience: In one particularly hideous beating, the stepfather murders the boy.

C. A story that attempts to locate the truth of the young man's experience. *Truth* in this case is not limited to historical accuracy; the practice of art allows the imagination to be used as an investigative tool. The story that searches for what this bad news means to this young man—how it has affected his life, what he thinks about it, how he intends to live with it—will probably require him to use his imagination. As Chekhov did in writing "A Dead Body," this young author may have to make up things that didn't actually happen; he may have to leave out things that actually did happen. He may have to change the characters, the place, even the nature of the beatings—in order to reach his personal truth of the experience.

Almost anyone would advise this young man to choose option C. Aside and apart from how good or how bad a story it turns out to be, chances are that writing it as a journey toward personal truth will have a liberating effect on the young man. He will better understand his past, will free himself from the pain of it, and will diminish the likelihood of its affecting him negatively later in life. He'll feel better; he'll improve his life. Who could argue with those results?

The reader who has never met this young man and who knows nothing about him might well ask, *Why should I read a depressing story about a kid getting beat up by his stepfather? Great: He wrote it, and he feels better, but I don't have to read it, thank you. Besides, I'm going to the movies.* Such a reader, if he had to read some kind of a story by this author, might request option A (for its uplifting qualities) or even option B (for its entertaining horror).

Writers have been known to get huffy over the question *Why should I read a depressing story?* and to respond like the salesperson at an ultraexpensive store: *If you have to ask why you should read it, then you definitely shouldn't read it.*

It is, however, a tough and reasonable question, one that's worthwhile for a writer to try to answer. We can see why a *writer* might want to write a bad-news story. But why should anyone spend time and intellectual energy *reading* a story that's going to deliver bad news to them?

- Because a work of art is a thing of beauty, and beauty is a noble opponent of suffering and death. Orth's "Handling Charges" is exemplary: The writing is musical, rich in detail, comforting in its wisdom, honesty, compassion, and intelligence; the elegance of its form is testimony to the possibility of immortality within the scope of human endeavor.
- Because the imagination is our only resource when facing the unknown, and works of art inform and strengthen our ability to imagine. Sooner or later each of us will have to face the imminent death of someone we love. We can't know exactly how that experience will be for us, but Orth's "Handling Charges" will be on file in our resident memory; it is already available for reference, should we wish to speculate about how we might

think and feel and behave as we face the approaching death of a child, parent, brother, sister, or friend.

- Because we live but one life, but to live fully and deeply we must know many lives. "Handling Charges" tells us about a woman who makes up an ongoing story to tell her adopted, dying, three-year-old son while he undergoes the suffering of radiation therapy. (Tova's spontaneous storytelling for Jeff during his radiation therapy sessions is a practical example of how we use "beauty [as] a noble opponent of suffering and death.") For having known this experience—even if our knowledge is limited to having read only this single page of prose—we are more complete human beings.

- Because in spite of our desire to escape the fact of our mortality and to avoid any reminder of it, each of us knows—and suffers in the knowing—that we are going to die. Works of art may disturb us by reminding us of that fact, but they reassure us that others—even children!—have faced death with dignity. Whether they show it being faced heroically or ignominiously, whatever news they have to deliver to us about this topic, they help us prepare for death.

- Because the ugly truth is more valuable than the pretty lie. Tova's lying to the polite lady in the rose-printed dress, refusing to share her troubles when the occasion presents itself, is not an example of ideal human behavior, but it holds a truth that may help a reader who finds him- or herself acting similarly. Had Tova chosen to "have a good talk" with the lady, we might enjoy the warm, fuzzy feeling of the moment, but the scene would be of less value to us in our own future difficulties and failures of behavior. However much we may prefer to be deceived in the short run, each of us knows—because we are the species designated to be conscious of death—the truth of the long run. Finally, truth achieved through the struggle to forge experience and imagination into art—truth such as that offered by "Handling Charges"—is comfort that lasts.

ABOUT

Allen Shepherd

Allen Shepherd, born in Boston in 1936 and a graduate of Harvard University, Brown University, and the University of Pennsylvania, teaches American literature at the University of Vermont. He has published fiction, poetry, and personal, critical, and scholarly essays in numerous periodicals. With Arthur W. Biddle he contributed a chapter on fiction to *Reading, Writing, and the Study of Literature* (1989), and with Ghita Orth a chapter on short fiction to *Angles of Vision* (1992). Allen Shepherd, Ghita Orth, and David Huddle are currently collaborating on *About These Poems,* a companion volume to *About These Stories.*

Lightning

Allen Shepherd

One evening after supper the four Powledges—father, mother, and two girls—all careful in their bare feet, walked up and down the beach together collecting dead sea urchins and saw a porpoise just off shore which followed them attentively back and forth. For no reason in particular, Fred Powledge whistled to it and it turned quickly on its tail in the water and came in very close and floated, rolling gently in the small waves.

Pulling his big-billed cap down firmly on his head, Fred waded slowly out into the warm water and whistled again. Because the porpoise still seemed interested and unalarmed, Fred with the water at his knees began to talk to it, saying what he usually said to their dog at home. He said, "Come here, Jesse. Come here, boy." The porpoise backed off into deeper water.

The girls were amazed and a little frightened—their father whistling and then talking to a fish—but for the last six months they hadn't known quite what to make of him. He was going to be a senator soon and he had to be president and something else of their grandfather's company and he was almost never home. And he'd been on T.V. twice. Their mother had discussed it with them and they all knew he would be a good senator, not in Washington.

Back on the beach, the porpoise having disappeared, Fred took his wife's hand. He couldn't bring to mind Owen Glendower's speech about calling spirits from the deep but remembered there was a crushing response. There was always a prince. The trip to Fort Myers he had proposed as a kind of reparation; he hadn't been himself for some while. Or had he just begun to be? It didn't seem that he knew any longer. At forty-three, a man ought to, he thought.

His bathing suit was tight, his legs chafed. A man a little more than medium-sized (no bigger than he'd been at fifteen), Fred was starting to get fat but hadn't gotten used to it. He didn't eat very much; he'd never eaten desserts. He couldn't understand it. Most of his life he'd weighed 160, 165, but for months he hadn't been able to get under 180. His blood pressure was up and he had to take a diuretic and potassium.

The Powledges regrouped, Fred and Marjorie before, the girls behind, they all filled their plastic bags with sea urchins, and headed back to their white, three-story apartment building—a condominium it was called—a hundred yards or so from the Gulf, with a small heated swimming pool and blacktop tennis courts and car ports and comfortable, garish furniture and an elevator whose inspection certificate had expired a year before. Fred had rented the apartment for ten days.

When the legislature convened on the fifteenth, there he'd be in Montpelier, Senator Powledge (R-Addison), who had taken on that decent, white-headed old man of twelve terms' service, William T. Pelkey (D) and stung him into unheard-of public debate on television and driven him into one corner after another, made him look like a complete fool, and beaten him in November almost 2–1. Powledge remembered Pelkey, blinking in the clear white light, rubbing the sweat from his red nose, saying (because he knew nothing else to day): "But everybody knows me."

Since they'd arrived in Florida, it had been better. Fred slept with his head out the sliding door onto the balcony to hear the waves. For months before he'd risen in dreams, full of false power, smashing Pelkey and a whole string of successors, older men, declaring many things palpably untrue: that they lied and sold their votes and fornicated and beat their children and cheated monstrously on their income tax. Once he had sworn that World War I hadn't ended until 1925. And no one ever picked him up on anything. He had run against Pelkey simply because he'd been asked to, but that was no excuse for the way he'd done it.

Fred hoped that Marjorie and the girls would have a good time; they'd never been to Florida before. He rented a big car, drove them to look at the alligators (FEEDING THE ALLIGATORS IS STRICTLY PROHIBITED), dutifully toured the gift shops, and sat with them every day in the sun by the pool as long as he could stand it. He did not like to be hot and with his fair skin he burned badly. Nor did he particularly like swimming. He was a hell of a man to be in Florida with anybody, he thought.

Watching a seagull prepare to sneak a drink of fresh water (if the bird got in the water, the boy cleaning the pool would chase him with a vacuum tube), Fred thought how fortunate he was to be married to whom he was married; to have the children he had. And Father and Mother, of course. Though why, all of a sudden, his father had retired, handed everything to Fred, and gone off to Arizona he couldn't understand. From their letters, they seemed happy and meant to stay.

As they were sitting by the pool one lightly overcast afternoon—their sixth and no rain yet—Fred looked out over the water and saw a peculiar looking plane flying in low from the left, from the direction of Punta Gorda. It was relatively small, had two engines, and a twin tail. It wasn't a civilian plane. Fred had never actually seen one except in pictures, but he knew, or thought he knew, from a long time ago, what it was. The plane turned in, over the beach, and disappeared. It must have landed. Later while Marjorie and the girls were resting and having baths and curling their hair and deciding what to wear out to supper, Fred took out the car alone for the first time. He was looking for an airport or a landing strip down the road beyond the condominiums where they'd never explored. He was excited.

Their car was a metallic gold Chrysler LeBaron, just two weeks old, with automatic transmission, power brakes, power steering, power seat, air conditioning, tinted glass, and FM-stereo; it was more expensive than anything Fred had ever owned. With the dial set at MAX COOL he drifted down the road, two fingers on the wheel, coming in slow after a few miles to the edge of a long, close-cut brown field.

The plane sat at the far end, bright silver at the dark tree line, with no one in sight. He got out and walked, squinting even with his sunglasses. From five hundred feet he knew it was what he'd thought it was: he'd made two of them, models, during the war. A P-38, the Lockheed Lightning. The pair of them had hung on catgut leaders from his ceiling, diving on his bed.

Two men had seen him and were coming out of a tent pitched under the trees. With a dog, a big dog, a German Shepherd, on a leash. Both young men wearing baseball caps and green jackets and not smiling, side by side, burned brown. They could have been brothers. It was their plane.

"Mister," the left-hand one said, "you didn't see the sign?"

He was pointing back where Fred had left the car. He had a fuzzy blonde beard and a thin, high voice. Fred hadn't seen any sign; there wasn't one. He wouldn't trespass. So he explained seeing the plane over the water. They listened, they heard him out, they nodded. The right-hand one unsnapped the leash and sent the dog back to the tent. "Go" was all he said. Fred introduced himself; they were brothers, Phil and Hal Cunningham. Going to the air show in Palm Beach and be glad to be gone. People stole the KEEP OUT signs.

Fred told them they had a beautiful plane, and he asked them where they'd gotten it. They knew it was beautiful, and Phil told him how they'd found three in New Mexico, Las Cruces (an old man who'd stored them for twenty-five years and then died), and how they had cannibalized the other two so that "Baby Doll"—their plane—was all authentic. Once they knew Fred knew and that he appreciated what they had, they were friendly enough and gave him a printed card with all of the Lightning's statistics.

The Cunningham brothers were not twins, though they looked it; they were twenty-five and twenty-eight, had two B.S.s in aerospace engineering from UCLA, were both rated commercial pilots. They had had "Baby Doll" for eighteen months and were just about out of money. So they said as the three of them sat under a gauzy pine tree having a beer, the plane shining in the sun directly in front of them, the Cunninghams' Toyota pickup parked in the shade behind the tent. One flew, one drove; then they changed off. They'd come down from Durham where it had been getting too cold; below forty degrees "Baby Doll" tended to stall out.

Fred thought for a moment of inviting them to dinner but remembered that one of them had always to stay with the plane. Then Hal said to him, "Hey, you want to go up? Air her out. You want to go, ten minutes?" Yes, yes, he did.

They pulled up the long aluminum pegs that held her down in case of wind; they wound up the cord. Then Hal got a step ladder out of the back of the Toyota and—following him—Fred climbed up and into the cockpit, the center nacelle. That's what it's called, he knew. The engines are in the outer nacelles. Painted on the fuselage were two small red rising suns, perfectly round; climbing in, Fred touched them with his finger. They were hot: two Japanese planes shot down. Inside, Fred pointed toward the back. He wasn't sure. "That's it," Hal said. "Sit easy." Sitting—squatting—behind him was like being in the rumbleseat with his father driving the old Ford.

Ahead, Hal was saying something—he seemed to be reciting numbers. What you did before you started the engines, pre-flight. The engines turned over, coughed, and one fired, blowing oily smoke through the exhaust. The noise shook the air. Fred swallowed and blew his nose and could not hear the sound he made. He hugged himself. The other engine started; the plane shivered and rattled. Over his head Fred watched the plexiglass canopy vibrating. On the wings the rivets danced in the sun. They moved, turned; "Baby Doll" picked up speed, bouncing. A new noise—high whining: the supercharger. There wasn't enough room—the trees, fifty feet high, were coming. Then off and up and banking easily. Trees and the road he'd driven on, the car and their truck in the brown field.

Fred straightened one leg, got his elbows up on the canopy ledge to brace himself, and Hal took off his baseball cap. Fred saw clouds coming. Below was the ocean, half a dozen beautiful shades of blue. A boat, two boats together. Then nothing. As Hal dropped her down, the horizon shrank. Over his shoulder he said, "There's a dope boat." It was a freighter, green and red, not very big, steaming slowly up the coast. Fred looked down on the deck, at packing cases and masts and booms and other things he didn't know the names of; he could see three men, but they didn't look up. Five minutes beyond the freighter, miles, without warning, Hal kicked "Baby Doll" sharply around, dropped her down almost to the waves, and began a broadside run at the freighter. On deck for a second they were running, falling and rolling, and then "Baby Doll" jumped and they were gone.

Shortly they cruised down the beach, waggling their wings occasionally, just mooching along, and Fred actually saw the tennis courts and the little pool and people lying on the beach, three who might have been his family, except that he remembered they were all inside, getting ready.

Hal was going in, just about to go in, had put his cap on again, but Fred touched his shoulder. He didn't want to go in, not yet. When Hal turned his head, Fred made a circling sign with his hand. Hal smiled and said, "O.K., man, once more." She took them up and up, climbing on her tail, did a few slow, meticulous rolls, looped once; then they circled easily back and dropped onto the field.

By the tent Fred shook hands with both of them, clapped Hal on the shoulder, and told him it was the best thing he'd done in years. "Yeah, it's good," he said. "It's good." Fred had no more to say; he did not want to embarrass them or himself, make a speech.

Marjorie and the girls had seen the plane, had heard it and looked out the window when it came in so low. They thought it was going to crash. And he was in it! Was he flying it, the girls wanted to know, and seemed disappointed that he was not, that he'd squatted behind. Fred did not mention their raid on the dope boat. Alone with his wife for a moment in the living room, he kissed her. She smelled good.

After shrimp and red snapper and lime pie but no coffee, Fred pulled his bed back into the room, reattached it to Marjorie's, and invited her (he blushed fiercely) to take a shower. His stomach embarrassed him. They didn't wake up until almost 9:30 the next morning when the girls got tired of cartoons.

With the three of them lying out in their sun hats and sunglasses by the pool, Fred edged down toward the water, the waves. He hated cold water, which this wasn't, and he wasn't sure that he was going in now, right this minute. He felt he ought to; twice after the porpoise he'd refused, even though they'd all asked him. As if looking for shells, he walked out to his knees; the best shells were collected before they reached the beach, before they broke and the birds cleaned them out.

After trying one, two, three to get under, Fred tripped on something and almost went down. It was good and he decided. And under, down to the bottom. He did a backward flip under water, he touched both hands flat on the bottom. Then swam straight out, floated on his back, dived once, let himself drift in. He wished they had seen him, up at the pool, but they'd see that he was wet, and he could invite them to come back with him, all go in.

He sat and watched as under eight inches of water a small hermit crab walked up and over his bare foot. He caught it with two fingers, watched it disappear inside its shell, then buttoned it into his bathing suit pocket. He didn't think the girls had seen one close up; afterward they could put it back. On one knee digging out a cache of auger shells to have something else to show, to contribute to Marjorie's collection of shells for a necklace, he found a beauty, green and gold, perfect. Then he heard the plane, the Lightning, bound for Palm Beach, knew what it was, and walked up past the pine tree toward the pool, where he knew they were waiting for him.

Getting It Almost Right

Allen Shepherd

Because I throw away almost nothing to do with fiction writing, I knew that I could locate all the drafts of "Lightning" (there turned out to be six), with alternative titles, whatever notes there were from friends who'd offered commentary (three), periodic queries and memos to myself, a sending list with letters of rejection, and, finally, the letter which begins "I am pleased to inform you that . . ."

Why keep all this stuff? What is probably the best answer is intimated in the last sentence of the most satisfying, useful rejection letter I've unearthed: "Powledge is rich material for a story, but one I think either much shorter or much, much longer"—this from the editor of *Ploughshares*. Grateful as I am for that comment, it's difficult for me to imagine the story much shorter. But because the story as published is just a little more than half the size of the longest draft, there is in fact a lot of material patiently waiting around down in the file cabinet in my cellar, spare parts of Dr. Shepherd's laboratory.

I had on hand a number of vignettes, overheard conversations, evocative details, a few jokes that badly wanted to be used. Even though none of them made the final cut, let me give you two examples. As Powledge was sitting at the pool, for instance, he was to listen to a conversation from the next bank of chairs. It was hair these people were talking about, or haircuts. There were to be two couples, and one of the men would tell the other that he had spent three years getting his hair right. Fred would sneak a look and perhaps be caught in the act. One of the women (the speaker's mother-in-law, probably) would urge him not to get a permanent and he would say, "For God's sake, Mitzi, I have no intention." Although I could argue that the overheard exchange was, for Fred, an encounter with another, alien culture, that it let the world in, so to speak, even that it was mildly funny, I couldn't argue that it was really functional, that it was worth 150 words.

One more, much shorter example: Fred encounters in the elevator, perhaps twice, an elderly, nearly blind man carrying a check from his son which he means to cash at the condominium office. The man asks Fred to read for him what his son has written after "FOR" on the check. The word, neatly printed, is "EXPENSES." Here, it seemed to me, are epitomized issues of family, money, responsibility, love or the lack of it, all pertinent to the Powledge narrative. And suppose Fred in his reading were to substitute for "EXPENSES" a word of his own choice? But finally I couldn't make a good case for the incident, not in a story ten to twelve pages long.

What size the story was to be depended on such matters as structure, focus, plot, characterization, and the like, to which I will return shortly. After looking through a fat file folder, reading drafts of the story variously titled "Up," "Up, Down and Around," "The Senator, the Lightning and the Hermit Crab," "Nil Admirari," and "Lightning," I realized (with gratifying objectivity) that I was wonderfully ambitious and/or wildly unrealistic as to what "Lightning" could conceivably carry. For openers, however, better to have too much than too little.

I wanted to write about Vermont, where I'd lived for a dozen years. What do you have to know about a place to write about it convincingly? You need to know, I suppose, something about the topography, the weather, what the people talk about and sound like, what their names are, how they're employed. I was gratified, for instance, when a native Vermonter told me that Pelkey was a good name for Fred's defeated opponent. It occurred to me afterward that perhaps she couldn't think of anything else to speak well of.

I wanted to write about politics, which had always interested me. Early in getting ready to write I made the mistake of sketching an overview of local politics, complete with lists, as if I were preparing to do an article or essay. Later on, with some difficulty, I excised almost all such material from the story, but my mistake illustrates a point, I believe: that the kind of preparation you do substantially affects what you'll produce. Thus for a time "Lightning" was burdened with some distinctly undynamic and fairly parochial exposition.

I also wanted to write of family, three or four generations' worth, and perhaps of the descent of a family business. People are better understood and characters in fiction more economically depicted, I think, if we know of (preferably *see*) the apartment, the condominium, the house they live in. The connection of house and householder is exemplified, in Gothic fashion, by Edgar Allan Poe in "The Fall of the House of Usher." I wanted somehow to incorporate at least a sense of the Powledge establishment, but I never managed it. At poolside Fred was to review the security precautions (lights, snow shoveling) he'd taken before leaving, thus allowing (me) as extensive a tour of the premises as there was room for. There wasn't room for any, as it turned out. All of this—Vermont, politics, family, business, Florida—would have filled at least one novel.

My protagonist was to be a middle-aged man in whose life nothing had ever seriously gone wrong and who, paradoxically, I suppose, felt incomplete as a result. Some years after I wrote the story a friend resolved on his fiftieth birthday to become, or at least try to become, more optimistic; that is a resolution my character would understand perfectly. Fred Powledge is a man to whom (good) things have been happening—he's won a state senatorial election, he has become president of a flourishing business, he is married to a woman he loves very much. Yet he doesn't understand why things happen, why other people, his parents, for instance, behave as they do, nor why he has himself behaved so uncharacteristically in his recent campaign. As the cliché has it, he is well into a midlife identity crisis.

I need to pursue Fred a little further. He is what lawyers mean when they refer to the "reasonably prudent man"; that is, he is rational, cautious, circumspect. He balances his checkbook, remembers birthdays, and is suspicious of free gifts. He is given to fairly rigorous self-scrutiny and is seldom altogether pleased with what he discovers. For some time, he thinks, he has not done what he ought to do; thus taking his wife and children to Florida constitutes compensation, reparations. To cite the *Ploughshares* editor once more, he resembles the protagonist of Evan Connell's *Mr. Bridge,* or at least I'm happy to think so, since I admire that novel.

After all this, you're certainly not going to ask me whether the character is autobiographically derived. I didn't think so. I don't know that it's a very profitable question anyway. You start with some things you know about and then, because writing truly is a process of discovery, you go on to see what you can find out, what the characters are going to do. Thus it took me quite some time to find out that the resolution of Fred's crisis would be a ride in an antique World War II fighter plane.

The centrality of the P-38 will make better sense, perhaps, if considered in the context of structural problems that I'm not sure I ever solved. How in ten pages or so to integrate, structurally and thematically, Fred as businessman, politician, son, husband and father, and vacationer, without a sense of too much left out, of a character whose background and foreground don't come together? This was substantially the judgment of the editor of *San Jose Studies*, who wrote that she "kept searching for more pages, looking for some resolution of the situations you set up." How much of the context and the protagonist's feelings may safely be left to the reader's inference? As one of my friends remarked in a note, "Understatement is a virtue—as everyone believes in that old title: 'Run Silent, Run Deep.' And yet the psychological *depth* is lost (and the point unclear) if so little is allowed to surface." Her point was well taken, I think; it's the writer's responsibility to focus the story, not to emulate a character who has little to say for himself. These are essentially the same issues raised by an encounter with the two versions of Raymond Carver's "So Much Water So Close to Home."

How to focus "Lightning" required considerable experimentation. The story in its present form begins at page twelve of an earlier twenty-one-page draft, in which the Powledges are first encountered on a plane somewhere between Montpelier, Vermont, and Fort Myers, Florida. During the rest of the flight Fred reflects uneasily on the state of his world as the narrative cuts back and forth from present circumstances to recent and even not-so-recent history. However, although the plane flies steadily on, nothing else does, for the exposition is leadenly inert. It was in undertaking to correct this problem, I think, that I was moved to such brisk development in the first sentence of the final draft. Indeed, if I had continued at that rate, the story would have been over in a page. In an early draft I created foils to my focal aircraft, the P-38—from the Continental Airlines DC-10 that carried the family south to several smaller planes glimpsed on the ground. All these avatars having gone to rest in my cellar filing cabinet, however, I have to hope that the Lightning can carry on alone.

Whether it does is of course for you to say, but I can tell you what, after living with Fred for some time, I had in mind. As a child Fred had built model airplanes, as was common, I think, during World War II, when I built them. The P-38 was in reality a one-person plane, but as the story developed, it became clear that fact would be no match for psychic necessity. From having made twelve-inch models Fred could feel that the plane was already his, that he knew it, understood it, was ready to claim the real thing. The realness of the aircraft in this fantasy-fulfilling flight I insisted upon in all drafts except the last by equipping the Cunningham brothers with printed cards citing all the plane's vital statistics. It was probably overkill, but the text read:

> "Baby Doll" is a mid-wing, cantilever, single-seater pursuit monoplane, built in 1943, one of 6900 1942–1945, has a wingspan of 52 feet, length of 38 feet, powered by two 1400 h.p. Allisons, weight unloaded 5.7 tons, max. loaded

weight 8.2 tons, max. speed 414 m.p.h. at 24,000 feet, radius of action without drop-tanks 360 miles, armament four 13-mm. machine guns and one 20-mm. Hispano cannon. All metal construction. "Baby Doll" had two confirmed kills in the South Pacific in 1944. She is not for sale.

All of this, by the way, is accurate information, which does not redeem it for fictional use.

I do not usually trade very much in literary allusion, although (or perhaps because) it is a staple of academic life and writing. But I did incorporate into the fourth paragraph a Shakespearean reference, though only after several revisions had suggested it to me. Owen Glendower, a Welsh braggart, boasts of his ability to call up spirits out of the ocean; it is Prince Hal, as I remember, who asks, cuttingly, whether they come. Thus "There was always a prince." The longer I pursue this point, the more mechanical and inconsequential it seems, but I wanted Fred to meet and bond with—not be denied by—a latter-day Hal, one of the Cunningham brothers, the Lightning man.

Fred's preflight preparation is focused in the paragraph recounting his piloting the rental Chrysler LeBaron to the airfield. He is already flying in such a sentence as the following: "With the dial set at MAX COOL he drifted down the road, two fingers on the wheel, coming in slow after a few miles to the edge of a long, close-cut brown field."

Though in real time the plane ride lasts only about ten minutes, it is (for him) an experience of fear and beauty and adventure, control and power, aggression and glamour. When Fred calls the creatures, that is to say, they come, if only for the duration of the flight. After Baby Doll lands, he is ready for a happy ending, which promptly follows, and one measure of which is that what he wants to do coincides exactly with what he believes he ought to do. As I think about it, "happy ending" is perhaps not quite the phrase, not for the provisional perspective with which I wanted to close. Are people capable of such change as Fred seems to display? Sometimes. Or is he, metaphorically, a hermit crab who has just located a somewhat larger, more comfortable, more readily defensible shell?

Trusting the Tale

Ghita Orth

A porpoise, a World War II fighter plane, the Florida ocean—how do such disparate entities come together in "Lightning" to allow its protagonist, who "did [not] particularly like swimming," to be, at story's end, not only swimming but doing "a backward flip under water"? Just as in a writing workshop we're often tempted to ask a story's author, "What did you mean by that?" I could simply have walked down the hall to my colleague

Allen Shepherd's office and asked him to explain the "meaning" of his story. But no matter what writers know, or tell us, about their work, it's the work itself that speaks to us most strongly. A story acquires a life of its own separate from whatever its author's intentions and purposes may have been, and it's to the words on the page and the way they affect us that a reader needs to turn for understanding. Trust the tale, not the teller.

This tale interested me just because it seemed to resist easy explanation. I knew something of import had happened to change Fred Powledge during the course of the story, and I wanted to know what it was, so I began to ask questions—not of Allen Shepherd but of the story itself. I noticed, first, the timorousness of the vacationing Powledges, "all careful in their bare feet" on the shell-strewn beach—they seemed vulnerable and uncertain somehow. And why is Fred so strangely "whistling and then talking to a fish"? His comical interaction with the porpoise furthered my sense that this was a man, like his family, out of his natural element. The only way Fred knows to relate to this creature "from the deep" is to treat it as he would his dog, to domesticate it, ignore its difference.

But the porpoise backs away from him. I had to refresh my memory of Shakespeare's *Henry IV* to recognize the allusion here as a reference to Prince Hal's "crushing" rejoinder to Owen Glendower—one may summon "spirits from the deep," but they will not necessarily heed one's call. In life, Fred thinks, "There was always a prince" to invoke one's human limitations in controlling unfamiliar territory.

And much of Fred's life when we meet him, a dislocated vacationer, has become strangely unfamiliar; he no longer understands his body, which is going to fat, or even who he is. His thoughts suggest the fragility of his sense of identity at the beginning of the story: "He hadn't been himself for some while. Or had he just begun to be? It didn't seem that he knew any longer." Fred's question mirrors my own; we both want to know the answer.

The crucial circumstances that have so jarred Fred's sense of self arise from his newly acquired responsibilities as a state senator and as head of his father's company. These responsibilities, having been thrust upon him, seem to have caught him unawares. Fred hasn't chosen these roles, they have chosen him; he had run "simply because he'd been asked," and his father had inexplicably retired and just "handed everything to Fred."

Even though he has not actively sought these positions of power, however, his thoughts make clear his guilty unease in them. Ashamed of his reprehensible behavior toward his political opponent, Fred even dreams of his "false power," exaggerating his unpunished dirty dealing, suffering from the fact that he has "no excuse" for his ugly attacks on Senator Pelkey. Fred's new circumstances have, like Glendower, called up "spirits of the deep"; something has been loosed in him, and he seems surprised and taken aback by its uncontrolled virulence.

I too am surprised, and look to the story's language to find some reason, if not excuse, for his behavior. Senator Pelkey, we're told, was a "decent, white-headed old man," and in Fred's dreams he smashes politicians who are "a whole string of successors, older men." Whatever aggressions and angers he is playing out before the TV cameras and in his dreams, they are directed at men who may look much like his father, and seem so to him. Fred has thus usurped his father in both his political and business lives; it is understandable that, guiltily, he doesn't know what to make of himself and feels a need for the "kind of reparation" the vacation may provide. The comic image of Fred sleeping "with his head out the sliding door onto the balcony to hear the waves" is nonetheless one of a man who is oppressed and stifling, who needs the cleansing potential of fresh air and ocean.

Yet Fred isn't comfortable in Florida; he can't immerse himself in its sun or water, or in his family's tourist activities or souvenir shopping. Though his nightmares have lessened, he seems just to be "dutifully" going through the motions of rehabilitation and renewal until his initial sight of the Lightning. For the first time in the story he comes alive, and the simple sentence "He was excited" signals the plane's powerful attraction for him.

What is so special about this plane, and Fred's flight in it, that could explain its pivotal role in the story? Again I looked for answers on the page. Even seeing the plane from afar, Fred recognizes it, thinking "he knew, from a long time ago, what it was." In contrast, then, to the flashy, expensive, and temporary rental car that is so different from "anything [he] had ever owned," the plane is a familiar machine to Fred, an icon of his childhood suddenly become reality. The model he had made and hung over his bed is now life sized and actual in front of his eyes.

Here, as odd and out of place as it is in a Florida field, is something with which Fred feels comfortably familiar. I don't know if Allen Shepherd really made a model P-38 when he was young or if he had to research its identifying details; what matters here is that I believe Fred knows this plane and that the writer is describing it accurately. It seems the less a reader knows about some object or setting in a story, the more the *writer* has to know about it to convince us of its fictional reality.

And it's precisely Fred's knowledge of, and admiration for, the reconstructed Lightning that leads its owners to allow him into its "all authentic" world, one in which Fred seems more at ease than in any other evoked in the story. "Once they knew Fred knew and that he appreciated what they had," the Cunningham brothers offer their camaraderie. Here he can sit around "under a gauzy pine tree having a beer" and chat with the two men while his wife and daughters are "resting and having baths and curling their hair and deciding what to wear out to supper" in alien female rituals in which he has no place.

Although the plane is entirely familiar to Fred, being up in the air in it is a new experience. From what we've seen of Fred's prior responses to unaccustomed environments, whether Florida or the political arena, we might expect him to be hesitant now, unsure of whether flying would be like "himself" or not. Instead he jumps at the opportunity—"Yes, yes," he wants to go up in the Lightning. Here is where he may discover what being "himself" entails.

The description of Fred's flight helps to explain its climactic role in the story. Confident of Baby Doll's abilities as he is not of his own, he doesn't fear engine noises and approaching trees and, contrary to his previous role in debates and dreams, is aligned with the "good guys" when the plane makes a "raid on the dope boat." Although he is still being passively carried along, Fred is clearly free and happy for the first time in the story.

What in this plane ride has freed him? For me, the answer comes in Fred's sense that "sitting—squatting—behind [Hal] was like being in the rumbleseat with his father driving the old Ford." Huddling in the elderly fighter that had successfully shot down two Japanese planes evokes for Fred a companionable childhood relationship with his father. Surrounded by the ambience of "long ago," he seems to have given himself over, even if momentarily, to the comforting dependencies that have been distorted in his later hostility to "older men." Fred is once again his father's child, rather than his usurper; he seems to have made peace with the past. When Fred then hugs himself in anticipation of the flight, he almost appears in that gesture to be forgiving himself, as well as his father, for whatever had since come between them.

The new perspective that his flight has afforded Fred is mirrored in his changed view of the formerly alien ocean; now, from high above, he sees in it "half a dozen beautiful shades of blue." As Fred explains to Hal, this flight in a resurrected relic of his childhood is "the best thing he'd done in years."

Fred is so moved by his experience that he cannot articulate his feelings to Hal, wanting to avoid sentimentality or anything like political speech making. If I'm to gauge its effect on him, then, I must look at his consequent behavior. Although unwilling to risk embarrassment with Hal, he risks it with Marjorie and approaches her with clearly sexual intentions we've had no sign of before. He can now live more comfortably in the circumstances of his life; he "pulled his bed back into the room, reattached it to Marjorie's."

Just as Fred has reconnected with his wife, he now connects with the previously unwelcoming ocean. Although Fred is first timorous as before, a chance accident brings him into the water. Again he has not chosen, but finding, surprisingly, that "it was good," he actually cavorts underwater, porpoiselike. Fred's pride in his swimming, his wanting his family to witness it, seems also a pride in the freer "self" his plane flight has generated; he brings his wife and daughters souvenirs from this new territory he can now inhabit. In fact, when Fred returns to the family he knows is "waiting for him," he also brings them what they were waiting for—a man with a surer sense of himself than they had seen "for the last six months," one who can fly the air in a plane and dive under water into "the deep," whose terrors have been domesticated. Seemingly comfortable now in the elements of an expanded world, Fred is ready to resume his life.

The porpoise, the plane, and the ocean have come together in the story just as they have for Fred. That "Lightning," the plane's generic name, is also the title of the story reinforces my sense of the import of Fred's experience. The flight has struck new sparks in him and enlightened him as well. One sometimes wonders, though, when reading a story, how much one may be reading "into" it. For me, the word "lightning" has suggestive connotations that work with what the story has shown about Fred's encounter with the plane and with himself. Although Allen Shepherd probably chose this type of plane because of his familiarity with it and not for its potentially symbolic name, if a P-38 had been called a "Thunderhead" or a "Blizzard," I think he might have chosen a more appositely named fighter to be central to his story. A writer, he makes use of the evocative power of language.

Whatever understanding of the story I've come to, then, has been through its language—the images and implications its words evoke. It's to them, not the author, that I've looked for answers to my questions. And I still have questions.

For some of these, the story simply won't provide answers; there is no way, for example, to discover in its diction or detail *why* Fred feels unconscious antipathy toward his father. To conjecture about this withheld information seems irrelevant—Allen Shepherd is interested in effects, not causes. So, too, Fred's relationship with his wife and daughters isn't fully dramatized, although they all seem to care for and about one another. The central issue in the story, however, is Fred's coming to himself as a person, not as a husband or father.

Some of my remaining questions, though, could, I think, ultimately be answered. Not all readers of "Lightning" will wonder about the same things, but I wonder why, for example, early on, Fred suddenly feels blessed to have his family; or if there's any connection between the Cunninghams' easy control of their dog and Fred's inability to control the porpoise as though it *were* a dog; or how the four elements—earth, air, fire, and water—might be operating here; or what could be made of the hermit crab Fred finds underwater that "disappear[s] inside its shell"—will he do that again himself?

When I reread "Lightning" tomorrow, or next week, I may find the answers, ones that even Allen Shepherd might not be able to provide as fully as his story can. One reading of "Lightning," then, as of any piece of fiction in this book or elsewhere, isn't enough. Another reader will find in it additional meanings and suggestions for writing just as, another time around, this reader will.

Glossary

allusion Reference to some well-known person, place, event, or piece of literature outside the work itself.

atmosphere Mood surrounding the action in a narrative.

characterization Means of evoking the personality and attitudes of a character through his/her speech, action, and thoughts, and through direct description.

character narrator Character who tells a story in which he/she is a participant.

climax Decisive turning point in a plot.

colloquial Diction level employing the language of informal speech.

conflict Opposition of two elements that creates the focus of tension in a plot.

denouement *Untying,* or conclusion, of a plot.

dialogue Presentation of conversation between characters.

diction Level or pattern of word choice.

exposition Presentation of essential background information.

flashback Enactment of a past event.

flat character One-dimensional character.

foil Character who serves as contrast to another.

foreshadowing Detail that implies the outcome or import of a later event.

image Word or group of words that evoke a sensory response.

in medias res Opening of a story "in the middle of things."

inner monologue Evocation of a character's thought processes.

irony Discrepancy between two things—between what is said and what is meant (verbal irony), what is expected and what occurs (situational irony), or what reader/audience knows and what character knows (dramatic irony).

minimalism Fictional style often using the present tense, simple diction and characterization, and little surface detail.

motif Pattern of recurrent images or references.

motivation Psychological imperatives of a character.

narrator Teller of the story, either a character (first-person narration) or an anonymous voice (third-person narration) which can assume various degrees of knowledge from limited to total omniscience. See *point of view.*

open-ended narrative Narrative which does not come to a definitive conclusion or resolution.

place Environment in which action occurs.

plot Significant order of events in a narrative.

point of view Assumed eye and mind through which a story is told; focus of narration. See *narrator.*

protagonist Main character in a plot.

rising action Plot structure that begins with exposition (presentation of essential background information), passes through complication (the protagonist is opposed), and reaches a crisis or climax (decisive turning point).

round character Multidimensional character.

satire Form of comedy in which a character or institution is held up to some standard and found wanting.

scene Enactment of an event in a plot, including dialogue and surrounding detail. Also, location of an event.

sentiment Feeling, emotion.

sentimentality Effort to induce an emotional response disproportionate to the situation depicted.

setting Physical and temporal background against which action occurs.

structure General plan or form of a piece of literature.

style Selection and use of words, including diction, abstract and/or concrete language, imagery, syntax, and tone.

summary Narration telling about, rather than enacting, an event.

suspense Uncertainty, even anxiety, as to what will happen.

symbol Object, action, setting, character, or image pattern which suggests abstract meanings in addition to its literal, concrete significance.

symmetry Beauty based on excellence of proportion and balance.

syntax Pattern or structure of the word order in a sentence.

thematic concerns What a work of literature is about, its central ideas.

tone Author's attitude toward subject and audience.

unreliable narrator Character narrator who, because of limited interpretive ability, cannot be depended upon to present events objectively.

what if? Supposition on which a story is based.

Acknowledgments

Julia Alvarez "The Kiss." From *How the Garcìa Girls Lost Their Accents*. Copyright © Julia Alvarez 1991. Published by Plume, an imprint of New American Library, a division of Penguin Books USA Inc. First published in hardcover by Algonquin Books of Chapel Hill. Reprinted by permission of Susan Bergholz Literary Services, New York.

Toni Cade Bambara "My Man Bovanne." From *Gorilla, My Love* by Toni Cade Bambara. Copyright © 1971 by Toni Cade Bambara. Reprinted by permission of Random House, Inc.

Benjamin Carlisle "In the Woods." Copyright © 1995 by Benjamin Carlisle. Reprinted by permission of Benjamin Carlisle.

Raymond Carver "So Much Water So Close to Home" (short version). From *Furious Seasons*, copyright © 1977 by Raymond Carver. Reprinted with permission of Capra Press, Santa Barbara.

Raymond Carver "So Much Water So Close To Home" (long version). From *Fires*, copyright © 1983 by Raymond Carver. Reprinted with permission of Capra Press, Santa Barbara.

Anton Chekhov "A Dead Body." From *The Image of Chekhov* by Anton Chekhov, trans. Robert Payne. Copyright © 1963 and renewed 1991 by Alfred A. Knopf, Inc. Reprinted by permission of the publisher.

Anton Chekhov Excerpt from a letter to Nikolay Leikin. From *The Image of Chekhov* by Anton Chekhov, trans. Robert Payne. Copyright © 1963 and renewed 1991 by Alfred A. Knopf, Inc. Reprinted by permission of the publisher.

Louise Erdrich "Fleur" from *Esquire*, August 1986. Copyright ©1986 by Louise Erdrich. Reprinted by permission of the author.

Barry Hannah "Love Too Long." From *Airships* by Barry Hannah. Copyright © 1978 by Barry Hannah. Reprinted by permission of Alfred A. Knopf, Inc.

David Huddle "Little Sawtooth." From *Intimates* by David Huddle. Copyright © 1993 by David Huddle. Reprinted by permission of David R. Godine, Publisher, Inc.

Maria Hummel "The Music of Detail: Creating a Character's Perception." Copyright © 1995 by Maria Hummel. Reprinted by permission of Maria Hummel.

James Joyce "Eveline," from *Dubliners* by James Joyce. Copyright 1916 by B. W. Heubsch. Definitive text Copyright © 1967 by the Estate of James Joyce. Used by permission of Viking Penguin, a division of Penguin Books USA Inc.

Franz Kafka "A Hunger Artist," trans. Willa and Edwin Muir. From *The Metamorphosis, The Penal Colony, and Other Stories* by Franz Kafka. Copyright © 1948 and renewed 1975 by Schocken Books, Inc. Reprinted by permission of Schocken Books, Pantheon Books, a division of Random House, Inc.

291

Index